Classical Mythology

Second Edition

by Kevin Osborn and Dana L. Burgess, Ph.D.

A member of Penguin Group (USA) Inc.

ALPHA BOOKS

Published by the Penguin Group

Penguin Group (USA) Inc., 375 Hudson Street, New York, New York 10014, U.S.A.

Penguin Group (Canada), 10 Alcorn Avenue, Toronto, Ontario, Canada M4V 3B2 (a division of Pearson Penguin Canada Inc.)

Penguin Books Ltd, 80 Strand, London WC2R 0RL, England

Penguin Ireland, 25 St Stephen's Green, Dublin 2, Ireland (a division of Penguin Books Ltd)

Penguin Group (Australia), 250 Camberwell Road, Camberwell, Victoria 3124, Australia (a division of Pearson Australia Group Pty Ltd)

Penguin Books India Pvt Ltd, 11 Community Centre, Panchsheel Park, New Delhi - 110 017, India

Penguin Group (NZ), Cnr Airborne and Rosedale Roads, Albany, Auckland, New Zealand (a division of Pearson New Zealand Ltd)

Penguin Books (South Africa) (Pty) Ltd, 24 Sturdee Avenue, Rosebank, Johannesburg 2196, South Africa

Penguin Books Ltd, Registered Offices: 80 Strand, London WC2R 0RL, England

International Standard Book Number: 1-59257-289-8
Library of Congress Catalog Card Number: 2004110066

06   05   8   7   6   5   4   3

Interpretation of the printing code: The rightmost number of the first series of numbers is the year of the book's printing; the rightmost number of the second series of numbers is the number of the book's printing. For example, a printing code of 04-1 shows that the first printing occurred in 2004.

Printed in the United States of America

Note: This publication contains the opinions and ideas of its authors. It is intended to provide helpful and informative material on the subject matter covered. It is sold with the understanding that the authors and publisher are not engaged in rendering professional services in the book. If the reader requires personal assistance or advice, a competent professional should be consulted.

Most Alpha books are available at special quantity discounts for bulk purchases for sales promotions, premiums, fund-raising, or educational use. Special books, or book excerpts, can also be created to fit specific needs.

For details, write: Special Markets, Alpha Books, 375 Hudson Street, New York, NY 10014.

Publisher: *Marie Butler-Knight*
Product Manager: *Phil Kitchel*
Senior Managing Editor: *Jennifer Chisholm*
Acquisitions Editor: *Tom Stevens*
Development Editor: *Michael Thomas*
Production Editor: *Megan Douglass*

Copy Editor: *Ross Patty*
Illustrator: *Shannon Wheeler*
Cover/Book Designer: *Trina Wurst*
Indexer: *Heather McNeil*
Layout: *Angela Calvert*
Proofreading: *John Etchison*

Contents at a Glance

Part 1:   **The Beginning of All Things**   1

  1   Tell Me a Story   3
*What a myth is, the functions myths play in a particular cul-
ture, and the sources of our knowledge about the mythology of
ancient Greece and Rome.*

  2   O Brave New World   13
*How the world was created, how men were created, and how
and why women were created.*

  3   Hey, I've Heard That Before! The Roots of
Classical Myth   25
*Earlier myths from other cultures that may have influenced
classical mythology—including the Babylonian genesis and
the story of the first hero, Gilgamesh.*

  4   Author, Author   39
*The ancient poets, playwrights, and other writers whose
works have informed us about classical mythology.*

Part 2:   **Welcome to the Pantheon: The Greek Gods**   55

  5   Tales of the Titanic   57
*The birth of the first immortals, the ascent and brief reign
of the Titans, and their fall to the Olympians.*

  6   The Reign of Thunder and Lightning: Olympus
Under Zeus   67
*The six original Olympians, all children of the Titans Cronus
and Rhea: Zeus and Hera (and their stormy marriage), their
brothers Poseidon and Hades, and their sisters Hestia and
Demeter.*

  7   The A Team: Olympians All   81
*The seven other major players on Mount Olympus: the
goddesses Aphrodite, Athena, and Artemis, and the gods
Hephaestus, Ares, Apollo, and Hermes.*

  8   Friends, Fairies, and Fairy Tale Monsters   97
*The "lesser" gods and goddesses, satyrs, and nymphs, and
the battles between the Olympians and both the Giants
and the terrifying monster Typhon.*

9   Eat, Drink, and Be Merry: Dionysus   109
    *The frenzied and ecstatic rites of the god of wine and
    his followers—as well as his persecution and ultimate
    ascent to Olympus.*

Part 3:   **Everyone Needs a Hero**   121

10   The Model Hero: Perseus   123
    *The hero who slew Medusa, rescued his wife from a sea
    monster, and saved his mother from a human monster.*

11   What the Hell? Adventures in the Underworld   133
    *How Hades found a wife, how Orpheus pursued his wife
    even after death, and the eternal tortures of the damned.*

12   Even the Wisest Cannot See: Oedipus the King   145
    *The blindness that caused a visionary hero to kill his father
    and marry his mother.*

13   The Labors of Heracles   157
    *The greatest of classical heroes: his persecution by his step-
    mother Hera and his many thrilling adventures.*

14   Crimes of Passion: Jason, Medea, and the Argonauts   173
    *The fabled quest for the Golden Fleece, Medea's crimes on
    Jason's behalf—and her revenge after he dumped her.*

15   Lucky in War, Unlucky in Love: Theseus   187
    *The hero who defeated the Minotaur and escaped the
    Labyrinth—and his unfortunate choice of women.*

16   All's Not Fair in Love and War: The Fall of Troy   199
    *How a crasher at a wedding party sparked a rivalry among
    goddesses, the abduction of Helen, and the greatest conflict in
    classical mythology: the Trojan War.*

17   Achilles: The Angry Young Hero   213
    *The greatest of Greek war heroes: his birth, his near invinci-
    bility in combat, his withdrawal from and return to the
    Trojan War, and his ultimate death on the battlefield.*

18   Take the Long Way Home: Odysseus   223
    *Why it took Odysseus 20 years to return to his faithful wife
    Penelope—and his many adventures along the way.*

19   Not in Our Stars: Tragic Heroes and Their Fates   237
    *Tales that illustrate the pain of unrequited love, the treachery
    of in-laws, the perils of distrusting your mate, the virtue of
    listening to your parents, and reasons why you should never,
    ever lend your child the keys to the family chariot.*

Part 4:   Friends, Romans, Countrymen   249

20   When in Rome, Worship as the Romans Worship   251
     The personal relationship that ancient Romans maintained
     with their gods and goddesses—and the rituals they used to
     keep these deities strong and vital.

21   Meet the New Boss(es), Same as the Old Boss(es):
     The Gods and Goddesses of Rome   259
     The hodgepodge of Roman deities—native Latin gods, immi-
     grant Olympians, deified Greeks, and nature spirits.

22   All Roads Lead to Rome: The Odyssey of Aeneas   273
     How Aeneas escaped the sack of Troy and undertook his own
     odyssey to found the Roman race.

23   Rome Wasn't Built in a Day   285
     How Romulus and Remus battled over the founding of Rome,
     legends of the city's early kings, and how a rape led to the
     founding of a republic.

Appendixes

A   Glossary of Terms   297

B   Who's Who in Classical Mythology   301

C   What's in a Name? Greek and Roman Gods
    and Heroes   361

D   Be Careful What You Wish For: The Fates of
    Mortals Who Slept with Gods or Goddesses   363

E   Read More About It   367

    Index   369

Contents

Part 1:   **The Beginning of All Things**   **1**

1   **Tell Me a Story**   **3**

Stories That Mean Something 4
> *Why Does the Rain Fall from Up Above? (Why Do Fools*
>   *Fall in Love?)* 5
> *Which Came First: The Chicken or the Egg?* 7
> *The Sacred and the Profane (and the Heroic)* 8

The Tellers and Their Tales 9
> *The Big Eight* 9
> *A Dash of Heroism, a Handful of Fate* 11
> *Myths? What Myths?* 12

2   **O Brave New World**   **13**

The Big Bang Theory: Creation Through Procreation 14
> *What a Mess!* 14
> *A Garden of Earthly Delights* 15
> *All You Need Is Love* 15

Mama Laid an Egg 17
A Work in Progress: The Ages of Man 18
> *Golden Years* 18
> *Hi-Ho Silver* 19
> *Coming in Third: The Bronze Medal* 20
> *Hard as Nails: The Iron Man* 20

Quest for Fire 20
> *Where's the Beef?* 21
> *Sugar and Spice and Everything Nice? Not Quite!* 22

3   **Hey, I've Heard That Before! The Roots of Classical Myth**   **25**

In the Beginning ... .26
Meet the New Boss 27
> *Quiet Up There!* 27
> *Clash of the Titans* 27
> *Recipe for Creation: Take One Divine Body, Break It in Two ...* 29
> *Hey, That Sounds Familiar!* 30

I Need a Hero: Gilgamesh 30
> *Gods' Gift* 31

Going for the Gusto *32*

The Goddess of (Unrequited) Love: Ishtar *32*

The Secret of Life *33*

A Hero in the Classical Mold *35*

The Mother of All Goddesses 36

A Goddess by Any Other Name *36*

A Hell of a Journey *37*

There's No DNA Test for the Paternity of Mythologies 38

4   Author, Author   39

Do Tell 40

The Poet as Performance Artist 40

Homer, Sweet Homer *41*

Never Refuse a Muse: Hesiod *42*

The Play's the Thing 43

Chorus Lines *43*

The Dramatist as War Hero: Aeschylus *45*

The Dramatist as Civic Leader: Sophocles *46*

The Dramatist as Realist: Euripides *47*

All Greeks to Me 48

Poetic License *48*

The Myths of History, Biography, and Geography *49*

The Grandeur That Was Rome 50

The Poet as Propagandist: Vergil *51*

The Poet as Storyteller: Ovid *52*

When in Rome … *52*

Part 2:   Welcome to the Pantheon: The Greek Gods   55

5   Tales of the Titanic   57

Raise the Titanic! 57

Too Many Hands, Not Enough Eyes *58*

Not-So-Fatherly Love *58*

No Womb to Move *59*

Mother's Little Helper *60*

A Titanic Struggle 61

The New Generation *61*

A Tale That's Hard to Swallow *61*

'Scuse Me, I Burped *63*

Clash of the Titans 63
Three Hundred Helping Hands 63
To Hell with the Titans 64

6 The Reign of Thunder and Lightning: Olympus Under Zeus   67

Master of the Universe 68
King of Gods, God of Kings 68
Trouble in Paradise 70
The First Sex Addict? 70
A Heavenly Marriage? Hera and Zeus 72
Cuckoo for Love 72
Hades Hath No Fury Like a Goddess Scorned 73
Surf and Turf: The Brothers of Zeus 75
Turf Wars 75
Beastly Couplings, Beastly Children 75
The Prince of Darkness 77
Home and Harvest: The Sisters of Hera 78
Home Is Where the Hearth Is 78
Earth Angel 79

7 The A Team: Olympians All   81

First in War, First in Peace: Athena 82
A Surefire Cure for a Migraine: Athena's Birth 82
War! What Is It Good For? 83
A Not-So-Immaculate Conception 83
Three's a Crowd: The Olympian Love Triangle 84
The Heavenly Castoff: Hephaestus 84
Fear and Loathing on Mount Olympus: Ares 86
First of the Red-Hot Lovers: Aphrodite 86
A Fine Romance? 87
Love Child 88
Night of the Hunters: Artemis and Apollo 89
Wild Queendom: Artemis 90
The Temperamental Musician: Apollo 92
The Little Rascal: Hermes 94

8 Friends, Fairies, and Fairy Tale Monsters   97

Children of Lesser Gods 98
Here Comes the Sun King 98
From Dusk to Dawn: The Sisters of Helius 99

Dark Goddesses: Hecate and Styx *100*

The Good-Time God: Pan *102*

Hemi-Demi-Semi-Deities *103*

The Fairy Tale World: Giants, Ogres, and Monsters *104*

Big Trouble on Olympus: The War with the Giants *104*

The Mother of All Monsters! *106*

9 Eat, Drink, and Be Merry: Dionysus **109**

Turning Water Into Wine: How Dionysus Came to Be *110*

Be Careful What You Wish For *110*

Kids Will Be Kids—Literally *111*

Sex, Drugs, and Rock 'n' Roll: Dionysus on Tour *112*

The Original Flower Child *113*

The Star and His Groupies *113*

Don't Make Him Mad *114*

Yo Ho Ho and a Bottle of Wine! *115*

Homecoming Queen: Pentheus of Thebes *116*

Madness Is the Best Revenge *117*

The Kindness of Strangers *117*

Swing Time *118*

All That's Gold Does Not Glitter *119*

Mama's Boy *119*

Part 3: Everyone Needs a Hero **121**

10 The Model Hero: Perseus **123**

Against All Odds: Perseus's Conception, Birth, and Youth *124*

The Golden Shower *124*

A Fine Kettle of Fish *125*

Something Fishy Going On *125*

A Face Only a Mother Could Love *126*

A Little Help from My Friends *126*

The Gray Women: Their Sisters' Keepers *127*

Medusa Loses Her Head *128*

Homeward Bound *128*

The Mountain Man: Atlas *129*

A Damsel in Distress: The Rescue of Andromeda *129*

The Marrying Kind *130*

A Family Reunion *131*

Welcome Home *131*

11 What the Hell? Adventures in the Underworld **133**

Hades Takes a Wife: Persephone 134
  Where Have All the Flowers Gone? *134*
  The Long Winter of Her Discontent *134*
  The Renewal of Spring *135*
  Queen of the Underworld *136*
The Cunning Rogue: Sisyphus 137
  All in the Family *137*
  No Honor Among Thieves *138*
  Cheating Death *138*
The Not-So-Heavenly Host: Tantalus 140
Undying Love: Orpheus 142
  Following Love to Hell and Back *142*
  Life After Death *143*

12 Even the Wisest Cannot See: Oedipus the King **145**

A House Divided: Oedipus's Ancestors 146
  Watch Where You're Looking: The Heirs of Cadmus *147*
  The Sins of the Father *148*
Exile and Triumphant Return 149
  Abandonment and Adoption *149*
  At the Crossroads *150*
  Riddle Me This *151*
  Hail the Conquering Hero *152*
The Blind Leading the Blind 152
A Tainted Legacy: The Curse of Oedipus 154
  The Curse Becomes a Blessing *154*
  The Sins of the Father—Part II *155*

13 The Labors of Heracles **157**

The Wonder Years: The Birth and Youth of Heracles 158
  The Labors of Alcmene *158*
  Training a Hero *159*
  Marriage, Madness, and Murder *161*
The Labors of Heracles 162
  Beastly Chores: The First Four Labors *162*
  Even More Beastly Chores: The Second Four Labors *164*
  The Far Corners of the Earth: The Final Four Labors *166*

Love and Death 169
    Lydia, Oh Lydia, Oh Have You Seen Lydia? *169*
    Vengeance Is Mine *170*
    Fatal Attraction: Deianira *170*

14 Crimes of Passion: Jason, Medea, and the Argonauts   173
Assembling the Argonauts 174
    The Other Shoe Drops: The Return of Jason *174*
    Golden Fleece? What Golden Fleece? *175*
    Help Wanted *176*
In Search of Adventure 177
    The Island of Women *177*
    Surprise Attacks *178*
    Winged Avengers and Clashing Rocks *179*
    Witch Way to the Golden Fleece *180*
Crime and Punishment: The Long Way Home 182
    Am I My Brother's Keeper? *182*
    Dangerous Waters *183*
    Dry-Docked *183*
    No Place Like Home? *184*
A Woman Scorned 185
    Beware of Colchians Bearing Gifts *185*
    The Aftermath of Tragedy *186*

15 Lucky in War, Unlucky in Love: Theseus   187
Who's Been Sleeping in My Bed? 188
Road Warrior 189
    Batter Up *189*
    Up a Tree *189*
    Look Out Below *190*
    Wanna Wrestle? *190*
    The Perfect Fit? *191*
A Lot of Bull 191
    Maternal Instinct Gone Wild *191*
    Birth of a Beast: The Minotaur *192*
    No Way Out: The Maze and the Minotaur *193*
    Loss and/or Abandonment *194*
King Theseus Wants a Wife 194
    Attack of the Amazons: Antiope *195*
    Forbidden Love: Phaedra *195*
    Midlife Crisis: The Abduction of Helen *196*

16 All's Not Fair in Love and War: The Fall of Troy   **199**

One Bad Apple Does Spoil the Bunch 200
Who's the Fairest of Them All? *200*
But She's Already Married! *200*
The Face That Launched a Thousand Ships 201
Which Way to Troy? *202*
The Long Siege of Troy Begins *202*
Heroes of the Battlefield *203*
The Final Battles: The Tenth Year of the War 206
The End of Achilles *206*
A Recipe for Winning the War *207*
Beware of Greeks Bearing Gifts! *208*
The Agony of Defeat *209*
The End of Heroes 209
Welcome Home? *210*
The House of Blood: Agamemnon's Return *211*

17 Achilles: The Angry Young Hero   **213**

How to Create an (Almost) Invulnerable Hero 214
A Lover, Not a Fighter: His Father Peleus *214*
A Marriage Made in Heaven *215*
Don't Try This at Home! *216*
Hey, This Kid's Got Potential! *217*
Draft Dodging? Try Dressing in Drag *218*
To War! 218
A Curious Cure *219*
First Blood: The Early Battles *219*
Never Insult Your Greatest Warrior *220*
The Final Battles 221
I Have Not Yet Begun to Fight *221*
Love Among the Ruins *222*

18 Take the Long Way Home: Odysseus   **223**

Is This the Stuff Heroes Are Made Of? 224
Choosing Wisely *224*
Draft Dodging? Try Feigning Insanity *225*
Going Home So Soon? Not Bloody Likely 226
What Are We Doing Here? *226*
My, What a Big Eye You Have! *227*

The Poseidon Adventures 228
  Good Host, Bad Host 228
  Pigging Out 229
  A Ghost of a Chance 230
  Eeek! Sea Monsters! 231
  Don't Have a Cow 231
  The Hard Life of a Love Slave 232
Hi, Honey, I'm Home! 233
  Reports of My Death Have Been Greatly Exaggerated 233
  No Contest 235

19 Not in Our Stars: Tragic Heroes and Their Fates   237

He Loves Me, He Loves Me Not 238
  No Voice of Her Own 238
  My Eyes Adored You 238
  Mirror, Mirror, on the Wall 239
Switchblade Sisters 240
  Sister Act 240
  Dinner—and Vengeance—Is Served 241
Mutual Mistrust: The High Cost of Jealousy 242
  A Test of Fidelity 242
  The Spy Who Loved Him 243
The Limits of Craftsmanship 244
  Towering Ambition 244
  Fly Like an Eagle, Drop Like a Stone 245
  The Shell Game 245
Dad, Can I Borrow Your Car? 246
  Son of the Sun 246
  Hold Your Horses 247

Part 4:   Friends, Romans, Countrymen   249

20 When in Rome, Worship as the Romans Worship   251

A *Practical* Guide to Roman Mythology 252
  Greek Immigrants: The Gods of Olympus Arrive in Rome 252
  Pick a God, Any God 253
  Gods in the Balance 254
  Say a Little Prayer for Me 254
  The Rituals of Everyday Life 255

Every Home a Temple 257
   Bless This House: The Lares 257
   What's in the Pantry? The Penates 257
   Spirits Everywhere 258

**21 Meet the New Boss(es), Same as the Old Boss(es):
The Gods and Goddesses of Rome**   **259**

The Magnificent Seven 260
   The Great Civilizer: Saturn 260
   By Jove, It's Jupiter! 261
   Marrying Money: The Goddess Juno 262
   Like a Virgin: Vesta 262
   Eyes in the Back of His Head: Janus 263
   War and Peace: Mars 264
   Love Makes the World Go Around: Venus 265
Ye Gods! Lesser Deities of the Romans 266
   New to the Neighborhood: The Other Olympians 266
   Greeks in Togas: The Lesser Deities Go Roman 268
   *Everything Old Becomes New Again: The Ancient
    Italian Deities* 270
   Bit Players: Minor Italian Deities 272

22 All Roads Lead to Rome: The Odyssey of Aeneas   **273**

A Born Hero 274
   The Son Also Rises 274
   The Good Soldier 275
   The Bitter End 276
A Man Without a Country 276
   Are You My Mother(land)? 277
   Islands in the Storm 277
   Juno Acts as Matchmaker 278
Veni, Vidi, Vici 280
   Passport to the Underworld 280
   Arrival of a Rival 281
   This Means War 282
   Friends, Romans, Countrymen 283

23 Rome Wasn't Built in a Day   **285**

Double Visionaries: Romulus and Remus 285
   Dancing with Wolves 286
   The Lost Generation Returns 287
   Sibling Rivalry Is for the Birds 288
If You Can't Come to Rome, Rome Will Come to You 289
   Personals: SM Seeks SF × 100 289
   Imperialist Rome 291
Rome Rules! 291
   Long Live the Kings 292
   I Just Can't Wait to Be King 293
   Et Tu, Junius Brutus? 295

Appendixes

A Glossary of Terms   **297**

B Who's Who in Classical Mythology   **301**

C What's in a Name? Greek and Roman Gods and Heroes   **361**

**D Be Careful What You Wish For: The Fates of Mortals Who
Slept with Gods or Goddesses**   **363**

E Read More About It   **367**

Index   **369**

Foreword

Many people in years past absorbed the rich details of Greek mythology from the earliest phases in their educations, but times change. While classical allusions must be at least as ubiquitous as ever, in novels, op-ed columns, and computer games, our readiness to decipher these erudite nuggets and appreciate their contribution to our thoughts and our feelings has perhaps declined somewhat as our educational curricula have grown more diffuse in approach and more varied in quality. That's why this comprehensive new edition of *The Complete Idiot's Guide to Classical Mythology* seems to me so perfectly timed and calibrated.

This book is not really for idiots, of course. It is just what you want, however, if you ever played a computer game that uses characters from classical mythology (or watched your child play it) and felt curious about those oddly powerful divinities with their distinct spheres of interest. It's just what you want, if you wonder what it means when pundits on current events describe our persistent national enemies as "hyra-headed" or label a notorious prison as "Stygian" or call someone who makes a dire warning about "sowing dragon's teeth" a "Cassandra." It's just what you want, if you would like to know the stories behind "Andromeda" and "Orion's Belt" and "Ursa Major." You can very quickly find out about these names and phrases (and hundreds more) in the helpful glossary at the back of the book, but you won't want to miss out on reading the fuller accounts within the chapters. The new edition also has a fascinating new chapter on how and why Romans appropriated Greek mythology as their own, the changes they made, and the unique deities and other elements they added. Readers may rest assured that this introductory, beginners-level book covers everything that one would likely encounter in an introductory college-level course on classical mythology.

The authors' fine sense of humor permeates this book, and their light touch makes it great fun to read. You will enjoy the clever and entertaining tone of their section headings throughout. From the chapter on Achilles: "Don't Try This at Home!" (about the way the divine Thetis tempered her infant son Achilles over hot coals); "Hey, This Kid's Got Potential!" (on early indicatons that Achilles was destined for a life of greatness and fame); "Draft Dodging? Try Dressing in Drag" (about the attempts of Achilles' anxious father, Peleus, to keep his son out of the war at Troy by hiding him among the princesses in the court of Lycomedes on the island of Scyrus); "I Have Not Yet Begun to Fight" (on the return of an absolutely manic Achilles to battle following the death of his beloved friend Patroclus); and "Love Among the Ruins" (about the bizarre passion Achilles felt for the Amazon queen Penthesilea at the very moment when he killed her in battle). But at the same time the learned authors haven't trivialized their subject, nor omitted too much. I find an excellent balance between the real substance and scholarly precision within each of the chapters, on the one hand, and the deft summaries ("The Least You Need to Know") presented as bullet points at the end of each chapter, on the other.

By Zeus, read this book! Enjoy this book! And I'll just bet that after you do, you might feel inspired to pick up a translation of *The Odyssey* and read that story next, the way Homer told it. *The Complete Idiot's Guide to Classical Mythology, Second Edition*, includes wonderful suggestions for further reading.

Ross Scaife, Ph.D.

Ross Scaife is Associate Professor of Classics at the University of Kentucky and co-editor of "The Stoa Consortium for Electronic Publication in the Humanities" (www.stoa.org)

Introduction

Oh, sure. You were supposed to have learned this stuff in school. But how much (if anything) did you really learn about classical mythology in high school or college? And how much (if anything) do you remember?

Knowledge of the mythology of the Greeks and Romans was at one time considered the hallmark of a person's education. After all, classical mythology has permeated virtually every type of literature and nearly every medium of art in the Western world over the last two thousand years.

If you visit any major art museum in the United States or Europe, you will see images of Greek or Roman gods. But when you see these gods and goddesses, can you tell them apart (without peeking at the titles)? Can you distinguish between Aphrodite and Athena—or between Zeus and Apollo?

Classical mythology has exercised a powerful influence on Western culture, both high and low art. We're not just talking Shakespeare, Tennyson, and James Joyce here either. We're talking Walt Disney, NBC, HBO—even the USA Network. Pop singers from Frankie Valli to Bananarama have sung songs about Venus. Our planets and several of our months are named after the greatest of Roman gods. And let's not forget Kevin Sorbo (TV's Hercules).

Unfortunately, most of us feel totally clueless when it comes to classical mythology. If it weren't for our elementary school children, most of us would have no notion of how Disney changed the adventures of Hercules. If you saw *The Odyssey* on TV or video, did you notice that they left out the Sirens? When you saw *Troy* in the movie theaters, did you wonder where the Greek gods and goddesses were? Assuming you knew that the planets were named after Roman gods, did you know why each got its name? Here are a few examples:

- The biggest planet was named after the greatest god (Jupiter).

- The planet with the quickest orbit was named after the fleet messenger of the gods and patron of astronomy (Mercury).

- The red planet was named after the god of war (Mars).

- The darkest and most distant planet was named after the lord of the Underworld (Pluto).

If you don't know this stuff, you may feel like a complete idiot. But that's being too hard on yourself. The classical myths are seldom taught in primary or secondary schools anymore. So where would you have learned about them? Nowhere. Until now.

Relax! They're Only Stories

You may feel somewhat intimidated or perhaps put off by the "educational" content of classical mythology. If you do, forget about it. Yes, these stories have an educational value: They're essential pieces of our culture. But don't get too hung up on that—because they're also just plain terrific stories. *The Complete Idiot's Guide to Classical Mythology, Second Edition,* will introduce you to these fantastic yarns. You'll read about battles that pit men against monsters more fearsome than Godzilla, and of the 10-year struggle between the Greeks and the Trojans outside the walled city of Troy. You'll try to solve the riddle of the Sphinx.

The Complete Idiot's Guide to Classical Mythology, Second Edition, will transport you on some amazing adventures. Travel onboard the *Argo* on a quest for the Golden Fleece. Head for Italy and join Romulus and Remus as they argue about their plans for the new city of Rome. Follow the flight of Perseus as he tracks down and decapitates the Gorgon, Medusa. This book will even take you to hell and back.

In this book, you will also meet some of the greatest characters in literature. Of course you will encounter the gods of Mount Olympus, but you will also meet mortals who suffered agonizing tragedies or achieved glorious victories. You'll meet the likes of:

- Oedipus, who unwittingly engineered his own downfall by killing his father and marrying his mother
- Procne and Philomela, who transformed into birds to escape the treachery and lechery of Procne's husband
- Heracles, the greatest of classical heroes, buffoonish yet unbeatable
- Medea, who helped Jason capture the Golden Fleece and then exacted a horrible price when he abandoned her
- Achilles, the greatest Greek hero of the Trojan War
- Odysseus, the cunning rogue who invented the famed Wooden Horse that allowed the Greeks to breach the walls of Troy

These gods and heroes—and the tales of their adventures—are guaranteed to entertain, amuse, and occasionally appall you. And they're almost certain to stick in your mind. So you'll learn something regardless of your intentions.

But again, you don't have to learn anything from this book. Just enjoy the stories. *The Complete Idiot's Guide to Classical Mythology, Second Edition,* invites you to join a host of memorable characters who undertake incredible adventures. We think the characters and their escapades are so memorable that by the time you finish this book, you'll be a virtual expert on classical mythology.

How This Book Is Organized

The Complete Idiot's Guide to Classical Mythology, Second Edition, aims to make the myths of the Greeks and Romans as accessible, entertaining, and enjoyable as possible for you. The book is divided into four parts. The adventures of both mortals and immortals form the heart of this book—and therefore find their place in the middle of the book. The next three central parts retell the most famous and significant myths of ancient Greece and Rome. In each of these parts, you will find some of the greatest tales of adventure in the world—stories that describe the nature and deeds of the gods and goddesses and stories that continue to influence our notions of heroism.

Sandwiched around these tales of the lives of mortals and immortals of the classical world, you'll find sections devoted to mythic beginnings (the conception and birth of the myths) and the mythic endings (the death and afterlife of the myths).

Part 1, "The Beginning of All Things," begins with an exploration of just what makes a myth and the functions myths play in a society. Here you will also find entertaining and enlightening stories from neighboring Babylon and Sumer that may have influenced the development of classical myths. This part also provides information on the Greek and Roman poets, playwrights, and other writers who recorded, retold, and/or reinterpreted the myths—those to whom we are indebted for our knowledge of classical mythology. Finally, you will also enjoy your first introduction to the Greek and Roman myths: the classical account of the creation of the universe—and of humankind.

Part 2, "Welcome to the Pantheon: The Greek Gods," will introduce you to all the divinities of the Greek world. This part features tales of the births and lives of the Olympians and will acquaint you with the powers, domains, and responsibilities of the classical gods and goddesses. You will also meet their forerunners, the Titans, and read how Zeus and the Olympians defeated them to conquer Olympus. Here you will also find tales of fairies and monsters, satyrs and nymphs. Finally, you will enjoy the stories of the youngest god—Dionysus, the god of wine—who overcame the persecution of the disbelievers to establish his place on Olympus.

Part 3, "Everyone Needs a Hero," presents some of the greatest adventure stories ever told. Of course, you will find here the story of the labors of Heracles—the greatest hero of them all. But you can also sail off with Jason in quest of the Golden Fleece, accompany Perseus as he sets out to slay the snake-haired Medusa, and navigate the Minotaur's Labyrinth with Theseus. You can also bemoan the fate of Oedipus and other tragic heroes—or take a trip or two to the Underworld. You will stand shoulder to shoulder with Achilles on the battlefields of Troy, then join Odysseus on his long and treacherous journey home.

Part 4, "Friends, Romans, Countrymen," will introduce you to the gods and goddesses as well as the greatest heroes of ancient Rome. You can start by meeting the Roman deities, and seeing how the Romans worshipped them. Some of these divine beings have counterparts in the Greek pantheon, but others were native nature spirits and household or ancestral gods and goddesses. You can then join Aeneas as he flees the ruins of Troy to found a new home—and the Roman race—in Italy. Then you will meet the brothers Romulus and Remus, founders of Rome, whose heroics yielded to tragic sibling rivalry. Finally, you will meet the legendary kings of ancient Rome: some benevolent, some malignant, but all adding to the glory and grandeur of their kingdom.

Extras

The Complete Idiot's Guide to Classical Mythology, Second Edition, not only offers clear, concise, and entertaining versions of the greatest tales of the Greeks and Romans, it also provides extras that will help add to your appreciation or understanding of the stories themselves—and the ways in which classical mythology has shaped our culture, ancient and contemporary. You can easily spot these extras by looking for the following icons:

> **The More Things Change …**
>
> The myths of different cultures often share similarities or common elements. Here you will find comparisons between two or more classical myths or between a particular classical myth and a mythic story from another culture.

> **Read All About It**
>
> These boxes will refer you to classical source material on particular myths—the epic poems and great tragedies from which all of our knowledge of classical mythology is derived.

> **Logos**
>
> These boxes offer definitions of unfamiliar terms and the meanings of Greek or Latin words from which English terms are derived. In addition, these boxes give you clues to the meanings of names for both people and places, explore certain word origins, and take a look at a storyteller's choice of words.

> **Mythed by a Mile**
>
> Since mythologies are neither consistent nor universally accepted, significant variations of specific myths—one storyteller's tale of divine intervention that prevents a human sacrifice described by other storytellers, for instance—can be found in these boxes.

> **What a Life!**
>
> In these boxes, you will find fascinating or amusing biographical information on secondary characters who cross paths with the main character in a myth. You will also find biographical nuggets on more prominent characters that would digress from the main story being told.

Acknowledgments

We owe special thanks to a great number of people who contributed to the genesis and creation of this book. Sharon and Timothy Kaufman-Osborn brought us together on this quest. Richard Parks guided us through the nuts and bolts of collaboration. Deb Simon clarified the astronomical explanation of why seasons change as the year progresses. Amy Zavatto, Carol Sheehan, Mike Thomas, Megan Douglass, and Ross Patty offered valuable suggestions and critical editorial advice. Tom Stevens guarded the integrity of this edition as fiercely as the hundred-headed dragon Ladon guarded the Golden Apples. Clio, Thalia, and Melpomene—the Muses of history, comedy, and tragedy—provided us with inspiration and guidance throughout this project.

Dana Burgess would also like to thank George for the Odyssey at San Galgano and Emma for Fairy Tales on the North Fork Trail.

Kevin Osborn would like to thank Megan and Ian, who eagerly embraced his rather odd choice of Ovid's *Metamorphoses* as bedtime reading, and Molly and Casey, who will soon learn to do the same.

Special Thanks to the Technical Reviewer

The Complete Idiot's Guide to Classical Mythology was reviewed in its first edition by an expert who double-checked the accuracy of what you'll learn here, to help us ensure that this book gives you everything you need to know about classical mythology. Special thanks are extended to David Sacks.

Trademarks

All terms mentioned in this book that are known to be or are suspected of being trademarks or service marks have been appropriately capitalized. Alpha Books and Penguin Group (USA) Inc. cannot attest to the accuracy of this information. Use of a term in this book should not be regarded as affecting the validity of any trademark or service mark.

Part 1

The Beginning of All Things

Everything has a beginning; mythology has many beginnings. In classical mythology, you can see the creative hand of the gods, other ancient cultures, and the poets who recorded the myths.

We develop myths in large part to explain things that we find incomprehensible. Where did the world come from? Who created the first human being? Why do the moon and stars light up the night? As many cultures have, the ancient Greeks and Romans developed their own answers to these unanswerable questions through myths of creation.

But who created the creation myths of the Greeks and Romans? After all, they did not give birth to themselves. And who were the authors who recreated these stories in written form?

The best place for us to begin looking at classical mythology is to explore exactly what a myth is. We may consider them merely entertaining stories, but the ancients regarded them as much, much more … in the beginning.

Chapter 1

Tell Me a Story

In This Chapter

- ◆ What is a myth?
- ◆ The various functions of mythology
- ◆ The recorders of classical mythology
- ◆ The ingredients of classical mythology
- ◆ Ancient attitudes toward myths

Do you like a good story? Do you enjoy stirring tales of battles fought and won (or lost); moving stories of loves thwarted by fate or by human nature and of loves that endure against all odds; tragic tales of lives torn apart by sibling rivalry, jealousy, or simple foolish pride? Do you draw a sense of satisfaction when a villain's betrayal, arrogance, or cruelty lead directly to his or her downfall? Are you enchanted by fantastic tales of superhuman strength, magical powers, and remarkable transformations?

If so, you've come to the right place. Classical mythology covers all the bases. Here you can find:

- ◆ Heroic adventure stories
- ◆ Tales of superhuman heroism on the field of battle
- ◆ Passionate love stories

- Fantastic tales of gods and monsters

- Moral tales in which pride goeth before the fall

- Tear-jerkers about lost loves and tragic lives

- Tales of fantastic beasts and their battles with men

- Marvelous accounts of the creation of the universe and the creatures who inhabit it

- Gripping domestic dramas in which tensions rise to a fevered pitch

- Wondrous fairy tales that transport you to magical worlds

- Tales of sorcery and witchcraft

- Magical stories in which humans change into beasts or flowers

- Tales of virtue rewarded and of treachery avenged

Logos

Our word **myth** comes from the Greek word *mythos*, which has a wide range of meanings. Some of these include "word," "saying," "speech," "tale," "story," "purpose," "plan," "fact," "plot," and "fiction."

The *myths* of the ancient Greeks and Romans offer a wide variety of tales that will appeal to the tastes of virtually every reader. So feel free to dive right in.

Try not to feel intimidated by the "classical" label. Yes, these myths are classical: They come from ancient Greece and Rome. But these stories are classics, too—in the same sense that movies like *It's a Wonderful Life* or *The Wizard of Oz* or *E.T.* or *Gone With the Wind* are classics: They're not to be missed.

Don't worry. We won't be testing you later, so you won't need to memorize the difference between Eris and Eros, Pelias and Peleus, or Leda and Leto. In fact, at the end of each chapter, rather than quizzing you, we offer up the answers, highlighting the most important points about each myth. So pour yourself a glass of mead (or a cup of tea or coffee or anything else you'd like), settle down in your favorite comfy chair, and enjoy these stories.

Stories That Mean Something

Undoubtedly myths are entertaining stories. But myths are—or were—much more than just that. In their time, myths serve many important functions for the society and culture that believe in them.

Why Does the Rain Fall from Up Above? (Why Do Fools Fall in Love?)

Many myths have an explanatory element. They attempt to provide an *aetiology*, to explain otherwise unanswerable questions, to provide reasons that things are the way they are.

The current state of our scientific knowledge, for example, allows us to know that the earth has seasons because of the tilt of the earth's axis. When the tilt of the axis points the northern hemisphere toward the sun, the sunlight's energy falls more directly on the northern surface of the earth. This makes it summer in the north and winter in the south. But because the tilt of the planet's axis remains fixed, as the earth gradually revolves halfway around the sun over the course of six months, the northern hemisphere increasingly faces away from the sun. As a result, the sun's light hits the northern hemisphere less directly and the seasons change. In the north it becomes colder as summer turns to autumn and then winter; in the south, it becomes hotter as winter gives way to spring and then summer. When, over the course of the next six months, the earth completes its revolution around the sun, the seasons change again.

Logos

Aetiology or **etiology**, derived from the Greek word *aition* ("cause"), means the study of first causes. Classical mythology was fascinated with first causes, the origins of the conditions we experience in our lives. Why, for example, do we hear an echo in the mountains? Aetiology leads us to the story of a lovelorn nymph who lost her body and became nothing but a voice (see Chapter 19).

The Greeks and Romans, however, unaware of the tilting of the earth (or the fact that it revolves or the spherical shape of the globe), came up with another explanation of why the seasons change. The story of Demeter and Persephone (see Chapter 11) filled this gap in the knowledge of the ancients.

Providing a moving or entertaining story to explain puzzling natural phenomena makes the "explanation" much more memorable. In the case of Demeter and Persephone, the heart-wrenching story of a mother's grief over her missing daughter etches itself into the listener's (or reader's) brain. The "explanation" of seasonal changes—the re-emergence of Persephone from the Underworld and her reunion with her mother, the goddess of fertility—satisfies not only our curiosity, but also our sense of divine justice and our faith in an ordered universe.

Many Greek and Roman myths answered such unanswerable questions as:

♦ Why does the sun move across the sky every day—and where does it go at night? (See Chapter 8.)

♦ How did humankind learn to harness the power—the light and the heat—of fire? (See Chapter 2.)

♦ Why do certain flowers—the hyacinth, for example—display the patterns of color they do? (See Chapter 7.) Or why does the heliotrope turn its bloom to follow the sun throughout the day? (See Chapter 8.)

♦ Why do the people of Africa have dark skin? (See Chapter 19.)

Of course, classical myths also tackle the biggest questions:

♦ How was the world created? (See Chapter 2.)

♦ What's the difference between humans and gods? (See Chapters 13 and 17.)

♦ Where did the first humans come from? (See Chapter 2.)

♦ What is love? (See Chapter 19.)

♦ Why do humans suffer? (See Chapter 2.)

♦ What happens to us when we die? (See Chapter 11.)

Many myths also serve a religious function—an obvious consequence of stories that concern themselves with the nature and actions of gods and the way they relate to the human race. Though the gods of the ancient Greeks and Romans were often arbitrary in their treatment of human beings (a reflection of the difficult living conditions at that time), the myths nonetheless testify to the belief in an ordered universe. Nearly every aspect of nature and human life fell under the domain of one or more gods or goddesses.

Stories of the gods and their various aspects spelled out for the Greeks and Romans which god they should petition for specific types of help. Some of the gods to whom these ancients prayed included:

♦ Hestia (Vesta) for the safety of home and family

♦ Athena (Minerva) for wisdom or courage

♦ Demeter (Ceres) for an abundant harvest

♦ Artemis (Diana) for a successful hunt

♦ Ares (Mars) for military might

- Hermes (Mercury) for traveler's aid

- Poseidon (Neptune) for a safe sea voyage

- Zeus (Jupiter) for justice

- Aphrodite (Venus) for love

While providing a soothing sense of order, myths also explore incomprehensible and possibly terrifying aspects of life. Love can be painful, as both Echo and Narcissus discovered (see Chapter 19). Guilt can be meaningless, as Oedipus—who sinned without knowing it—found out (see Chapter 12). Even the gods can be hostile. Witness the persecution of Heracles by Hera (see Chapter 13).

Among the Greeks and Romans, myths also pointed the way toward acceptable behavior in interactions with both gods and fellow humans. Those who transgressed the laws of Zeus—or otherwise offended the gods—invariably suffered from retribution at the hands of those gods. Those who committed crimes against family members would be tormented by the Erinyes (Furies). Hosts who scorned the laws of hospitality—or guests who sinned against their hosts—would suffer the wrath of Zeus. By encouraging socially acceptable behavior and discouraging crimes and other sins, such myths helped to uphold and protect the social order, while recognizing and respecting its fragility.

Which Came First: The Chicken or the Egg?

Other myths helped to justify particular religious rites or practices. When the Greeks offered up a sacrifice to the gods, for instance, they burned the bones of the slaughtered animal while saving the meat for themselves. Why? Because in the sacred narrative (myth) of the first sacrifice, Prometheus reserved the meat for humans and gave the gods the bones and fat (see Chapter 2).

Some classical myths explained, justified, or perhaps led to the development of particular religious rituals and practices—or even gave rise to the birth of cults devoted to a specific deity. The myth of Dionysus, for example, justified (or spawned) an elaborate set of religious rituals and ecstatic rites performed by the Dionysian cults (see Chapter 9). The story of Orpheus gave rise to an Orphic cult with its own set of religious rites (see Chapter 11). The myths of Demeter—and the importance of the goddess of the harvest in the day-to-day lives of the ancients—gave rise to the Eleusinian *mystery religion*.

Logos

Mystery religions were secret cults in both Greece and Rome that offered religious experiences that the more established, officially sanctioned religious practices could not offer. The Dionysian cults, the Orphic cults, and the Eleusinian Mysteries were all mystery religions. Initiates in these secret cults would seek spiritual fulfillment through arcane ceremonies and rituals, religious feasts, and dances—activities that also strengthened the bonds within the cult.

Stories that complement, explain, or justify religious practices or rituals raise a chicken-and-egg problem: Which came first, the myths or the religious rituals? If the story was created first, then the complementary ritual was developed later to honor that story. But if the religious ritual was performed before the creation of the complementary story, then was the myth created solely to justify these religious practices?

We cannot know which came first. We can only appreciate them as different but complementary methods of religious expression: the myths in symbolic narrative form, the rituals in symbolic actions.

The Sacred and the Profane (and the Heroic)

Not all myths became the basis for religious beliefs or religious practices. Often, a culture's myths can serve to justify or validate social standing or political power in the secular world. The Romans, for example, used mythology to establish a grandiose lineage for their rulers. Roman myths showed their line of kings and later emperors to be descended not only from great *heroes*, but from the gods themselves (see Chapters 22 and 23).

Logos

Our word **hero** comes from the Greek word *heros*. In one of its senses, this term refers to great men who have died and have become protective local divinities through burial in the soil. Through their direct connection to the earth, these heroes defend their homeland during times of crisis. Although people could invoke the protective services of these heroes through prayer and sacrifice, the heroes belonged solely to that one place.

Similarly, Babylon's *Enuma Elish* (see Chapter 3)—a possible precursor of classical myths—told the story of how the god Marduk brought order to chaos, becoming the first lord to govern the universe. This myth established (though much more obliquely than the Roman myths) the authority of earthly kings as well, giving the royals a divine mandate to rule over their people.

Other myths in the secular realm (though often guided by the hands of the gods) are the tales of heroes. The heroes of such stories usually embody human characteristics that the society holds up as admirable, heroic, or ideal.

In wartime, heroism—in almost all cultures, not just Greece and Rome—has meant fearlessness in battle, loyalty to one's allies and their united cause, an ambition for glory, and a ruthless efficiency in slaughtering the enemy (see Chapters 16 and 17). In more peaceful times, it meant honor, hospitality, loyalty, devotion to family, and often a thirst for adventure (see especially Chapters 10 and 14).

Though hero myths sometimes describe valued human traits, they are almost never as didactic as fables. You will only rarely find any explicit "moral" attached to a myth. Myths seldom offer specific "recipes for life."

The Tellers and Their Tales

The myths of Greece and Rome come from an oral tradition. In an almost entirely illiterate society, these stories were passed down from generation to generation or from storytellers to an audience. Who created these myths? And how did their listeners respond to these stories?

We cannot know who originally created the myths of ancient Greece and Rome. It seems reasonable to assume that they existed for generations—or even centuries—before anyone thought to write them down. Indeed, we only know the mythology of ancient Greece and Rome because these oral traditions became part of a written tradition. The Greek poets Homer and Hesiod, who composed their works in the eighth or seventh century B.C.E., are recognized as the oldest sources we have only because they—or someone else who had heard their recitations—took the trouble to write down the stories they narrated.

The Big Eight

Our knowledge of classical mythology comes primarily through the works of eight poets and writers. Though others have also contributed, these eight stand out among the recorders of Greek and Roman mythology:

◆ *Homer*, the Greek poet who (probably) composed the two greatest Greek epics: *The Iliad* (about the final months of the 10-year Trojan War) and *The Odyssey* (about the torturous 10-year return voyage of one of the heroes of that war)

- *Hesiod*, another Greek poet who composed *Theogony*—a poetic narrative of the creation of the world and the succession of the gods

- *Aeschylus*, one of three great Greek dramatists, whose seven surviving plays include *the Oresteia* (three plays about the tragic house of Atreus), *Prometheus Bound*, and *Seven Against Thebes*

- *Sophocles*, another Greek dramatist, whose surviving plays include *Electra*, *Ajax*, *Antigone*, and two plays about the tragic figure Oedipus

- *Euripides*, the third great Greek dramatist, whose 19 surviving works include *The Bacchae*, *Medea*, *Iphigenia in Aulis*, *Hippolytus*, *Heracles*, and *The Trojan Women*

- *Apollodorus*, a mysterious mythographer about whom nothing is known except his work: *The Library*, a wide-ranging description of everything from the creation of the world to tales of the gods and heroes

- *Vergil*, the Roman poet who wrote Rome's greatest epic, *The Aeneid*, which tells of the hero Aeneas and his journey from Troy to Italy, where he founded the Roman race

- *Ovid*, another Roman poet whose best work, *Metamorphoses*, collects a great variety of mythic tales of people transformed into other shapes and sizes (such as animals, plants, or rocks)

The Greek poets Homer and Hesiod told their versions of the Greek myths around the eighth century B.C.E. The three dramatists had their heyday in the fifth century, and the two greatest Roman poets in the first century B.C.E. (Apollodorus remains a mysterious and shadowy figure.)

How much of what these authors have given us is tradition and how much the author's invention? We'll never know.

Fortunately, the culture of myth is expressed not only through literature, but through other arts as well. Painted pottery and sculptures from ancient Greece and Rome seem to support versions of these tales that have survived. But how much these artists were influenced by the same era's storytellers we can never know. We can reasonably assume that since they read their works aloud to an audience, most of the poets generally adhered to the traditions of stories known by their listeners and their forebears for centuries. But we can just as reasonably assume that for their own particular reasons—whether poetic license, metrical consistency, dramatic effect, or a personal or political agenda—these poets also added or subtracted certain details, changed others, and perhaps even invented entire stories that became, through telling and retelling, an integral part of the ancient culture.

A Dash of Heroism, a Handful of Fate

The recorders of the myths each served up a different dish, some focusing on specific mythic events but touching on a wide range of related stories, others aiming for a more comprehensive recording of the tales. But each author basically had the same ingredients to work with. The elements of classical mythology included:

♦ *The pantheon of gods and goddesses, each with his or her own domain and attributes.* Putting each god and goddess in his or her place lent the world a sense of order—even when the deities themselves behaved irrationally or arbitrarily.

♦ *Human and often superhuman characters; heroes who—though usually mortal—descended from the gods themselves.* The tales of these heroes inspired awe and perhaps emulation and also glorified or sanctified the heroes' homelands.

♦ *Tales of extraordinary events, things that did not happen in everyday life (divine intervention, encounters with terrifying monsters, journeys to Olympus or the Underworld).* Though these stories were fantastic and often implausible, no attempt was made to justify them as true. Some may have accepted them as true tales, while others no doubt recognized a wisdom in the tales that did not depend upon a literal understanding.

♦ *A specific place at an unspecified time.* Mythic events usually occurred in places known to the listeners: Athens, Sparta, Thebes, Rome. But they took place in mythic time—outside of our day-to-day experience. The tales of heroes can be placed in a roughly chronological order, but even these took place in an unspecified time.

♦ *Separation or distance from ordinary, everyday human experience.* Though gods often intervened in the lives of heroes or other mythic characters, they rarely had direct contact with the poets or their audiences.

♦ *The strong hand of destiny.* Future events were often foretold by *oracles* in mythic stories. But no matter how hard people—or even gods—attempted to avoid fulfilling these prophecies, they could not escape the hand of fate.

♦ *A reflection of the culture that gave rise to them.* Through myths, cultures often explore and express the way people think about themselves and the world. The myths therefore give us insight into how the ancient Greeks and Romans thought and felt about nature, society, gender, and many other aspects of their culture.

Logos

An **oracle** was a priest or priestess who received divine knowledge about future or past events. The term also referred to the often cryptic prophecies received and transmitted by these diviners.

Myths? What Myths?

In reading classical myths today, we can—and most likely do—take them as entertaining, and perhaps enlightening, stories. We may see the myths as symbolic stories about the relationship between humans and the natural world, between humans and other humans, or between individual humans and the larger society. But the Greeks and Romans did not have this detachment. For these ancient peoples, the myths were an essential part of their culture.

All myths carry with them as an essential element an air of authority. The stories they tell are unproven, but they were also unquestioned by the culture that gave rise to them. How much the ancients actually believed in the truth of these tales no doubt varied from person to person, ranging from the rural peasant who might have accepted as literal the tales of local ancestral heroes to the urban sophisticate who found in this rich body of tales not gospel truth, but philosophic insight or pure amusement. Myths address truths ranging from weather patterns to family feuds, from the colors of a flower to the sorrows of a grieving parent. Whether accepted literally or examined for their "deeper" meaning, these myths offer insight to all people, ancient or modern.

The Least You Need to Know

- Classical myths are terrific, entertaining stories. For the ancients, they undoubtedly had a religious significance. But for us, they're just fun.

- Most myths helped to explain (to their original audiences) what would otherwise be unexplainable: the creation of the universe, the condition of the natural and social worlds, the authority of kings, or the genesis of religious rituals.

- The greatest of ancient Greek poets were Homer and Hesiod. The greatest dramatists were Aeschylus, Sophocles, and Euripides. The greatest of ancient Roman poets were Vergil and Ovid.

- The essential elements of classical mythology—the intervention of deities in human affairs, the non-specificity of time, the superhuman heroes, the fantastic creatures, and the extraordinary events—all helped to establish a distance between the world of myths and the everyday worlds of ancient peoples.

2

O Brave New World

In This Chapter

- ◆ The Creation of all things
- ◆ The supreme importance of Eros in Creation
- ◆ The succeeding ages of man
- ◆ How the Titan Prometheus, champion of mankind, earned the wrath of Zeus
- ◆ The revenge of Zeus: Pandora, the first woman

The place to begin, of course, is always at the beginning: the beginning of all things. Although particular myths or certain stories may begin *in medias res*—"in the middle of things"—Creation stories never can. Classical mythology starts, as it must, with the Creation of the universe and the creation of the human race.

The mythologies that cultures create—the stories that people elaborate to make sense of life's mysteries; to impose structure and order on the universe; and to define the place of individuals, races, and all people in that universe—must start with a story explaining the origins of all things. For how can people fully define where they are without first explaining where they came from?

The Big Bang Theory: Creation Through Procreation

To the Greeks, the universe began with a mystery. The physical world was not born from nothing. The existence we know did not spring from any primeval, primordial void. Instead it sprang from the unknown, from Chaos.

> **Read All About It** _____
>
> The most detailed account of early classical Creation myths comes to us from *Theogony*, a poem composed by Hesiod, a Greek poet, in the eighth century B.C.E. The first book of *Metamorphoses*, a narrative poem written by the Roman Ovid early in the first century, also offers a compelling version of the Creation.

What a Mess!

Chaos, which Hesiod conceived of as an enormous chasm, came first, born into darkness. Ovid, who agreed that everything in the world began with Chaos, saw it somewhat differently. Ovid viewed Chaos as shapeless, mutable matter—an idea that fit in well with the theme of his *Metamorphoses*, which focused on gods, humans, and other creatures who changed their form.

In Ovid's primordial Chaos, land and sea and air existed. Yet all matter remained formless, shapeless, forever changing, and at war within. No one could stand on this mutable land; no one could swim in this ever-changing water; no one could breathe this inconstant air. The confused atoms of this Chaos constantly warred with one another. Heat fought with cold; liquid battled against solid; wet warred with dry; hard battled with soft; the weighty struggled with the weightless. Every quality clashed with its opposite.

After Chaos came *Gaia*, the Earth, either born of Chaos or simply rising on its own. The Earth surrounded and engulfed Chaos. From where Chaos and Gaia came is neither explained nor elaborated. Hesiod simply states that they came first—and that the Earth came into being to serve as a solid foundation for the home of the gods.

> **Logos** _____
>
> **Gaia** means both Earth itself and the early goddess of the earth. Most of the early gods and goddesses have this kind of dual function: as both the personification of a natural object or phenomenon and the deity associated with that object. So Uranus is both the Sky and the early god of the sky. Pontus is the Sea and the god of the sea. Nyx is the Night and the goddess of the night.

Ovid does not explain the sudden appearance of Earth either—attributing the molding of Earth to God or Nature, but refusing to take sides in a debate over which. In either case, he insisted the emergence of Earth brought harmony and order to Chaos. Its "birth" separated heaven from Earth, water from land, and air from airless space. Each thing in the universe found its place through this orderly separation.

A Garden of Earthly Delights

Here Hesiod and Ovid part ways. Ovid continued to see the hand of a Divine Creator (or personified Nature). This Creator, having shaped the globe, then added the waters: ponds, marshes, rivers, and oceans. He (Ovid saw the Creator as male) then formed the land into widespread plains, towering mountains and settled valleys, and full, leafy forests.

The Creator then moved from Earth to Sky. He spread the air above all things and filled it with clouds and winds and dreaded thunder and lightning. Over all of these, the Creator placed the pure and weightless ether, untainted by Earth. Within the Sky, the Creator brought forth the stars, forever earlier shrouded in darkness. The stars beamed throughout the heavens, home of the gods. Finally, the Creator added fish to the seas, beasts to the land, and birds to the air. All was almost complete—shaped throughout by a divine hand—in Ovid's world. The stage was set. Now all that was needed were the players.

By contrast, Hesiod presented the progression of Creation—at least initially—without explanation or attribution to a divine hand. The first four beings—and the natural phenomena or abstract qualities they personified—Hesiod proclaimed, sprang into being without cause or explanation. After Chaos and Gaia came Tartarus, which—located deep within the earth's depths—would become the lowest level of the Underworld. Then came Eros, the fairest of all the immortals. Only after these four have emerged do Hesiod and Ovid begin to explain the rest of Creation.

Logos

Parthenogenesis, which refers to creation resulting from just one gender, pops up in many different world mythologies. In Greek mythology, both Aphrodite and Athena owe their births to parthenogenesis. In Norse mythology, Freya, a mother goddess, has no mother herself, but only a father: Njord, the god of fertility. The Bible's Eve, created from the rib of Adam, is another example.

All You Need Is Love

Through Gaia and Chaos all else comes into being. Yet though these primeval beings give birth to the universe, the driving force behind almost all Creation from this point is Eros: Love. For the birth of almost everything else in the universe came only after powerful erotic attraction. From the mountains and seas to the creatures that would inhabit them, all emerged as products of procreation through good old-fashioned sex.

First came the few beings who were born through *parthenogenesis:*

◆ Chaos gave birth to Erebus—the darkness of the Underworld—and Nyx (Night). All other forces of darkness or negativity sprang from this originator.

◆ In her sleep, Gaia (Earth) gave birth to Uranus (Sky and the god of the sky) and Pontus (Sea and the god of the sea). Uranus came first—and emerged as Gaia's equal.

After the emergence of Erebus, Nyx, Uranus, and Pontus, virtually all of Creation came through mating. Uranus, the Sky, emerged as big as his mother Gaia, so that he might envelop her—which he quickly did. Radiant with love for his Mother Earth, the Sky showered her with fertile rain. Gaia then gave birth to the rest of the physical world: the mountains, bodies of water, flora, and fauna.

Gaia and Uranus also brought forth the 12 Titans (see Chapter 5). Two of these children, Oceanus and Tethys, continued the Creation themselves—in prodigious fashion. Their mating produced the 3,000 rivers of Earth—all of which draw their waters from the mighty stream of Oceanus—as well as 3,000 Oceanids, ocean goddesses all.

CAUTION **Mythed by a Mile**

The great Greek poet Homer, author of the epics *The Iliad* and *The Odyssey*, attributed an even greater role in Creation to Oceanus and Tethys. Homer held that Oceanus—the great stream that circles the world, flowing on the earth's outermost edge, and the god of that primordial stream—provided the source not only for all the seas and rivers, but all living creatures, including the gods. And Tethys—the ancient sea goddess, daughter of Earth and Sky—was the mother of all these children.

Afterward, Oceanus and Tethys quarreled and parted. This, too, was a gift to the world. If their unbridled creation had continued, the overstuffed world would never have either order or stability.

Nyx mated with Erebus, producing a daughter, Hemera (Day) and a son, Aether (the upper air). Night (Nyx) and Day (Hemera) share a house, forever shrouded in darkness by the grim clouds of Tartarus. Yet they never dwell in the house together. Instead they take turns, each waiting for the other to depart before crossing the bronze threshold and entering the house. When Night departs, cradling Sleep

(Death's brother) in her arms, she greets her daughter Day—but only in passing. Each has her own domain. Night also spawned a breed of mostly unpleasant abstractions, personified:

- Moros (Doom)
- Thanatos (Death)
- Hypnos (Sleep)
- Nemesis (a goddess of retribution)
- Eris (Strife)
- The Keres (female death-spirits who would be charged with collecting and carrying off the bodies of the dead)
- The Moirai (Fates)

Eris, or Strife (according to Hesiod, who became increasingly abstract and philosophical), then bred a host of woes ranging from Famine and Sorrows to Lies and Murder.

What a Life!

The Three Fates—Clotho, Lachesis, and Atropos—would later have the responsibility of determining the course of events in mortal lives—including the span of each life. Clotho spun the thread of life, Lachesis measured it with a rod, and Atropos snipped it with shears, thereby ending it. They also saw that violators of divine laws received due punishment, though they remained remote and disinterested in meting out this divine justice.

Mama Laid an Egg

Nearly 3,000 years before the time of Hesiod, the Pelasgians—immigrants to Greece from Asia Minor—had quite a different take on Creation. The Pelasgians brought with them a tradition of devotion to a mother goddess. So for them, the Creation could only have sprung from Eurynome, the Goddess of All Things.

The Pelasgians, like later Greeks, envisioned the beginning as Chaos. Eurynome arose naked from Chaos. She then separated the sea from the sky so that she would have something to stand on. As the Goddess danced across the waves, she spun around and caught the wind created by her own wake.

Rubbing this wind between her hands, Eurynome created Ophion, a great serpent. To keep warm, the Goddess danced with more and more frenzy. Her gyrations excited the lust of Ophion, who entwined himself about her limbs and mated with her.

Now pregnant, Eurynome transformed herself into a dove and laid the Universal Egg upon the waters. She then ordered Ophion to wrap himself seven times around the egg. In time, the egg hatched, releasing the universe inside: all the heavenly bodies, including the Earth—already shaped with mountains, seas, and rivers, already blessed with all manner of flowers and beasts.

When Ophion, who lived with Eurynome on Mount Olympus, later claimed to have created the universe himself, Eurynome kicked him in the head, bruising him and knocking out his teeth. She then banished him to the dark realms well beneath the Earth's surface, where he and his descendants would dwell forever.

Mythed by a Mile

The Orphic cult, reputedly founded by the mythological hero Orpheus (see Chapter 11), developed a Creation myth that incorporated elements of both the Pelasgian myth and the tradition recorded by Hesiod. The Orphic myth holds that in the beginning, Nyx (Night) mated with the Wind, then laid a silver Egg in the lap of Darkness. From this Egg emerged Eros, the golden-winged god of love. Eros, who also went by the name Phanes, then brought the whole world out from the hidden depths of the Egg into the light. Oceanus and Tethys, who emerged from the Egg, became the first to marry—a coupling that would ultimately lead to the races of Titans, gods, and humans.

A Work in Progress: The Ages of Man

Even with the creation of land, air, and sea, something was still missing: human beings. Humans, however, were not the first mortal beings created by the immortals. Several stages of mortals led up to the creation of the mortal human race:

+ The Golden Age

+ The Silver Age

+ The Bronze Age

+ The Iron Age

Golden Years

The immortals first created a race of mortal men during the reign of Cronus, the Titan who overthrew Uranus as king of the immortals (see Chapter 5). This first race of mortals—all males—were fashioned from gold and they lived a golden life, full of laughter, dancing, and other pleasures.

The golden men lived free from pains, cares, miseries, sorrows, fears, and anxieties. Even death, when it came, did not disturb their peace, for it always came as sleep. Neither diseases nor the ravages of aging afflicted them, as they spent their lives in eternal spring.

The fragrant land freely yielded its abundant harvest without back-breaking toil. Mountainsides gave them berries and cherries and edible acorns. The fields were forever filled with wheat and other grains. Rivers flowed with milk and honey. And the leaves of the trees dripped with nectar. Though unplanted by men, flowers decorated every field and hillside.

Throughout the world, these golden men lived in peace, free from any aggression. No walled cities sprang up, because no one warred on their neighbors. Indeed, neither weapons nor armor even existed. The golden men needed neither laws nor judges. No threat of retribution or punishment was ever required, for justice and right were cherished by each and every one of these golden mortals. They never constructed ships, for everything they wanted or needed could be found at home.

In short, this golden race lived like gods—but they were mortal nonetheless. When this race died (and with no women, they could not perpetuate the race), they became the holy spirits of the earth. In later ages, they protected mortals from injustice and bestowed wealth upon men.

Read All About It _____

Both Ovid (in *Metamorphoses*) and Hesiod (in *Works and Days*) detail these ages of man: the stages through which the gods created mortal men.

Hi-Ho Silver

During the reign of Zeus, the ruler of the Olympian gods who overthrew Cronus and the Titans (see Chapter 5), a second mortal race was fashioned. By this time, Earth no longer basked in eternal spring, but moved through summer, autumn, and winter as well. The change in seasons forced men to build houses. The caves and the canopies of trees in the woods and forests no longer provided enough shelter. The seasons also meant that the earth now demanded cultivation: Men needed to plow the fields, plant the seeds, and harvest the crops.

As for the silver mortals (again, all men), they fell short of the standards set by the golden race, but still proved superior to the bronze men who would follow. The silver race remained infantile for most of their lives, spending 100 years nurtured as babies. Adulthood was very brief, for the silver mortals—moved by greed and the lust for power—committed reckless violence against one another.

These foolish men offended the gods of Olympus, for they never performed any sacrifices to honor them. Stung by this slight, Zeus destroyed the silver race. After death, these silver men became the spirits of the Underworld.

Coming in Third: The Bronze Medal

The third mortal race—men fashioned from ash trees—continued the downward progression. A mighty and violent race fashioned by Zeus, the bronze men proved much more aggressive than those who had come before them. Though not entirely evil, they did not hesitate to take up weapons to serve their ends or protect their interests.

Since iron had not yet been mined, they forged weapons, tools, and even their homes out of bronze. By their own hands, fighting brother against brother, they killed themselves. Despite all their strength, they could not avoid Death. Nameless, they sank down to the icy palace of Hades, lord of the Underworld.

Hard as Nails: The Iron Man

Finally, the last race of mortals came: our own human race. Here Ovid and Hesiod agree: This was by far the basest race of all. Ours was the race that first gave evil free rein over the earth. Modesty gave way to shamelessness; truth to deceit; and righteousness to vice and violence. This race of men—later abetted by the creation of women—would scheme and cheat and even kill to fulfill their greed.

The life of men born in the Iron Age is one of constant work. Neither day nor night offers any rest from man's pain and labor. No longer content with the fruit of natural harvests, men began mining for gold and precious metals—and, of course, for iron. Iron men invented the concept of private property, plotting out their acreage and marking off boundaries on the land—once as free as air or water or sunlight.

The iron men took up arms and went to war against one another. Gold became its object; iron, its weapon. Civility and the bonds of society dissolved. Hosts attacked their guests; guests plundered their hosts. Brothers killed brothers and sons pushed their fathers toward death.

This sinful race, the classical poets agree, is the one into which all of us are born. And this race has banished justice, loyalty, and piety from the world.

Quest for Fire

Who were the first of this cursed race of mortals? And how did they come into being? Many Greeks believed that the gods—working far beneath the earth's surface—built the first men of earth and fire and other elements. Others believed that men were created *autochthoniously:* They simply sprang out of the earth, children of Gaia, the mother of all Creation. The Pelasgians may have believed that the first men—including their ancient ancestor Pelasgus—sprang up from the serpent Ophion's teeth after Eurynome kicked them out of his mouth.

The most compelling tale of early mortals, however, centers on a Titan: *Prometheus.* Many Greeks credited Prometheus as the originator of humankind: He fashioned humans out of clay and water in the likeness of the gods. But whether or not Prometheus created the human race, he was the greatest champion of humankind among the immortals.

The father of Prometheus was Iapetus, one of the original Titans (the children of Uranus and Gaia). His mother was Clymene, one of the Oceanids (the 3,000 daughters of Oceanus and Tethys). Iapetus and Clymene had three other children, all boys: the famed Atlas, Menoetius, and *Epimetheus.* Epimetheus would become his brother Prometheus's constant companion, his loyal—but far less cunning—sidekick.

Where's the Beef?

At one point early in the history of this new race of men, the gods and men came together and argued over which portion of a sacrificial bull should go to men and which to the gods. The Olympians asked Prometheus to arbitrate the dispute.

Prometheus first carved up the bull. From the bull's hide, he fashioned two open-mouthed bags. Into one, he placed the choicest flesh, but covered the meat with the unappetizing stomach of the beast. Into the other bag, he placed bare bones—but hid them beneath a layer of rich and gleaming fat.

Logos

Autochthony, derived from autos ("self") and chthon ("earth"), means the spontaneous creation of people from the soil. Many peoples, from the Greeks to Native Americans, have claimed that they sprang directly from the soil they now inhabit. Such myths justify a tribe's special relationship to a certain piece of land. Both the Athenians and the Thebans, among others, traced their origins to autochthony.

Logos

Prometheus means "foresight," a quality the Titan demonstrated in abundance. Prometheus sided with the Olympian gods in their war against his fellow Titans (see Chapter 5) and persuaded Epimetheus to do the same. The brothers thus became the rare Titans to find favor among the Olympian gods. **Epimetheus** means "hindsight." This name suited him well, too, for he seldom learned anything until after he had suffered the consequences of his ignorance.

Prometheus, delighting in his own cleverness, then told Zeus to choose the portion that should go to the gods. Zeus saw through the deception, but chose the fat-covered bones in order to create an eternal hostility between gods and humans, a hostility that would forever maintain the distance between the realm of the divine and domain of mortals. (Ever since this trick, humans offer only the bones when burning offerings to the gods in *sacrifice*.)

Logos

Sacrifice, from the Latin sacrum ("sacred") and facere ("to make"), means "to make sacred." People in the ancient world ate much less meat than we do today. Essentially an antiquated version of the backyard barbecue, the special occasion of a sacrifice afforded a rare opportunity to feast on meat.

Zeus, however, enraged that Prometheus would even think about tricking him this way, decided to withhold the gift of fire from humankind. Man might get the choicest meat, he sneered, but they would have to eat it raw.

Crafty Prometheus stole the fire anyway—either from the workshop of Hephaestus, the god of fire, artisans, smiths, and other metalworkers (see Chapter 7) or from the hearth-fire of Zeus's palace, or by lighting a torch from the flaming chariot of Helius (the Sun). After plucking a glowing ember from this everlasting fire, he hid it in a hollow stalk of a fennel plant. Joyfully, he raced to man with the divine gift of fire.

Sugar and Spice and Everything Nice? Not Quite!

When from his palace on Olympus Zeus spied the glow of men's fires below, his rage shook the heavens. He proclaimed the fire a curse on Prometheus and his descendants as well as on humankind. To avenge himself on man, Zeus prepared an evil yet seductive gift. Zeus laughed as he set in motion his plot of vengeance, for he knew that men would eagerly welcome this evil gift.

Until this time, all mortal races had been exclusively male—a condition that goes a long way toward explaining why none of them lasted very long. The female counterparts of earlier mortals, if any, were *nymphs* of the lakes and forests and mountains. But mortal women had not yet been seen on Earth.

Logos

Nymphs were semi-divine, female spirits of nature who inhabited trees, mountains, and bodies of water.

To punish man for receiving the fire—and perhaps to complete the creation of this final human race—Zeus decided to change all that. He ordered Hephaestus—the greatest of all craftsmen—to mix earth with water and fashion a clay woman. Hephaestus sculpted the form of a shy, modest maiden and molded a face modeled after the goddesses. Other immortals also contributed to the creation of this wondrous new creature, the world's first woman:

♦ The goddess Athena dressed her in white, veiled her face, and decorated her with jewels.

♦ Hephaestus forged a golden crown that Athena placed on her head.

♦ Aphrodite, the goddess of love, anointed her with both grace and charm, but also filled her with ravenous lust.

♦ Hermes, the god of thieves and rogues, endowed her with an intoxicating voice, but also with lies, flattery, seduction, treachery, and shamelessness.

♦ Peitho (Persuasion) provided her with golden necklaces.

♦ The Horae (Seasons) wreathed her head with spring flowers.

♦ The four winds breathed life into her.

When all was finished, Hermes named this maiden Pandora (which means "all gifts"), since all the gods had given her a "gift," sealed inside a special box or jar, to carry to mankind: an evil that would long torment this race of men. Hermes then swiftly brought the figure down to Epimetheus, the brother of Prometheus. Though his brother, who had foreseen that Zeus would retaliate, had cautioned him never to accept a gift from Zeus, Epimetheus did not heed this warning.

Before the arrival of Pandora, men had lived free of painful illness, free of suffering, free of the need for toil and hardship. But Pandora had not been on Earth long before she became curious about the gifts that lay inside the vessel the gods had given her. When she opened this jar or box to see, the contents overflowed and scattered throughout the earth. The "gifts" released from *Pandora's box*—such sources of woe as vice, passion, labor, old age, insanity, sickness, and even death—brought only grief and trouble to men. Heeding the instructions of Zeus, Pandora recapped the jar before Hope could come out. It alone remained securely inside that woeful container. As for the rest, the innumerable evils and miseries released by Pandora would wander forever more among humans, causing nothing but pain and sorrow.

Logos

Our expression **Pandora's box**, meaning something that produces an enormous amount of unforeseen and/or uncontrollable difficulties, comes from the myth of Pandora, who unwittingly unleashed a sea of ills.

The arrival of Pandora thus weakened man just as much as—or even more than—the gift of fire had strengthened him. This first woman not only unleashed a host of evils upon the world—she also became, according to Hesiod, the mother of all wicked women.

Prometheus—who not only disobeyed the decrees of Zeus, but delighted in trying to deceive and later steal from the Olympian gods—then suffered the wrath of Zeus. He was bound with adamantine chains to a rock at the base of the Caucasus mountains. A stake that pierced his middle held him fast to this rock. To add to his torment, an eagle swept down and devoured the Titan's liver every day. During the course of the night, the liver grew back—just in time to make another meal for the predatory bird.

The daily torture of Prometheus lasted throughout 13 generations of humankind. Ultimately, Heracles, a mortal son of Zeus, added to his own glory by shooting the ravenous eagle (see Chapter 13). Heracles thus freed the Titan who had given such a great gift—and endured so much suffering—all for the sake of lowly humankind.

The Least You Need to Know

- Nearly all classical Greek and Roman mythmakers agree that after the mysterious creation of two to four immortal beings, almost all of Creation sprang from Eros, from acts of divine procreation.

- Gaia is regarded as the mother of all Creation in most classical myths.

- Our human race was not the first race of mortals. Three or four other ages of man came before ours. Women did not exist in any of these long-gone races.

- Prometheus, a Titan, stole fire from the gods and brought it to man. Zeus punished him by chaining him to a mountain, where an eagle gnawed at his liver every day for 13 generations.

- Zeus ordered the creation of Pandora, the first woman, to punish mankind for receiving the fire from Prometheus. Pandora opened a container from the gods, unleashing all the ills that plague mankind to this day.

3

Hey, I've Heard That Before! The Roots of Classical Myth

In This Chapter

◆ The cultures of Mesopotamia

◆ Creation through destruction: *Enuma Elish*, the Babylonian Genesis

◆ Birth of the hero: the story of Gilgamesh

◆ Inanna (or Ishtar or Astarte): the Great Goddess of Mesopotamia and her descent to the Underworld

The stories of the gods and heroes of classical mythology did not spring fully formed from the mouths of Greek and Roman poets as Athena did from Zeus's head (see Chapter 7). They evolved from the myths of neighboring cultures—particularly those in the Middle East. Among the neighbors who may have influenced the development of Greek mythology were the Sumerians, the Babylonians, and the Assyrians.

These three peoples flourished along the fertile valley that lay between the Tigris and Euphrates rivers. This region, stretching from the Persian Gulf northwest for about 500 miles through present-day Kuwait and Iraq, was known as Mesopotamia.

Control of Mesopotamia shifted from one of these peoples to another in the 2,500 or more years preceding the first written recording of Greek myths:

- *The Sumerians.* Settling in the southern part of Mesopotamia around the thirty-fourth century B.C.E., the Sumerians founded a society of city-states, each under the protection of a particular deity. This intertwining of political and religious systems would remain the basis for life in Mesopotamia for thousands of years. (Later the Greeks would found their own city-states, each associated with a particular Olympian.)

- *The Babylonians.* Around the nineteenth century, Semitic invaders from Akkad in central Mesopotamia invaded Sumer. Together, these two peoples—the Akkadians and the Sumerians—became known as the Babylonians and built Babylon, a well-fortified capital city that stretched across the Euphrates.

- *The Assyrians.* The inhabitants of northern Mesopotamia, the Assyrians, conquered Babylon—and all of Mesopotamia—in the early ninth century. They established their new capital, Nineveh, along the Tigris River in the late eighth or early seventh century. After Nineveh fell in the late seventh century, a new Babylonian empire controlled Mesopotamia until the Persians conquered the region in 539 B.C.E.

In the Beginning ...

One of the most important stories of Mesopotamian mythology was the *Enuma Elish* (also called the Babylonian Genesis), which detailed the Babylonian account of the Creation of the universe. The mythic account spread northwest through Assyria (although the Assyrians substituted the name of their high god, Ashur, for the Babylonian god Marduk).

Logos

The Babylonians may have called their Creation story by a different name. We call it **Enuma Elish**, which means "when above," because these are the opening words of the Babylonian Genesis story.

During the 1840s, an excavation of the library of King Ashurbanipal, who ruled Assyria in the seventh century B.C.E., led to the discovery of seven clay tablets on which the *Enuma Elish* was inscribed. The tablets date back to about 1000 B.C.E., but the story may date back another thousand years or more.

Meet the New Boss

The story of the *Enuma Elish* goes something like this ...

In the beginning, all that existed were the male Apsu (the ancient sweet-water—that is, unsalted—ocean), the female Tiamat (the salt-water ocean), and their son Mummu (probably a rising mist). Yet even they were indistinct, mingled into an undefined mass.

Apsu and Tiamat conceived two pairs of divine children. Little is known of the older pair. But the younger pair, Anshar and Kishar, had a son they named Anu. Now this son Anu—the god of the sky—begot Ea (also called Nudimmud or Enki) and many other children. An exceptionally wise and strong god—the god of underground sweet waters as well as the god of powerful magic—Ea would become the master of all gods, even his fathers.

Quiet Up There!

The older generations of gods—who wanted nothing more than undisturbed peace and quiet—were upset by the younger gods' constant revelry. The elders asked the children to quiet down, but the young gods could not curb their exuberance.

Finally, Apsu could take no more. Supported by his primeval son Mummu, Apsu resolved to end their clamor once and for all by destroying his offspring, despite Tiamat's protests.

Hearing of Apsu's rage, the other gods fretted about their impending destruction. But Ea protected them by casting a magic spell on his great-grandfather, the father of the gods.

Bewitched, Apsu finally gained the sleep he wanted. But as he slept, Ea stripped Apsu of his splendor and his might. Ea took the crown off Apsu's head and put it on his own. Though Ea spared Tiamat, who had opposed her husband's plot, he killed Apsu and imprisoned Mummu. Ea now held all power over the gods.

Clash of the Titans

Ea lived gloriously with his wife, Damkina. They had a wondrous child, Marduk. By sucking on the breasts of goddesses, Marduk acquired even more divine power and divine characteristics. From the very beginning, Marduk inspired awe—even before his proud and overjoyed papa, Ea, doubled his child's dimensions and gave him two faces.

Yet Tiamat was disturbed by her husband's violent death at the hands of Ea. Egged on by a faction of other gods, Tiamat decided to avenge her husband's death by declaring war on the gods who had taken part—or sided with those who took part—in Apsu's murder. Gearing up for the battle, Tiamat gave birth to 11 kinds of bloodthirsty monsters, serpents, and dragons and rallied the rebel gods to her side.

Tiamat chose the rebel leader, Kingu (whose whispers had helped create this strife), as her mate. Giving him the "tablet of destinies," which had formidable magic power and gave its owner control over the divination of the future, she granted Kingu dominion over all other gods. Kingu fastened the tablet to his chest as a sign of his new power.

Ea, forewarned, launched a counterattack that failed. Anshar, Ea's grandfather, asked his son Anu (Ea's father) to intervene and calm Tiamat. But Anu returned quaking with fear, for he knew that Tiamat could neither be persuaded by diplomacy nor tamed by magic. Physical violence alone was all that might defeat her—and Anu feared that no one could survive in battle with the mighty Tiamat.

The prospects looked very grim for the young gods, but Anshar suddenly remembered the strength, wisdom, and supreme divinity of his great-grandson: Ea's son Marduk. Petitioned by Anshar, the powerful, confident Marduk quickly rallied the gods behind him. He promised to deliver them from the powerful threat of Tiamat—but only if they granted him supreme and undisputed authority over the gods.

The gods assembled for a feast, built Marduk a throne, gave him supreme power over the pantheon and the universe, and urged him to go cut the life out of Tiamat.

Marduk armed himself with a bow, a quiver of arrows, and a club. The god of storms, Marduk caused lightning to go before him. He fashioned a net, which the four winds—a gift from his grandfather Anu—carried for him. In addition, he created the hurricane, the cyclone, the whirlwind, and four more winds of his own. Causing a flooding rain to precede him, Marduk drove his fearsome storm chariot to his showdown with Tiamat.

Read All About It

The full story of the Creation battle between the gods can be found in numerous translations published under the titles *The Babylonian Genesis* or *Enuma Elish*.

Kingu and all of Tiamat's followers trembled at the sight of mighty Marduk. But Tiamat herself taunted Marduk and let loose a terrifying roar. Unfazed, Marduk condemned Tiamat's wickedness and challenged her to a duel. Though shaken by his fearlessness, Tiamat accepted the challenge of single combat.

Marduk quickly enmeshed her in his net. When Tiamat opened her mouth to devour him, Marduk sent the evil wind into her mouth to prevent her from closing it. As the raging winds inside her swelled her body, Marduk sent a shaft flying down her throat. The arrow pierced her heart and killed her.

The rebel gods, terrified, tried to escape. But Marduk quickly rounded them up, stripped them of their weapons, and imprisoned them. Marduk tore the powerful tablet of destinies from Kingu's breast and fastened it to his own.

Recipe for Creation: Take One Divine Body, Break It in Two ...

Marduk split the skull of Tiamat's corpse with his club, opened her arteries, and bid the north wind to carry her blood far and wide. He then split her body in two, forming the sky from one half of her corpse and the earth from the other. Next Marduk created the rest of the universe. He set up stations for the great gods in the sky, assigning 300 gods to heaven and 300 to Earth and delegating unique responsibilities to each. He placed constellations to help organize the calendar. He erected the east and west gates through which the sun could enter and depart the world each day. And he created the moon to watch over the night.

The victorious gods, led by Marduk, enslaved the gods who had rebelled, forcing them to feed their conquerors. When the enslaved gods petitioned Marduk for mercy, the lord of all gods resolved to set the captive gods free. But for Kingu, who had incited Tiamat to revolt and created strife among the gods, Marduk reserved a special punishment. Marduk's father Ea killed Kingu, cutting his arteries and creating humankind from his blood. This new race then assumed the responsibility that the freed gods no longer performed: feeding the Babylonian divinities (through sacrificial offerings).

The More Things Change ...

The Sumerian myth of Creation has elements in common with the Babylonians, the Greeks, and the Romans. In the beginning only the primeval sea, the goddess Nammu, existed. (The primeval sea—with its waters swept by a mighty wind—also predated the Creation in the Bible's book of Genesis.) Nammu gave birth to An and Ki—a sky god and an earth goddess (like Uranus and Gaia). The union of brother and sister produced the "great gods" such as Enlil, the god of vegetation, cattle, agricultural tools, and the art of civilization. (Enlil is not unlike the Roman god Saturn, the agricultural deity who brought civilization to Italy.) The gods then created humankind to provide them with sustenance and serve them in other ways.

Hey, That Sounds Familiar!

Whether or not the Greeks actually borrowed any elements of the Babylonian Creation myth in devising their own, certain parallels do exist:

◆ As in Hesiod's version, the waters Apsu and Tiamat mysteriously came first.

◆ Within this primeval mass were contained all the elements later known, but all without form—a description that Ovid would echo in *Metamorphoses*.

◆ An older generation of gods plotted the destruction of the younger generation. But the younger generation ultimately defeated and overthrew the elders who wanted to destroy them (see Chapter 5 for the Greek version).

◆ Just as the Greek story of the strife between immortals represented the victory of a male-dominated over a female-dominated tradition, so did the story of Marduk's rise to power over all the gods and all creation.

◆ Like the Greek Earth Mother Gaia, the Babylonians' first goddess—the Mother Goddess Tiamat— gave birth to the greatest of gods and later incited a revolt by giving birth to the world's monsters and demons. (See Chapter 8 for Gaia's demons.)

◆ Both Marduk and Zeus were armed with lightning. Babylonians, Greeks, and Romans all raised a storm god above the rest of the pantheon.

◆ The gods of the pantheon (whether Babylonian, Greek, or Roman) were arbitrary, willful, and unpredictable—not unlike the world in which these ancient peoples lived.

I Need a Hero: Gilgamesh

What's a story without a hero? Mythic stories of the Creation and the battles of the gods would mean much less if unaccompanied by mythic tales about the humans whom the gods placed on Earth, for such stories—the tales of heroes—set ideal standards for human behavior. Of the heroic myths that came from cultures neighboring ancient Greece, none surpassed the story of Gilgamesh.

Written down (actually, inscribed on tablets) at least 1,300 years before Homer composed *The Iliad* and *The Odyssey*, the story of Gilgamesh is the oldest major work of literature in the world. Like the *Enuma Elish*, the story of Gilgamesh was discovered in excavations of the library of Assyrian King Ashurbanipal in Nineveh in the 1840s. The tablets that record various portions of the story date from 2100 to 627 B.C.E.

No doubt grounded in the oral tradition of the Sumerians, the story was probably first recorded in 2100.

The first hero in literature, the character of Gilgamesh was based on a real king of that name who ruled Uruk in southern Mesopotamia sometime between 2700 and 2500 B.C.E. But as it so often does, history in this case has given way to mythology. We know nothing of the real Gilgamesh; all that remains is the myth.

Gods' Gift

The son of a wise goddess, Ninsun, and a heroic mortal, Lugalbanda, Gilgamesh was one-third man and two-thirds god. Even before his conception, the gods had favored Gilgamesh:

- ◆ Nintu, the great Mother Goddess who created the human race, made a special effort to create him.

- ◆ Adad, the storm god, gave him great courage.

- ◆ Shamash, the sun god, gave him great beauty.

- ◆ Ea, the god of wisdom, gave him a tremendous capacity for wisdom, for no man ever learned as much from his experiences as Gilgamesh did.

An arrogant, fearless, and willful young man, Gilgamesh did not respect tradition and never considered the effect of his actions on others. (Among his abuses was extending beyond one night the right of the king to sleep with any bride on her wedding night.) So the gods decided to humble him by creating his match: Enkidu, who was fashioned in the form of the sky god Anu. When brought to life, however, Enkidu turned out wild: a hairy beast of a man who lived on the plain among the wild animals.

Enkidu protected his companions by filling in hunters' pits and releasing the animals from traps. An exasperated hunter finally sent for a temple prostitute—and for Gilgamesh, the king of Uruk.

Entranced by the priestess, a smitten Enkidu sat down with her. But because she civilized him, teaching him the ways of men, the animals shunned him from that day forward.

Brought together to fight, Enkidu and Gilgamesh instead became the greatest of friends. At first, they fought like two bulls, wrestling so fiercely with each other in the gates of Anu's temple that the wall of the temple shook. But in the end, the two combatants recognized each other as equals and embraced.

Going for the Gusto

After cementing their friendship, Enkidu and Gilgamesh set out to slay the evil giant Humbaba—and thus banish evil from the land. Humbaba had the fierce face of a lion, a dreadful roar, the teeth of a dragon, and breathed fire. Enkidu initially seemed reluctant to take on this beast, but Gilgamesh—who recognized mortality as his fate—convinced his friend to join him in seeking adventure, glory, and the immortality achieved through the memory of great deeds. Gilgamesh then invited the like-minded men of Uruk to join him on this heroic adventure. With 50 brave young men, Gilgamesh and Enkidu set out to seek their glory.

After traveling for many days and arriving deep within the Cedar Forest where Humbaba roamed, Gilgamesh stopped to chop down a tree, trying to lure the monster into a confrontation. Humbaba, though two miles away, heard and rushed toward them with rage in his eyes. Shamash the sun god, who had promised to protect the two friends, bound the monster with eight winds and foretold victory as long as Gilgamesh did not allow Humbaba to return to his house.

Paralyzed by the winds and staring into the face of defeat, Humbaba begged for mercy, vowing to become Gilgamesh's servant on Earth. But Enkidu warned Gilgamesh not to listen to the lies of this clever and dangerous enemy. With three mighty blows from their axes, the two friends killed the giant.

The Goddess of (Unrequited) Love: Ishtar

When Gilgamesh returned to Uruk, he quickly caught the eye of Ishtar, the supreme goddess of sexual love, fertility, and war. Ishtar greatly admired Gilgamesh's beauty and wanted to marry him. The goddess wooed him with promises of a golden, jeweled chariot pulled by storm demons, the constant fragrance of cedar, tributes from all the kings of Earth, and twins and triplets born to all his goats and sheep.

Despite these rich offers, Gilgamesh refused, for he knew that it might kill him to marry the goddess. Instead of offering a simple no, however, Gilgamesh unwisely listed the ways she had abused previous mates. These included her husband Dumuzi, who wept for years and years after she abandoned him, and a herdsman whom she turned into a wolf. (His own sons then drove the shepherd away as his dogs nipped at his heels.)

Grievously insulted, Ishtar resolved to kill Gilgamesh, too. She begged her father, the sky god Anu, to allow her to let loose the Bull of Heaven inside Uruk. When she saw her father hesitate, the goddess threatened to smash the gates of the Underworld, causing the dead to rise among the living, if he refused her. Anu reluctantly agreed, but Enkidu and Gilgamesh easily dispatched the beast. The killing of this sacred beast enraged Ishtar even further. She resolved that Enkidu would pay for his part in the slaying. Tormented by Ishtar with dreams of his own death, Enkidu swiftly wasted away and died.

The Secret of Life

The death of Enkidu crushed Gilgamesh. He suffered from loneliness—and from the new consciousness of his own mortality. Though he was two-thirds god, the one third of him that was man ensured that, like Enkidu, he too would die.

What a Life!

Enlil, ruler of all gods, had created the Great Flood because the world had too many people and they made too much noise. But Ea, who loved humans and had taught them agriculture, warned Utanapishtim. By building an ark, Utanapishtim saved himself, his family, and animals both wild and tame. Enlil was furious that a human had survived. But Ea persuaded him to show mercy. Enlil not only spared Utanapishtim and his family, but gave them everlasting life.

In search of the secret to immortality, Gilgamesh set out to find *Utanapishtim*—also called "the Faraway"—the sole survivor of the Great Flood.

In order to find Utanapishtim, Gilgamesh had a few obstacles to tackle en route:

◆ He battled two enormous lions with the help and protection of Sin, the moon goddess. Managing to kill both beasts, Gilgamesh skinned them and wore their hides over his own tattered clothing.

◆ The hero next had to pass through an almost endless tunnel. He walked 36 miles in complete darkness, unable to see anything ahead of him or behind him. However, when he finally got through the tunnel, Gilgamesh found himself in a heavenly garden with trees bearing jewels that dazzled him. He knew now that he was approaching the land of the gods.

Logos

The name "Utanapishtim" is derived from *uta* ("he found") and *napishtim* ("life"). It accurately describes the one man who survived the Great Flood.

The More Things Change ...

A great flood—and the favored humans who survived it—figures prominently in the mythologies of many cultures. Like Utanapishtim, Noah survived the Biblical flood by building an ark for himself, his family, and two animals of every species. Similarly, the Greek characters, Deucalion and Pyrrha, were spared from the Great Flood, forewarned by Prometheus (see Chapter 6).

♦ Continuing his journey, Gilgamesh next encountered the cottage of an old fisherman's wife named Siduri. Siduri, initially frightened by the lion's hide he wore, fled from him. He managed to gain her trust and explained what was troubling him and where he was headed. Siduri wisely advised that he accept his mortality, living each day to the fullest.

Despite Siduri's wise words, Gilgamesh continued on his way to seek out Urshanabi, Utanapishtim's boatman. Only Urshanabi, under the protection of sacred stone figures, could safely cross the Waters of Death to reach Utanapishtim.

Gilgamesh wasn't feeling all that patient after his long, arduous journey, so when he couldn't find the boatman near the sacred images, he angrily destroyed the stone figures. Urshanabi ran to the site and chided Gilgamesh for foolishly breaking the protective statues. Still, Gilgamesh wasn't going to let the loss of a couple of rocks stop him now. By cutting down 10 dozen trees and fashioning them into 100-foot poles, Gilgamesh and Urshanabi managed to cross the Waters of Death.

The More Things Change ...

Gilgamesh's long voyage through the dark tunnel and then across the Waters of Death seem similar to the trips to the Underworld taken by many later heroes. Heracles, Odysseus, and Aeneas all travel to the Underworld and back (see Chapters 13, 18, and 22). The greatest Italian poet of the Renaissance, Dante Alighieri, undertook a similar journey—with Vergil as his guide—in *The Inferno*, the first book of his *Divine Comedy*.

When Gilgamesh arrived, Utanapishtim greeted him and told him about the flood and how Enlil had made him immortal. But he doubted that the gods would do the same for Gilgamesh.

Utanapishtim then challenged Gilgamesh to stay awake for seven nights and six days to prove that he had the strength of a god—and thus warranted immortality. Gilgamesh tried, but couldn't do it. Humbled, he began to despair. But, echoing Siduri's advice, Utanapishtim urged Gilgamesh not to lament over the gift the gods had *not* given him, but rather to rejoice in the gifts the gods had bestowed upon him:

- His unparalleled might

- His undeniable heroism

- His undiminished power as a king

- The wisdom that made him a leader of his people

Before Gilgamesh left, Utanapishtim gave him a magic plant. Though it would not give him immortality, it would give him everlasting youth throughout his mortal life. On his way home, Gilgamesh stopped by a freshwater pool to take a dip. Unfortunately, a snake slipped onto the shore while he bathed and stole the magic plant. As the serpent slid back into the water, it shed its skin, uncovering a new, youthful appearance. To this day, snakes have continued to shed their skins to renew themselves.

Gilgamesh accepted his mortality and resolved to make the most of the time he had. The king returned to Uruk, where he ruled wisely over his people for many more years and grew old gracefully.

> **The More Things Change …**
>
> Urshanabi bears a striking resemblance to the Greek Charon—the ferryman who transports souls across the river Styx to the land of the dead.

A Hero in the Classical Mold

The story of Gilgamesh shared some elements with the later stories of classical heroes:

- Like the Greek hero Theseus, Gilgamesh undertook some of his adventures alone and some with his pal, Enkidu. Just as Gilgamesh and Enkidu began as adversaries but then forged a friendship, so did Theseus and Peirithous, who provoked a confrontation by stealing some of Theseus's cows before the two became the best of friends (see Chapter 15).

- Gilgamesh shared with classical heroes a conscious quest for glory. In setting out to slay the evil giant Humbaba, Gilgamesh made the same choice that Achilles would make during the Trojan War (see Chapter 17): He would rather risk a short but glorious life than settle for a long, safe one.

- As Jason would do when recruiting a crew to join him on the *Argo* as they set out to capture the Golden Fleece (see Chapter 14), Gilgamesh invited others—the best and the bravest—to join him in this quest for glory.

- Another theme that binds the Gilgamesh story with classical sagas is the hero's need to endure the trials imposed by the wrath of the gods. The Sumerian goddess Ishtar established a pattern of vindictiveness that such Olympians as Hera and Poseidon would share. But just as Heracles overcame the wrath of Hera, just as Odysseus survived the wrath of Poseidon, Gilgamesh proved his heroism—at least in part—by meeting the challenge of Ishtar's wrath.

The Mother of All Goddesses

Another mythic element that the Greeks and Romans shared with many cultures in the Middle East—as well as many other cultures throughout the world—was the worship of a Great Goddess. The Great Goddess, usually considered the Great Mother of the Gods, often had three major aspects: love, Earth's fertility, and motherhood.

In Greece, this great triple Goddess, originally Gaia, was split not once, but twice. The daughters of Gaia's daughter Rhea formed one triad: Hera (motherhood), Demeter (fertility), and Hestia (the home). The other three goddesses formed a second triad: Aphrodite (love), Artemis (the hunt), and Athena (war and practical arts).

A Goddess by Any Other Name

In the Middle East, the Great Goddess went by many different names:

- The Sumerians called her Inanna.

- The Akkadians in central Mesopotamia called her Ishtar.

- The Assyrians called her Mylitta.

- The Egyptians—as well as the Ugarits on the Mediterranean coast of present-day Syria and the Hittites in Asia Minor, between the Black and Mediterranean seas—called her Astarte.

Logos

In Sumerian mythology, **me** was a set of more than a hundred preordained decrees that determined the development of all religious, cultural, and political institutions for the Sumerian people.

Yet though her name changed from culture to culture, the character of the goddess remained essentially the same. Astarte—or, if you prefer, Ishtar or Inanna—was the supreme goddess of sexual love, fertility, and war. Indeed, according to the Sumerians, Inanna would become the most powerful goddess of all.

Enki, the god of wisdom, originally had absolute power because he owned *me*. Ambitious Inanna, however, got the great god drunk one night and stole the me away from him (or convinced him to give it to her).

When Enki sobered up, he tried to catch Inanna and recover the me, but the goddess easily disposed of his agents with magic spells. Inanna safely reached her home city of Erech and thereafter became the most powerful goddess of all.

A Hell of a Journey

Perhaps the best known Sumerian story about Inanna (or Akkadian story about Ishtar) involved her descent to the Underworld. (Perhaps Inanna made her hellish trip in hope of gaining some dominion over the Underworld, but exactly why she undertook such a perilous journey remains a mystery.)

Inanna descended through seven gates to reach the Underworld. At each gate, she had to remove one item of clothing and jewelry. By the time she reached the Underworld and confronted her sister Ereshkigal, who ruled the nether regions, Inanna stood before the Underworld goddess entirely naked—and stripped of all the powers that her garments symbolized. When the powerless goddess nonetheless boldly tried to seize Ereshkigal's throne, her sister goddess condemned Inanna to death and hung her corpse on a wall.

Fortunately, the wisest of goddesses had anticipated that she might run into trouble. So before she had set out for the Underworld, Inanna had instructed her most trusted aide, Ninshubur, to ask three gods for their help if she did not return. Ninshubur did so, first seeking the help of Enki, the god of wisdom.

> ### The More Things Change ...
>
> Among the Greeks, Apollo would trick the Fates into providing King Admetus of Pherae a surrogate offer similar to Ereshkigal's deal with Inanna (see Chapter 11).

Enki quickly formed two sexless beings from the dirt under his fingernails. After bringing them to life, Enki sent them down through the earth to rescue Inanna. The two creatures succeeded in bringing her back to life, but Ereshkigal would let Inanna leave only if she agreed to provide a substitute for herself.

Fierce demons then escorted Inanna out of the Underworld. As her surrogate, Inanna chose her husband Dumuzi, a god of fertility. When Dumuzi left for the Underworld, the plants and crops of Earth withered and died. So Dumuzi arranged to alternate his time in the Underworld with his sister Geshtinanna, the "Lady of the Grape Vine." Forever afterward, each spent half of the year in the Underworld.

The myth of Inanna in the Underworld explained the disruption and restoration of fertility with the passing cycle of seasons. (The Greeks would explain the same cycle of fertility with a similar tale involving a descent to the Underworld in the story of Demeter and Persephone—see Chapter 11.) Every year, the Mesopotamian people lamented the passing of Dumuzi as the hot season approached. And they no doubt celebrated his return with some sort of joyous rite of spring.

There's No DNA Test for the Paternity of Mythologies

Tracing the lineage of one culture's myths to the myths of another culture can be a tricky business. Just because two myths from different cultures share certain similarities of plot or character does not necessarily indicate that one has evolved from the other. After all, cultures throughout the world have developed myths to explain everything from the earth's fertility cycle to the divine right of kings. It shouldn't be surprising that even cultures that have no connection to one another sometimes come up with strikingly similar explanations for natural phenomena.

Nonetheless, the closeness of the Middle East peoples and the similarities in terms of theme, character, and sometimes plot suggest that the Greeks may have borrowed at least some of their mythology from their neighbors to the east. And why not? They're great stories. No matter how much they borrowed, however, the Greeks transformed this material from other cultures into a rich mythology all their own.

The Least You Need to Know

- According to the Babylonian Genesis, the *Enuma Elish*, the creation of the world resulted from a generational war between the gods. The human race was created to feed and serve the gods.

- The Sumerian Gilgamesh, the first hero in literature, sought the meaning of life in the face of his own mortality. The character of Gilgamesh and the nature of his exploits share many similarities with Greek and Roman heroes and their stories.

- Inanna, Ishtar, Astarte: The name may change, but the character of the Great Goddess remains strikingly similar from culture to culture.

- Dumuzi, a fertility god, took his wife Inanna's place in the Underworld for six months every year. His withdrawal from the world coincided with the infertile dry season in Mesopotamia.

- If not explicitly derived from ancient Mesopotamian mythology, classical mythology shares many of their themes, plot elements, and character archetypes.

Chapter 4

Author, Author

In This Chapter

- The great ancient poets: Homer and Hesiod
- The great Greek tragedians: Aeschylus, Sophocles, and Euripides
- A variety of Greek sources on classical mythology: historians, poets, biographers, and even travelogue writers
- The great Roman poets: Vergil and Ovid
- Other Roman sources: Livy, Horace, and Seneca the Younger

As much as we might enjoy it, we can't go back more than 2,500 years to hear the ancient storytellers spin their tales around the town square. We can't listen in as parents in Greek villages and towns hand down to their children the mythic stories that they once heard from their own parents. We can't spy on the priests of old performing their ceremonial rites or dedicating a sacrifice to the gods and goddesses.

With direct experience of such cultures beyond our reach, what we know of classical mythology depends solely upon ancient source material. What's more, we can know only those stories that some scribe had the time, energy, and ability to write down. No matter how widespread, tales that never made it onto the written page are lost to us forever.

Who were these ancient storytellers who handed down mythic tales in a form that we can still grasp today? What were their lives like? In what forums did they share their versions of the myths with which surely everyone in their audience had at least some passing familiarity? Read on to find out.

Do Tell

The most ancient authors of classical mythology whose work survived were two Greek poets: Homer and Hesiod. Yet when you read about the works of Hesiod or Homer, keep in mind that in all likelihood they never *wrote* the works that we attribute to them.

No one knows precisely when Homer and Hesiod composed their greatest works. Our best guess is that both poets flourished during the eighth or seventh century B.C.E. The Greek world during this age was almost entirely illiterate. In fact, no written literature existed at all!

The Greek alphabet, derived or imported from Phoenicia in the late eighth century B.C.E., was used only in a very limited way during the age of these poets. Neither Homer nor Hesiod probably read *anything* in their lives—and almost certainly never wrote any of their poems. Indeed, if their poems were transcribed at all during their lifetimes, it probably occurred in their twilight years. Even if the poets had been able to write their verses down, very few people at that time could have read them anyway. Word of mouth was king.

In all likelihood, then, someone else wrote down the poems we know as Homer's *The Iliad* and *The Odyssey* or Hesiod's *Theogony* and *Works and Days*. The anonymous scribes transcribed the poems as they heard the poets—or others perhaps generations later—recite them.

> **What a Life!**
>
> According to legend, Homer died of mortification when he couldn't figure out the answer to a young boy's riddle—something about catching lice. After his death, so lore has it, the Homeridae—the descendants of Homer—assumed a duty to preserve and disseminate his poetry.

The Poet as Performance Artist

Since reading and writing weren't the pastimes of choice in ancient Greece, Homer and Hesiod used recitations or dramatic performances to get their words to a greater audience. The recitations of *rhapsodes* were almost always accompanied by an instrument—in most cases a lyre or some other stringed instrument.

If all or part of their poetry was sung, meter or rhythm would play a very important role in their composition. But composing their stories in verse primarily functioned as a mnemonic device—a safeguard to protect the poets from drawing a blank during a performance. Or perhaps they simply enjoyed verse as a medium for exploring the beauty and rhythms of language.

Hesiod and Homer, then, were performance artists—live entertainers who brought their art directly to their audiences. They told stories in verse, reciting them aloud before a crowd of listeners.

Logos

Rhapsodes traveled from town to town telling their stories. To appeal to the local audience, Homer and other rhapsodes no doubt highlighted the heroism of characters who hailed from that town, perhaps even altering stories to find favor with their listeners.

In telling stories, of course, the tale depends on the teller. No two eyewitnesses ever describe an accident or a crime or anything else they've seen in exactly the same way. Each focuses on particular aspects of the incident that seem important *to that teller* at the time. In the same way, these great poets—though they drew from a common mythology—shaped the tales they told, bringing incidents to life and adding (or subtracting) details as the occasion for recitation or their own talents directed. In all likelihood, no poet ever told the same story exactly the same way more than once. After all, performance art does have its improvisational moments.

Does this make Homer and Hesiod suspect as authoritative sources on the mythology of the age? Well, no. Keep in mind that the stories they told had probably been told and retold, sung and resung, in different forms for many generations before Homer and Hesiod put their imprints on them. And since most of their listeners were probably familiar with these stories, the basic outlines no doubt remained the same. Besides, all myths allow for a certain amount of variation. So we can safely regard Hesiod and Homer as the earliest surviving sources of classical mythology.

Homer, Sweet Homer

Although undoubtedly the most famous of all epic poets, Homer himself remains shrouded in mystery. He became so renowned and so revered that nearly every city in Asia Minor claimed him as their own. In addition, Chios, Athens, Argos, Salamis, and Rhodes—among many other Greek cities—embraced the poet as a son of their own.

And why not? No one could prove otherwise, because little or nothing is known of Homer's birth, life, or death. We know that he probably composed his poetry during the eighth century B.C.E., but nobody really knows just when he lived. We believe that his parents were Greek and that he lived and "wrote" in Ionia, a Greek region on the western coast of Asia Minor and nearby islands. He may (or may not) have been blind.

But all that we really know about Homer is his work, which provides one of the oldest sources of classical mythology. Even here, we don't know as much as we think we do. Not everyone agrees that Homer wrote both *The Iliad* and *The Odyssey*. Some scholars argue that Homer wrote *The Odyssey* as a sequel to *The Iliad*, while others go so far as to suggest that the two poems don't even come from the same period, much less the same hand. (The *Homeric Hymns*, which sing praise to various Greek gods, were definitely *not* written by Homer. But since the ancients had traditionally ascribed these hymns to him, we still call them "Homeric" today.)

What a Life!

Though the tale is probably only a legend, Hesiod and Homer reportedly went head-to-head in a poetry contest—each reciting selections from their poetry—and by popular acclaim Hesiod won! Yet aside from this legend, no evidence exists to suggest that the two poets were even contemporaries.

Whoever wrote the epics (let's call him Homer), he was a terrific storyteller. *The Iliad* focuses on the final year of the Trojan War; *The Odyssey*, on its hero's long trip home from that war. Yet both works provide a wide-ranging cultural history of ancient Greece. While focusing on immediate and concrete tales, the epic poems also touch on disparate myths and legends that had come down through many centuries.

Never Refuse a Muse: Hesiod

Hesiod, too, is somewhat of a mystery—though we know more biographical details simply because he put them into his poetry. Among the earliest of Greek poets and teachers, Hesiod probably composed his poems in the late eighth to early seventh century B.C.E.

Yet we know little about Hesiod's life other than the snippets he provides in his own poems. According to his own account, Hesiod was a poor farmer and shepherd whose father had immigrated from Asia Minor, settling in Askra, a village near Mount Helicon in Boeotia, in central Greece. One day, the Muses came down to Mount Helicon as Hesiod tended his sheep and gave him the gift of song, a poet's voice, and a poet's staff. What choice did he have? He became a poet.

Like Homer, Hesiod composed two major works that still survive. (*Shield*, a description of the shield of Heracles, has long been attributed to Hesiod, but was almost definitely written by someone else.) His *Theogony* offers an account of the Creation. In it,

Hesiod also describes the line of deities from Uranus to Zeus, the origins of monsters, the Olympians' war against the Titans, and the battle between Zeus and Typhoeus (or Typhon).

What a Life!

In *Works and Days*, Hesiod wrote angrily about Perses, who apparently lied and bribed judges in an attempt to cheat Hesiod out of some of his inheritance. Hesiod also provided something of the flavor of life in seventh-century Boeotia—descriptive contemporary and personal details completely absent from Homer's poems, which focus solely on events 500 years before the time when Homer and Hesiod lived.

In *Works and Days*, Hesiod advises his brother Perses—and anyone else willing to listen—on the value of work and on ways in which he might pursue self-interest without doing harm to others. Although essentially a farmer's almanac, *Works and Days* offers some mythology, too. Hesiod included stories about Prometheus and Pandora as well as a detailed description of the ages of man (see Chapter 2).

The Play's the Thing

From the (probably) eighth-century works of Homer and Hesiod, we need to move forward nearly three centuries to find the next source of classical mythology: the Ancient Theatre of Athens, also known as the Theatre of Dionysus. Those who came before the fifth century B.C.E.—Thespis, Pratinas, and Phrynichus—are unknown to us, their works lost. But the fifth century saw the rise to prominence of the three greatest Greek tragedians: Aeschylus, Sophocles, and Euripides.

Among them, these three dramatists wrote more than 300 tragedies. Though most of these—like the works of earlier dramatists—have faded from existence, 33 of their tragedies still survive: 7 plays each by Aeschylus and Sophocles and 19 by Euripides.

Chorus Lines

The Theatre of Dionysus was well established long before the emergence of Aeschylus, Sophocles, and Euripides. Every spring, the Great Dionysia—an Athenian festival honoring the god Dionysus (see Chapter 9)—would feature a dramatic competition among three invited dramatists, each with his own group of players. Each acting troupe would perform four plays: a set of three dramas based on Greek myths and legends followed by a satyr play, a broad burlesque. The set of dramas did not necessarily have to be connected either thematically or by plot, though dramatists did sometimes produce a unified trilogy.

Classical Greek drama probably began as choral lyric poems—storytelling sung or chanted by a *chorus*. In time, dramas started to feature actors who would impersonate characters to enact the action of the plot. Nonetheless, by the turn of the fifth century, each group of players that competed in the Great Dionysia still had just one actor and the all-important chorus.

Logos

The word **chorus**, like so many of the terms we still use to describe the theater, originated with the Ancient Theatre of Athens. The chorus commented on the actions of the play through song, dance, and poetry. Other terms we still use include *scene* ("skene," meaning tent, the backdrop for ancient plays), *proscenium* ("proskenion," the area in front of the skene), and *orchestra* ("orkestra," meaning dancing place, the area in front of the proscenium where the chorus was situated).

Dramatic tension, if any, was confined to exchanges between the actor—who could change roles by using different masks, but could play just one role at a time—and the chorus. The dramatists of this age are therefore more accurately described as dramatic poets than playwrights.

The chorus dominated Greek dramas during the age of single actors. During the fifth century, however, the number of actors expanded to two and then three. The chorus would remain an irreplaceable element of Greek drama. But as the century progressed and the roles of individual actors took on greater importance, the role of the chorus steadily diminished.

A degree of remoteness was an important ingredient of Greek tragedy. Most violence, indeed most physical action, occurred offstage—though the chorus would then usually describe it. The actors and chorus dressed in formal costumes and used masks at all times. Until the end of the century, when Euripides began moving Greek drama in the direction of naturalism, all characters remained heroic and oversized rather than human. The reliance on mythic source material for these dramas contributed to their remoteness.

The Dramatist as War Hero: Aeschylus

The oldest of the three great Greek tragedians, Aeschylus was born in 525 or 524 B.C.E., probably in the Athenian town of Eleusis. During this era, Greece was pre-occupied with matters of internal politics and the repeated repulsion of foreign aggressors, most notably the Persians.

Aeschylus fought in the most famous battle of the sixth and fifth century B.C.E. Persian Wars: the Battle of Marathon in 490. Sent by King Darius of Persia, a vast force of infantrymen launched an invasion of Greece, landing at Marathon, a plain on the sea just 26 miles from Athens. Although greatly outnumbered, the small defending force of Athenians stood their ground, forcing the Persians back out of the country. The Greek historian Herodotus put the number of dead at 6,400 Persians and just 192 Greeks. Aeschylus was only wounded, but his brother was one of those who died.

Aeschylus, who had first entered the dramatic competition at the Great Dionysia in 499, won his first victory 15 years later. He would go on to win first prize 13 times during his lifetime. After losing in 468 to young Sophocles, who may have studied under him, the old master came back to win again in 467. (One of the plays in this set has survived: *Seven Against Thebes*.) His crowning achievement came in 458 with the staging of the *Oresteia*—a three-play cycle all focused on the tragic House of Atreus (see Chapter 16).

The first Greek tragedian to add a second actor, which allowed dialogue between characters and not simply between the actor and the chorus, Aeschylus may have written as many as 90 plays. Only seven have survived: six on mythological subjects and one—the oldest surviving Greek drama, dated 472 B.C.E.—on the war with the Persians.

Following the production of his *Oresteia*, Aeschylus—nearly 70 years old—left Athens for Sicily. His death in 456 or 455 was followed by an elaborate public funeral with performances and sacrifices. His grave at Gela, a Sicilian town, became a pilgrimage site for later generations of writers.

What a Life!
Legend has it that Aeschylus, who was bald, died when an eagle—thinking the shell would crack on this "rock"—dropped a tortoise on his head.

The two sons of Aeschylus also became prominent tragedians. In fact, Euphorion defeated both Sophocles and Euripides to win first prize at the Great Dionysia in 431.

The Dramatist as Civic Leader: Sophocles

The consummate Athenian—a poet and civic leader who lived and died in the city—Sophocles was born around 496 B.C.E. in the village of Colonus, outside Athens. A generation younger than Aeschylus and 10 to 15 years older than Euripides, Sophocles was the son of a wealthy armor manufacturer. He received an excellent education, his father hiring only the best tutors. He studied music under Lamprus, the most renowned musician of his day. And he reportedly received instruction in tragedy from none other than Aeschylus himself.

> ### What a Life!
>
> Sophocles lived to an extreme old age (90), an achievement much less common in antiquity than it is today. The Greek philosopher Plato later reported that the aged Sophocles was asked whether he still enjoyed sex. "Be quiet!" Sophocles replied. "I am happy to be done with that. I feel that I have been liberated from a savage master."

A remarkably beautiful boy, Sophocles excelled in dancing, playing the lyre, and wrestling. At 16, he was chosen to lead a chorus of boys who celebrated the Greek victory over the Persians that year in Salamis.

Sophocles grew up to become a well-loved, highly respected, and gracious citizen of Athens as well as a revered poet. He presided over the board that collected tributes from other cities under Attic rule. He served as a foreign ambassador. In his mid-50s, Sophocles was one of only 10 men elected as military and naval commanders in the war against the rebellious Samians. A patron of the arts as well as an artist, Sophocles founded a society dedicated to the arts of the muses (music, literature, and so on).

The most successful of the three major tragedians, Sophocles introduced the third actor to tragedies, allowing more dramatic conflict and smoother expositions of plot. Sophocles first won the annual dramatic competition in 468, defeating his former tutor. Though Aeschylus won again the following year, Sophocles went on to win at least 18 (and perhaps as many as 24) first prizes—and never finished lower than second.

Even more prolific than Aeschylus, Sophocles wrote perhaps 123 dramas. Yet, like Aeschylus, only seven of his tragedies have survived. All draw on mythology as their source material.

His three most famous tragedies—*Antigone, Oedipus the King,* and *Oedipus at Colonus*—center on the myth of Oedipus (see Chapter 12). But unlike Aeschylus's *Oresteia,* these tragedies were not written as a set to be performed together. Indeed, they were written over the course of about 40 years, as Sophocles kept returning to and reinterpreting this central myth.

Sophocles outlived the younger Euripides by several months. Following his fellow poet's death in 406, Sophocles led a chorus of public mourning before that year's Dionysian festival. He himself died later that year.

The Dramatist as Realist: Euripides

The youngest of the three dramatists, Euripides was born sometime between 485 and 480 B.C.E. In a marked contrast with his two predecessors—not to mention the majority of citizens in Athens—Euripides took almost no part in politics or civic affairs. Considered an eccentric by his contemporaries, Euripides reportedly spent a great deal of time sitting in a cave overlooking the sea. A skeptic and devotee of philosophy, Euripides constantly questioned traditional Greek religious beliefs and practices.

Euripides presented his first set of tragedies at the festival of Dionysus in 455, the probable year of Aeschylus's death. Though he wrote 22 four-play sets in his lifetime, he won first prize only five times (the first in 441)—one of them posthumously.

The invitation to compete 22 times indicates that Euripides was considered one of the top three laureates of his age. Yet he never gained the critical acceptance won by both his predecessor and his older contemporary. He became the butt of mocking jokes and the object of satire for countless comic poets such as Aristophanes. (In the two centuries after his death, however, Euripides became the darling of the stage. His plays were played in revivals to a much greater extent than those of his rivals.)

Read All About It

Aristophanes was the greatest of Greek comedians. Born around 448 B.C.E., Aristophanes wrote between 40 and 50 comedies and satires before his death in 386. Eleven of these—including *Lysistrata, The Frogs,* and *The Birds*—have survived.

Undoubtedly, Euripides alienated the judges of the Dionysian competitions by questioning the virtue and worthiness of the gods and by injecting greater and greater realism—especially psychological realism—into his dramas. Euripides offered not the oversized heroes of his contemporaries, but characters more like people Athenians might have seen every day. Sophocles pinpointed the difference between himself and his colleague when he said—if indeed he ever said it—that he showed men as they ought to be while Euripides showed them as they really were.

Euripides wrote perhaps 92 dramas—about the same number as Aeschylus. But 19 of his works survived—more than those of Aeschylus and Sophocles combined. All 19 draw their characters and subjects from classical mythology. Yet in keeping with his own position as an outsider and a "failure" (despite his numerous successes), Euripides most often focused on misfits, the dispossessed, and victims of injustice. His leading characters included slaves, captives, and, for his time, an inordinate number of women. (Eleven of his nineteen surviving dramas—such plays as *Iphigenia in Aulis*, *Medea*, and *The Phoenician Women*—feature women as their title characters).

Like Aeschylus, Euripides abandoned Athens at the end of his life. Underappreciated as a dramatist and disillusioned with Athenian politics, he exiled himself in 408. Accepting an invitation by King Archelaus of Macedonia, he remained in the king's court until his death two years later.

All Greeks to Me

For our knowledge of classical mythology, we owe a huge debt to the two great ancient poets and the three incomparable Greek dramatists. But others have also contributed to our storehouse of classical myths. These sources include a widely disparate cast of characters: poets, mythographers, biographers, historians, and even a writer of travel guides.

> **What a Life!**
>
> Pindar, a Theban, suffered a serious setback to his reputation when Thebes collaborated with the Persians, who invaded Greece in the early fifth century B.C.E. Years later, having reestablished his reputation, Pindar wrote a famous tribute to the city of Athens. Legend has it that Thebes fined him heavily for extolling the virtues of its not-so-friendly rival city.

> **What a Life!**
>
> A century after Pindar's death, Alexander the Great was reportedly a great admirer of Pindar's work. When his Macedonians destroyed the city of Thebes in 335 B.C.E., Alexander ordered that the family townhouse of Pindar remain untouched.

Poetic License

A Greek lyric poet of the fifth century B.C.E., Pindar was born to nobility. As an aristocrat, he was more likely to have become a patron of poetry than a poet himself. Pindar, however, used his poetry to celebrate his fellow aristocrats and men of power at a time when ideas of democracy were only in their infancy.

Pindar wrote odes (poems set to music) that praised the athletes in the Olympic Games (as well as the Pythian, Nemean, and Isthmian Games). Each of his 45 surviving odes open with praise to the gods whose festivals provided the reason behind such athletic games. The poet made frequent comparisons between the athletes he observed and mythological heroes, thereby linking contemporary glory to an even more glorious mythological past.

Two centuries after Pindar, another Greek poet, Apollonius Rhodius (of Rhodes), addressed mythological material much more directly. Apollonius, who served for many years as the chief librarian at the Greek Egyptian city of Alexandria, wrote the epic *Argonautica*. This poem offers the most complete account of the fabled journey of Jason and the crew of the *Argo* (see Chapter 14).

The Myths of History, Biography, and Geography

Most of the other ancient Greeks who added to our understanding of classical mythology never addressed the subject directly. Though each of these writers included mythological elements and sometimes explored particular myths in detail, they examined myths only as a way of shedding light on their own subjects: history, biography, or geography:

- *Herodotus.* The famed fifth-century (B.C.E.) Greek writer renowned as the "Father of History," was the first person to think of writing a history, thus inventing a genre of writing that has become central to our way of thinking. His account of the Persian Wars conveys much factual material, but also interweaves it with mythology.

- *Plutarch.* The first- and second-century (C.E.) Greek writer and biographer, Plutarch was a versatile man. A priest of Delphi and initiate in the mysterious rites of Dionysus, Plutarch also served as a small town chief magistrate and the head of a school that emphasized the teaching of ethics.

  A citizen of both Rome and Athens, Plutarch compared Greek and Roman heroes (soldiers, statesman, and orators) in his *Parallel Lives*. In highlighting the similarities between such figures as the Greek hero Theseus (see Chapter 15) and the Romans Romulus and Numa (see Chapter 23), Plutarch hoped not only to encourage his readers to embrace a moral life, but to foster mutual respect between Greeks and Romans. Twenty-two of his paired biographies survive.

- *Apollodorus.* No one knows exactly when this Greek mythographer wrote (though it was probably sometime in the first two centuries of the Common Era). (A writer named Apollodorus did live in Athens in the second century B.C.E., but he was probably not the author of *The Library*.) No one even knows if his name was really Apollodorus. Yet his *Library* provides an invaluable guide to classical mythology. Unlike the Greek epic poems that focused on a single event, the scope of *The Library* encompasses everything from the origins of the universe to the adventures of both gods and heroes. His scrupulous citation of earlier sources lends significant validity to his mythology as both accurate and representative.

◆ *Pausanias.* This second-century writer of travelogues drew heavily on the mythological associations of sites he visited in his tour guide to Greece. In his 10-volume *Description of Greece*, he begins each portrait of a Greek city with a sketch of its history—including religious rites, superstitious customs, legends, folklore, and mythology.

Pausanias had a special interest in architecture and his *Description of Greece* provides an invaluable guide to the buildings of that age. His work made it unnecessary for us to guess the original function of ancient Greek ruins, for he told us in great detail.

The Grandeur That Was Rome

Though the Romans borrowed heavily from Greek sources for their mythology, they also had their own myths—and their own mythmakers as well. The best of the Roman poets who told or retold the familiar myths—especially Vergil and Ovid—approached, even equaled, the poetic heights and storytelling skills of Homer and Hesiod.

The greatest Roman poets wrote during the Augustan Age, which lasted from about 43 B.C.E. to 14 C.E. The Augustan Age began following the assassination of Julius Caesar and the dissolution of the Roman Republic. Julius's grandnephew and adopted son, Octavian, became one of the three rulers given absolute authority over the Roman state in 43 B.C.E. A year later, after defeating Brutus and Cassius (the assassins of Julius Caesar), Octavian and Mark Antony divided the empire. Yet the struggle for power led to a series of civil wars that did not end until 31, when Octavian defeated Antony and Cleopatra, the Queen of Egypt. Renamed Augustus Caesar four years later, Octavian assumed unchallenged power over the Roman Empire. By 23 B.C.E., he had become the Empire's first emperor.

> **What a Life!**
>
> Born around the same year as Vergil, the wealthy Gaius Maecenas extended his patronage to such poets as Vergil and Horace. A close friend and confidant of Augustus Caesar, Maecenas exercised his patronage with a political aim in mind: He persuaded both poets to use their poetry, at least in part, to glorify the Roman Empire—and specifically the reign of Augustus.

The Augustan Age, marked by peace and unrivaled prosperity within the Roman Empire, became the richest literary period in the region's history. Patrons of the arts supported the efforts of poets, who in turn often addressed their work to them—or to Emperor Augustus himself. The verse of these poets became polished, sophisticated—and often patriotic. Many found that by linking the current ruler of the empire to mythological heroes—or even gods—of the past, they not only exalted Augustus but lent a divine authority to the entire Roman Empire.

The Poet as Propagandist: Vergil

The greatest of all Roman poets, Vergil was born in 70 B.C.E. in the village of Andes, on the River Po near the city of Mantua. The son of a well-to-do farmer, Vergil studied in Cremona, Milan, and Rome. Naturally, the great Greek and Roman writers who came before him figured prominently in his studies. Vergil devoted himself completely to his schooling, living life as somewhat of a recluse throughout his early adult years. He was rarely in good health and never married.

Despite his solitary nature, the quality of his poetry attracted an influential circle of friends. When the state of Rome took over many family farms in 42 to provide housing for resettled veterans of the Battle of Philippi, Vergil may have won back his family's land through appeals to his powerful friends. And he became a member of the Augustan court, even though unlike most other members of the court, he never really participated in either the military or politics. There he enjoyed the patronage of Gaius Maecenas, a counselor to Augustus and famed patron of the arts.

> **What a Life!**
>
> Vergil reportedly made a deathbed request that his epic be burned. Augustus, however, would not allow it—and so the *Aeneid* has survived to this day.

Vergil wrote his first major work, a collection of pastoral poems called *Eclogues*, from 42 to 37. In 30, a year after Augustus consolidated his rule, Vergil began an epic poem, the *Aeneid*, that added to Augustus's glory. The *Aeneid* follows the hero Aeneas as he flees Troy, settles in Italy, and defeats the native Rutulians to found the Roman race (see Chapter 22). The poem deliberately glorifies and idealizes both Rome and the Julian family (the family of Emperor Augustus) by connecting them to mythological heroes of the past. By linking his emperor with the gods, Vergil bestowed upon Augustus and Rome a divine mandate to conquer and then civilize the world.

Unfortunately, Vergil never finished writing the *Aeneid*. Though he had reached the tale's end, the poet was not yet satisfied with the work. Believing that he would complete his epic in three more years, Vergil set out for Greece in 19, perhaps intending to do more research for his final revision of the *Aeneid*. But he contracted a fever and died after returning to Brundisium (present-day Brindisi on the "heel of the boot" in Italy).

The Poet as Storyteller: Ovid

Perhaps the most widely read of all the ancients, Ovid was a wonderful storyteller. Ovid filled his tales with gripping details, some handed down and many wholly his own invention. The poet introduced characters and events of his own making—and may even have invented his own myths. Yet no doubt about it, the man knew how to spin a yarn.

Born in 43 B.C.E., just one year after the assassination of Julius Caesar, Ovid spent his boyhood in Sulmo, a town in the hill country about 90 miles east of Rome. His father—the driving force behind both his education and his writing—sent Ovid and his brother to Rome to study. After traveling extensively throughout Greece, the poet settled in Rome.

A popular artist, Ovid became famous even during his own lifetime. He wrote a great many works, the most famous being the long narrative poem *Metamorphoses* or *Stories of Changing Forms*. This poem pays particular attention to mythological stories in which characters transform themselves or are transformed into other forms.

Ovid demonstrated an incredible versatility in his writing. In *Heroides* he offers a series of imaginary love letters written by mythological women. *Fasti* (Feasts) describes both mythological events and Roman festivals. But in addition to these, Ovid also wrote on love and sorrows, and—following his exile—a series of letters from the Black Sea. He even wrote a poem titled *On Make-Up*—perhaps the world's first self-help poem.

Ovid married three times. And though the first two were brief, the third was the charm, lasting for the rest of his life. At the height of his career, however, Ovid was charged with immorality, high treason, or both. In 8 C.E., Augustus banished the poet from Rome to Tomis—a town on the Black Sea, on the distant edge of the Roman Empire. The embittered poet, who died in 17, spent the last 9 years of his life complaining about life on the shores of the Black Sea and begging to return to Rome. He insisted that he had committed no crime, but had been banished simply for making a mistake. The exact nature of the charge was never revealed.

When in Rome ...

Though Vergil and Ovid were the greatest Roman poets and without a doubt the richest Roman sources of classical mythology, they were not alone. Especially during the Augustan Age, other Roman writers drew on classical mythology—or invented and promoted new myths—to add to the grandeur of Rome. Like the Greek writers who contributed to the mythic storehouse, these Roman writers represented a grab bag of the literary arts: history, satires, and tragedies:

- *Livy*. A Roman historian during the time of Augustus, Livy wrote the definitive history of Rome from its founding through the early days of the Roman Empire. Livy's "history" included the legends of early Rome: the line of kings that led to the establishment of a republican government (see Chapter 23).

- *Horace*. The great Roman lyric poet and satirist Horace, the son of a former slave, at age 21 joined the army of Brutus, one of Caesar's assassins. Soundly defeated by the forces of Mark Antony and Octavian (Augustus) in the Battle of Philippi, Horace returned home only to find that the state had confiscated his family farm. Despite his early opposition to Octavian, Horace later won the patronage of Gaius Maecenas. Given a house and farm in the Sabine hills, he wrote different types of verse, the most famous of which are his four volumes of *Odes*.

- *Seneca*. The Roman statesman, philosopher, and writer Lucius Annaeus Seneca, also called Seneca the Younger, composed nine plays that focus on such classical figures as Hercules, Oedipus, and Medea. As a tragedian, he falls short of the Greek standard. Seneca's plays, meant to be recited rather than performed, feature shrill and undramatic speeches and focus on lurid or supernatural events.

Seneca's life was more fascinating than his work. As a young lawyer and politician, Seneca got caught up in the intrigues of the emperors Caligula and Claudius in the 1st century C.E. Seneca so infuriated Caligula that the emperor might have executed him, but was persuaded that the sickly young man would not live long anyway. (Seneca outlived both Caligula and Claudius.)

Claudius, the fourth emperor of Rome, banished Seneca to Corsica for sleeping with the emperor's niece. After eight years in exile, Seneca returned at the behest of Agrippina, Claudius's wife. Within five years, he had built a political base so secure that when Claudius was murdered and his son Nero—just 16—ascended to the throne, Seneca assumed joint management of the Roman Empire with Burrus, another politician. The two were preeminent for eight years, but when Burrus died, Seneca—fearful of challenges to his power—resigned. Three years later, he was charged with conspiring against the government and sentenced to kill himself. He did so with great grace and courage.

The Least You Need to Know

◆ Homer and Hesiod composed (but almost certainly did not write) their poems in the eighth or seventh century B.C.E. Homer "wrote" the epic poems *The Iliad* and *The Odyssey*. Hesiod "wrote" the poems *Theogony* and *Works and Days*.

◆ Aeschylus, Sophocles, and Euripides, the three greatest Greek dramatists, all wrote their works—and often competed against one another in the Great Dionysia—in the fifth century B.C.E. Only 33 of their more than 300 tragedies have survived.

◆ Apollodorus—whoever he was—collected hundreds of Greek myths in his *Library*.

◆ Vergil and Ovid both wrote during the Augustan Age, just before the dawn of the Common Era. Vergil wrote the epic *Aeneid*, while Ovid's greatest work was the narrative poem *Metamorphoses*.

◆ Livy collected and published the legends of early kings of Rome as "history."

Part  2 Welcome to the Pantheon: The Greek Gods

Like many ancient peoples, the Greeks had not just one god, but many. The 12 gods and goddesses recognized as the original Olympians were led by Zeus, who overthrew his father Cronus, leader of the race of Titans, and secured the place of the gods and goddesses on Mount Olympus. You'll recognize many of these gods by name: Zeus, Hera, Aphrodite, Ares.

Though you might think a dozen deities would be more than enough, the Greeks had many others, such as Hades, Lord of the Underworld, and Dionysus, the young god of wine. They also hosted dozens of minor deities: nymphs and lesser gods and goddesses.

So come let us introduce you to the Pantheon. You don't have to get all dressed up to meet them. Just come as you are and enjoy your visit.

Chapter

Tales of the Titanic

In This Chapter

- ◆ The first immortals are born: the Hundred-Handed Giants, the Cyclopes, and the Titans
- ◆ Why Cronus castrated his cruel father, Uranus
- ◆ How Zeus was saved from his father's appetite for infanticide
- ◆ How Zeus tricked Cronus into vomiting up his siblings
- ◆ The war between the Titans and the future Olympian gods

No doubt about it, the Creation, as detailed in Chapter 2, was a monumental feat. One might have thought that Gaia, Mother Earth, might have rested on her laurels after such a display of creative force. Yet Gaia knew that giving birth to the universe, however impressive, merely set the stage for the drama to follow.

The story still needed its players. So after giving birth to Uranus and Pontus, Gaia enlisted them to fill up the stage with more than mere scenery.

Raise the Titanic!

Gaia lay with her son Uranus, encouraging him to envelop her with his love. Through this union arose the famed Titans, the first rulers of the universe. Yet even before the Titans were born, Gaia and Uranus had six other formidable children: the Hundred-Handed Giants and the Cyclopes.

Too Many Hands, Not Enough Eyes

Though not as well known as the Titans who came after them, the first children of Gaia and Uranus were three giants: Cottus, Briareus, and Gyges. Each of these three brothers had 50 heads and 100 arms. These Hundred-Handed Giants would prove the mightiest of all Gaia and Uranus's children. Their great strength and imposing presence caused even Titans and later Olympian gods to quake with fear.

What a Life!

Gaia also lay with her other son, Pontus. She gave birth to five children by him (whose name means "sea" in Greek). Nereus, a sea god who would become known as the Old Man, was renowned for his truthfulness, gentle manner, and fairness. Phorcys, another sea god, and Thaumas were the brothers of Nereus. The Old Man also had two sisters: Ceto, a sea monster, and Eurybia.

The next children born to Gaia and Uranus were no less intimidating. They were three Cyclopes: Brontes, Steropes, and Arges. Each had only one eye, yet their enormous stature and mighty limbs more than made up for their limited vision.

These three Cyclopes were not the man-eating monsters of later myths (see Chapter 18), though some storytellers suggest that they might have fathered this later race. On the contrary, these Cyclopes were almost godlike. Inventive smiths and builders, they would later become the forgers of thunder and lightning.

Not-So-Fatherly Love

Unfortunately, these nearly divine Cyclopes were also arrogant, powerful, and unwilling to bow to authority. To punish them—and prevent them from becoming a threat—Uranus hurled them down into Tartarus, imprisoning the Cyclopes in the deepest, gloomiest section of the Underworld. But the Cyclopes need not have felt singled out by this cruel act. Uranus, who envied the incredible strength of the Hundred-Handed Giants, tossed these sons into Tartarus as well.

No Womb to Move

In addition to the Hundred-Handed Giants and the Cyclopes, the mating of Gaia and Uranus—Earth and Sky—also produced a line of gods. The primordial couple had a dozen more children, who later became known as the Titans.

The 12 children, conveniently enough, included six daughters and six sons—the perfect balance for later couplings. The daughters were named:

- *Theia*, who would become an early goddess of light
- *Rhea*, an earth goddess who would later become mother of the Olympian gods
- *Themis*, another earth or mother goddess—like her mother, Gaia, and her sister, Rhea
- *Mnemosyne*, a personification of memory
- *Phoebe*, who would become an early moon goddess
- *Tethys*, who would become the most ancient goddess of the sea

The sons were named:

- *Oceanus*, the first-born of the Titans, both the god of the primordial river and the river itself, which flowed from the Underworld in a circular and never-ending stream around the edge of the earth
- *Coeus*, who would become the father of Leto
- *Crius*, who would become the father of Astraeus
- *Hyperion*, who would become an early god of the sun
- *Iapetus*, who would become the father of Prometheus
- *Cronus*, the youngest of the Titans, but the craftiest and most daring

The youngest of the Titans, Cronus, hated his father, Uranus. In fact, all of the Titans hated their father—and with good reason. Uranus hated all of his children with a passion. Unlike mortal fathers who age and die, thus passing the torch to a younger generation, immortals like Uranus never wanted to give up their power. So no sooner had Gaia given birth to one of these children than Uranus thrust the baby back into the darkness of Gaia's womb. Forcing his own children to remain in the deepest, darkest hollows of the earth, Uranus refused to let them into the light again. What's more, the father of the Titans seemed to take great pleasure in this cruelty toward his children.

Gaia was, to say the least, uncomfortable with so many already-born children still borne in her womb. She now carried a dozen Titans inside her—not to mention the three Hundred-Handed Giants and the three Cyclopes trapped in Tartarus. Groaning with pain and the oppression of this forced burden, Gaia finally reached her breaking point.

Mother's Little Helper

Gaia devised a scheme to avenge the injuries inflicted by Uranus on both herself and her children. She crafted an enormous and very sharp sickle of iron. She then complained to her children about their father's shameful behavior and called upon them to punish him. From deep inside her, she felt the Titans quake with fear. But no one volunteered until Cronus, the youngest, boldly promised to do his mother's bidding.

Cronus hid and awaited his father's arrival. When Uranus finally entered at nightfall, he embraced Gaia and lay upon her in the fullness of his love. But Cronus took him by surprise. Seizing his father's genitals with his left hand, Cronus swiftly sliced them off with the right hand, which wielded the iron sickle. The deed done, Cronus tossed the castrated organ into the sea.

What a Life!

In the sea behind Cronus, the severed organ bobbed on the water, giving rise to a white foam. From this foam emerged the fully formed goddess of love: Aphrodite (whose name means "out of foam"). Naked and riding on a scallop shell, Aphrodite first touched land on the island of Cythera, but found the place too small for her comfort. Instead she stepped ashore on Cyprus. Wherever her feet touched down, grass and flowers popped up from the earth.

In honor of Aphrodite's landing sites, the goddess was sometimes also called *Cythereia* (meaning "from Cythera") or *Cypris* ("born on Cyprus").

From Uranus's severed manhood (or godhood) fell countless drops of blood, which spattered all over Gaia. From this not-so-immaculate conception, Gaia bore many more children, including:

- The Erinyes (Furies)—Alecto, Tisiphone, and Megara, who avenge perjury and crimes against one's own family (such as patricide—or castrating one's own father)

- The race of Giants, who were born in full armor with spears in their hands

- The ash tree nymphs, who would soon come to inhabit the forests of Greece

Uranus, understandably furious at Cronus and the rest of his children, cursed them all with the name "Titans" (which means "Overreachers"). He screamed a warning that their monstrous act would one day be avenged.

A Titanic Struggle

After gaining their own freedom, the Titans made Cronus their king and freed the Cyclopes and their Hundred-Handed brothers from Tartarus. But Cronus proved no more benevolent a ruler than his father. The Cyclopes and the Hundred-Handed Giants—as powerful, arrogant, and resistant to authority as before—had hardly tasted liberty when Cronus once again imprisoned all six in Tartarus.

The New Generation

The 12 Titans and Titanesses, however, retained their liberty—and began pairing off and breeding a new generation of Titans. Of the dozen, at least eight—four brothers and four sisters—married and had children:

- Theia and Hyperion—both associated with the sun—fell in love and married each other. Theia soon gave birth to a son—actually *the* sun (Helius)—and two daughters, Selene (the moon) and Eos (the dawn).

- Phoebe and Coeus—brought together by the moon—conceived two daughters: Leto, the sweetest and most gentle of the goddesses, and Asteria.

- Oceanus and Tethys—the Titans associated with the sea—joined in a most prolific union. Their offspring included all the 3,000 rivers—each with its own (usually male) god—and the 3,000 female Oceanids (see Chapter 2).

- The most impressive union of all—that between Cronus and Rhea, the father and mother of the gods—produced six divine children. All three daughters—Hestia, Demeter, and Hera—and all three sons—Hades, Poseidon, and Zeus—would soon take their place as gods on Mount Olympus.

A Tale That's Hard to Swallow

As lord of the immortals, Cronus became even more of a tyrant than his father. His parents, Gaia and Uranus, had warned him when he first seized the heavenly throne that despite his great power, he would one day be overthrown by his own son. But Cronus relished his power and would not tolerate any potential challengers to his position as king of the immortals.

To secure his power, Cronus came up with a dastardly scheme. Recalling that he and his Titanic siblings had escaped from the darkest depths of Mother Earth only because she became unwilling to bear the burden of keeping them inside her, Cronus decided to assume the burden of his own children himself. With the birth of each of his children—one a year—Cronus scooped up the child just as he or she emerged from Rhea's womb and immediately swallowed the child whole.

Rhea, grieving for her lost children, built up a tremendous rage toward her husband. When she conceived her sixth child, Zeus, Rhea pleaded with her parents to devise some scheme to conceal the child's birth. Gaia and Uranus, who foretold the future of both father and son, quickly consented to their daughter's request.

Gaia and Uranus quietly sent their daughter to Lyktos in Crete. In the dead of night, Rhea gave birth to Zeus and immediately turned him over to her Mother Earth. Gaia hid her grandchild in a cave on Mount Dicte, and nourished him with both food and love.

Meanwhile, Rhea returned to Cronus bearing a large stone wrapped in swaddling clothes. Without bothering to examine this bundle, Cronus swallowed it whole.

Zeus grew up on Crete in the care of the ash nymphs Adrasteia and Io and the goat nymph Amaltheia, who nursed him with her own milk. By the time he attained manhood, Zeus had become invincibly strong and swift.

> ### What a Life!
>
> In gratitude for her nurturing, Zeus later transformed the goat nymph Amaltheia into the constellation Capricorn. Zeus also fashioned one of her horns into the famed Cornucopia. This "horn of plenty" always contains the food or drink its owner most desires. What's more, no matter how much anyone takes from it, the Cornucopia never becomes empty.

> ### Mythed by a Mile
>
> When Rhea substituted a stone for her youngest son Zeus, it may not have been the first time she got away with this kind of trick. Some storytellers say Rhea spared her son Poseidon from her husband's digestive tract using a similar ruse. When Cronus demanded that she give up her newborn son, Rhea presented him with a foal in Poseidon's place.

> ### What a Life!
>
> When war between the Titans and the future Olympians seemed certain, Zeus promised the other immortals to restore any rights denied them by Cronus if only they would stand by his side in the battle ahead. Styx, a daughter of Oceanus and Tethys, and her children volunteered first—despite her marriage to the second-generation Titan, Pallas. Zeus rewarded her not only with great honors and gifts, but by inviting her children to live forever with him. Zeus later decreed that the gods should swear their greatest oaths by Styx, who had sworn an oath to him.

'Scuse Me, I Burped

Before confronting his father, the young Zeus traveled to the Ocean stream—the waters that circled around the edge of the earth—to find his cousin Metis, a wise Oceanid. Metis advised him to go first to his mother Rhea and volunteer to serve as Cronus's *cupbearer*. She then outlined a scheme that would allow Zeus to wreak vengeance on his father and release his brothers and sisters.

Logos

A **cupbearer** served his or her master food or drink. In essence, a cup-bearer was nothing more than a private waiter.

When Zeus approached his mother, she eagerly embraced the plan. Rhea prepared an emetic potion to make her husband vomit. Zeus then mixed the emetic into a honeyed drink and humbly carried it to Cronus.

As soon as Cronus had taken a long draft of this noxious drink, he began throwing up. First came the stone that Rhea had substituted for her youngest child, then Zeus's five brothers and sisters followed. All emerged unharmed. By acclamation, the siblings immediately chose Zeus to lead them in a war against Cronus and the Titans.

Clash of the Titans

Not all the Titans chose to fight against the children of Cronus. In fact, of the 12 original Titans, only five took up arms. None of the six original Titanesses got involved in the conflict. And Oceanus, who feared the power of Zeus, prudently refrained from taking sides in the conflict. Indeed, Oceanus and Tethys reared Hera, their niece, whom their sister Rhea entrusted to them.

The second generation of Titans—the children of the original Titans—had its holdouts, too. Helius refused to take sides, remaining neutral throughout the war. Prometheus and Epimetheus not only failed to support their parents, but sided with their cousins instead.

Three Hundred Helping Hands

The war did not resolve itself swiftly. After all, it pitted the nearly invincible Titans against the equally formidable children of Cronus. Every day for 10 years both sides fought fiercely on the battlefield, with each side stubbornly alternating attacks and retreats. The daily combat weakened both groups of immortals. Yet even after 10 years, neither side could claim victory.

Gaia foretold that the children of Cronus would triumph if joined by their allies in Tartarus. She assured Zeus that an alliance between the three Hundred-Handed, 50-headed Giants and the new Olympians would claim victory and the glory that comes with it.

Zeus heeded this oracle and headed straight down to Tartarus, the darkest depths of the Underworld. After killing Campe, the jailer, and stealing her keys, Zeus freed all six of his uncles: the Cyclopes and the Hundred-Handed Giants. He immediately relieved them of both thirst and hunger with offerings of nectar and ambrosia, which revived both their bodies and their spirits.

After leading them up out of Tartarus, Zeus enlisted all six, reminding them who had pulled them out of the earth's depths—and who had put them there in the first place. Briareus, Cottus, and Gyges—the Hundred-Handed Giants—quickly pledged their lives to protecting Zeus's power. The Cyclopes also needed little convincing. Indeed, they showed their gratitude by contriving new weapons and presenting them to the sons of Cronus:

- For Zeus, the Cyclopes forged thunder and lightning, which would become his weapons of choice.

- To Hades, the Cyclopes proffered the helmet of darkness, a magical hood that makes its wearer invisible.

- For Poseidon, they forged a trident, which would become emblematic of the future god of the sea.

After Zeus, Hades, and Poseidon held a war counsel, the fighting resumed with a new enthusiasm on the younger generation's part. By contrast, the Titans— now led in battle by Atlas, whom the other Titans had hand-picked to replace their not-so-invincible former leader, Cronus—seemed weary of the endless battles.

To Hell with the Titans

Briareus, Cottus, and Gyges proved to be formidable warriors. The Hundred-Handed Giants attacked the Titans with barrages of massive boulders—hurled in crushing volleys of 300, one from each of their mighty arms. The clash of warriors was so fierce that the sound of their fighting made the earth rumble, the sea swell, and the heavens shake. Even the depths of Tartarus resounded with the sound of their blows and the landing of their missiles.

Zeus also showed his mettle in this renewed campaign. The god steadily advanced upon the Titans, hurling his new thunderbolts in front of him. The earth itself became scorched with his flames. Vast forests were eradicated and the oceans and rivers steamed with the heat of Zeus's blasts. The earth-born Titans, overcome by the steam and blinded by the thunderbolts, soon fell to the Olympian gods.

The gifts offered by the Cyclopes proved invaluable weapons, especially in the attack on Cronus. Invisible under the helmet of darkness, Hades slipped inside Cronus's stronghold and stole his weapons. Poseidon quickly followed and began attacking his father with the trident. Though this assault did not harm Cronus, it distracted him enough to allow Zeus to hurl a thunderbolt at his defenseless father. Cronus finally had to concede victory to his sons.

Having crushed Cronus and the Titans, the army of Zeus drove all of their enemies down to the lowest depths of Tartarus. Zeus decreed that the Titans should remain imprisoned in Tartarus, hidden away far below the earth, forever. Securely locked behind its marble gates and bronze threshold, deeply rooted in the ground, the Titans had no chance of escape. But just in case they did, Briareus, Cottus, and Gyges—three Giants with 150 heads among them—stood watch outside the walls of Tartarus.

Mythed by a Mile

The followers of Orpheus—who rejected the more prevalent classical notion that conflict shaped the world, embracing instead the concept of a world ordered by pre-destined structures—told quite a different tale of what happened to Cronus after the fall of the Titans. Zeus wrapped his father in chains and dragged him to the outermost regions of the earth, depositing him on the Islands of the Blessed—idyllic islands where the Golden Age of Man (see Chapter 2) still lived. According to this more peaceful worldview, Cronus then ruled these islands, where mortal heroes who have become immortals resided forever.

Only one Titan who had opposed Zeus avoided eternal imprisonment in Tartarus. For Atlas, who had led his fellow Titans in battle, Zeus reserved a special punishment. The god placed Atlas at the westernmost end of the earth and ordered him to lift up the sky and bear the weight of the heavens forevermore on his head and shoulders.

As for his supporters, the new king of the immortals rewarded them handsomely. To Briareus, Zeus gave his daughter, Cymopoleia. The Titans who did not oppose the Olympians—the six Titanesses, Oceanus, Helius, Prometheus, and Epimetheus—all retained their places of honor and their functions. The Olympians showed particular reverence for Themis, Oceanus, and Tethys. By remembering his supporters, Zeus helped to ensure that his reign—unlike those of his father and grandfather—would last forever.

The Least You Need to Know

- Gaia and Uranus conceived not only the 12 Titans, but the three Cyclopes (one-eyed giants) and the three Hundred-Handed Giants, who had many arms and heads.

- Uranus hated his children and shoved them all back into Mother Earth's womb right after their birth.

- At Gaia's urging, Cronus castrated his father and became ruler of the immortals.

- Cronus swallowed all of his children except Zeus, who escaped ingestion when his mother Rhea substituted a boulder instead of a baby.

- Zeus slipped his father a drink that forced him to throw up the rest of his children.

- After a 10-year war, the new Olympian gods—the sons and daughters of Cronus—overthrew the Titans and established the rule of Zeus over the immortals.

Chapter 6

The Reign of Thunder and Lightning: Olympus Under Zeus

In This Chapter

- ◆ The reign of Zeus
- ◆ The turbulent marriage of Zeus and Hera
- ◆ Poseidon and Hades: the brothers of Zeus and their realms
- ◆ Hestia and Demeter: the sisters of Hera and their responsibilities
- ◆ The Olympians' failed rebellion against Zeus

Having disposed of their father, the six children of Rhea and Cronus became the first of the Olympian gods. Unlike their predecessors, these Olympians would—despite some challenges—hold on to their power to rule the universe, governing the affairs of both gods and men for the rest of time.

At Gaia's urging, the gods of Olympus—supremely grateful to their little brother for freeing them from their father—implored Zeus, the greatest of the gods, to rule over them. The ambitious Zeus readily accepted this honor.

But how would they divide the spoils of their victory over the Titans? Who would rule the heavens? Who would rule the sea, the earth, and the Underworld? Zeus decided to cast lots to determine the dominion of each god. (The goddesses were excluded from this division of power.) The three brothers—Zeus, Poseidon, and Hades—placed their names in a helmet and drew them out to determine the lords of the sky, sea, and Underworld.

By chance, Zeus drew the sky; Poseidon, the sea; and Hades, the dark Underworld. The brothers agreed that both the earth and Mount Olympus—the home of the gods—would remain under their common jurisdiction, the realm of no one god.

Master of the Universe

Some storytellers depicted Zeus, the Supreme Ruler of the universe, as the all-knowing and all-powerful ruler of all things. But with his power also came many responsibilities:

- ◆ Zeus handed down the laws that governed the behavior of mortals and immortals alike and made sure they were obeyed.

- ◆ In addition to upholding the laws, Zeus enforced any oaths sworn—by either mortals or immortals—upon the gods.

- ◆ Zeus pronounced certain oracles, for, like many of the gods, Zeus often knew what the future held.

- ◆ As ruler of the heavens, Zeus imposed order on the universe. He placed all the planets and the stars in the sky.

- ◆ He also commanded meteorological phenomena. It was he who sent the rains that fertilized the earth and made it productive. He also commanded the thunderstorm, wielding thunder and lightning as his most potent weapons.

King of Gods, God of Kings

Despite the initial agreement that no single god would rule Olympus, Zeus—as Lord of the Heavens—in effect ruled Olympus as well. But he did not lord over the other gods with an iron fist. Zeus maintained his power not through force alone, but through wisdom and justice.

If not exactly a benevolent ruler, Zeus was, for the most part, sensible, shrewd, and fair. In mediating conflicts among the gods, Zeus demonstrated both impartiality and good judgment. Many of these arguments involved border disputes—such as when

Poseidon and Athena both wanted to serve as the patron of Athens. Zeus chose to remain neutral, putting the question before a tribunal of other gods. In a similar dispute between the same two Olympians over Troezen, Zeus ruled that Poseidon and Athena should share that city equally—a solution that satisfied neither of them.

Zeus often found compromise the quickest route to justice. When Demeter demanded the return of her daughter Persephone from Hades, Zeus ruled that the girl should spend part of the year with her mother and part of it with her new husband (see Chapter 11). Similarly, when both Persephone and Aphrodite claimed the right to rear Adonis, Zeus found a solution that demanded mutual compromise (see Chapter 7).

As for his relations with mortals, Zeus was never overly impressed with humankind. He would have withheld fire from the human race had not Prometheus stolen it from Olympus and presented it to man (see Chapter 2). Later, Zeus—grossly offended by the mortal Lycaon, who had served the god human flesh to eat—intended to wipe out the entire race with a great flood. Once again, however, Prometheus saved the day.

What a Life!

King Lycaon, who had 50 sons, ruled Arcadia when Zeus came down from Olympus to investigate human wickedness. Lycaon (or perhaps his sons) rashly tried to test the nature of their divine visitor. So they mixed human flesh in with the stew that they served Zeus. Enraged by this impiety, Zeus turned Lycaon into a wolf, destroyed all but one of the king's sons, and created the great flood.

Deucalion, a son of Prometheus, married Pyrrha, a daughter of Epimetheus and Pandora. When Prometheus learned of the flood Zeus had planned, he warned Deucalion and Pyrrha, who swiftly built a boat and stocked it with food. The flood lasted for nine days and nights, but the couple then landed safely on Mount Parnassus. Zeus, showing some mercy, then helped them repopulate the earth by having them throw stones. Those that Pyrrha threw became women, while Deucalion's stones became men.

In the affairs of mortals, the justice of Zeus often involved chastening or punishing mortals for overreaching. Those mortals who dared to assume divine rights, privileges, or powers soon regretted having aroused the wrath of Zeus.

In addition to guarding the rights of the gods, Zeus sometimes protected mortal kings from overreachers (usurpers of the throne). Zeus also harshly punished those who violated the laws of hospitality toward guests and suppliants (those who humbly asked their hosts for some favor).

Trouble in Paradise

As ruler of Olympus by acclamation, Zeus experienced few threats to his power. The gods tried to challenge his rule just once. Hera, Poseidon, and young Apollo—soon joined by all the other Olympians, except Hestia—rose against Zeus.

As Zeus lay sleeping, they bound him to his couch with thongs of rawhide, tying 100 knots to hold him fast. Though Zeus could scarcely move a muscle, he boldly threatened the rebellious gods with instantaneous destruction. They only laughed and mocked him, knowing that his intimidating thunderbolts were far out of reach.

What a Life!

Zeus also forced Poseidon and Apollo to atone for their part in the failed rebellion. He sent the chastened Olympians to Phrygia to serve King Laomedon of Troy humbly for one year. The gods built the impenetrable walls around Troy that would later keep Greek attackers from taking the city for 10 years (see Chapter 16).

The debate over who would best succeed Zeus as ruler of the gods grew heated, however. The argument might have led to civil war, but the Nereid Thetis—ancient goddess of the sea—saved the Olympians from war. Thetis summoned Briareus, one of the Giants. Using all of his hands at once, Briareus swiftly untied the 100 knots, freeing the god who had freed him from Tartarus.

To punish Hera for leading the rebellion, Zeus affixed golden bracelets to her wrists and hung her from the sky. To each of her ankles he attached an iron anvil. Zeus freed her only after her fellow Olympians, tortured by Hera's anguished cries, vowed never again to rebel against him.

The First Sex Addict?

If Zeus had one flaw (and most Olympians had at least one), it would have to be his insatiable lust. His mother Rhea recognized her son's enormous appetite for sexual intercourse and foresaw that it would create problems for both him and any wife he chose. So she forbade Zeus to marry.

Furious at his mother's interference, Zeus threatened to violate *her*. Upon hearing this threat, Rhea transformed herself into a vicious serpent. But Zeus did the same, tangled himself in a knot with his mother that could not be untied, and did indeed violate her—making her the first in a long line of victims of the god's lust.

Metis, the beautiful Oceanid who had advised him on how to free his brothers and sisters (see Chapter 5), became his first lover. A shape-shifter, Metis transformed herself many times in order to escape the lust of Zeus, but Zeus finally caught her. The couple conceived the goddess Athena. But during the pregnancy, Gaia prophesied that a second child by Metis would be a son who would overthrow his father and rule heaven in his stead. Zeus knew this story well: After all, he had deposed his father, Cronus, who had done the same to Zeus's grandfather, Uranus.

Rather than risk the fulfillment of Gaia's prophecy, Zeus emulated his father—but went even further. Instead of just swallowing the children, as Cronus had done, he swallowed Metis even before she could give birth to Athena. (See Chapter 7 to find out just how Athena was born.) Thereafter, Zeus claimed that Metis—who was considered wiser than even the gods—continued to provide him with advice and counsel from within his belly.

After Metis, Zeus mated with his beautiful aunt Themis, a Titaness. Themis and Zeus conceived several children—and this time Zeus allowed their birth. Themis gave birth to:

♦ The three Horae (Seasons): Eunomia (Law and Order), Dike (Justice), and Eirene (Peace)

♦ The three Moirai (Fates): the sisters Clotho, Lachesis, and Atropos, who mete out every mortal's life span and his or her share of good and evil. (For more on the Moirai, who were, according to Hesiod, not the daughters of Zeus and Themis, but of Nyx and Erebus, see Chapter 2.)

With the birth of these six daughters, Zeus—the father of all laws—completed the job of creation: bringing order to chaos.

Zeus chose as his third mistress a sister of Metis, an Oceanid named Eurynome. She gave birth to the three Graces—*Aglaia*, *Euphrosyne*, and *Thalia*—who personified the qualities of beauty, grace, and charm.

Logos

Aglaia means "beauty" or "splendor." **Euphrosyne** means "the quality of having a good heart." And **Thalia** means "flourishing" or "thriving abundance."

Zeus next slept with his sister Demeter. Their daughter Persephone, against her mother's wishes, would become Queen of the Underworld (see Chapter 11).

Zeus next lay with another aunt, the Titaness Mnemosyne. For nine nights, this divine couple made love, thereby conceiving the nine Muses. Though not all storytellers agreed on the specific functions of individual Muses, they are usually identified as follows:

♦ Clio, the Muse of history

♦ Euterpe, the Muse of music and lyric poetry

- Thalia, the Muse of comedy (not to be confused with Thalia, one of the three Graces)

- Melpomene, the Muse of tragedy

- Terpsichore, the Muse of dance

- Erato, the Muse of love poetry and marriage songs

- Polyhymnia, the Muse of sacred song and oratory

- Urania, the Muse of astronomy

- Calliope, the Muse of epic or heroic poetry

The sixth lover of Zeus was his cousin Leto, the daughter of the Titans Phoebe and Coeus. Leto gave birth to the most beautiful of all the Olympians: Artemis and Apollo (see Chapter 7).

A Heavenly Marriage? Hera and Zeus

After Leto, Zeus found a lover who put him in seventh heaven. For this lover, his seventh, was the one he chose to marry: his sister Hera. When he began courting her—in secret, so that his mother would not find out—Hera, who no doubt knew that Zeus had already had six different lovers, spurned his romantic overtures.

Cuckoo for Love

Zeus realized he needed another approach. So he appeared to her in the guise of a bedraggled, rain-soaked cuckoo. Hera saw the poor bird and kindly brought him into the shelter of her bosom to warm and dry him. Zeus immediately returned to his true form and—true to form, indeed—ravished her. He thus shamed Hera into marrying him.

What a Life!
Here's a neat trick! Hera regularly bathed in the spring of Canathus near Argos—and in doing so restored and renewed her virginity.

The first wedding of Olympians was no small occasion. All the gods and goddesses attended, bringing with them marvelous gifts. Gaia presented her granddaughter, Hera, with a wondrous tree. Hera planted this tree, richly hung with Golden Apples, in her garden under the care of the Hesperides, nymphs who were daughters of the Night (Nyx). Hera and Zeus had a glorious wedding night—one that lasted 300 years.

Zeus and Hera had three children together: Ares, the god of war; Hebe, a perpetually youthful beauty; and Eileithyia, the goddess of childbirth.

Hades Hath No Fury Like a Goddess Scorned

Although Hera was a goddess of both marriage and childbirth herself, she never had a happy or peaceful marriage. Zeus continued to have love affairs with goddesses, nymphs, and mortals long after he married Hera, much to her chagrin.

A full accounting of his conquests would humble Don Juan. The list of trysts included, among many, many others:

- Maia, a Pleiad (daughter of Atlas), by whom he fathered Hermes (see Chapter 7)

- Electra, another Pleiad, with whom he conceived Dardanus (see Chapter 22)

- Taygete, a third Pleiad, with whom he conceived Lacedaemon

- Semele, a mortal, who gave birth to Dionysus (see Chapter 9)

- Alcmene, another mortal, who became the mother of Heracles (see Chapter 13)

- Dana, the mother of Perseus (see Chapter 10)

- Leda, by whom he fathered Helen and Polydeuces

Zeus also had dalliances with boys, the most notable of which was Ganymede, a beautiful young Trojan whom Zeus abducted to become his cupbearer.

Needless to say, this parade of paramours caused quite a bit of marital tension between the King and Queen of Heaven. Hera was understandably jealous of all of her husband's infidelities. The goddess had a violent temper, and Zeus roused her fury more than once with his incessant seductions.

The scorned goddess poured most of her energy into pursuing, punishing, and persecuting her husband's mistresses and bastard children:

- She tried to prevent Leto from giving birth even though that affair had come before his marriage.

- She sent a relentless gadfly to torment the mortal Io after Zeus had changed her into a cow.

- She provoked Artemis into shooting and killing Callisto, whom Zeus had transformed into a bear (see Chapter 7).

◆ She killed nearly all the inhabitants of the island named after Aegina. (Zeus later repopulated the island by transforming ants into people who became the subjects of his son by Aegina: Aeacus, the first king of the island that bore his mother's name [see Chapter 17].)

◆ She goaded Semele into making a request to Zeus that ultimately destroyed her (see Chapter 9).

◆ She relentlessly persecuted Zeus's mortal son, Heracles, who rose to immortal status in spite of her (see Chapter 13).

What a Life!

Io, the daughter of the river god Inachus, was seduced or raped by Zeus. When Hera came looking for her husband, Zeus transformed Io into a cow either to protect her from Hera's wrath or to hide his own shame. Not fooled a bit, Hera sent a gadfly that repeatedly stung Io, driving her all the way through Asia Minor and into Africa. Only then did Zeus, finding Io on the banks of the Nile River, change her back into a woman.

Jealousy was not the only emotion that could rouse Hera's anger. The goddess was also extremely competitive about her beauty. When Side, the first wife of the great hunter Orion, boasted that she was more beautiful than Hera, the goddess dispatched her to Hades. And when Paris of Troy chose Aphrodite as the fairest of the goddesses, Hera naturally took the side of the Greeks in the Trojan War that followed (see Chapter 16). Zeus forbade divine interference in this conflict. Yet despite this prohibition, Hera once seduced her husband, distracting his attention so that Poseidon could incite the Greeks to attack the Trojans.

Zeus and Hera once argued about whether men or women derived greater pleasure from the act of making love. Each insisted that the other's gender reaped the greater share of pleasure. The great seer Teiresias, called in to decide the matter, insisted that a woman's pleasure was nine times that of man. Infuriated, Hera immediately blinded the seer.

What a Life!

Teiresias was uniquely qualified to mediate the dispute between Zeus and Hera, for only he had tasted the pleasures of life as both a man and a woman. As a young man, he had killed a female snake in the act of coupling, and was immediately transformed into a woman. After seven years of this life, he killed a male snake in the act of mating, and he changed back to a man on the spot.

Surf and Turf: The Brothers of Zeus

Though not as powerful as their younger brother, Poseidon and Hades could claim to equal his status. For just as Zeus ruled the sky, Poseidon was lord of the seas and Hades the supreme authority in the dark Underworld.

Turf Wars

Poseidon, who won the right to rule the seas, was also the god of horses and of earthquakes. Poseidon's domain actually extended beyond the oceans to include freshwater rivers, even though the river gods were the sons of Oceanus and Tethys.

Mythmakers often depicted Poseidon as gruff and quick to anger. He sometimes resented the greater dominion of Zeus. Perhaps for this reason, Poseidon lived not in Olympus, but in an underwater palace off the eastern coast of Greece.

His subordinate position to Zeus made him sensitive about his other rights. Poseidon argued more over city patronage than any other Olympian. He contested the patronage of Argos with Hera and the patronage of Corinth with Helius. Poseidon lost both disputes and had to settle for the patronage of various islands and seaports.

The most famous of these patronage disputes was the fight over Athens. Poseidon claimed the land by plunging his trident into the ground of the Acropolis and creating a salt-water spring. But Athena later planted the first olive tree beside this well and claimed the city as her own. Poseidon challenged her to combat, but Zeus intervened and put the matter before a divine tribunal. Wishing to remain neutral and above the fray, Zeus did not vote. That left four other gods, all of whom voted for Poseidon. (Hades, as was his custom, did not attend the Olympian hearing.) The five goddesses, however, all sided with Athena, giving her the right to the land by virtue of her greater gift to the city.

In a fury, Poseidon flooded the Attic plain. The Athenians adopted several measures to appease Poseidon's wrath. The city denied the women of Athens the right to vote. It ended the practice of men carrying on their mothers' names. And all Athenians continued to honor both Poseidon and Athena on the Acropolis.

Beastly Couplings, Beastly Children

Poseidon courted Amphitrite, one of the Nereids (daughters of Nereus, the Old Man of the Sea). Yet Amphitrite scorned the god's advances and fled to the Atlas Mountains. Poseidon refused to give up, sending messengers after her to plead his case. One of these, Delphinus, argued so persuasively for his master that he broke down Amphitrite's resistance. She agreed to marry Poseidon. (The god later showed his gratitude by placing his messenger's image in the sky as a constellation: the Dolphin.)

Like his brother Zeus, Poseidon was not exactly the poster boy for fidelity. He, too, had numerous affairs with goddesses, nymphs, and mortals. Like most sea gods, Poseidon had the power to transform his shape, and often did so in order to complete a seduction:

♦ He appeared to the maiden Medusa as a bird. Unfortunately, he chose as the setting for this seduction one of Athena's temples. The enraged goddess punished Medusa by turning her into a Gorgon (see Chapter 10).

> **What a Life!**
>
> Otus and Ephialtes, already 50 feet tall at age nine, literally moved mountains. Just because they could, they heaped Pelion, Ossa, and Olympus on top of one another, nearly reaching heaven itself. The twin giants later killed each other in a hunting "accident" orchestrated by Artemis and Apollo (see Chapter 7).

♦ To mate with Theophane, whom he had changed into a ewe in order to hide her from her many suitors, he transformed himself into a ram.

♦ When Demeter, overwhelmed by the loss of her daughter Persephone, attempted to escape her brother's attentions by becoming a mare, Poseidon was not fooled. He changed himself into a stallion and mated with her in an Arcadian pasture.

Poseidon also mated in the shape of a dolphin and a bull. These many transformations had a powerful influence on his offspring, too:

♦ Medusa's children were the winged horse Pegasus and the giant warrior Chrysaor.

♦ His union with Theophane produced the famous Golden-Fleeced ram (see Chapter 14).

♦ Demeter had two children by him: the nymph Despoena and a wild horse named Arion.

♦ Many of his children were giants, including Chrysaor, the Cyclops Polyphemus, and the trouble-making brothers Otus and Ephialtes.

As a father, Poseidon was very protective, not only toward his three children by Amphitrite, but toward the children of his many mistresses, too. Poseidon made his son

Cycnus invulnerable to weapons. He helped Theseus prove his parentage in a bragging contest with King Minos of Crete (see Chapter 15). And he avenged the blinding of Polyphemus by tormenting Odysseus for 10 years (see Chapter 18).

Perhaps because he mated with a goddess in that form, the horse became sacred to Poseidon. Some storytellers insisted he invented the horse by smashing his trident down upon a rock. In any case, it is said that he invented horse racing and perhaps the bridle as well. Wherever he went, he rode in a gold chariot drawn by two magnificent white horses with golden manes and brass hooves.

The Prince of Darkness

Hades, who by chance won dominion over the Underworld, soon came to prefer the darkness of his own domain to any other place on Earth or in heaven. For the most part, he remained out of touch with both Olympus and Earth, learning of events there only when someone invoked his name in oaths or curses. He seldom met with the other gods and goddesses on Olympus. And unless moved by lust, he rarely left the Underworld for the common ground of Earth.

Hades became as absolute an authority in the Underworld as Zeus was in the sky. Fiercely protective of his own rights, he claimed ownership of all metals and gems below the surface of the earth.

The most private of all the gods, Hades did not welcome "visitors" and rarely let anyone who entered the Underworld leave again. Cerberus, a vicious, three-headed watchdog, stood guard at the locked gate, making sure the dead remained in the Underworld.

For this reason, men feared and loathed the fierce lord of the Underworld. Indeed, he became so closely associated with the darkness and horror of the Underworld that the place itself eventually came to be called simply *Hades*.

Logos

Hades was originally the name only of the ruler of the Underworld, rather than the place itself. Homer, among others, began referring to the Underworld as the "House of Hades." In time, the "house" was omitted and the Underworld itself became known as Hades.

Yet Hades, though cold and grim, was neither vicious nor evil. True, he oversaw all punishments of the dead mandated by the gods, but most of these tortures were carried out by the Erinyes (Furies). In lording over the dead, he was simply doing his job. Nonetheless, mortals were reluctant to speak his name (or his somewhat longer title, Aidoneus, the "Unseen One") for fear of attracting his attention.

Home and Harvest: The Sisters of Hera

Though not given a share in ruling the universe, the sisters of Hera (and Zeus) were no less deserving of honors. The original Olympian goddesses assumed "traditional" female responsibilities derived from the functions of ancient earth goddesses. Hera protected marriage and childbirth, Hestia guarded the hearth and home, and Demeter promoted fertility and the harvest. Since these functions played no small role in the earthly lives of mortal men and women, the Greeks (and later the Romans) showed them great reverence. Ancient literature on mythology and religious practices—written exclusively by male authors—offers us few tales about Demeter and Hestia. However, other relics of antiquity—artifacts, graffiti, place names, and so on—provide strong evidence that women in particular directed religious practices and daily worship primarily toward female deities.

Home Is Where the Hearth Is

The first-born of the six children of Rhea and Cronus, Hestia was the kindest, most virtuous, and most charitable of all the Olympians. As goddess of the hearth and fire—the symbolic center of the home—Hestia watched over the home, household activities, and the family. Indeed, some storytellers assert that Hestia herself invented the art of building houses. By extension, she also protected the community, the civic affairs of the communal family.

Unlike most other gods and goddesses, Hestia had few shrines built to honor her. But she needed none, for every home was her shrine—as well as the public hearth of every city. Suppliants could seek her protection in any private home or in the city hall.

What a Life!
Only once did Hestia come close to losing her virginity. One night at a rustic feast, the gods ate and drank too much and fell asleep or passed out. Priapus, an incredibly ugly man possessed of grossly elephantine genitals, prepared to mount her. But just as he lowered himself on top of her, a braying ass woke Hestia up. The goddess screamed and Priapus skittered away like a scared rabbit.

The goddess of the home and family never had a family of her own. At one time, both Poseidon and the younger god Apollo pursued her, and the competition for her favor threatened to get ugly. But her supreme dedication to peace never allowed Hestia to take part in wars, rivalries, or other disputes. So in order to maintain peace on Olympus, Hestia turned down both rivals and swore by Zeus's head to maintain her chastity forever. Thereafter she withstood all amorous advances by gods, Titans, and mortals alike. Zeus rewarded her for this sacrifice by guaranteeing her the honor of receiving the first portion of every public sacrifice.

Earth Angel

Although the division of kingdoms among the three sons of Cronus left Earth as common ground, if anyone on Olympus ruled over Earth, it was Demeter. The goddess of the harvest, earth, and fertility, Demeter presided over all crops, but especially grains. (For some reason she was not fond of beans, regarding them as impure.)

Demeter, like Hestia, never married, but she did have several love affairs. With her first love, Zeus, Demeter had two children: a daughter, *Kore* (later called Persephone); and a son, Iacchus.

Attending the marriage of Ares' daughter Harmonia and Cadmus, the first king of Thebes, Demeter fell in love for the second time: with the bride's brother, Iasion, a Titan. The couple lay together in a thrice-plowed field. But when the lovers returned to the wedding feast, Zeus spotted the mud on their arms and legs and jealously killed Iasion on the spot with a thunderbolt. Her child by Iasion, Plutus, would become the god of the earth's wealth.

Logos

Kore means "maiden," one of the three principal aspects of ancient goddess worship. The ancients divided female divinity into The Maiden, The Mother, and The Crone—the three phases of an ancient woman's life.

For the most part, Demeter was gentle and mild. Very rarely, however, she exploded with anger. Her most notable outburst of anger came in the wake of her daughter Persephone's abduction by Hades. In her thirst for vengeance—and her sorrow—Demeter made the earth barren, forbidding trees to blossom and crops to grow and creating a year-long famine.

Even in the throes of despair, however, Demeter responded to kindness with kindness and generosity of her own. In the midst of her search for Persephone, the daughters of Celeus, king of Eleusis, invited Demeter—who had disguised herself as an old woman—to stay in their palace. In return for this kindness, Demeter schooled Celeus and the Eleusinians in the religious rites in her honor that came to be known as the Eleusinian Mysteries—the most widespread and influential of all Greek religious rites. (Celeus constructed a temple at Eleusis in her honor.)

What a Life!

One mortal who incurred Demeter's wrath was Erysichthon. Needing timber, he cut down trees in a grove sacred to her, refusing to heed the cries of the trees' dryads (nymphs who dwell in trees) or the blood flowing from their wounds. When Demeter, in the guise of her priestess, Nicippe, told him to stop, he raised his axe and told her to be gone. For this sacrilege, the goddess condemned him to eternal hunger. Erysichthon stuffed himself to no avail. Unable to afford feeding himself, he became a beggar. In the end, he gnawed on his own flesh until he died.

Queen Meteneira also offered Demeter a place in her home, asking the old woman to serve as her young son's nurse. Demeter adored the boy, Demophon, and—in gratitude to his parents—wanted to give him the gift of immortality. But Meteneira was horrified to discover the old woman laying the baby on the embers at night to burn away his mortality. As a result, Demeter never got the chance to complete this rite. (Demophon grew up to be a great, but mortal, leader of Eleusis.)

Demeter also rewarded Triptolemus, an Eleusinian (perhaps another son of Celeus) who gave her the first clue to her daughter's whereabouts. To thank him, Demeter taught him the art of agriculture. She then sent him throughout the world with seed-corn, a wooden plough, and her dragon-drawn chariot to sow these lessons everywhere.

The Least You Need to Know

- Zeus ruled, for the most part, with wisdom and fairness.

- Hera was jealous—with good cause—of her husband's countless infidelities. She often tormented his mistresses and their children. She also led a rebellion of the gods against Zeus, but it failed miserably.

- Poseidon, god of the sea, often looked for ways to expand his influence.

- Hades, lord of the dead, actually preferred the darkness of the Underworld to all other places.

- Hestia, the virginal goddess of the hearth and home, tried to keep the peace among families and communities—even among the Olympians.

- Demeter, goddess of the harvest, was kind and generous—but if crossed, imposed harsh punishments.

The A Team: Olympians All

In This Chapter

- ◆ Athena, the goddess of war and wisdom
- ◆ Hephaestus, the god of smithing and craftsmanship
- ◆ Ares, the god of war
- ◆ Aphrodite, the goddess of love
- ◆ Artemis and Apollo, the divine children of Leto
- ◆ Hermes, messenger of the gods and patron of thieves

The children of Rhea and Cronus did not remain the only Olympians for long. Joined by seven others, the Olympians soon became a baker's dozen of great gods. (Since Hades, however, rarely emerged from the Underworld, Olympian affairs were for the most part the province of just 12 deities: 6 gods and 6 goddesses.)

Zeus, of course, continued to rule the roost among this expanded pantheon. And no wonder: He was brother or father to 9 of the other 11 Olympians. Not counting Hades, who did not consider himself an Olympian, Zeus had four siblings on Olympus: Poseidon, Hera, Hestia, and Demeter. But he also fathered Ares (by Hera), Athena (by Metis), Artemis and Apollo (by Leto), and Hermes (by Maia). Zeus would also father Dionysus (by Semele), a god who would later claim his own place among the pantheon.

First in War, First in Peace: Athena

Of all the Olympians, few enjoyed the universal respect accorded to Athena—the virgin goddess of arts, crafts, and war. Athena was also the goddess of wisdom, which in her case meant the technical skill of artisans and craftsmen as well as practical sense and cunning.

As the goddess of arts and crafts, Athena received credit for inventing many useful tools and arts. Athena introduced the plow, rake, yoke, and bridle to farmers. She also invented the chariot and designed the first ship. Her other inventions included the earthenware pot, the flute, and the trumpet. In addition, Athena first taught the science of mathematics as well as such household arts as spinning, weaving, and cooking.

A Surefire Cure for a Migraine: Athena's Birth

Athena, you'll recall, had not yet been born when Zeus, her father, swallowed Metis, her mother (see Chapter 6). Zeus did not fear Athena, though it was foretold that her wisdom and strength would match his own. But he dared not risk the birth of a second child by Metis: a son destined to usurp his dominion.

After swallowing Metis, Zeus didn't give a second thought to the child she was carrying. But one day as he walked along the shore of Lake Tritonis, Zeus was suddenly racked with a splitting headache. He suffered from so much pain that he roared in agony.

Unable to bear the pain, Zeus called upon either Hephaestus or Prometheus, who brought an ax down upon his head, splitting open his skull. Dressed in full armor, an adult Athena emerged from her father's head with a shout that echoed throughout the world.

The birth of Athena completed the evolution from a mother-dominated mythology to one dominated by a supreme patriarch: Zeus. Through two generations, mothers had controlled the power structure of the immortals. In league with their sons, these mothers had toppled their mates. First, Gaia had conspired with her son Cronus to castrate Uranus. Next, Rhea—with Gaia's help—had saved her son Zeus in order to overthrow Cronus.

Zeus ended this pattern, however, by swallowing Metis and the unborn Athena. In appropriating the

What a Life!
Brave Tydeus—a warrior from Calydon, in central Greece—was a favorite of Athena's. She might have made Tydeus—who was mortally wounded in the war of the Seven Against Thebes—an immortal. But Tydeus slew his own slayer and began gorging on his enemy's brains. Athena recoiled in disgust at the sight, leaving him to die.

female function of giving birth, Zeus ended the line of female supremacy. For Athena, born out of Zeus's head, owed no loyalty to any mother.

War! What Is It Good For?

The goddess of war, unlike her aggressive half-brother Ares, the god of war, had little taste for blood. Though often depicted in full armor—helmeted, with spear and shield—Athena derived more pleasure from peaceful resolutions of disputes than from battle. In keeping with her aversion to bloodlust, Athena was also merciful. When seated on the tribunal that tried Orestes for murdering his mother after she had murdered his father, for example, Athena voted for acquittal (see Chapter 16).

Though she shunned warfare, when forced into battle she proved nearly invincible. A brilliant strategist, she twice defeated the war god Ares on the battlefield. She was also a dominant force in the war with the Giants (see Chapter 8).

The goddess of both war and wisdom often rewarded those who demonstrated bravery or ingenuity. For instance, she helped Perseus (another child of Zeus) kill the Gorgon Medusa. Afterward, she proudly displayed the head of the slain Medusa in the center of her shield.

Athena also acted as Odysseus's special protector. When the hero finally arrived back home in Ithaca after 20 years, Athena—though in disguise—appeared to greet him (see Chapter 18). Odysseus returned the favor of her deceit by lying about who he was. With a laugh, Athena revealed her true identity and admitted that she and Odysseus were two of a kind, shrewd liars both.

> ### What a Life!
> Athena hid the infant Erichthonius in a basket and presented it to the three daughters of King Cecrops of Athens. She warned them not to open the lid of the basket. But two of the girls disobeyed. Shocked to see a child with a snake's tail instead of legs, the two sisters ran off a cliff and died. So Athena took him back and reared him with great love and tenderness in her shrine on the Acropolis.

A Not-So-Immaculate Conception

A virginal goddess, Athena remained chaste despite many potential suitors. During the Trojan War, however, she experienced a very close call.

Athena needed both armor and weapons, for she went without them except when in battle. So she asked Hephaestus to forge some for her, which he gladly offered to do as a labor of love.

Athena apparently didn't appreciate the import of these words. When she entered his shop to check on his progress, Hephaestus—normally deferential toward the goddesses—attacked her. Poseidon had apparently played a trick on him, telling the smith god that Athena yearned for him to make passionate love to her.

Athena quickly pulled herself away from her attacker, but Hephaestus could not stop himself: His seed spilled out onto her thigh. Athena, greatly offended, took some wool and wiped off the god's semen.

When she tossed the wool to the ground, however, she unwittingly fertilized Gaia. The earth goddess—disgusted by this tale of violation—disavowed any responsibility for the offspring of this misadventure. So Athena vowed to care for the baby herself. The infant, Erichthonius, would grow up to become the first king of Athens to worship Athena.

Three's a Crowd: The Olympian Love Triangle

At times, Mount Olympus bore a resemblance to that later hotbed of intrigue and betrayal: *Dawson's Creek*. Start with Zeus, who fathered five of the Olympians—with four different mates! Add Hera, the archetypal jealous wife, constantly trying to catch her husband and plotting against his mistresses and his children by them. Don't forget the sibling rivalry between the three brothers—or that Hera's sister Demeter also slept with Zeus.

The second generation of Olympians was not exempt from participating in this soap opera. Hermes would steal from his half-brother Apollo. Hephaestus would immobilize his mother, Hera. And Aphrodite would make love to no less than four of the six gods on Olympus. Naturally, this created some tension—especially between her and her husband, Hephaestus.

The Heavenly Castoff: Hephaestus

Hephaestus, the god of smithing, metalworking, and craftsmanship, was born of the rivalry between Hera and Zeus. Hera, furiously jealous when Athena burst out of her husband's head, decided that if he could do it, so could she. So Hera resolved to bear her own child without his help. Sadly, the child, Hephaestus, was born sickly and lame. Hera, disgusted and embarrassed by her creation, threw the child out of heaven. Hephaestus landed on the Greek island of Lemnos, where he worked at his craft and became a brilliant artisan.

Mythed by a Mile

Some storytellers contend that Hephaestus landed in the sea. But, unknown to Hera, the sea goddess Thetis and the Oceanid Eurynome rescued him and brought him up in an underwater grotto. There he established his first smithy. In forging countless gifts to show his gratitude to his rescuers, he became a master craftsman.

A third version of his origins holds that Hephaestus was born hale and healthy. But when Zeus once punished Hera for opposing him, the boy ran to her defense. Zeus angrily threw Hephaestus out of Olympus. The boy fell from the sky for a full day before landing on the island of Lemnos. Only after this fall did Hephaestus become lame. But the islanders took good care of him and thus Lemnos became his favorite place on Earth.

Having become a master craftsman, Hephaestus won his way back into heaven by forging a magnificent golden throne for his decidedly unmaternal mother. Hephaestus was not hoping to win her favor, however, but rather to punish her for her ill treatment of him. As soon as she sat in it, the chair held her tight.

The gods and goddesses pleaded with Hephaestus to forgive his mother and even invited the exile back to Olympus. Still he would not release her. Finally, Dionysus (see Chapter 9) got Hephaestus drunk and persuaded him to let his mother go.

Welcomed back to Olympus, Hephaestus quickly made himself indispensable. An ingenious artist and artisan, he created countless beautiful, intricate, and often indestructible objects. The hands of Hephaestus created (among many other works):

♦ All the palaces of the Olympian gods

♦ The shield of Achilles

♦ Pandora, the first woman

What a Life!

Ares, who killed Halirrhothius, a son of Poseidon, was the first defendant ever tried for murder. During the trial, Ares claimed that Halirrhothius had tried to rape—or had indeed raped—his daughter Alcippe. Since Alcippe confirmed her father's story and no other witnesses came forward, the court acquitted him, ruling the killing a justifiable homicide. The hill at Athens where this trial took place—and later the Athenian court of law—was forever after called the Areopagus, the "hill of Ares."

Some say that Hephaestus constructed many mechanical creatures of gold—including the world's first robots!—to help him in his work. He also built three-legged tables with golden wheels that *moved themselves* around his workshop. Whenever the Olympians met, these wondrous tables would run to the meeting place and then run back again afterward.

Fear and Loathing on Mount Olympus: Ares

Hera had another son—this one by Zeus—who became one of the exalted of Olympus: Ares, the god of war. But Ares was the most hated among the gods. All of the immortals loathed him, with three notable exceptions:

◆ Eris, the goddess of discord, appreciated the way he took her work to a new level.

◆ Hades didn't necessarily like Ares, but recognized that he was good for business in the Underworld.

◆ Aphrodite loved him.

True, Ares was brave and strong—but he was also argumentative, impulsive, bloodthirsty, and destructive. In conflicts, the god of war chose sides capriciously and sometimes switched sides in the middle of a war. Ares simply took pleasure in the bloodshed, slaughter, and wanton destruction of war.

Ironically, the god of war was not so skillful as a warrior:

◆ Level-headed, disciplined Athena bested him twice.

◆ Otus and Ephialtes, the giant sons of Poseidon, also defeated him. Indeed, they humiliated him, trapping him inside a bronze jar for over a year before Hermes managed to release him.

◆ Heracles (see Chapter 13) knocked the god of war off his feet four times in a single battle and ultimately forced him to flee from the battlefield.

◆ Diomedes stabbed him with a spear and sent him running from the battlefield outside Troy.

Ares never married, but he fathered dozens of children with both mortals and immortals. The most notable of these many mistresses was the goddess of love: Aphrodite.

First of the Red-Hot Lovers: Aphrodite

Aphrodite, as noted earlier (see Chapter 5), actually predated Zeus and the other Olympians. She rose from the sea foam created when Cronus—the father of the Olympians—threw Uranus's severed genitals into the sea.

The goddess of love, lust, and mating never had to do a bit of work. Indeed, she had no other responsibility but to make love—and that she did with abandon.

Aphrodite, who possessed a magic girdle that made its wearer an object of desire for everyone who saw her, was always happy to help young lovers. She took particular delight in causing her fellow Olympians to fall in love with mortals. (Zeus paid her back in kind by making her fall in love with the mortal Anchises—and conceive the hero Aeneas. See Chapter 22.)

Like the other gods and goddesses, however, Aphrodite also harshly punished those who refused to honor her properly (in her case, this meant celibates or others who withstood the pleasures of love). Hippolytus (see Chapter 15) was just one of the mortals whom Aphrodite punished for denying himself erotic joys.

> **What a Life!**
>
> Aphrodite was caught working just once. Athena spotted her working at a loom and complained that this was her domain. Greatly apologetic, Aphrodite immediately abandoned her work and never took it up again.

A Fine Romance?

Hera, reconciled with her son Hephaestus, arranged for him to marry the goddess of love. Zeus, Aphrodite's adoptive father, agreed. Unsurprisingly, the marriage of the enchantingly beautiful, sensual, and insatiable Aphrodite and the powerful, but gruff, ugly, and lame Hephaestus was not a happy one. Aphrodite could not confine her love to just one other. The goddess did not remain faithful to Hephaestus—not by a long shot. She had countless affairs with both gods and mortals.

The most long-standing and significant of all of Aphrodite's lovers was Ares. But one night, the lovers tarried too long together. As Helius hitched up his golden chariot of the sun, he saw the lovers in Ares' palace in Thrace.

> **What a Life!**
>
> Aphrodite had three children by Ares. Their sons, Phobus (Panic) and Deimus (Fear), became Ares' constant companions, driving his chariot on the battlefield. Their daughter Harmonia (Harmony) fell in love with the mortal Cadmus, who served her father for eight years to atone for killing a dragon sacred to Ares. After a wedding attended by all the Olympians, Cadmus became the founding king of Thebes, in central Greece.

When Helius told Hephaestus what he had seen, the smith god forged an unbreakable bronze net and secretly attached it to the posts and sides of his bed. Then he bid Aphrodite adieu, saying he was going to relax on Lemnos for a while.

As soon as he had gone, Aphrodite sent for Ares. When the morning came, Hephaestus walked in—"Surprise! Hi, honey, I'm home!"—and found the two ensnared in the net. The cuckolded god quickly gathered all the other gods at his bedside to witness the shame of the naked, helpless couple and to heap ridicule upon them.

Hephaestus then demanded the return of the marriage gifts he had given to Zeus. But the ruler of the gods refused, calling the adultery a marital dispute and ridiculing Hephaestus as a fool for making it a public spectacle. (Hermes and Apollo snickered that they would gladly make such a public spectacle if it meant lying with Aphrodite.)

With his first glance at the naked goddess, Poseidon fell in love. So the sea god suggested that Ares should pay for the marriage gifts. Poseidon gladly offered to serve as guarantor: If Ares defaulted on the payment, Poseidon would pay the price and take Aphrodite as *his* wife. Ares did ultimately default on the debt, but Hephaestus—still smitten with his wife—did not really want a divorce at all, so he never brought it up again.

Poseidon, however, was not the only god to envy Ares' position. Hermes too fell in love with naked Aphrodite. When Aphrodite spurned his advances, Hermes sought the help of Zeus. The king of gods dispatched an eagle to steal one of Aphrodite's sandals. To retrieve it, the goddess was forced to submit to Hermes. This union produced a double-sexed child: *Hermaphroditus*.

Logos

Our word **hermaphrodite**—meaning a person born with both male and female reproductive organs—is derived from the offspring of Hermes and Aphrodite.

Aphrodite also slept with the youngest of gods, Dionysus. But Hera, who disapproved of Aphrodite's free ways, deformed their child Priapus. She made the boy incredibly ugly and endowed him with gargantuan genitals—an ironic comment on his mother's behavior.

Love Child

Like Hera, Aphrodite was vain regarding her own beauty. So when Cinyras, the king of Cyprus, boasted that his daughter Smyrna was more beautiful than Aphrodite, this braggadocio could not go unpunished. The goddess made Smyrna fall in love with her own father. One night, she climbed into his bed, where Cinyras—oblivious with drink—impregnated her.

When Cinyras discovered what he had done, he chased his daughter out of the palace at swordpoint. Aphrodite transformed Smyrna into a myrrh tree just as Cinyras overtook her and split her in half. The infant Adonis emerged from the cleft. Repentant

Aphrodite loved the infant, whom she hid in a chest and gave to Persephone, Queen of the Underworld, for safekeeping.

Not unlike Pandora, Persephone grew curious about the contents of the chest. When she peeked inside and saw the stunningly beautiful baby, Persephone, too, became enamored. She reared Adonis in the palace of Hades. When Aphrodite finally showed up to claim the child, Persephone, infatuated with the boy, refused to give him up.

Zeus put the dispute to the Muse Calliope to decide. Calliope ruled that Adonis should spend four months of each year with Persephone, four months with Aphrodite, and four months on his own.

Aphrodite was not pleased with this ruling, so she used her magic girdle to bewitch Adonis. The beautiful boy soon gave the goddess not only his own four months, but the four months he was slated to spend with Persephone as well.

Persephone was not pleased either. She went to Ares and aroused his jealousy of this lovely mortal. Ares then changed himself into a wild boar and gored the boy—who was hunting on Mount Lebanon—to death. The blood of Adonis yielded beautiful anemones. But the soul traveled to the Underworld, Persephone's realm, and stayed with her forever.

Night of the Hunters: Artemis and Apollo

Two other children of Zeus rose to take their place among the greatest of Olympians. These were the children of Leto, the beautiful daughter of the original Titans Coeus and Phoebe. Hera was tormented with jealousy of Leto. So the Queen of the Gods sent a serpent after Leto to vex her and to prevent her from finding a place to deliver her babies.

Leto frantically went from place to place, but found no welcome anywhere, since everyone feared incurring the wrath of Hera. She finally found refuge on *Ortygia*, the island of her sister Asteria, where she gave birth to Artemis.

Immediately after her own birth, the newborn Artemis precociously helped her mother through nine days of labor and delivery until her brother Apollo emerged. Themis, Leto's aunt, took care of the young gods and nourished them on ambrosia and nectar—the food and drink of the gods.

Logos

Ortygia means "quail island." Asteria, Leto's sister and the mother of the goddess Hecate, had escaped the lecherous pursuit of Zeus by turning herself into a quail and diving into the sea. The island of Ortygia appeared on the spot. After the births of Artemis and Apollo, the island's name changed to **Delos**, which can mean "famous." It was renowned as one of the holiest places in ancient Greece.

Artemis and Apollo cherished their mother, who had gone through such an ordeal to bring them into the world. Not long after their birth, the giant Tityus attempted to rape Leto in a sacred grove near Delphi. Leto called out the names of her children, who quickly rescued her by showering arrows upon the giant, killing him instantly. For Tityus's offense, Zeus consigned the giant (who was his own son) to eternal torment in the Underworld (see Chapter 11).

Artemis and Apollo also defended their mother's honor (or perhaps their own pride) when Niobe, the daughter of Tantalus, boasted of having more and better children than Leto. The two killed most (or all) of Niobe's children, leaving Niobe to weep eternally.

Artemis and Apollo remained close to each other forever. Both siblings would become associated with the skill of archery, and they enjoyed hunting together. In addition, both had the power to send plagues upon mortals.

Wild Queendom: Artemis

Artemis grew to become the virgin goddess of the hunt, of wild animals, and of childbirth (due to her participation in the birth of her brother). She and her brother also became the protectors of young children.

When she was just three, Artemis was asked by her father, Zeus, to name any gifts she wanted. Among many others, she named:

◆ A bow and arrows (just like her brother's)

◆ All the world's mountains (as her home and playground)

◆ Just one city (for she preferred to live in the mountains)

◆ Eternal virginity

Zeus gladly provided her with everything she wanted and more. He ordered the Cyclopes to forge a silver bow and fill a quiver with arrows for her. He promised her eternal virginity. Zeus gave her all the mountains as her domain. And he presented her with 30 cities—and named her as guardian of the world's roads and harbors.

Artemis, constantly attended by nymphs, could almost always be found in the mountains she loved. Though she was the guardian of wild animals, Artemis enjoyed nothing more than hunting. Orion, a giant hunter, joined both Artemis and her mother on many of their hunts.

Like most of the Olympians, Artemis reacted strongly whenever she did not receive the honors due her as a goddess. After Apollo had helped Admetus win Alcestis as his bride, for instance, the groom neglected to sacrifice to Artemis at his wedding. Imagine his horror that night when he found his bridal bedchamber teeming with snakes! Admetus quickly followed Apollo's advice and made the necessary sacrifices to the god's sister.

King Oeneus of Calydon similarly offended Artemis by forgetting to dedicate the first fruits of the harvest to her one season. Artemis sent a monstrous boar to ravage and terrorize his kingdom. To rid the kingdom of this vicious beast, Oeneus was forced to call on some of the greatest heroes of the age to participate in the hunt. (For more on the Calydon boar hunt, see Chapter 17.)

> ### What a Life!
>
> The hunter Orion greatly offended Gaia by boasting that his hunting skill was so great he could kill all of the animals on Earth. Gaia decided to protect her domain by sending a giant scorpion after the hunter. After the scorpion stung and killed Orion, Artemis and Leto prevailed upon Zeus to immortalize him as a constellation—but with the scorpion similarly honored.

Actaeon, the son of Autonoe and grandson of Cadmus, offended the goddess by stumbling across her once while she was bathing in the woods. Furious that a mortal had seen her naked, Artemis transformed the hunter into a stag. His own hounds then ripped Actaeon to pieces.

The biggest penalty paid for offending the goddess was that of King Agamemnon of Mycenae, who foolishly boasted that his hunting prowess outstripped even hers. On the eve of the Trojan War, Artemis stranded the Greek fleet with ill winds. To appease her, Agamemnon sacrificed his daughter Iphigenia—though, according to some accounts, the goddess showed mercy at the last minute and substituted a deer on the altar.

Having won the right to eternal virginity from her father, Artemis sometimes found it necessary to fiercely defend it. Buphagus, son of the Titan Iapetus, once tried to rape her, but she shot and killed him. The twin sons of Poseidon, Otus and Ephialtes, also met their doom trying to violate the goddess—and Hera as well. Otus chased after Artemis while Ephialtes pursued Hera. But suddenly a deer—either Artemis herself after a transformation or a real deer sent by her brother Apollo—darted between the two brothers. Distracted, the brothers quickly hurled their spears at it, but it sped away. Otus's spear pierced Ephialtes and Ephialtes' hit Otus—and both giants died instantly.

Artemis required the nymphs who attended her to remain virgins, just as she did. But her father once raped Callisto, a favorite of Artemis's. Hoping to help her escape Hera's notice, Zeus then transformed her into a bear. But Hera—not fooled at all—tricked Artemis into shooting and killing the bear.

The Temperamental Musician: Apollo

Artemis's brother, Apollo, was just as sure a shot. The god of archery—as well as of music, prophecy, healing, and youth—got an early start on his art. Apollo was just four days old when he demanded a bow and arrows, which Hephaestus created for him. He immediately set out in pursuit of the serpent that Hera had sent to torment his mother, Leto. The serpent, Python, sought refuge at Delphi. But Apollo heedlessly followed Python into the shrine of the Oracle of Mother Earth and killed him there.

Gaia was outraged at this defilement of her shrine. Yet after Apollo was purified for his crime in Crete, he learned the art of prophecy—perhaps from Pan, the goat-legged god of the flock and herds. In any case, he soon took over the Oracle at Delphi. Through the Oracle of Apollo (as it was renamed), the god became so closely associated with the art of prophecy that almost all seers soon claimed to have been either taught or fathered by him.

Originally a herdsman, Apollo was the first god charged with protecting flocks and herds. (Pan was associated primarily with goats and sheep that grazed in rural and wild areas; Apollo more with cattle that grazed in fields on the outskirts of the city.) But he later turned this duty over to Hermes in exchange for some musical instruments the younger god had devised. Apollo demonstrated such talent as a musician that he soon became a god of that art, too. Some even credit the god with having invented the *cithara*.

Logos

The **cithara** was a musical instrument that resembled a large lyre.

What a Life!

Pan also lost a musical contest to Apollo. Though Tmolus, the judge, awarded the prize to Apollo, King Midas of Phrygia remarked that he himself liked Pan's playing best. Apollo punished Midas by giving him the ears of an ass.

Some dared to challenge Apollo's musical talents—but never more than once. A satyr named Marsyas once found a flute made from the bones of a stag. (Athena had made this flute, but had angrily thrown it away when the laughter of the other immortals made her realize how ridiculous she looked when she puffed out her cheeks to play it.) Still inspired by Athena, the flute played rapturous music. Listeners even compared the satyr's playing favorably to Apollo's playing of the lyre.

This comparison enraged Apollo, who immediately challenged Marsyas to a contest. The contestants agreed that the winner could choose any punishment for the loser. The jury of Muses found both players magnificent. So Apollo dared the satyr to try to do what he himself could do: turn his instrument upside-down and play it—and sing while playing. Marsyas, of course, could do neither with a flute.

Impressed by his versatility, the Muses judged Apollo the best musician. Not content with merely winning, Apollo then chose a brutal punishment for Marsyas: He skinned the satyr alive and nailed his skin to a pine tree.

Apollo never married, but he was by no means a celibate. He fathered more than a dozen children by at least nine different partners.

> **What a Life!**
>
> Apollo also wooed a beautiful young man, Hyacinthus. Sadly, while Apollo was teaching the boy how to throw the discus, the West Wind—who also desired Hyacinthus—redirected the missile straight into the boy's head, killing him instantly. The drops of blood that fell from his head yielded the flower hyacinth.

Yet his most persistent courtship—that of Daphne, a mountain nymph—was never rewarded. Apollo first eliminated the competition. Leucippus, the son of King Oenomaus of Pisa, also loved Daphne—so much that he once disguised himself as a girl just to be with her while she engaged in her mountain revels with other nymphs. But Apollo knew of this charade—and so the god quietly advised the nymphs to bathe naked. When Leucippus was exposed—literally and figuratively—the nymphs tore him to shreds.

Though Apollo alone now wooed her, Daphne still refused him. Ultimately, she changed into a laurel tree rather than submit to his desires. Thereafter, Apollo made the laurel his sacred plant.

Others refused Apollo, too. When Zeus ruled that Marpessa, daughter of the river god Evenus, could choose between her two suitors, she chose the mortal Idas. (She suspected that Apollo's amorous interest would wane as she grew older.)

The nymph Sinope used cleverness to escape Apollo's advances. Sinope agreed to surrender herself to the god, but only if he first granted her a wish. When Apollo swore to give her anything she wanted, Sinope revealed her wish: to remain a virgin for all of her days. (Some storytellers say that Sinope had used this same trick to avoid Zeus's embrace.)

The Little Rascal: Hermes

The herald and messenger of the gods, Hermes was like a breath of fresh air on Mount Olympus. For Hermes, a friendly, likable young god, became the patron not only of travelers and merchants, but of thieves and rogues as well.

The son of Zeus and Maia (a daughter of the Titan Atlas), Hermes was born in a cave on Mount Cyllene in Arcadia in southern Greece. Nursed by the nymph Cyllene, the precocious young boy grew incredibly fast. Within hours of birth, he had wandered out of his cave, killed a tortoise, and stretched seven strings of sheep gut across it to build the first lyre. He then quickly taught himself how to play.

That same day, the baby Hermes slipped out of his mother's sight and went searching for adventure. When he found himself in the pastures of the gods, Hermes impulsively stole 50 cows from Apollo, then still the herdsman of the gods. Though he had been in the world less than a day, Hermes already had a cunning mind. He disguised his tracks by cobbling together "shoes" made of bark from a fallen oak tree. To make it even harder to track him, he confused the herd's trail by driving the cows backward and traversing sandy places that left no prints.

While driving the cattle, he came across an old man named Battus. Hermes bought the old man's silence, but the young god doubted whether he could trust the stranger. So he disguised himself and returned, offering a reward for any news of the stolen cattle. Battus quickly sold him out, telling him what he knew, so Hermes punished the old man by turning him to stone.

At the river Alpheus, Hermes stopped to sacrifice two of the cows. Once again he demonstrated his wiliness, burning the hooves and heads to leave no trace of his actions. After hiding the cows, Hermes returned home, slipped through the keyhole, again put on his swaddling clothes, and lay down to sleep. Despite his attempted deception, Hermes did not fool Maia. His mother warned him that the gods would be angry at his pranks.

Meanwhile, Apollo searched throughout the world, but could not find his cows. An omen led him to the cave where he found Hermes. The boy god feigned innocence, swearing by his father's head that he had not stolen the cows. He may have protested too much, however, when he claimed he didn't even know what a cow was.

Apollo, disbelieving the scamp, carried Hermes before Zeus and charged him with theft. Though he found his son's devilishness amusing, Zeus prompted Hermes to confess and lead Apollo to the herd. When Apollo spotted the two slaughtered cows, Hermes explained that he had divided the meat into 12 equal portions for the gods. Raising an eyebrow, Apollo asked who the twelfth god was. "Me, of course," acknowledged the not-so-humble but lovable Hermes. Reportedly, this was the very first sacrifice of flesh to the gods.

While Apollo gathered his herd together, Hermes began playing on his new lyre. Enchanted by the music—and by the song that flattered Apollo for his cleverness, nobility, and generosity—the older god offered to exchange the entire herd of cattle for the younger god's lyre.

Hermes agreed, and immediately began building another musical instrument for his amusement: a reed-pipe. Equally charmed by this instrument, Apollo asked Hermes to name his terms for it. Hermes agreed to trade it for Apollo's golden staff—and with it, the honor of being the god of herdsmen and shepherds—as well as instruction from Apollo's old nurses in how to use pebbles to divine the future.

When Zeus called Hermes to Olympus to chide him for stealing and lying, Hermes promised he would never again lie if Zeus named him as his messenger and herald. Zeus quickly accepted this offer, and told his son that his duties would also include protecting travelers, promoting trade, and negotiating treaties.

To ensure rapid delivery of his messages, Zeus presented Hermes with golden winged sandals as swift as the wind. He also gave the young god a round hat to protect him from rain and a herald's staff. Zeus's brother Hades soon asked Hermes to serve as his herald as well. As the herald of death, Hermes thereafter gently collected and guided the dead to the Underworld.

> **What a Life!**
>
> Hermes was also credited with helping the Fates to invent the Greek alphabet. On his own, he reportedly invented the musical scale, astronomy, and the sports of boxing and gymnastics.

Hermes did not remain a boy forever. The god fathered several children. Among them were several who displayed at least one of his most defining characteristics:

♦ Echion, who served as herald for the *Argo* (see Chapter 14)

♦ Autolycus, a notorious thief

♦ Myrtilus, the swiftest of all charioteers

As the herald of Zeus, Hermes kept his promise not to lie. (On the other hand, he didn't always tell the *whole* truth.) In gratitude, Zeus made Hermes his most constant companion. Whenever Zeus visited Earth, Hermes went with him.

Though usually in disguise, Hermes often visited Earth on his own, too. Despite his roguishness, Hermes truly enjoyed helping travelers. His acts of kindness did not go unnoticed by the mortals of Earth. Soon every traveler who became lost or suffered from some hardship called upon Hermes for help. And more often than not, the god swiftly arrived to deliver them.

The Least You Need to Know

- The goddess of war, Athena—born from Zeus's head—did not enjoy war at all. She preferred her other domains: practical wisdom, arts, and crafts.

- Hephaestus, the lame and grotesque god of smithing and craftsmanship, was a Frankenstein monster: the result of Hera's attempt, without a mate, to create a child.

- Ares, the detested god of war, cuckolded Hephaestus by having a long affair with his wife Aphrodite, the promiscuous goddess of love.

- Artemis, the goddess of hunting and wild animals, guarded her chastity as her most prized possession.

- Apollo demonstrated extreme versatility. Originally a god of shepherds and herdsmen, his talents led him to become the god of music, medicine, prophecy, and youth.

- Hermes, herald of the gods, demonstrated cunning, deception, thievery, and roguery within 12 hours of his birth. He became the patron of thieves and rogues as well as travelers, merchants, and messengers.

Chapter 8

Friends, Fairies, and Fairy Tale Monsters

In This Chapter

- ◆ Helius, Selene, and Eos: three siblings who retained their godhood under Zeus
- ◆ The dark goddesses: Hecate and Styx
- ◆ The nature of satyrs, silens, and nymphs
- ◆ How the Olympians defeated the rebellious Giants
- ◆ The terrible battles of Zeus and the monster Typhon

Though the 12 gods and goddesses quickly came to dominate Mount Olympus (while solitary Hades ruled the Underworld), there were other immortals who shared their world, if not their power. Some were gods and goddesses in their own right—but with the rise of Zeus and company, they lost some of their power and influence.

Far more menacing among the other primordial creatures were the breeds of Giants and other monsters. These monstrous creatures would not only terrorize the mortals on Earth, but would threaten to topple the Olympians from heaven. Though Zeus—the god who imposed a lasting order on chaos—defeated all challenges to his authority, even he needed a hand to overcome his monstrous enemies.

Children of Lesser Gods

Under Zeus, Olympus quickly set up its starting lineup of gods:

- Zeus
- Hera
- Poseidon
- Demeter
- Hestia
- Athena

- Hephaestus
- Aphrodite
- Ares
- Artemis
- Apollo
- Hermes

Though these 12, along with Hades in the Underworld, were the mightiest of the gods, they were not the only gods. Indeed, with the ascent of Dionysus (see Chapter 9), many storytellers would relegate Hestia to the bench, her place taken by this young god of wine and revelry. Most of the remaining gods, however, predated the Olympians. By winning favor with Zeus, these older gods and goddesses had maintained their divine powers and some share in the rule of the universe.

Here Comes the Sun King

One of the greatest of these "lesser" gods was Helius, the indefatigable giver of light. The god of the sun, Helius was the son of the Titans Hyperion and Theia, early deities of sun and light themselves.

Helius cut quite a dashing figure as he drove the four magnificent horses that pulled his chariot of the sun. Heralded and accompanied by his sister, Eos (Dawn), golden-helmeted Helius would each day emerge in the east, race across the sky, and disappear as he passed the westernmost horizon. During the night, he would make his way back east unseen to reemerge the next morning. Since the world was not round in those days, Helius rode the river Oceanus around the perimeter of the earth in a gargantuan golden cup.

Zeus greatly respected Helius, who had steadfastly maintained neutrality during the war between the Titans and the Olympians (see Chapter 5). Indeed, Zeus might have included him in the division of the universe among the gods, but Helius was driving his golden chariot when the gods drew lots.

Helius didn't completely miss out, though. When he saw an island rising in the Aegean Sea and expressed interest in it, Zeus gladly yielded the piece of land to him. Helius thus became the patron of the island of Rhodes. The people of the island later erected an enormous statue of Helius overlooking the harbor: the famed "Colossus of Rhodes."

Later, in a dispute with Poseidon that Briareus (one of the Hundred-Handed Giants) moderated, Helius also gained rights to all of Corinth except the isthmus.

With his fierce gaze, Helius saw everything that happened on Earth during the day. The all-seeing sun god was not very discreet, either: It was he who told Hephaestus that his wife Aphrodite was having an affair with Ares (see Chapter 7)—and told Demeter that Hades had stolen her daughter Persephone (see Chapter 11). Since no one could hide from the sun's gaze, mortals often swore oaths by him, knowing that if they broke their vows, Helius would see it.

What a Life!

Aphrodite later avenged herself by making Helius fall in love with the mortal Leucothoe. But the nymph Clytie, once Helius's lover, jealously told Leucothoe's father—Orchamus, king of Persia—of the affair. Orchamus angrily buried his daughter alive, but Helius, torn with grief, transformed her into a frankincense bush. Helius detested Clytie for her treachery. She died of longing for Helius … and turned into the heliotrope, a flower that each day turns its head to follow the sun as it passes across the sky.

Helius had several children who would figure prominently in later myths. He had seven sons by Poseidon's daughter Rhode, the nymph of his island. His wife Perse (or Perseis), one of the Oceanids, had several children, including:

◆ Aeëtes, the notoriously unfriendly king of Colchis, land of the Golden Fleece (see Chapter 14)

◆ Circe, the sorceress famous for turning men into animals (see Chapters 14 and 18)

◆ Pasiphaë, the Queen of Crete, who had an infamous affair with a prized bull and gave birth to the monstrous Minotaur (see Chapter 15)

Finally, Helius also had a son by the Oceanid Clymene: the tragic Phaethon, who found the chariot of the sun far too much to handle (see Chapter 19).

From Dusk to Dawn: The Sisters of Helius

In addition to their son Helius, the Titans Theia and Hyperion had two daughters: Selene and Eos. Selene, the white-armed goddess of the moon, brought a great gift from heaven to Earth: the light of the moon that shone through the darkness of night. Like her brother, Selene drove a chariot drawn by gleaming horses, enveloping Earth with the glow of her great beauty.

Few tales are told of Selene. The god Pan once seduced her with the offer of a beautiful fleece. At another time, Zeus gave Selene a daughter, a stunning beauty named Pandia. But the affairs with both Pan and Zeus were fleeting.

Selene fell deeply in love with handsome Endymion, the king of Elis, in southern Greece. Some say she had 50 daughters by him. But when Zeus offered Endymion the rare opportunity to determine his own fate, the vain king foolishly chose to preserve his own beauty by sleeping forever without ever aging a day. Selene was alone once more.

The sister of Helius and Selene was the rosy-armed goddess of dawn, Eos. The goddess of dawn arose each morning from a golden throne in her palace in the east to announce the coming of her brother, Helius. Despite her name, however, Eos personified the light of day, not merely the light of morning. For Eos rode with her brother all day in the chariot of the sun.

Eos fell in love with Astraeus (whose name means "Starry")—a son of Crius, a Titan, and Eurybia, a daughter of Pontus and Gaia. The mating of this heavenly pair produced the winds: Zephyrus (west), Boreas (north), and Notus (south). Through this coupling also came Eosphorus (the Dawn Star) as well as all the stars that light the heavens.

Eos also had an ill-advised affair with Ares, the god of war. Jealous Aphrodite punished Eos by making her fall in love with a series of beautiful young men, most of whom did not return her love. (For the story of one of these loves, Cephalus, see Chapter 19.)

The most storied of her lovers was Tithonus, a brother of Laomedon, king of Troy. Smitten with Tithonus, Eos petitioned Zeus to make him immortal. When the king of gods granted her request, Eos eagerly carried him off to her palace. But foolishly, Eos had forgotten to ask Zeus to make her lover ageless as well as immortal. As her lover's hair started to turn gray, Eos—though she continued to pamper Tithonus and feed him on ambrosia—stopped sharing her bed with him. In time, of course, Tithonus became a wrinkled, endlessly babbling, and nearly immobile old man. Unable to bear his company, Eos locked him in a room in her palace forever.

Dark Goddesses: Hecate and Styx

Hecate, once a powerful and benevolent goddess, underwent one of the most mysterious transformations in all of classical mythology. As time passed, she became increasingly identified with the darkness of the Underworld and the art of sorcery.

Hecate was the daughter of Perses, a brother of Astraeus, and Asteria, a sister of Leto. In his *Theogony*—one of the oldest surviving sources of classical mythology—Hesiod depicted Hecate quite rosily. Hesiod insisted that though Zeus defeated and imprisoned most of the other Titans, he honored Hecate greatly. Indeed, Zeus gave her a share of divine power over the earth, the sea, and the sky.

Mortals who found her favor received great blessings, for Hecate had great power to assist men—when she wanted to do so. She could, for example:

- Exponentially expand the herds of cattle, goats, and sheep for farmers who worshipped her

- Bestow abundant catches on fishers who prayed to her

- Grant victory and glory to the soldiers and athletes she preferred

Yet all this changed and Hecate became a force of darkness—though no one ever explained how or why. The change may have come after she helped the goddess Demeter find her lost daughter Persephone. Some storytellers claim that Hecate served as an attendant and follower of Persephone, who became the Queen of the Underworld following her abduction.

In any case, later mythmakers almost always depicted Hecate in her darker, more terrible aspects. A goddess of the night, Hecate became the patron of sorcery. After coming to a crossroads or a graveyard—the favorite haunts of the goddess—sorceresses and sorcerers would call out her name in weaving a spell. With a band of hellhounds baying beside her, Hecate would approach bearing a torch. Only if the offerings made to her met with her liking would the sorcery take hold.

Those who wished to curse an enemy would also invoke the name of Hecate. Seeking vengeance, a person might, for example, write a curse out on lead foil, address it to Hecate, roll it up, and drop it down a well. (Archeologists have actually discovered such "curse tablets" in excavations of ancient wells.)

What a Life!

Woe to the immortal who swore a false oath to Styx. If an Olympian lied while swearing to Styx, he or she would fall into a breathless coma for at least a year—unable to eat, drink, or speak. When the immortal awoke, the other Olympians would treat him or her as an outcast for another nine years. The liar would be unwelcome to meet, mingle, or dine with the other immortals.

Another goddess of the Underworld was Styx, the goddess of the main river of Hades. A daughter of Oceanus and Tethys, Styx had four sons with Pallas, a brother of Astraeus and Perses. These sons were the personified abstractions:

- Zelus (Zeal)
- Nike (Victory)
- Cratus (Strength)
- Bia (Force)

During the Olympian war against the Titans, Styx was the first of the minor deities to commit herself and her four sons to the side of Zeus and his siblings. Zeus rewarded her by promising to keep her sons—Zeal, Victory, Strength, and Force—by his side at all times. He then added to the honor by making all Olympians swear their greatest oaths to Styx.

The Good-Time God: Pan

Half-goat, half-god, Pan—sometimes called Aegipan (although some storytellers insist these two were distinct characters)—was a god of shepherds, forests, wildlife, and fertility. Pan was the son of Hermes and a fair-haired daughter of Dryops, one of Apollo's sons. (Some storytellers, however, claim that his father was Zeus and his mother was either a nymph or a goat.)

When she first saw that her baby had the horns, ears, tail, and legs of a goat, Pan's mother was horrified. Although even as a newborn Pan was laughing and full of life, both his mother and his nurse ran away to escape his monstrous appearance. Hermes, however, could not have been happier. Filled with joy at the birth of his son, Hermes whisked his baby to Olympus and proudly introduced him to the other immortals.

A mountain dweller, Pan roamed the ranges in the company of nymphs. He hunted mountain wildlife and pursued quite a wild life himself: Pan lived to dance, sing, play his pipes, and chase after nymphs (playful god though he was, Pan could also be lewd and lecherous).

Once while hunting, Pan spotted a beautiful nymph named Syrinx. When he attempted to seduce her, she ran away, for she admired and emulated Artemis, the virgin huntress. In her flight, she came to a river and found herself unable to cross. So Syrinx begged the river nymphs to change her into marsh reeds—and they gladly accommodated her.

Just then, Pan caught up with her, but as he reached out to embrace her, he saw and felt nothing but reeds. His sigh of disappointment was echoed by a breeze blowing through the reeds. The sound enchanted Pan, who quickly tied several of the reeds together to fashion his first *syrinx*, or Pan pipes.

Hemi-Demi-Semi-Deities

Not quite deities, but not quite human either, were the creatures that inhabited the natural worlds of the forests, mountains, and waters of Greece. These included the satyrs, the silens, and the nymphs.

Woodland spirits who took the form of men, the satyrs had decidedly animalistic features as well. Most looked similar to Pan—with a goat's legs, a horse's tail, and horns or pointed ears. In addition, most satyrs sported exceedingly large genitals.

Like Pan, the satyrs were revelers who sang, danced, got drunk, and ran after nymphs and other females. Frequent followers of Dionysus (see Chapter 9), the satyrs represent the untamable fertility of the forests.

The silens were physically similar to the satyrs, but were generally regarded as somewhat older, somewhat wiser, more powerful—and much more prone to drunkenness. They were experts in the arts of both music and prophecy. Gods of the forest, the silens followed Pan and later Dionysus.

Minor female divinities, the nymphs often served as attendants to greater gods: Hermes, Dionysus, Pan, Artemis, Apollo, and Poseidon all enjoyed the company of nymphs. And why not? Nymphs are typically described as beautiful, eternally youthful, and amorous.

> **What a Life!**
>
> The satyrs and silens would often serve their master Dionysus by initiating drunken revels. In the sixth-century B.C.E. playwriting contests at the Great Dionysia (see Chapter 4), each dramatist would submit not just three tragedies, but a satyr play as well. The chorus of these farces usually consisted of satyrs and silens, often in service to Dionysus, engaging in their wild pursuits.

These "nature spirits" usually resided in a particular place or within a particular object. Nymphs seldom traveled far, for each was confined to a localized tree, mountain, or spring. Some of the many different kinds of nymphs were:

- *Dryads.* Nymphs of the wood who lived in trees
- *Hamadryads.* Nymphs who inhabited oak trees
- *Meliae.* Nymphs who lived in ash trees
- *Naiads.* Water nymphs who might be found in springs, rivers, lakes, fountains, or brooks
- *Oreads.* Nymphs who lived on mountains and in grottoes

In addition to these, some call the Oceanids—the 3,000 daughters of Oceanus and Tethys—sea nymphs, though they roam throughout the sea, demonstrating much more mobility than other types of nymphs. For this reason, the Oceanids might more properly be called sea deities. The term "sea nymphs," however, does suit their nieces, the Nereids—the 50 daughters of Nereus (the Old Man of the Sea) and Doris (an Oceanid).

All in all, thousands of nymphs, satyrs, and silens inhabited the natural world of classical mythology. And though a few might be considered dangerous, most of these spirits of nature were friendly, playful, and fun-loving hedonists.

The Fairy Tale World: Giants, Ogres, and Monsters

Unfortunately, not all of the immortals and primordial creatures were as benevolent as the gods and goddesses of Olympus (though they, too, had their moods) nor as benign as the nymphs and other nature spirits. The world of classical mythology also featured forces of destruction, chaos, and barbarism that opposed the order and civilization represented by the Olympians. Giants and monsters tore up landscapes, devoured humans, and bedeviled the immortals. If not properly called evil, these bugaboos nonetheless wreaked havoc on the world and threatened the peaceful reign of the gods.

Big Trouble on Olympus: The War with the Giants

In defeating the Titans after 10 years of war, the Olympians vanquished a formidable opponent. But even with the Titans locked away in darkest Tartarus, the Olympians still faced another challenger to their power to rule the universe: the mighty race of Giants.

The Giants, you'll recall, were bred from the blood shed from Uranus's manhood (or godhood) when Cronus castrated his father. This blood spattered on the womb of Gaia, who then gave forth the Furies (Erinyes), the meliae (ash nymphs), and the Giants (see Chapter 5).

The Giants, whom some storytellers described as having legs that ended in the tails of snakes or the scales of dragons, settled near Phlegra in Thrace. Although the spawn of gods, they didn't enjoy the power of the Olympians. So, egged on by their Mother Earth, the Giants rose up against the Olympians.

That Gaia would turn on the Olympians—including her beloved grandson Zeus, whom she had nurtured as an infant—should not come as too much of a surprise. Twice before Gaia had aroused the spirit of rebellion against the ruling powers:

urging Cronus to castrate her husband Uranus, and then supporting Zeus in overthrowing her son Cronus. After helping to oust her husband and son, why not attempt to overthrow her grandson as well?

The Giants started the war by hurling boulders and flaming oak trees at the sky.

Led by Zeus, the Olympians fought valiantly against the superior strength of the massive Giants. But the gods learned from an oracle that they could not win this war without the aid of a mortal. So Zeus sent Athena to enlist his son by the mortal Alcmene: Heracles (see Chapter 13).

> ### What a Life!
>
> To ensure their victory—or some say, to give the Giants immortality—Gaia attempted to find a magic herb. But Zeus, who knew of her plans, enlisted the help of Eos, Helius, and Selene to thwart them. Zeus forbade the dawn to rise nor the sun or moon to shine, leaving the world in utter darkness until he himself had found the magic herb.

Heracles immediately helped turn the tide in favor of the Olympians. He first attacked the Giant Alcyoneus, who could not be killed on his own soil. Heracles shot an arrow that should have delivered a fatal wound, but the Giant staggered back to his feet. So heeding Athena's advice, Heracles carried him across the border into a neighboring land, where Alcyoneus soon died.

The Giant Porphyrion then attacked both Heracles and Hera. But Zeus distracted Porphyrion from battle, using his wife as a decoy and inflaming the Giant with lust for her. Porphyrion tore off Hera's robe and attempted to ravish her, but before he could violate her a shaft from Heracles' bow and a bolt from Zeus's hand struck him simultaneously, killing him.

After these two champions—the strongest of the Giants—fell, the Olympians seemed certain to prevail. Nearly all the Olympians contributed to the victory:

◆ Apollo shot Ephialtes in the left eye just as an arrow from Heracles' bow pierced the Giant's right eye.

◆ Hephaestus hurled red-hot metal at Mimas, killing the Giant (though some say Ares defeated Mimas in battle).

◆ Athena, the goddess of war, killed two Giants. She threw the island of Sicily on top of Enceladus, who had been trying to retreat. And after slaying Pallas, Athena tore the Giant's skin off and used it as a shield.

◆ Hecate destroyed Clytius with her torches.

◆ Poseidon chased Polybotes across the Aegean Sea to the island of Cos, where he threw part of the island on top of him.

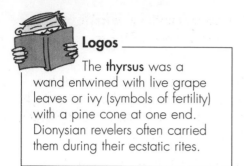

Logos

The **thyrsus** was a wand entwined with live grape leaves or ivy (symbols of fertility) with a pine cone at one end. Dionysian revelers often carried them during their ecstatic rites.

♦ Hermes "borrowed" the cap of darkness from Hades and, rendered invisible, stole up on the Giant Hippolytus and killed him.

♦ Artemis the archer shot Gration.

♦ Dionysus killed Eurytus by beating him with his *thyrsus*.

♦ Even the Fates took part, using bronze clubs to beat the Giant brothers Agrius and Thoas to death.

Zeus destroyed all the rest with his thunderbolts, with Heracles supplying the death blows that killed all of the Giants as they lay dying. In this way, the Olympians prevailed and maintained their rule over the universe.

The Mother of All Monsters!

Perhaps to avenge the defeat of the Giants, Gaia soon lay down with Tartarus, begetting the most frightening monster of all Greek mythology: Typhon (sometimes called Typhoeus). The youngest yet largest of all her sons, Typhon shot flames from the eyes of one hundred serpentine heads that spoke in the voices of both men and animals. His legs were tireless and his arms were mighty.

Typhon wanted to overthrow the gods. If not for Zeus, he might have done just that, for even the gods fled from the sight of this horrifying creature. Following the advice of Pan, the Olympians transformed themselves into various animals and fled to Egypt. Hermes, for instance, turned himself into an ibis (a long-legged wading bird), while Aphrodite assumed the form of a fish. This left Zeus alone to oppose the monstrous Typhon—and some storytellers claim that even the mightiest of the gods took the form of a ram and hid himself away for some time.

Zeus and Typhon engaged in fierce combat. Their series of battles produced quakes so violent that they frightened Hades, Cronus, and the other Titans now deep below the earth. The keen-eyed Zeus began by hurling a thunderbolt that echoed throughout heaven and hell, causing the earth, sea, and sky all to tremble. The thunderbolts of Zeus weakened the monster, burning each of his hundred heads. Seizing the advantage, Zeus descended to Earth to engage Typhon in hand-to-hand combat.

But Typhon did not fall easily. The monster seized Zeus's sickle from his hand and cut out the sinews from both of the god's hands and feet. Unable to walk or to fight, Zeus was helpless. Typhon carried the Olympian to Cilicia in southeast Asia Minor and held him captive in a cave. The monster hid the sinews under a bearskin and ordered the dragon Delphyne to guard them. But the crafty pair of Hermes and Pan managed to steal the sinews back.

After Hermes and Pan restored Zeus to health, the god returned to Olympus. There Zeus outfitted himself with more thunderbolts and, harnessing winged horses to draw his chariot, set out in pursuit of Typhon. The monster threw mountains at his pursuer, but Zeus used his thunderbolts to deflect them right back at Typhon.

After several more bloody battles, Typhon fled across the sea to Sicily. There Zeus threw Mount Etna on top of the monster, trapping him under its weight. To this day, the volcanic mountain still spits out flames from Typhon's breath (or perhaps his eyes). Or maybe the eruptions are lingering blasts from Zeus's thunderbolts. Some say that Zeus instead cast the vanquished monster down to Tartarus, where he became the source of all the deadly winds that rage over the seas, tossing ships and claiming sailors' lives.

Having defeated both the Giants and Typhon, the Olympians could now rest on their laurels. The mightiest and the most monstrous had failed to wrest power away from them, and never again would they face such formidable challengers for the throne of heaven. The reign of the Olympians was secure for all time.

The Least You Need to Know

- The 12 Olympians (and Hades) recognized as the greatest of gods were joined by many other "lesser" gods. These included Helius (the Sun), Selene (the Moon), Eos (Dawn), Hecate, Styx, and Pan.

- Hecate, feared as the goddess of sorcery, was once revered as one of the greatest and most benevolent of goddesses.

- The world of classical mythology teemed with nature spirits. Woodland satyrs and silens roamed the forests and nymphs lived in every tree, mountain, lake, river, and spring.

- The Giants waged war on the Olympians, but—with the help of the mortal Heracles—the gods and goddesses of Olympus crushed the mighty rebels.

- Typhon—an enormous, hideous monster with 100 fire-spitting snake's heads— also tried to overthrow Zeus and the Olympians. In one-on-one combat, Zeus stunned the monster with his thunderbolts and buried him under Mount Etna.

Chapter 9

Eat, Drink, and Be Merry: Dionysus

In This Chapter

- How Dionysus was conceived—and how he earned the epithet of "Twice-Born God"
- The ecstatic rites and revels of Dionysus and his followers
- How Dionysus dealt with those who disbelieved in his godhood or persecuted his followers
- The rewards of wine bestowed on his followers
- The reunion of Dionysus and his mother and their ascent to Olympus

Of all the gods of Olympus, none was quite so complex as Dionysus, the god of wine and revelry. Dionysus brought entirely new rites and a new spirit into Greek worship, yet he was accepted and even embraced by the gods and goddesses whom he joined. Indeed, some say that he became the twelfth of the great Olympians, taking the place of Hestia, whose importance and influence gradually faded away.

Yet unlike the other Olympians—who often seemed cold, forbidding, and distant—Dionysus lived many years in the company of mortals and concentrated his attention on the earthly sphere.

The other gods required the construction of temples, the enactment of sacrifices, and other rites that emphasized the vast separation between gods and mortals. Dionysus and his followers, on the other hand, taught that through a combination of wine, revelry, and religious ecstasy, mortals could achieve a mystical oneness with him. They could not only be like Dionysus, but in a certain sense, they could become Dionysus.

This seemed entirely foreign to the established Olympic pantheon. Yet the myth—and the rites—of Dionysus nonetheless became an integral part of classical mythology.

Turning Water Into Wine: How Dionysus Came to Be

Zeus, Father of the Gods, had already conceived five children (by four different mothers) who had taken their place on Mount Olympus: Athena, Ares, Artemis, Apollo, and Hermes. Yet Zeus apparently had it in him to create one more god—by yet another mother.

Zeus took a fancy to Semele, a daughter of King Cadmus of Thebes. So he disguised himself as a mortal in order to carry on a discreet love affair with her. With this subterfuge, Zeus hoped not only to keep his presence among mortals a secret, but also to protect Semele from the jealous wrath of Hera.

Together, Zeus and Semele conceived a son: Dionysus.

Be Careful What You Wish For

Though his disguise may have fooled the mortals he met, Zeus could not hoodwink Hera so easily. The Queen of the Olympians saw through his ruse and jealously set out to destroy Semele and her bastard son.

 Mythed by a Mile _____

The followers of Orpheus insist that Zeus did not originally conceive Dionysus by the mortal Semele. Instead, he took the form of a snake and conceived a child with Persephone, the daughter of Demeter. The child of this union, born with horns and a crown of serpents, was named Zagreus.

But ever-jealous Hera gave this infant to the Titans. Though the baby tried changing shapes to escape his captors, the Titans tore him limb from limb, boiled up the pieces, and ate him. Yet Athena managed to save the boy's heart. When she presented it to Zeus, he swallowed it and then seduced Semele in order to conceive the child a second time. Only after this second conception was the god renamed Dionysus.

No doubt inspired by her husband's trickery, Hera disguised herself as an old woman—perhaps Semele's nurse, Beroe—and appeared before the young girl during the sixth month of her pregnancy. After gaining her confidence, Hera urged the unsuspecting Semele to ask her lover to reveal his true self to her, to let her see him in the same form that his wife did. Hera insisted that this was the only way Semele could make sure that the father of the child inside her wasn't a monster.

Zeus loved Semele so much that when she asked for a boon, he swore he would grant her anything she desired. When he heard what Semele wanted, Zeus tried to talk her out of it, but she would not budge. Bound by his promise, the storm god granted her request. He appeared to her as a thunderbolt—or perhaps riding a chariot that blazed with thunder and lightning. Awestruck by the sight, Semele was consumed by her lover's lightning.

Though he had lost his lover, Zeus refused to lose his son, too. The god rescued the as-yet unborn child from the ashes of his mother. Summoned by his father, Hermes removed the baby son from Semele's womb, placed the child inside the god's thigh, and sewed up the tear. Zeus then carried the child to term in his thigh. After three months, the wound was reopened and the child, Dionysus, delivered. For this reason, Dionysus became known as the "Twice-Born God."

Mythed by a Mile _____

Pausanias, the writer of travelogues who described the mythology of a place as well as the place itself, related an obscure story regarding the birth of Dionysus that he had heard from the Laconians. In this tale, Semele did not die before giving birth to Dionysus. Her father, Cadmus, refused to believe that a god had seduced her. No longer able to bear the sight of her or her bastard son, Cadmus locked Semele and his grandson in a chest and tossed it into the sea. By the time the chest washed ashore on the Laconian coast, Semele had died. Yet her sister Ino, who had plotted to murder her stepchildren Phrixus and Helle before going mad (see Chapters 12 and 14), wandered to Laconia, too. There Ino brought her nephew to her own breast. Taking refuge in a Laconian cave, Ino nursed Dionysus during his infancy.

Kids Will Be Kids—Literally

Zeus did his best to keep his baby under wraps, far from the eyes of Hera. At his father's bidding, Hermes brought his stepbrother Dionysus to Ino, Semele's sister. Ino and her husband, King Athamas of Orchomenus, agreed to care for the child, whom they dressed as a girl in order to keep him hidden from Hera.

But once again, Hera easily saw through these attempts at subterfuge. She drove both Ino and Athamas mad. Athamas, deluded into seeing one of their sons as an animal, hunted and killed the boy. Ino boiled her other son in a cauldron and then leapt into the sea.

But Zeus once again managed to save his child, transforming *Dionysus* into a kid (not a child, but a young goat). This time, the deception succeeded. Unknown to Hera, Hermes brought Dionysus to the nymphs of Mount Nysa. The nymphs nurtured, cuddled, and nursed Dionysus through his youth. Hidden away in a sweet-smelling cave, the son of Zeus grew up as a goat-child.

Logos

Dionysus means the "god of Nysa." No one knows where Nysa was located. It may have been as close as Thrace or as far as India or across the Mediterranean in Libya or Ethiopia. Or it may never have existed at all, merely invented in order to explain his name.

Even more than the other Greek gods, Dionysus was called by many names. The most common was Bacchus, though some also called him Bromius. Dionysian revelers often called out a special word: *evoe!* This exclamation, however, did not name the god; it simply indicated the joy of the Dionysian worshipper.

After Dionysus was restored to human form, the nymphs of Nysa became the *maenads*, the female votaries of the god. Like Dionysus himself, the maenads would suffer intense persecution from those frightened or appalled by their frenzied, ecstatic rites.

Sex, Drugs, and Rock 'n' Roll: Dionysus on Tour

Dionysus grew up to be a beautiful—if somewhat effeminate—young man, boisterous and full of life. Unfortunately, after Dionysus had lived many years hidden in the cave on Mount Nysa, Hera—who had never given up the search for her bastard son—finally caught up to him. Though the god was still only a youth, Hera did not hesitate to drive the boy mad. For many years, Dionysus wandered aimlessly throughout Egypt and Syria.

Eventually, the young god arrived at Phrygia. Cybele, the Phrygian mother goddess, perhaps recognizing him as a kindred spirit, welcomed Dionysus. Cybele exercised a powerful influence on Dionysus. She not only purified him and cured him of his madness, she also initiated him in her religious rites. Dionysus learned well, and before long had begun creating his own rites based on those taught by Cybele. To honor her, the god also adopted the costume of the Phrygians: long, flowing robes and a crown of ivy.

The Original Flower Child

Thereafter, Dionysus declared himself the god of the grapes as well as all other vegetation, and, of course, wine. Indeed, some even say he discovered the vine and the use to which its fruit could be put, for Dionysus invented wine: the medicine for misery, the bearer of sleep and relief from human troubles.

Dionysus began frequenting woods, mountains, and valleys. Unlike some of the other gods, Dionysus enjoyed reveling with mortals. The god, who loved wine, women, and song, traveled with a sometimes raggedy band of Bacchants: maenads, satyrs, and silens (see Chapter 8) who worshipped him.

The Star and His Groupies

Worshippers celebrated Dionysus as a kind of fertility god. Through a combination of wine, music, dancing, and religious fervor, followers achieved a mystical communion with the god. Indeed, they even called themselves by his name: Bacchus.

Male and female followers alike dressed in long flowing robes that the traditional Greeks—those who had difficulty accepting the deity of this new god—considered girlish. While caught up in their revelry, the Bacchants covered their robes in animal skins, sometimes said to be fastened to their shoulders with snakes that enjoyed licking their cheeks. In addition, each reveler carried a thyrsus, a pole wrapped in live ivy and grapevines and topped with a pine cone.

High in the mountains, hidden in the secluded forests, Dionysus and his followers would engage in wild, frenzied rites, often at night. A parade of nymphs and Bacchants would dance through the forest, all making quite a racket. Under the influence of copious amounts of wine and religious ecstasy (and some say sexual ecstasy as well), revelers became one with their god. Even after he ascended to Olympus, his followers could still see Dionysus—often in the form of a bull or goat—in visions brought on by their religious rites.

In the orgiastic celebrations of Dionysus and his mostly female followers, women sometimes suckled gazelles, wolves, fawns, or kids. At other times, they engaged in *sparagmos*, ripping cows, goats, or sheep to pieces with their bare hands and eating them raw. By banging their thyrsi on the ground, the Bacchants sometimes created springs of water, wine, milk, or honey.

Logos

Sparagmos involves the ritualized dismemberment of a living animal. Its use in the rites of Dionysus contrasted sharply with the scrupulous preparations for slaughter and sacrifice observed in more traditional Greek religious practices. Sparagmos thus showed just how unorthodox the Dionysian religion was.

Don't Make Him Mad

Leaving Phrygia, Dionysus began doing his own missionary work. He traveled from land to land, spreading the culture of the grape. He introduced people to the cultivation of the vine and to the joys—and sometimes the perils—offered by wine. Equally important, he spread the word about his own divinity and initiated countless followers in his religious mysteries. This mission would take him throughout the Greek world and beyond—as far east as the land of the Amazons on the Black Sea, across the Mediterranean to Egypt—and even as far as the Ganges in India.

Needless to say, the young god aroused much anger and resentment. Not everyone embraced Dionysus, accepted his teachings, and adopted his ideas on worship and religious practice. The kind of worship that Dionysus and his followers preached was foreign to Greece. And the many tales of mythic battles between Dionysus and the kings he encountered no doubt reflect very real battles between those who preached the word of Dionysus and those who fought the spread of this cult.

Read All About It

The *Homeric Hymn to Dionysus* beautifully tells one version of the tale of Dionysus among the Tyrrhenian pirates. The hymn is the seventh of 33 songs of praise to the many gods and goddesses of ancient Greece. Though once attributed to Homer, these *Homeric Hymns* are now almost universally regarded as the works of another, unknown poet.

The first to insult and mistreat Dionysus in the course of his missionary work was Lycurgus, king of the Edonians in Thrace. Lycurgus brutally attacked Dionysus and his maenads with an ox-goad, forcing them to flee his kingdom. Many Bacchants were captured and imprisoned, but the Nereid Thetis offered Dionysus refuge deep beneath the sea.

To avenge this insult to himself and his followers, Dionysus drove the king mad—the first of many times the god would employ this weapon. The madness of Lycurgus first manifested itself when, after getting drunk, he attempted to rape his own mother. Temporarily restored to his senses, Lycurgus realized what he had done.

Blaming the wine, the king then attempted to destroy all the vines that Dionysus had taught the Edonians to plant. But Lycurgus again suffered a fit of madness. The king slaughtered his wife and son, thinking them vines, and then chopped off his own feet with his ax.

Dionysus vowed to keep the land barren until the king's death. As drought and famine wasted the land, his subjects brutally killed Lycurgus. They tied their king up and threw him among the wild, man-eating horses that roamed Mount Pangaeus.

Yo Ho Ho and a Bottle of Wine!

Once Tyrrhenian pirates spotted young Dionysus standing alone on the shore of the island Icaria. Believing he was a prince and hoping to ransom him for a handsome price, the pirates kidnapped Dionysus and sailed off with him. His captors tried to shackle Dionysus, but found it impossible. The shackles kept slipping off his wrists, while Dionysus just sat and smiled at them.

Acoetes, the helmsman for the pirate ship, realized that this divine-looking young man must be a god. Acoetes urged his fellow pirates to treat Dionysus gently. He even suggested that they drop him back off on the nearest shore and be done with him.

But the captain would not listen, and called the helmsman crazy. To the rest of the crew, the pirate captain explained away the god's exotic looks by insisting that he probably came from Egypt or Cyprus. Perhaps he received his looks as a gift from some god, the captain claimed, but he was no god himself. So he ordered the crew to hoist the sails and set off.

Almost immediately after setting sail, the miracles began:

- Despite strong winds, the ship halted, frozen in the water.
- Streams of wine, sweet and fragrant, flowed throughout the ship.
- A vine, rich with grapes, spread across the top sail.
- Ivy, bearing lush flowers and luscious berries, entwined itself about the mast.
- Wreaths crowned the thole pins where the oars rested.

Now the crew agreed with the helmsman. They wanted to get rid of this god before they made him so angry that he destroyed them all. But their change of heart came too late.

Dionysus transformed into a growling lion. A large bear—or bears, panthers, and lions—instantly materialized on the ship. The roaring of animals so frightened the crew that they retreated to the stern of the ship. When the lion Dionysus leapt on the pirate captain, the crew quickly abandoned ship. They all dived into the water, where they turned into dolphins. Acoetes was about to join them when the god—in human form once again—halted him, insisting that the helmsman had nothing to fear. Due to his kindness toward Dionysus, Acoetes had become dear to the god's heart.

Homecoming Queen: Pentheus of Thebes

After years of wandering, Dionysus finally returned to Thebes, his birthplace. Yet he did not receive much of a homecoming. Semele's sisters—whether through jealousy or disbelief—had spread the rumor that she had never slept with Zeus at all. Indeed, they insisted that Zeus had killed her with a lightning bolt to punish her for that false claim.

When Dionysus arrived announcing that he was not only a god, but the son of Semele and Zeus, few of the men of Thebes believed him on either count. Only the wise seer Teiresias and Semele's aged father Cadmus—who hoped it was true for the honor it would bring to his family—accepted Dionysus for what he said he was.

Unfortunately, Cadmus had already stepped down from the throne of Thebes. His grandson, King Pentheus, not only disbelieved the claims of Dionysus, he found the fervor of his followers and the nature of their rites distasteful. He banned the participation of Theban women in the rites of Dionysus, rounded up the maenads, and threw them and their priest (who was probably Dionysus himself in disguise) into prison.

To punish his aunts, Dionysus drove them—and all the women of Thebes—mad. Ignoring Pentheus's edict, the Theban women abandoned their homes and families and joined in the frenzied rites on Mount Cithaeron. Dionysus and the maenads easily escaped their jail cells and returned to the mountain, where Dionysus tricked his unknowing cousin Pentheus to dress up as a maenad in order to spy on the Bacchants.

His mother, Agave, and two aunts, in the grips of Dionysian madness, caught the transvestite voyeur in the act. They uprooted the tree in which Pentheus had been hiding and the king fell to the ground. Seeing him as a mountain lion, the revelers then ferociously tore Pentheus limb from limb and scattered his body parts all over the mountainside. Agave herself speared her son's head with her thyrsus and paraded back home with it. When she returned to her senses and recognized the "lion's head" as that of her own son, Agave recoiled in horror. For their crimes, Dionysus then exiled Agave and her sisters from Thebes.

Pentheus was succeeded to the throne by his uncle Polydorus (Semele's brother), who quickly and prudently chose to honor Dionysus. Polydorus officially instituted the Dionysian rites and established Thebes as the center of Dionysian worship in Greece.

Madness Is the Best Revenge

Continuing his mission, Dionysus left Thebes for the neighboring kingdom of Orcho-menus. But the daughters of King Minyas would neither recognize him as a god nor take part in his rites. Insulted again, Dionysus drove them mad. The daughters chose one of their infant sons by lot and ripped him apart. Dionysus then transformed them into bats.

Moving on to Argos, the god again met with disbelief as the three daughters of King Proetus also refused to recognize him as a deity. Again, Dionysus afflicted the dis-believers with madness. Thinking they were cows, the three young women grazed on the mountainsides.

Proetus sent for the great seer Melampus to cure the women. But when Melampus demanded one third of the kingdom as his payment, Proetus angrily turned him away. As a result, the madness soon spread to all the Argive women. When the young moth-ers of Argos began feasting on the infants that they had nursed and loved the day before, Proetus begged Melampus to return. Though the seer now demanded another third of the kingdom for his brother Bias, Proetus had no choice but to accede. Using herbs and purification rites, Melampus managed to cure the women of Argos.

The Kindness of Strangers

Though traditionalists tended to persecute the Bacchants for their belief in the divin-ity of Dionysus and for their wildly ecstatic rites, the young god did not meet with resistance everywhere he went. True, he often alienated kings and noblemen as he toured the Mediterranean, but he nonetheless attracted a great number of followers. And he had a particularly strong appeal among women.

Those who embraced his godhood and observed his rites were often rewarded hand-somely. The maenads, for example, eventually grew very old—as even nymphs do. But in gratitude for their lifelong devotion to him, Dionysus prevailed upon the sorceress Medea to restore their youth.

Mythed by a Mile _____

According to another version of the union between Dionysus and Ariadne, Theseus really did love Ariadne, but when Dionysus fell in love with her, too, the god forced the hero to go on without her. Still other storytellers suggest that Dionysus laid the groundwork for his marriage to Ariadne while visiting her father, King Minos. At that time, he bribed her to sleep with him by offering her a stunning crown.

Though he had countless lovers, Dionysus married only one: Ariadne, the daughter of King Minos of Crete. Ariadne had helped Theseus escape from the Labyrinth, an elaborate maze that housed the vicious Minotaur. But after getting him safely out of Crete, Ariadne was cruelly abandoned by her lover (see Chapter 15) on the island of Dia (later known as Naxos). Dionysus found her there, fell in love, and married her.

The Lemnians claim that the god and his bride settled on the island of Lemnos. Ariadne bore Dionysus several sons, among them:

♦ Thoas, a king of Lemnos whose daughter secretly spared him when the women of Lemnos killed all the other men on the island (see Chapter 14)

♦ Staphylus, who sailed with Jason on the *Argo*

♦ Phanus, who joined his brother on the *Argo*

♦ Oenopion, who became a king of Chios, an island famed for its wine

Swing Time

When he introduced wine to Attica (the region surrounding Athens), Dionysus chose to teach the cultivation of the grape and wine-making to an ordinary citizen, Icarius, and his daughter Erigone. (Some storytellers say that he picked Icarius in gratitude after having seduced Erigone.) They embraced his arts and learned their lessons well.

When Icarius went to his neighbors and began offering his wineskin, however, some local farmers unfortunately drank too much and passed out. When they awoke, still groggy, they accused Icarius of trying to poison them and beat him to death. Erigone, after much searching, discovered her father's body and hanged herself in despair.

What a Life!

Icarius had a remarkably loyal dog named Maera. The dog accompanied him when he introduced wine to his neighbors. Its howling over its master's body helped Erigone find her father. And it jumped into a well and killed itself when Erigone hanged herself. Dionysus rewarded the dog's incredible faithfulness by placing it, too, in the sky as the Dog Star.

Furious at the murder of his disciple, Dionysus drove the Attic women mad. Like Erigone, they started hanging themselves from trees all over town. After discovering the cause of these suicides through an oracle, the men of Attica quickly tracked down and punished the murderers of Icarius. They also instituted an annual "swinging festival" to honor Erigone, in which the young girls of Athens played on swings hanging from the town's trees. These acts of atonement appeased the wine god and persuaded him to restore sanity to the Attic women. To honor his Athenian disciples, Dionysus placed both father and daughter in the stars as the constellations Bootes and Virgo.

Oeneus of Calydon was the first Greek king to offer Dionysus a warm welcome. Indeed, Oeneus treated his guest to unsurpassed hospitality. Recognizing that Dionysus wanted to sleep with Queen Althaea, Oeneus even left his kingdom for a short time to allow the god to fulfill his desire. This recess allowed some storytellers to speculate that Dionysus, rather than Oeneus, was the father of Althaea's daughter Deianira— a beautiful girl who would one day marry the hero Heracles (see Chapter 13).

All That's Gold Does Not Glitter

Once while traveling through Phrygia, Silenus, the leader and namesake of the silens— the demigods of the forest skilled at both music and prophecy (see Chapter 8)— disappeared. Midas, a Phrygian king, had lured him away from the rest of his company by adding wine to a spring that flowed outside his castle—perhaps to take advantage of the goat-man's gift for prophecy. Midas played the perfect host, entertaining his guest for several days before sending him back to Dionysus.

To thank Midas for his hospitality, Dionysus offered the king any boon he desired. The avaricious king did not hesitate a second: He wanted everything he touched to turn to gold. Dionysus reluctantly granted him this power.

> ### What a Life!
>
> The three daughters of King Anius of Delos became devotees of Dionysus, and he rewarded them with a touch much more valuable than Midas's golden one. Simply by touching something, Oino (wine) could transform anything into wine; Spermo (seed) could change anything into corn; and Elais (olive) could turn anything into oil. Agamemnon, leader of the Greek forces, recognizing their value to troops on the move, seized the girls on his way to Troy. But they prayed to Dionysus, who released them by transforming the girls into white doves.

Midas enjoyed his golden touch for only a brief time before he discovered that he could no longer eat, because everything he lifted to his mouth turned to gold (which has little nutritional value). Recognizing his foolishness, Midas petitioned Dionysus to take back his gift. This lay beyond even a god's power, but Dionysus advised the king to bathe in the river Pactolus, which washed away his touch of gold forever.

Mama's Boy

Dionysus, unlike his half-brother Heracles, had always been divine. Once he completed his missionary work throughout the eastern Mediterranean, Dionysus made up his mind to join his fellow gods on Olympus.

But ever the devoted son, Dionysus wanted to bring his mother Semele with him. So the god headed first to the Underworld. A guide told him that he need not take the long land route to the Palace of Hades. He could go more quickly by diving down into the water at the bottomless Alcyonian Lake or the Bay of Troezen.

In talking to Dionysus, the guide became smitten with the beautiful god. Knowing his generosity to kind strangers, the guide asked Dionysus to sleep with him in return for the advice he had provided. But now that he had directions in hand, Dionysus urgently wanted to reunite with his mother. As he hurried off, however, he swore he would pay the guide whatever he wanted when he returned from the Underworld.

After fetching his mother, Dionysus returned to honor his oath, but the guide had died in his absence. So the god carved a wooden image of his own genitals and left it at the guide's tomb. It was the least he could do to repay the stranger's kindness.

His business on Earth completed, Dionysus then brought Semele up to Olympus, where she became known as Thyone. At last, Dionysus had taken his place among the Olympians.

The Least You Need to Know

- Semele, the mother of Dionysus, burned to a crisp when she saw her lover Zeus in his full glory. Dionysus, delivered prematurely from her body, completed his gestation in the thigh of Zeus.

- Dionysus—trailed by his devoted followers, the maenads, silens, and satyrs—haunted the forests and mountainsides of the Greek world. They engaged in ecstatic revels centered around wine, song, dance, and perhaps sex.

- Dionysus used madness as a weapon against those who persecuted him or his followers. The madness often led to horrifying acts of violence.

- Dionysus, the god of wine, rewarded those who embraced his godhood with the gift of wine—and relief from the troubles of daily life.

- Once he had completed the work of spreading the word and initiating followers, Dionysus took his proper place among the immortals of Olympus.

Part 3

Everyone Needs a Hero

Now that you've gotten to know the gods, let's introduce you to the heroes of the Greek world.

Often sons of deities, the Greek heroes won their fair share of glory, thrones, and even immortality through their adventures. Some Greek heroes became heroes on the battlefield. Others made terrifying journeys to hell and back or slew fierce dragons, one-eyed giants, and sea serpents. And a handful of heroes are remembered as much or more for their tragedies as for their triumphs.

Yet no matter what path to greatness they chose, these heroes have all become immortals—whether or not they rose up to Olympus—through the enduring stories of their adventures.

The Model Hero: Perseus

In This Chapter

- ◆ The hero's birth and his youth in exile
- ◆ The slaying of Medusa
- ◆ The rescue of Andromeda
- ◆ How Perseus saved his mother
- ◆ The accidental killing of his grandfather

Could there be a hero more virtuous than Perseus? A model of chivalry, he rescued his future bride, Andromeda, from a monster and his mother from a lecherous and powerful king. A brave and resourceful adventurer, he ranks among the greatest monster-slayers of classical mythology.

A paragon of fidelity—one of the rarest virtues seen in Greek and Roman myths—Perseus remained true to Andromeda throughout their marriage. A beloved king, he not only ruled Tiryns for many years, but founded the neighboring city of Mycenae and fortified Midea as well.

Little wonder, then, that Homer called Perseus the "most renowned of all men."

Against All Odds: Perseus's Conception, Birth, and Youth

As so many classical myths do, the story of Perseus actually begins two generations earlier. His grandfather, Acrisius, king of Argos, had a twin brother named Proetus. Talk about sibling rivalry! Acrisius and Proetus were enemies even before their birth. While still inside their mother's womb, the two brothers began their lifelong quarreling.

The two brothers were supposed to grow up to rule Argos (a city in southern Greece) together. But as soon as they reached manhood, Acrisius and Proetus fought for the throne of Argos. Acrisius emerged victorious and forced his brother into exile. Proetus then became king of Tiryns, a neighboring city in Argolis—the region surrounding Argos. (The mighty fortifications of this city were so impenetrable, and the blocks of stone that comprised the wall so large, that the construction had been attributed to the Cyclopes—one-eyed giants who were renowned stonemasons—rather than to mere men.)

> **The More Things Change ...**
>
> Sibling rivalry—over inheritance or political succession—pops up frequently in mythology. The most famous battling brothers in Greek mythology are the sons of Oedipus, Eteocles and Polyneices, who killed each other over the throne of Thebes. Romulus slew Remus in a fight for the leadership of Rome. Much more recently, J. R. and Bobby Ewing fought for control of their daddy's oil empire in *Dallas*.

The Golden Shower

After many years of marriage to Aganippe, Acrisius had but one child: a daughter named Danaë. Wanting a son to inherit his kingdom, Acrisius consulted an oracle and got nothing but bad news. He learned that not only would he have no sons, but his sole male heir, his daughter's son, would kill him.

Acrisius desperately tried to prevent this prophecy from coming true. He locked his daughter up in an underground chamber cast of bronze.

Despite these preventive measures, Danaë conceived a child. Though some rumors held that the exiled Proetus had stolen into his niece's cell and impregnated her, Danaë always insisted that Zeus had fathered the child. The god appeared before her in the form of a shower of gold, which poured through the roof of her chamber and fell into her lap. Thus Danaë, despite her imprisonment, gave birth to a child, whom she called Perseus.

Some storytellers insist that Acrisius, alerted by a baby's cry, discovered his grandson almost immediately after his birth. Others maintain that mother and child spent more than a year imprisoned together—until Acrisius heard the toddler playing in the underground chamber. In any case, Acrisius acted quickly upon the discovery. He placed both Danaë and Perseus in a large wooden chest and set it adrift in the Aegean Sea, consigning his daughter and his grandson to death.

A Fine Kettle of Fish

Fortunately for Danaë and Perseus, Zeus guided the chest across the sea to the island of Seriphus. This island had its own pair of brothers. Though not so hostile toward each other as Acrisius and Proetus, these brothers were by no means close. Polydectes, king of Seriphus, enjoyed royal privileges, while Dictys lived the life of a poor fisher.

Dictys was out fishing one day when he spied the chest floating nearby and caught it in his net. After rescuing and releasing Danaë and Perseus, kind Dictys took the two refugees into his home, claiming they were distant kin. (This claim turned out to be true, since both Dictys and Danaë were descendants of Danaus, a former king of Argos.) Dictys cared for Danaë and Perseus for many years, until the boy was fully grown.

Something Fishy Going On

While mother and son were living in Dictys's home, King Polydectes fell in love with Danaë. The king asked her to marry him, but Danaë rejected his offer. Polydectes might have taken her by force, but by this time, Perseus had become a formidable young man. Perhaps afraid of opposing Perseus, Polydectes pretended to accept Danaë's rejection with good grace. Yet he never stopped scheming to have her.

Soon after Danaë's rejection, Polydectes announced his intention to ask for the hand of Hippodameia, a daughter of King Oenomaus of Pisa, a city in southwestern Greece. Polydectes arranged for a banquet in which

Mythed by a Mile

Some storytellers insist that Polydectes, as king, claimed whatever his brother caught in his net. When he learned that Dictys had netted Danaë and Perseus, Polydectes either took Danaë as a slave or he married her. In either case, the king brought her into his home, while Perseus grew up as a ward of Athena in her temple on Seriphus.

The More Things Change ...

Like many heroes both ancient and modern, Perseus is called upon to do the impossible. Heracles (see Chapter 13) performs a series of impossible tasks, including fetching the three-headed dog Cerberus from the gates of Hell. Just so, Dorothy Gale must bring back the broom of the Wicked Witch of the West. In accomplishing what all thought impossible, our heroes show their mettle.

each invited guest must traditionally bring a present for the intended bride. Polydectes demanded that each of his subjects bring a horse as a contribution.

This demand left Perseus in quite a bind. Whether the ward of a poor fisher or the son of a slave, Perseus had no horses. In all likelihood, Polydectes hoped that Perseus would be shamed into fleeing the kingdom. Instead, Perseus offered what must have seemed to Polydectes an even better solution. The young man acknowledged that he had no horses, but rashly promised to bring to the king anything else he desired—even the head of Medusa!

Polydectes, his evil intentions toward Danaë well disguised, eagerly accepted Perseus's offer. For he knew that no man had ever survived a meeting with the Gorgon whose face turned men to stone.

A Face Only a Mother Could Love

Medusa was one of three monstrous sisters called the Gorgons. Of the three, only Medusa could be killed; her sisters Euryale and Stheno were immortal. The hideous Gorgons had the following features:

♦ Serpents for hair

♦ Penetrating eyes that turned anyone who looked upon them into stone

♦ Huge, snake-like tongues

♦ Teeth as long and sharp as the tusks of a wild boar

♦ Bodies covered with scales so hard that no weapon could pierce them

♦ Golden wings

♦ Claws forged of brass

A Little Help from My Friends

Considering Medusa's frightening features, Perseus must have begun having second thoughts about his foolhardy promise almost immediately. Defeating the mighty Medusa seemed an impossible quest.

What a Life!

According to some tellers, Medusa was once a beautiful maiden. Though she turned away all suitors, Medusa finally consented to lay with Poseidon either in a field of flowers or in the temple of Athena. This enraged the goddess, who was either jealous of Medusa's great beauty or furious that the maiden had bedded Poseidon in her shrine. In either case, Athena transformed Medusa's loveliness into hideousness.

To avoid the vigilant eyes of Medusa and her sisters, her slayer must approach their lair without being seen. To escape being turned to stone, the killer would have to slay her without looking at her face. Even if Perseus succeeded in killing Medusa, he would then need to flee with incredible speed to avoid the swift pursuit of her golden-winged sisters.

Perseus soon discovered, however, that he would have help in completing his quest. Athena, who hated Medusa, appeared before him and told him exactly what to do.

Athena first brought Perseus to a cave on Seriphus where some of the Naiads (the nymphs of springs, brooks, and lakes) lived. These nymphs lent to Perseus virtually everything he would need to overcome the Gorgons:

♦ Winged sandals, which would allow him to approach—and later escape—the lair of the Gorgons with great speed

♦ The helmet of darkness (or cap of Hades), which makes its wearer invisible

♦ A purse or pouch in which to carry his trophy: Medusa's head

Hermes then appeared and presented Perseus with the final tool he would need: a sword (or sickle) of adamant—a metallic stone so hard it was almost unbreakable.

 Mythed by a Mile

Some storytellers contend that it was not the Naiads, but rather Hermes, who gave Perseus the cap of Hades and one (or both) of his own winged sandals because he found the young man so attractive. This seems plausible, since Hermes—who guided the ghosts of the dead to Hades—had ready access to the cap and already possessed the sandals.

The Gray Women: Their Sisters' Keepers

With his weapons assembled, Perseus traveled to a cave on the mountain where Atlas stood. In this cave lived the Graeae ("gray women"), sisters of the Gorgons. The hair of the Graeae, three ancient witches who had just one eye and one tooth among them, had been gray from birth.

Perseus hid himself and waited until one of the sisters took out her eye and started to hand it to another. Since this was the only time when all of the Graeae were blind, Perseus surprised them and intercepted the eye. Holding the eye hostage, Perseus forced the crones to reveal the location of the Gorgons' lair. After getting the information he needed, Perseus tossed the eye into Lake Tritonis and hurried toward the Gorgons.

Medusa Loses Her Head

Swiftly, invisibly, his sword in his belt and his bag slung over his shoulder, Perseus approached the lair of the Gorgons. He found the lair at the end of the earth, in a land where neither the sun nor the moon ever shone. As he approached and entered the Gorgons' lair, he passed dozens of stone figures: the petrified bodies of both beasts and humans who had foolishly wandered into that dark and desolate land and glimpsed one of the Gorgons.

> **Mythed by a Mile**
>
> Some say that Athena actually guided Perseus's hand as he decapitated Medusa, making it unnecessary for him to use his shield as a mirror. Other storytellers suggest that Athena herself killed Medusa, afterward skinning her and using her skin to form a shield.

> **What a Life!**
>
> Medusa was pregnant by Poseidon at the time of her death. So when Perseus chopped off her head, her offspring sprang from her neck: Chrysaor, who would become renowned as a brave warrior, and Pegasus, the famous winged horse. Some taletellers claim that Perseus, while fleeing Medusa's sisters, may have been the first to mount Pegasus.

Perseus had painstakingly polished his bronze shield before approaching the Gorgons' lair. He now used this shield as a mirror to spy on the Gorgons without looking directly at them. He waited near the entrance of their lair until he could see that the Gorgons had fallen asleep.

Using his mirrored shield to reflect Medusa's image and direct his attack, Perseus cut off her head with a single blow from his mighty sword, stuffed the head into his pouch, and flew away on his winged feet. The other Gorgons awoke and flew into the air shrieking for vengeance. Medusa's monstrous sisters could not see Perseus, though, cloaked as he was by the helmet of darkness, and soon gave up their attack.

Homeward Bound

With his trophy securely in hand, Perseus flew back toward Seriphus on his winged sandals. Yet the journey back from the lair of the Gorgons was a long one. He would need to make several stops before he returned home. These layovers were by no means uneventful. As Perseus soon discovered, he had several more adventures in store for him before he reached Seriphus.

The Mountain Man: Atlas

According to Ovid alone, Perseus first stopped in the land of the Hesperides. He announced himself as a son of Zeus and asked the Titan Atlas, who ruled the Hesperides, if he could rest there for a while.

Yet Atlas recalled the prophecy of the Titaness Themis, who had warned him that a son of Zeus would one day steal the Golden Apples of the Hesperides. So the Titan, who fiercely guarded these apples, insulted Perseus, denied his parentage, and rudely attempted to expel him from the land.

Perseus could not hope to match the strength of Atlas. Yet his cleverness far outshone that of the dim-witted Titan. Perseus knew that the head of Medusa, even after her death, had not lost its power to turn anyone who looked upon it to stone. So before he left, Perseus offered to show Atlas what he had in his bag. Turning his own head away, Perseus lifted the head out of the bag and turned the Titan into a mountain, known afterward as Mount Atlas.

Mythed by a Mile

None but Ovid give any weight to this account of the encounter between Perseus and Atlas. One of the famed labors of Heracles—another heroic son of Zeus— required him to bring back three of the Golden Apples. Yet if Atlas were already a mountain, Heracles could not have tricked the Titan, stolen the apples, and thus made the prophecy of Themis come true (see Chapter 13). Since virtually all storytellers include this as one of the labors of Heracles, they generally discount Ovid's account.

A Damsel in Distress: The Rescue of Andromeda

As Perseus flew on winged sandals over the coast of Ethiopia on his way home, he saw the figure of a beautiful woman chained to a rock below. The radiance of this figure stunned him so that at first Perseus thought her carved of marble. But when he descended for a better look, he saw that this maiden was crying.

At first the girl seemed frightened of Perseus and reluctant to speak about her predicament. But using gentle persuasion, Perseus overcame this virginal beauty's shyness, and she shared with him her tragic tale. Her name was Andromeda, the daughter of Cepheus (depending on the source, the king of either Ethiopia or Joppa, a city on the Levantine seacoast) and Cassiopeia. Her mother had angered Poseidon by boasting that she was more beautiful than the Nereids, the sea nymphs who served as the sea god's attendants. To punish Cassiopeia's vanity, Poseidon had flooded the kingdom and sent a sea monster to ravage Ethiopia. Following the advice of an ora-cle, King Cepheus had chained the naked Andromeda to a rocky cliff as a sacrificial offering to appease Poseidon and save his kingdom.

As he listened to her tale, Perseus fell in love with Andromeda. She begged him to save her from being devoured by the sea monster and take her away from that spot as a wife or a slave. Perseus promised he would, but first secured a promise from Cepheus to reward him with Andromeda's hand in marriage and a kingdom if he res-cued her. Welcoming the opportunity to save both his kingdom and his daughter, the king eagerly accepted Perseus's demands.

When the sea monster surfaced, Perseus dived on top of the beast and—following a raging battle that stained the sea red with blood—killed it. (According to the people of Joppa, the spring where Perseus washed his hands after this battle ran red from that moment onward.)

Perseus then freed Andromeda from her chains and brought the girl to her parents. Having saved their daughter, Perseus now demanded that Cepheus honor his prom-ises.

The Marrying Kind

Unfortunately, Andromeda had already been promised to Cepheus's brother Phineus (called Agenor by some)—a detail that Cepheus had neglected to mention in his eagerness to see his daughter rescued.

Though Phineus had not lifted a hand to save his bride, he still refused to step aside for her savior. The grateful Cepheus, however, kept his promise to Perseus by arrang-ing for a quick wedding.

With an army behind him, however, Phineus interrupted the wedding of Perseus and Andromeda to assert his prior claim on her. Though greatly outnumbered, Perseus emerged victorious from the battle for Andromeda's hand by using Medusa's head to turn his rival and all of Phineus's allies to stone.

With Phineus out of the way, Perseus married Andromeda and—unlike most of the gods and heroes of classical mythology—remained faithful to her throughout his life. The couple remained with her parents for almost a year after their marriage, An-dromeda giving birth to their first son, Perses.

When Perseus finally resumed his journey back to Seriphus, he and Andromeda left the infant Perses with his grandparents. Since his grandfather Cepheus had no other heirs, Perses would inherit his kingdom. (The boy's descendants would travel east and rule Persia, the land that was named after Perses.)

A Family Reunion

Upon his return to the island of Seriphus, Perseus found his mother taking refuge at the altar of the gods. As soon as Perseus had set out on his quest, the lustful King Polydectes had attempted to ravish Danaë. The king's brother Dictys had thwarted Polydectes and led Danaë to the altar, sacred ground where the king dared not violate her.

Upon hearing of Polydectes' treachery, Perseus headed straight for the palace. Bursting in upon a banquet, he surprised the king, who had no doubt presumed that Perseus was dead. Perseus announced that he had brought the promised gift for the intended bride of Polydectes. The king scoffed at this claim, challenging Perseus's word and his honor. The young hero needed no further provocation. Averting his own eyes, he held up the severed head of Medusa, which instantly turned Polydectes and his guests into stone.

Having rescued his mother, Perseus rewarded Dictys for his loyalty and protection by giving him the throne vacated by Polydectes. He then returned his borrowed weapons to Hermes, who carried them back to the Naiads. In gratitude to Athena, Perseus mounted his trophy, the head of Medusa, on the shield of the goddess. The head, surrounded by snakes' heads on the center of her *aegis*, became Athena's most distinctive emblem. His heroic quest completed, Perseus set out for Argos with Andromeda and Danaë. There, in the kingdom of his birth, he hoped to make peace with his grandfather, Acrisius.

Logos

An **aegis** was a protective garment carried on the arm like a shield or occasionally worn over the shoulder.

Welcome Home

The exploits of his grandson, Perseus, had not gone unnoticed by Acrisius. Fearing that his daughter and her famed son would soon return to Argos and fulfill the prophecy he had desperately tried to avoid, Acrisius fled to Larissa, a kingdom in Thessaly. But Perseus, who apparently harbored no vengeance for his grandfather despite Acrisius's cruelty so many years before, followed the old man to Larissa. Perseus had not yet found his grandfather when he learned that the father of the king of Larissa had died.

While attending funereal games held in honor of the king's father, Perseus impulsively decided to join the discus-throw competition. Unfortunately, a discus thrown by Perseus got away from him. It accidentally struck and killed one of the spectators: his grandfather Acrisius. The prophecy had come true: Perseus had indeed caused his grandfather's death.

Mythed by a Mile

Some say that Perseus threw the discus that killed his grandfather not at funereal games, but at games held to celebrate the reconciliation between grandfather and grandson. The two had already met and made their peace with each other before the tragic competition.

With the death of Acrisius, Perseus inherited the throne of Argos. Yet he felt so ashamed to have won the throne by accidentally killing his own grandfather that Perseus vowed never again to return to Argos. Instead, he traded kingdoms (Argos for Tiryns) with Megapenthes, the only son of Acrisius's twin brother Proetus.

Perseus served as king of Tiryns for many years thereafter. While ruling Tiryns, he established the city of Mycenae (though some say he merely fortified it) and fortified Midea. He remained faithful to Andromeda, who bore him six more children.

One of the greatest heroes of Argos, Perseus was worshipped after his death in both Athens and Seriphus. Athena herself honored Perseus and Andromeda by making constellations in both their names after they died.

The Least You Need to Know

♦ Trying to escape the prophecy that he would die at his grandson's hand, Perseus's grandfather set the infant and his mother adrift in a wooden chest. The prophecy, however, eventually came true.

♦ Athena offered strategic advice to Perseus, while Hermes and the Naiads provided him with the equipment he would need to slay Medusa.

♦ After using his shield as a mirror to avoid looking directly upon her face as he approached, Perseus cut off the head of Medusa.

♦ Perseus rescued the virginal Andromeda from a sea monster and remained true to her all of his days.

♦ Perseus saved his mother Danaë from the lecherous king of Seriphus by showing the king and his court the head of Medusa and turning them to stone.

What the Hell? Adventures in the Underworld

In This Chapter

◆ How Persephone became Queen of the Underworld

◆ The trickery of Sisyphus in the Underworld—and the special punishment reserved for him

◆ The sins of Tantalus and his eternal punishment

◆ How Orpheus retrieved Eurydice from the Underworld and then lost her forever

Of all the dangerous adventures undertaken by heroes in classical myths, none held as much peril as a journey to the Underworld, the realm of the dead. Hades did not welcome visitors. For the living, the trek was long and hard even for those who avoided the main entrance. What's worse, a trip to the Underworld was almost always one-way; very few who entered the realm of Hades ever returned.

Despite the forbidding nature of the Underworld, quite a few mythic characters had adventures there. Surviving the dangers of the Underworld—experiencing the realm of the dead as well as the realm of the living—certified a hero as genuine.

Those who dared undertake this journey included goddesses, great heroes, tricksters, lovers, and fools. These adventurers were linked only in their general response to the Underworld: It's not even a nice place to visit, and I sure wouldn't want to live there.

Hades Takes a Wife: Persephone

The first living visitor to the Underworld, though an unwilling one, was the goddess Persephone. The only daughter of Zeus and Demeter (the goddess of grain, agriculture, and fertility), Persephone was an innocent maiden, a virgin who loved to play in the fields where eternal springtime reigned.

But Hades had other plans for Persephone: He would steal her innocence and virginity and turn her into the dreaded goddess of the Underworld.

Where Have All the Flowers Gone?

Hades, god of the Underworld, fell in love with Persephone and wanted her as his bride. His brother Zeus consented to the marriage—or at least refused to oppose it. Yet he warned Hades that Demeter would never approve this coupling, for she would not want her daughter spirited off to a sunless world. At Zeus's suggestion—or with his tacit understanding—Hades resolved to abduct the maiden.

Persephone was gathering flowers one day on a plain in Sicily. Hades suddenly appeared, thundering across the plain in his four-horse chariot. The god swooped down upon Persephone, scooped her up with one arm, and literally and figuratively deflowered her—leaving the plain scattered with blossoms of every color.

The appearance, abduction, and disappearance happened so swiftly that none of Persephone's companions witnessed the kidnapping. And though she called out to them—and plaintively called for her mother—no one heard her pleas. The earth opened up before Hades' chariot and the god drove the jet-black horses down into the chasm. As Hades and Persephone disappeared into the depths, the hole closed up behind them.

The Long Winter of Her Discontent

Demeter soon came to collect her daughter, but could not find a trace of Persephone. Distraught and desperate, Demeter searched high and low for her daughter. She traveled to the farthest corners of the earth, searching for nine full days and nights without ever stopping to eat, drink, bathe, or rest. Demeter was in a fury. She destroyed lands, crops, and livestock as she bewailed the loss of her daughter.

She threatened to make the earth barren forever and thus destroy all of humankind if she did not find Persephone.

Finally, on the tenth day, the goddess Hecate told Demeter that Persephone had been carried away, but she did not know by whom. The two goddesses went to Helius, the god of the sun, who saw everything that happened on Earth. Helius did tell her what had happened, but also tried to persuade Demeter that Hades—as Zeus's brother and ruler of one third of the universe—was not an unfit husband for Persephone.

Demeter refused to accept Hades as a suitable mate for her precious daughter. Enraged by the news of Persephone's abduction (and Zeus's possible complicity), she refused to return to Mount Olympus. Instead she roamed the earth in the guise of a mortal, forbidding the trees to bear fruit and the earth to nurture vegetables and herbs.

> **The More Things Change ...**
>
> The painful separation of mother and daughter has been a common theme in mythology from Greece to Indonesia. Carl Jung, the pioneering psychologist and scholar of mythology, saw in such tales the universal pain of this ordeal—for example, when a daughter marries. Recognizing this universality gave rise to Jung's notion of "archetypes."

After a full year of famine had plagued the earth, Zeus realized that if he allowed Demeter to persist, all of humankind would starve—leaving no one to honor and make offerings to the gods. Zeus sent a parade of gods and goddesses to Demeter to beg her to come back to Olympus and to restore fertility to the earth.

But Demeter refused to budge until her daughter stood by her side. Zeus had no choice: He relented, promising to bring Persephone back to her mother.

The Renewal of Spring

Hermes, summoned by Zeus, raced down to Hades to fetch Persephone. Hades shrugged compliantly and agreed to let her go. Persephone had not eaten a single thing—whether from sorrow, loss of appetite, or stubbornness—since her arrival in the Underworld. But before she left, Hades urged Persephone to appease her terrible hunger by eating a single pomegranate seed. Sadly, this apparent act of kindness was a trick: Anyone who tastes the food of Hades must remain in the Underworld.

The deed having been done, Rhea—the mother of Zeus, Demeter, and Hades—proposed a compromise that her children reluctantly accepted: Since Persephone had eaten there, she had to dwell at least part of every year in the Underworld. Rhea suggested that Persephone spend six months (or, according to some, three or four months) as Queen of the Underworld and the rest of the year with Demeter.

Mythed by a Mile _____

In another version of this story, Persephone innocently plucked some fruit from the trees in the gardens of Hades herself. To fight off her terrible hunger, she secretly ate seven pomegranate seeds. But a gardener of Hades had seen her and ratted her out to Hades. Persephone punished him for his indiscretion by turning him into a screech owl or Demeter punished him by burying him under an enormous rock.

After agreeing to the deal, Demeter restored Earth's fertility and returned to Olympus with Persephone. But when the time came for Persephone to return to the Underworld, the earth became colder and less fertile until her reemergence months later.

Since the abduction of Persephone, spring and summer have given way to autumn and winter, and the earth's fertility has followed the progression of seasons. In the fall, seeds—like Persephone herself—were buried underground. But in the spring, Persephone and the earth's crops came out into the sun once more.

Queen of the Underworld

Although she spent only half of her life in the Underworld, little is known of Persephone's life above ground after her abduction. Below ground, however, she was dreaded forever afterward as the goddess of the Underworld. So feared was she that mortals often invoked her name in curses.

Despite her forbidding image, Queen Persephone did sometimes show a capacity for mercy. When Alcestis offered her own life in place of her dying husband's, Persephone sent her back from the Underworld and spared them both. Persephone also exhibited strong maternal feelings when Aphrodite entrusted her with safeguarding the infant Adonis (see Chapter 7). Indeed, she became so enamored of the baby that she refused to give him back. (Zeus ultimately ruled that Adonis would spend one third of his life with Persephone, one third with Aphrodite, and one third with whomever he wished.)

Persephone had no children by Hades, but she remained faithful to him—and saw that he remained faithful to her. When Hades attempted to seduce Minthe, Persephone transformed the nymph into a fragrant mint plant. Similarly, she thwarted her husband's attempt to seduce Leuce by changing that nymph into a white poplar tree.

Read All About It _____

An alternative version of the story of Alcestis and her husband Admetus can be found in *Alcestis* by Euripides. In this drama, Heracles restores Alcestis to life by wrestling with Thanatos (Death).

Hades returned the favor when Peirithous journeyed to the Underworld in an attempt to abduct Persephone and bring her back to Earth as his bride. When Peirithous arrived with his friend Theseus and announced his intentions, Hades graciously offered the visitors a seat. The two sat down in the Chairs of Forgetfulness: stone seats that enveloped and intertwined with their naked flesh. Though Theseus was later freed by Heracles (see Chapter 13), Peirithous remained in the Underworld forever.

The Cunning Rogue: Sisyphus

If you could cheat death, would you? Most people would. But few have ever had the cunning of Sisyphus, the legendary rogue who cheated death not just once, but twice. Sisyphus ultimately paid a heavy price for his trickery: The reprieve he gained through his cunning was brief; the torture he suffered in the Underworld was eternal.

All in the Family

The son of Aeolus, king of Thessaly, Sisyphus was born heir to the throne. Sisyphus and one of his brothers, Salmoneus, hated each other, however, and Salmoneus took the throne of Thessaly from him.

Eventually Sisyphus would become a king—but never of Thessaly. The sorceress Medea (see Chapter 14) gave Sisyphus the throne of Ephyra, later known as Corinth. (Some say that Sisyphus earned the crown by founding the city, which he populated with people grown out of mushrooms.)

Sisyphus married Merope, the only one of the seven Pleiades (daughters of the Titan Atlas and Pleione) to have wedded a mortal rather than consorting with the gods. The couple would have three children: Glaucus, Ornytion, and Sinon.

Glaucus would inherit the throne of Ephyra, but would suffer a gruesome fate. A renowned horseman, Glaucus fed his mares on human flesh. Having whetted their appetites for flesh, Glaucus unwittingly served them up a full meal. After losing a chariot race, his mares tore Glaucus to pieces and ate him on the spot. For generations afterward, horses on Corinth seemed unusually skittish—haunted no doubt by the ghost of Glaucus.

Sinon would inherit his father's talent for trickery. Near the end of the Trojan War (see Chapter 16), Sinon allowed himself to be captured by the Trojans. His lies convinced Priam to bring the giant Wooden Horse into the heavily fortified city of Troy. The Greeks hidden inside the horse then launched a surprise attack and seized Troy.

No Honor Among Thieves

Sisyphus, called "the craftiest of men" by Homer, was extraordinarily clever. His ingenuity came in handy when Autolycus began grazing cattle near the herds of Sisyphus.

Autolycus was a notorious thief. He would steal anything he could get his hands on. But he always escaped detection because he could change the form or color of anything he stole. Horned cattle would lose their horns; brown cattle would become white.

Autolycus repeatedly stole cattle from Sisyphus's herd. Sisyphus noticed that cattle were missing—and that the herd of Autolycus seemed to be expanding in number—but could not prove any theft. In an attempt to catch Autolycus in the act, Sisyphus secretly marked the inside of the hooves of his cattle. (Some say he wrote the words "Stolen by Autolycus," while others maintain he wrote only the letters "SS.") The later discovery of his mark on cows in Autolycus's herd proved that his neighbor was a thief.

Sisyphus was not satisfied merely with proving Autolycus a thief and recovering his cattle. Seeking revenge, he seduced Anticleia, the daughter of Autolycus and later the mother of Odysseus (see Chapter 18). Given the cunning that Odysseus later demonstrated, many have suggested that Sisyphus, rather than Anticleia's husband Laertes, was his father.

This was not the only occasion when Sisyphus used an enemy's daughter in order to take revenge on the father. When he consulted the oracle at Delphi to find out how he might exact revenge on his hated brother, Salmoneus, he learned that if he had children by his brother's daughter, they would destroy their grandfather. Without a second thought, Sisyphus violated his beautiful niece Tyro. The oracle went unfulfilled, however, because Tyro, learning of the prophecy, killed both of her sons.

Cheating Death

In his time on Earth, Sisyphus killed, raped, and stole. The special place of Sisyphus in the lore of the Underworld, however, comes not from his ill treatment of his niece or other mortals, but from the application of his cunning in his relations with the gods.

His crimes against the gods began with Zeus. Asopus—a river god whose father was Poseidon—was looking for his daughter Aegina, who had disappeared. Sisyphus promised to tell Asopus what had happened to Aegina if the river god would create an eternal spring for Sisyphus's kingdom, Corinth. Once Asopus created this endless source of fresh water, Sisyphus named Zeus as Aegina's abductor. Enraged, Asopus pursued Zeus until the god's thunderbolts forced him to retreat.

Even though Zeus had in fact taken Aegina, to punish Sisyphus for his betrayal, Zeus sent Thanatos (Death) after him. Yet Sisyphus managed to outwit Death. He may have asked Thanatos to demonstrate how a pair of handcuffs worked and then locked them on Death himself or he may have used some other trickery to entrap Death in heavy chains. In any case, Death found himself a prisoner in Sisyphus's house.

With Death locked up, no one could die—no matter how gruesome the injuries suffered. The headless, bloodless, mortally wounded, and disease-torn continued to walk the earth, racked with pain and begging for release. Finally, the war god Ares set Death free and delivered Sisyphus to him.

Yet still, clever Sisyphus managed to elude his fate. Before descending to Hades, he instructed his wife Merope not to bury him, give him a funeral feast, perform any sacrifices to Hades or Persephone, or place a coin under his tongue (which was used to pay Charon, who ferried the dead for passage across the river Styx to the Underworld home of Hades). Sisyphus thus arrived at the Palace of Hades as an unburied pauper.

Appealing to Queen Persephone, Sisyphus told her that he had no right to be there. As one of the unburied, who had no fare for Charon, he should have been abandoned on the far side of the river Styx. Furthermore, Sisyphus argued, his wife's neglect of funeral ceremonies and sacrifices might set a bad example for other widows in the future.

What a Life!
Like his brother Sisyphus, Salmoneus also offended Zeus. After becoming king of Elis, Salmoneus demanded that his subjects call him Zeus. To add to the insult, Salmoneus mocked Zeus by driving his chariot through the city dragging bronze kettles to simulate thunder and throwing torches to simulate lightning. Zeus killed Salmoneus with a thunderbolt and reserved a special place for him in the Underworld: not far from his hated brother, Sisyphus.

Sisyphus pleaded for permission to return to the surface of the earth for just three days. This brief time would allow him to arrange for his funeral, to punish his wife for neglecting her duties, and to teach her respect for the lords of the Underworld. Persephone fell for his pleas and allowed Sisyphus to go home.

Sisyphus, of course, had no intention to return to the world of darkness. He reneged on his promise to descend again in three days. Indeed, he lived many more years until old age claimed him at last.

For his offenses to both Zeus and Hades, Sisyphus was condemned to eternal punishment in Tartarus, the lowest region of the Underworld. The king of Corinth would forever roll a massive boulder to the top of a steep hill. But his efforts were always in vain, for whenever Sisyphus neared the top, the rock would roll right back down again. Sisyphus was thus forced to start his labor all over again.

The Not-So-Heavenly Host: Tantalus

Sisyphus and Salmoneus were not the only ones who suffered eternal punishment for offending the gods. Condemned to a similar fate was Tantalus, a king of Sipylus (a mountainous region in Lydia) and the earliest ancestor of the tragic house of Atreus.

Tantalus was the son of Zeus and an Oceanid named Pluto (not the Roman god of the Underworld). Like Sisyphus, Tantalus married one of the Pleiades, Dione. The couple had three children, all of whom suffered tragic fates:

- *Niobe*, who would later marry Amphion, a king of Thebes, and make the mistake of boasting that she had more children—and what's more, better children—than the goddess Leto. To avenge this insult, Leto called on two of her children, the deities Apollo and Artemis, to kill all 12 of Niobe's offspring. The grief-stricken Niobe found herself forever unable to stop weeping, even after she returned from Thebes to Sipylus and her sorrow turned her to stone.

- *Broteas*, who when grown would refuse to honor Artemis. To punish him, the goddess drove Broteas mad. Thinking that he was invulnerable to flames, Broteas threw himself into a fire and died.

- *Pelops*, who committed no offense against the gods himself but would play an important part in his father's ill treatment of the gods.

> ### What a Life!
>
> Two other great sinners also suffered eternal torments. Ixion, named by Aeschylus as the first murderer "in history," killed his father-in-law and attempted to seduce Hera. In the Underworld, Ixion was lashed with serpents to a fiery wheel that never stopped turning. Tityus, a giant, attempted to rape Leto (see Chapter 7). After her children, Apollo and Artemis, killed him, the giant's body was nailed to the ground of Tartarus, where it covered nine acres. Tityus then suffered the same torment inflicted on Prometheus (see Chapter 2): Every day an eagle arrived to gnaw on his liver, which then grew back with each new moon.

Tantalus became an intimate and favorite of Zeus. The other gods, too, showed Tantalus extraordinary favor, inviting him to dine with them on Mount Olympus. But Tantalus proved himself unworthy of these honors.

Tantalus committed several crimes against the gods. First, while sitting as a guest on Mount Olympus, he stole ambrosia and nectar (the food and drink of the gods). He then served these divine treats to his mortal friends in order to impress them. Tantalus further abused the gods' hospitality by revealing divine secrets that Zeus had confided in him or that he had overheard in the conversations of the gods and goddesses.

Tantalus also stole a golden dog, one of Zeus's favorite pets. Or if he himself did not do it, Tantalus kept the dog hidden for the thief Pandareus—and then refused to give it up.

Though these crimes insulted the gods and betrayed their hospitality toward him, Tantalus committed an even worse offense. He invited the gods and goddesses to a feast of his own. Then, either as a test of their wisdom or simply because he feared he lacked enough food to offer them, Tantalus supplemented his pantry in a ghastly way. He killed his son Pelops, carved up the body, roasted the pieces, and served his son to the gods and goddesses in a stew.

His omniscient guests saw through this horrific trick and refused to eat the meal offered by Tantalus. The sole exception was Demeter, who—perhaps still addled by the loss of Persephone—ate a piece of Pelops's left shoulder. (Zeus later restored Pelops to life, while Demeter gave him a shoulder of ivory to replace the one she had eaten.)

To punish him for his criminal contempt of the gods and goddesses, Zeus killed Tantalus himself—crushing him under a crag of Mount Sipylus—and ruined his kingdom. Zeus then condemned Tantalus to eternal torment in Tartarus.

Hanging from the bough of a fruit tree, Tantalus was doomed to suffer from burning thirst and hunger. Although the tree's tantalizing fruit seemed within his reach, a wind would blow the boughs away from his desperate fingers whenever Tantalus attempted to grasp a piece. The bough on which Tantalus hung hovered over a pool of water. Though this water rose up to his waist and sometimes as high as his chin, it receded whenever he would bend his head to take a drink. To make matters even worse, an immense boulder forever loomed over his head, threatening to fall and crush Tantalus at any moment. The frustration of his hunger and thirst were punishment for his infamous banquet, while the hanging rock was the penalty for his theft of Zeus's dog.

Undying Love: Orpheus

Not all who visited the Underworld suffered eternal torment, but few ever returned happy. The saddest of all was the poet and lyrist Orpheus, perhaps the greatest of all the musicians in Greek mythology. The son of Apollo, the god of music and poetry, and Calliope, the muse of epic poetry, Orpheus became such a master of the lyre that his playing enchanted every living thing. His playing not only soothed the savage breast, taming the wildest of beasts, but moved all of nature as well. Rivers silenced their flowing, trees bent, and mountains moved—all in order to listen.

As a young man, Orpheus joined the voyage of Jason and the Argonauts (see Chapter 14). His playing was often all that kept the fractious crew from attacking one another. On the return voyage of the *Argo*, Orpheus did more than merely keep the peace. His lyre-playing saved the ship from the Sirens, bird-women who lured sailors to their destruction with hauntingly sweet songs. As the ship passed the island of Anthemoessa, off the coast of Italy, Orpheus drowned out the singing of the Sirens by playing loud and fast on his lyre. The confusion of sounds that resulted significantly reduced the allure of the Sirens.

Near the end of their voyage, when the *Argo* became stranded in Lake Tritonis, Orpheus suggested offering the gods the bronze tripod that Apollo had given him. In response to this offering, Triton (a son of Poseidon) appeared and guided them to the sea—and home.

Following Love to Hell and Back

When Orpheus returned to his homeland of Thrace, he fell deeply in love with a young girl named Eurydice, married her, and enjoyed a happiness that eclipsed all joy that had come before. Yet their marriage—and Orpheus's happiness—did not last long. A beekeeper named Aristaeus, a son of Apollo like Orpheus, lusted after Eurydice, too. Aristaeus soon attempted to ravish the girl. While fleeing from his advances, Eurydice stepped on a poisonous serpent, which bit her on the foot. Within minutes, Eurydice died from the wound.

Heartbroken, the mourning Orpheus found he could not live without his bride. He quickly resolved to do everything he could to bring her back from the Underworld. Carrying his lyre with him, Orpheus descended to the Underworld.

Even in the dark despair of the Underworld, the music of Orpheus proved enchanting. The ferryman Charon, the guard-dog Cerberus, and the three Judges of the Dead all let him pass. The spirits of the dead crowded around to hear Orpheus play and sing.

Even the damned received release from their tortures while he played. Sisyphus, for example, took a break from his labors and Tantalus forgot his hunger and thirst.

Orpheus's art softened Hades and Persephone, too. They agreed to restore Eurydice to life. There was a catch, however. As he traveled back to the surface of the earth, Orpheus was forbidden to turn and look back upon her even once—not until both of them were safe in the light of the sun.

Orpheus began the long ascent from the Underworld, and Eurydice silently followed the enchanting sound of his lyre. Several times, he feared she was no longer behind him, but resisted the temptation to look back. But as he caught the first glints of sunlight before him, Orpheus could contain his doubts no longer. He turned his head, only to see his beloved fade away, becoming a shade once again. Orpheus had lost Eurydice forever.

Life After Death

Orpheus tried to return once more to Hades, but found he could not pass that way again. Anguished, he returned to Earth.

Without Eurydice, Orpheus did not live long himself. He established a rite of sacrifice to his father, Apollo, hailing him as the greatest of all gods. Dionysus, angered by Orpheus's refusal to honor him, sent the maenads (his female devotees) to punish Orpheus. The raving maenads tore the musician to pieces—and then murdered their own husbands.

> **CAUTION**
>
> ### Mythed by a Mile
>
> Some taletellers insist that these women tore Orpheus apart not because they were inflamed by the vengeful Dionysus, but because each wanted him for herself and none would give up her claim. Others suggest that his continuing fidelity to Eurydice—and his renunciation of love forever—enraged the women of Thrace. Still others say that Orpheus gave his love solely to young boys—and for this reason the women tore him to pieces.

After the death of Orpheus, his mother and the other Muses collected the scattered pieces of his body. They buried all but the head in Pieria—Orpheus's birthplace and one of the chief haunts of the Muses. The head of Orpheus, still singing, and his lyre floated across the sea to the island of Lesbos. The people of Lesbos, who buried his head, were rewarded forever after with a gift for music. His lyre became part of the heavens: the constellation Lyra.

Mythed by a Mile _____

No, no, no! That's all wrong. The head of Orpheus, some tellers of the tale insist, indeed came to rest on the island of Lesbos. But unburied, it prophesied day and night, drawing worshippers away from Apollo's oracles, until that god, Orpheus's father, ordered the head to be silent forever more.

The Least You Need to Know

♦ Persephone, abducted by Hades, made the mistake of eating food while in the Underworld and had to remain as Hades' Queen for at least part of every year.

♦ The reappearance of Persephone each spring explains the renewal of Earth's fertility (ruled over by her mother Demeter).

♦ Sisyphus twice cheated Death and suffered the punishment of endlessly pushing a boulder up a hill.

♦ Tantalus offended the gods by serving them his son in a stew. He was condemned to eternal hunger and thirst despite being within reach of both food and water.

♦ Orpheus, whose enchanting music persuaded Hades and Persephone to release his wife from the Underworld, lost Eurydice forever because he could not resist the temptation to look back and make sure she was following him.

12

Even the Wisest Cannot See: Oedipus the King

In This Chapter

- ◆ The founding of Thebes and the ill fortune of the House of Cadmus
- ◆ The future foretold: Oedipus would kill his father and marry his mother
- ◆ How Oedipus came to Thebes and solved the riddle of the Sphinx
- ◆ The blind fulfillment of the prophecy
- ◆ The aftermath of tragedy: Oedipus's blinding and exile

The bare bones of the Oedipus story are familiar today to many people—even to those who know little of classical mythology: He killed his father and married his mother. Thanks to pioneering psychoanalyst Sigmund Freud, the story of Oedipus is in the twentieth century perhaps the best remembered of the classical hero myths.

Despite our familiarity with Oedipus and the notorious events of his life, few of us know the full story. Well, hang on: It's a tale of intrigue, deception, and family rivalries that spans generations and makes the Tony Sopranos and Michael Corleones of our world seem like children in a sandbox.

A House Divided: Oedipus's Ancestors

The story begins long before the tragic hero's birth. Thebes, the city that Oedipus would one day rule, had been founded by his great-great-grandfather, Cadmus.

Cadmus had come from Phoenicia to Greece in search of his sister Europa, whom Zeus had spirited away. At the site that would become Thebes, Cadmus met with a ferocious dragon that destroyed his army. Yet Cadmus ultimately defeated the dragon.

At the command of Athena, Cadmus then sowed the teeth of the dragon in the ground. At each spot where he planted a tooth, an armed warrior rose up out of the ground. The army of *Spartoi* ("sown men") seemed ready to attack when Cadmus, again at Athena's bidding, threw a stone into the crowd. In the chaos that followed, all but five of the warriors killed one another. The five Spartoi who survived allied themselves with Cadmus and helped him build the city of Thebes.

Cadmus—the city's first king—later married Harmonia, a daughter of Aphrodite (the goddess of love) and Ares (the god of war). The first rulers of Thebes had four daughters—Agave, Autonoe, Ino, and Semele—and one son: Polydorus. (See the following figure.)

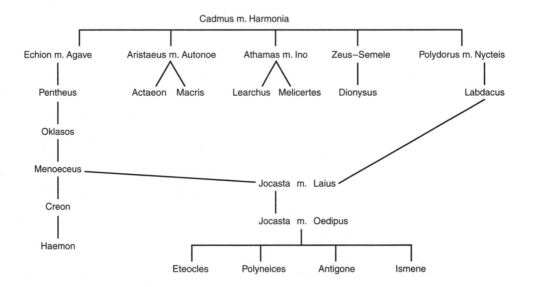

The House of Cadmus.

Watch Where You're Looking: The Heirs of Cadmus

The next two generations of the House of Cadmus did not fare well. Most suffered grave misfortune or, even worse, died horrible deaths:

♦ *Semele.* Semele became one of Zeus's many mistresses and conceived a son: Dionysus, the god of wine and revelry (see Chapter 9). Deceived by jealous Hera, Semele demanded that Zeus show himself to her in his true form. Awe-struck by the sight of the storm god, Semele was consumed by his lightning. (Zeus rescued the unborn Dionysus, however, carrying the child to term in his own thigh.)

♦ *Autonoe.* Autonoe had a son, Actaeon. A hunter, Actaeon came across the goddess of hunting, Artemis, and saw her bathing with her nymphs. Allowing a mortal to see her naked was something Artemis could not endure. She transformed the young man into a stag and his hounds ripped him to shreds and devoured him.

♦ *Ino.* Ino became the second wife of Athamas, king of Orchomenus. The couple had two sons and Ino had great ambitions for them. To clear their way to the throne, Ino plotted to kill her stepchildren: Phrixus and Helle. But Zeus saved these children by sending a golden, winged ram to carry them to safety. (For more on this ram and its "Golden Fleece," see Chapter 14.)

Ino and Athamas also earned Hera's wrath by honoring Zeus's request to care for their nephew: the god's son, Dionysus. To punish them, Hera drove Ino and Athamas mad. Athamas, under the delusion that his son was a deer (or a lion cub), killed one of their children with a bow and arrow. Ino plunged their other son into a boiling cauldron, then leaped with the boy into the sea. (The two then became sea deities: Leucothea and Palaemon.)

♦ *Agave.* Agave married Echion, one of the surviving Spartoi. They had a son, Pentheus, whom his grandfather Cadmus chose to succeed him as king of Thebes.

Read All About It

In his tragedy *The Bacchae*—which tells the tale of Pentheus and Agave—Euripides points out the parallels between their punishment and the fate of Actaeon at several crucial moments during the play.

Agave and her son made the mistake of offending Dionysus by denying that he was a god. Pentheus made matters worse by forbidding the women of Thebes from taking part in the wild rites held in Dionysus's honor. To punish them both, Dionysus drove

Agave mad and tricked Pentheus into spying on a Dionysian festival open only to women. When they caught Pentheus, the revelers, deluded into believing he was a mountain lion, ferociously tore the king apart. Like his cousin Actaeon and his aunt Semele, Pentheus had suffered a gruesome death brought on by witnessing something he should never have seen.

The Sins of the Father

Two generations later, Laius—a great-grandson of Cadmus and Harmonia—should have ascended to the throne. But usurpers forced the young boy to run away to Olympia, site of the future Olympic Games. After he grew to manhood, Laius returned to Thebes to reclaim the throne.

Yet before he left Olympia, Laius betrayed King Pelops—and the hospitality the monarch had shown in welcoming the boy into his home. Laius had become enamored with Chrysippus, Pelops's illegitimate son. Laius kidnapped the boy, bringing him to Thebes to serve as his sexual plaything. Chrysippus soon killed himself to escape his shame.

> **Mythed by a Mile**
>
> Some storytellers contend that Hippodameia, Pelops's wife, spurred two of her sons, Atreus and Thyestes, to go to Thebes and kill Chrysippus to prevent Pelops from naming the boy as his successor. Others suggest that Hippodameia killed the boy herself, using Laius's sword after creeping into his bedchamber at night. Laius escaped punishment because Chrysippus named his stepmother as his murderer with his dying breath.

As king of Thebes, Laius married within the House of Cadmus. His wife Jocasta (called Epicasta by Homer and others) was the daughter of Menoeceus, a Theban noble descended from Agave and Echion.

Laius and Jocasta remained childless for many years. Troubled by this misfortune, Laius decided to consult the oracle at Delphi for a cure.

The oracle offered Laius no cure. Instead, he heard a warning: Have no child by this bride, for if you do, that child will kill you. Three times the oracle cautioned that a child of Laius would bring ruin not only upon his father, but on the city of Thebes as well.

Laius took this warning to heart. He quickly came to regard his childlessness not as a curse, but as a blessing. To guard against the possibility of begetting a child, Laius ceased having sexual relations with Jocasta altogether. Sadly, though, he never told her why.

Jocasta was not pleased. Whether impelled by maternal desire or amorousness, Jocasta contrived to get Laius drunk on wine one night. She then brought him into her bed, where the two conceived a son: Oedipus.

Exile and Triumphant Return

The only son of Laius and Jocasta was not well loved by his father. Fearful of the prophecy of doom for himself and his city, Laius and Jocasta (who now knew the secret) pierced the infant's feet with an iron spike and gave the baby to the king's shepherds, who were instructed to leave him exposed on Mount Cithaeron.

Abandonment and Adoption

The shepherds, pitying the defenseless child, disobeyed their king and queen. They saved the child and presented him to Periboea, the childless wife of Polybus, king of Corinth.

 Mythed by a Mile _____

According to one tale spinner, the shepherds neither saved the baby nor left him on the mountaintop. Instead, they put the child in a chest and threw it into the sea. The chest soon washed up to shore near Corinth, where Periboea (also called Merope) was overseeing her servants as they did the royal laundry. The servants were too busy to notice the child, but Periboea found him, hid herself and the child in a thicket, and pretended to give birth. The queen told the truth about the baby's arrival only to her husband, Polybus.

No matter how the baby came to Periboea and Polybus, the Corinthian rulers welcomed him, named him *Oedipus*, and vowed to rear the child as their own. So Oedipus, like his father before him, grew up in exile—with the important distinction that Oedipus was entirely ignorant of his parentage.

After growing to adulthood, Oedipus, like Laius, received a warning from the oracle at Delphi. One night, a drunk taunted Oedipus for not resembling his father. Perhaps, the

 Logos _____

Oedipus means Swollen Foot—a name that derives from the wounds on the tragic hero's feet.

lout suggested, Oedipus was not really Polybus's son. Distraught by this thought, Oedipus traveled to Delphi to consult the oracle about his true parentage. But Oedipus never had a chance to pose his question. The Pythia, Apollo's prophetess, drove him from the shrine, shrieking that he would murder his father and marry his mother. His presence would defile the shrine.

Horrified by this prophecy, Oedipus headed toward the east, as far from Corinth as possible. Not knowing that the couple who had raised him and whom he loved so dearly were not really his parents, Oedipus vowed never again to see Periboea and Polybus.

In his ignorance, Oedipus headed straight for Thebes.

At the Crossroads

Meanwhile, back in Thebes, Laius was preoccupied with forebodings of his own. The Sphinx, a monster, was devouring the citizens of Thebes. In addition, Laius had recently learned of omens foretelling that, despite his ill treatment of his infant son, the king of Thebes had not escaped his fate.

Once again, Laius set out in his chariot for Delphi. Some say he went as the king—to ask the oracle how to get rid of the Sphinx who was terrorizing his city. Others suggest he went as a man—to seek further information on how he might avoid his fate.

As Laius's chariot approached a crossroads where the narrow road split—one road leading to Delphi, the other to Daulis—the king's party saw a solitary man traveling on foot.

Read All About It

The most fully realized version of the Oedipus myth can be found in three of Sophocles' plays: *Antigone, Oedipus Tyrannus* (called *Oedipus Rex* in Latin or *Oedipus the King* in English), and *Oedipus at Colonus.* The plays, written over the span of about 37 years, show Sophocles' enduring interest in this mythic cycle.

"Step aside!" the charioteer shouted. "Make room for those better than you!"

But the young man—Oedipus himself, of course—refused to give way to let the chariot pass. He insisted that no one—save the gods and his own parents—was better than he.

As the chariot passed, Laius or one of his servants struck the stranger on the head or a wheel banged against the young man's foot—or both.

In any case, the young man became enraged. He furiously pulled Laius from the chariot and beat him, the charioteer, and all but one of his servants to death with a stick.

Entirely unaware that the dreaded fate he had tried to avoid for so long had now come to pass, Laius died at the hands of this stranger, his son. Equally unaware, Oedipus left the dead where they lay. Laius was later buried with his attendants at this spot.

Trying to avoid their fate, both Laius and Oedipus had run headlong into it—and into each other—at the crossroads.

> **Mythed by a Mile**
>
> Who was really at fault at the crossroads? Sophocles—the most renowned teller of this tale—points a finger at the arrogance of Laius, who scorned the anonymous wayfarer. Other storytellers point to the arrogance of Oedipus, who refused to make room for the king.

Riddle Me This

Without a clue that he had already fulfilled the first part of the oracle, Oedipus continued on to Thebes. When he arrived, he found the city at the mercy of the Sphinx. A monster who had the head of a woman, the body of a lion, the tail of a serpent, and the wings of an eagle, the Sphinx was devouring the young men of the city. Hera had sent the monster to punish the House of Cadmus, perhaps for Laius's abduction of Chrysippus.

Perched on nearby Mount Phicium—or, according to some, on the citadel's walls or on a pillar in the city's marketplace—the Sphinx tormented the Thebans with a riddle:

"What creature walks on four legs in the morning, two at midday, and three in the evening?"

Whoever answered the riddle of the Sphinx correctly, the oracle had foretold, would set the city free from the Sphinx. Unfortunately, whoever answered the riddle incorrectly was immediately strangled and devoured by the ravenous Sphinx—and no one had yet solved the riddle.

> **The More Things Change ...**
>
> Myths involving riddles have occurred in many cultures through the ages. In the famous fairy tale "Rumpelstiltskin," the Brothers Grimm tell of a magical dwarf who would claim the firstborn child of a queen if she could not guess his rather peculiar name. Through luck and quick wits, the queen discovered the name and the little man was destroyed with rage when she solved his "riddle." So, too, the Sphinx destroyed herself when her riddle was solved.

Just before Oedipus entered Thebes, the Sphinx had eaten Haemon, the son of Creon and nephew of Jocasta. (Creon, Jocasta's brother, was serving as regent of Thebes while his in-law King Laius was "away" at Delphi.)

Shortly after Oedipus arrived, the news came that King Laius and his attendants had been slain. Yet the city could spare no one to seek out and bring the murderer to justice. The Sphinx posed a much more immediate problem.

Creon, grieving over the deaths of both his son and his brother-in-law, offered up a handsome reward to anyone who could defeat the Sphinx. The solver of the riddle would win the hand of his sister, the recently widowed Jocasta, and a share in the kingdom of Thebes.

Oedipus volunteered to try and save the city. His answer to the riddle of the Sphinx? "Man—who crawls in his infancy, walks upright in his prime, and leans on a cane in his old age." The enraged monster—furious that someone had solved her riddle—threw herself from her perch to her death.

Hail the Conquering Hero

Oedipus was hailed as a hero in his new hometown. As Creon had promised, the riddle-solver won the hand of Jocasta and was acclaimed king of Thebes. The one man who had seen the answer to the Sphinx's riddle and won praise as the cleverest of all men was blind to the fact that he had married his mother, fulfilling the entire prophecy of the oracle at Delphi.

The one attendant who survived the death of Laius might have identified Oedipus as his master's killer. When he returned to Thebes, the servant recognized King Oedipus. Fearing the new king's power as well as the bloody rage he had already witnessed, the servant invented the tale that Laius and his retinue had been slain by several highwaymen (robbers who preyed upon travelers). To escape recognition himself, the servant then asked to be given the duties of a shepherd far from the city.

The Blind Leading the Blind

Oedipus ruled Thebes—or as some narrators tell it, shared rule with Jocasta and Creon, the only *known* descendents of Cadmus—for perhaps two decades. As ruler, Oedipus enjoyed the blessings of fame, fortune, and power.

With Jocasta, Oedipus had four children: two sons named Eteocles and Polyneices and two daughters named Antigone and Ismene. The king would not discover until much later that he was not only father, but also brother to these children.

After 20 years or so, a great plague descended upon Thebes. Crops and livestock suffered from blight, women stopped bearing children, and a deadly pestilence swept across the land. Oedipus sent the aged Creon to Delphi to find out the cause of this plague.

Creon returned with word that the city was suffering because the murderer of Laius still lived unpunished among them. Oedipus—cursing Laius's unknown murderer and promising to banish him upon discovery—ordered an immediate investigation of the ancient crime.

Oedipus immediately sent for aged Teiresias, a blind seer. Teiresias told Oedipus that the plague would end only if a sown man (one of the descendents of the Spartoi) died for the city. Menoeceus, Jocasta's father and great-grandson of Echion, threw himself from the city's walls and earned the praise of all Thebans for his sacrifice and devotion to the city.

What a Life!

One legend holds that Teiresias, too, was blinded for seeing what he should not have seen. As Actaeon had, Teiresias stumbled upon a bathing goddess: Athena. After Athena blinded Teiresias by laying her hands over his eyes, his mother, who served as one of Athena's attendants, appealed to the goddess for mercy. Athena acquiesced, commanding the serpent Erichthonius to clean Teiresias's ears with its tongue. This treatment gave the blind man the ability to interpret the language of prophetic birds.

Teiresias then announced that though the plague would indeed end, the gods had expected the sacrifice not of Menoeceus, but of Menoeceus's grandson, who had killed his father and married his mother. Evidence of Oedipus's true identity and his guilt began to come to light. According to various sources, these included:

- The testimony of the shepherd charged with leaving Laius's infant son on a mountaintop, who confessed that he hadn't done so.

- A letter from Periboea that confided the details of Oedipus's adoption.

- The testimony of the attendant who had survived the attack on Laius, who confirmed that Oedipus was indeed the murderer.

Confronted with these facts, Oedipus (and Jocasta) could no longer deny the truth: Wife and husband were truly mother and son. And the son had murdered the father.

A Tainted Legacy: The Curse of Oedipus

The verdict having been reached, all that remained was the sentencing. Jocasta, learning that she had married and bedded her own son, hanged herself.

> **Mythed by a Mile**
>
> In *The Phoenician Women*, Euripides placed Jocasta's suicide much later than the discovery that her husband was her son. Euripides contended that Oedipus's sons, Eteocles and Polyneices, imprisoned him when they grew to adulthood. They had hoped that their fortunes would remain intact if the crime and scandal were forgotten. But during the war of the Seven Against Thebes, the two brothers battled each other to the death. Upon discovering her son's bodies, the distraught Jocasta picked up one of their swords and killed herself. Creon then banished Oedipus to lift the curse from the city.

Appalled by his own actions and disgusted by his figurative blindness, Oedipus used the pin of one of Jocasta's brooches to jab out his eyes, literally blinding himself. Creon then carried out the sentence that Oedipus himself had imposed: banishment of Laius's killer. When his two sons (and brothers) refused to oppose his exile, the departing Oedipus cursed them.

The Curse Becomes a Blessing

An outcast and a beggar, Oedipus wandered for years accompanied only by his loyal daughter (and sister) Antigone. Because his awful fate horrified everyone he met, he was expelled from every city he visited. Finally, the wandering pair arrived at Colonus, a country region in Athenian territory, the threshold of both Athens and the Underworld.

Oedipus determined to end his wanderings here. Oedipus knew that the site of his burial would be a defense to the land in which it lay. For when a great man—a hero—died, his power always went back into the soil in which he was buried.

Each of his sons, Eteocles and Polyneices, wanted to bring Oedipus back to Thebes to serve his own purposes in the struggle to succeed their father. Oedipus refused his self-serving sons and chose to remain—and die—in Athens.

King Theseus of Athens granted Oedipus the refuge that every other city had denied him. So though he had spent his life as a curse to the city of Thebes, Oedipus ended his life as a blessing to the city of Athens.

The Sins of the Father—Part II

After their father's banishment, Polyneices and Eteocles were named co-rulers of Thebes. The brothers agreed to alternate their years of reign. At the end of the first year, however, Eteocles refused to give up the throne. Instead, he accused Polyneices of having an evil bent, and banished him from the city.

The battle of brother against brother fulfilled the curse of Oedipus. Polyneices took refuge in Argos, where he married the daughter of King Adrastus. Supported by six mighty warriors from Argos, Polyneices led an army back to Thebes to reclaim his throne. This bloody war became known as the Seven Against Thebes.

Read All About It

The war of the Seven Against Thebes is drama- tized in great detail in both *The Phoenician Women* by Euripides and *Seven Against Thebes* by Aeschylus. Sophocles relates the aftermath of this war in *Antigone*.

After most of the Argive champions had died on the battlefield, Polyneices offered to decide the contest for the throne in a hand-to-hand battle with his brother. In the struggle, each mortally wounded the other.

Following the deaths of Eteocles and Polyneices, their uncle Creon ruled once again. Creon denied the rites of burial to Polyneices and the city's attackers. According to Sophocles, the ever-loyal Antigone disobeyed the new king's orders and either cere- moniously sprinkled dirt over the corpse of Polyneices or built a funeral pyre for him. Creon then ordered his son Haemon (who was apparently *not* devoured by the Sphinx in this version) to bury Antigone alive in the tomb of her brother Eteocles.

Instead Haemon secretly married Antigone and sent her to live among his shepherds. Years later, Creon recognized a young boy as Haemon's son. (All the descendents of Cadmus had the mark of a serpent on their bodies.) Infuriated by Haemon's disobedi- ence, Creon sentenced his newly discovered grandson to death. Upon hearing this news, Antigone hanged herself. Haemon then discovered his beloved's corpse and killed himself with his sword. This ended the tragic saga of the House of Cadmus.

The Least You Need to Know

- ◆ Many descendents of Cadmus, founder of the city of Thebes, suffered horrible deaths because they had seen things that should not be seen.

- ◆ Oedipus unknowingly fulfilled the prophecy of the oracle at Delphi by killing his father, Laius, and marrying his mother, Jocasta.

◆ Oedipus's greatest victory—solving the riddle and defeating the Sphinx—led directly to his marriage to Jocasta and his downfall.

◆ After discovering what he had done, Oedipus blinded himself and doomed himself to a life as a tormented outcast.

◆ The cursed sons of Oedipus took arms against each other in the war of the Seven Against Thebes. The brothers died at each other's hands.

Chapter **13**

The Labors of Heracles

In This Chapter

- ◆ The conception, birth, and early days of Heracles
- ◆ The madness of Heracles
- ◆ The 12 labors of Heracles
- ◆ The further adventures of Heracles
- ◆ The death of Heracles—and his ascent to Mount Olympus

If you saw the 1997 Disney movie called *Hercules*, forget almost everything you think you know about the hero (called Heracles by the Greeks). Disney skipped virtually all of the labors of Heracles, gave him at least one new parent, reduced his many teachers to one, limited him to just one wife (and no concubines), and ignored his tragic death altogether.

What's more, Hollywood created a new villain for the piece, an archenemy who conforms more closely to our current conceptions of Satan: Hades. This casting of the villain gave the climactic battle that pitted Hercules and the gods against Hades and the Titans (rather than the Giants) more echoes of Milton's *Paradise Lost* than of classical mythology.

Virtually the only element of the Heracles myth that Disney depicted faithfully was the overall theme: The story of Heracles centers on a hero who gains immortality through accomplishments in the mortal sphere.

The Wonder Years: The Birth and Youth of Heracles

Like so many Greek heroes, Heracles was a son of Zeus by a mortal woman. Alcmene, the daughter of King Electryon of Argos, married her cousin Amphitryon. (Electryon and Alcaeus, Amphitryon's father, were sons of the hero Perseus: see Chapter 10.) Before they could consummate their marriage, however, Amphitryon accidentally killed his father-in-law. His uncle Sthenelus accused Amphitryon of murder and forced him into exile.

Alcmene fled to Thebes with her husband, but refused to share his bed until he had avenged the murder of her eight brothers by pirates. Amphitryon gladly did so. But as Amphitryon journeyed homeward after his victory, Zeus impersonated him, told Alcmene in great detail how "he" had avenged her brothers and took her to bed. Zeus had the sun god Helius unharness his chariot for a day. So the world remained dark an extra 24 hours, and Zeus romanced Alcmene for the length of a 36-hour night.

When Amphitryon arrived home the following evening, his wife's lack of ardor disappointed him. Alcmene, for her part, grew impatient at hearing her husband recount the same stories "he" had told her the night before. Puzzled, Amphitryon consulted the blind seer, Teiresias, who told them what had happened. Since Zeus had deceived Alcmene, Amphitryon quickly forgave her for her unwitting adultery. Indeed, after his first night home, Amphitryon—fearful of inciting Zeus to jealousy—never slept with his wife again.

The Labors of Alcmene

Just before Heracles was born, Zeus boasted on Olympus that a son of his blood would be born that day who would rule over the House of Perseus. The always jealous Hera, who knew of her husband's tryst with Alcmene, made Zeus swear to this boast.

Thwarting Zeus's plans, Hera arranged with Eileithyia, the goddess of childbirth, to delay Alcmene's delivery. Eileithyia sat outside Alcmene's bedroom with her legs and fingers tightly crossed and her clothing tied into knots, a charm that effectively blocked the delivery. Meanwhile Hera hastened the labor of Nicippe, the wife of

King Sthenelus, who had driven his nephew Amphitryon from Argos. As the grand-son of Perseus (see Chapter 10), this premature child, Eurystheus, was indeed a son of Zeus's blood. Reluctantly, Zeus kept his vow to make this child the ruler of Argos, Tiryns, and Mycenae.

Zeus then enlisted the aid of Athena to trick Hera into suckling the infant Heracles. Athena "found" the infant Heracles outside the walls of Thebes, where Alcmene had abandoned him in fear of Hera's jealousy. Athena showed the child to Hera and urged the goddess to pity the beautiful child so cruelly neglected. Without thinking, Hera bared her breast to the baby, but Heracles sucked with such force that she tore him from her breast. (The milk that spurted across the sky became the Milky Way.)

> **What a Life!**
>
> Iphicles was born on the same day as his more famous half-brother Heracles. Alcmene and her husband had conceived Iphicles on the night Amphitryon returned home—the night after Alcmene and Zeus had con-ceived Heracles.

The suckling of the infant Heracles apparently awoke none of Hera's maternal instincts. She would remain for the rest of Heracles' life a hostile stepmother. Still jealous of Alcmene, the goddess sent two poisonous serpents with flaming eyes to destroy both Heracles and his half-brother Iphicles. Yet the mighty infant seized one in each hand and easily strangled the serpents.

Training a Hero

Zeus had it in mind to rear a son who would have the strength and skills to become not only a hero among men, but an ally and agent of the gods as well. So the god arranged for Heracles to receive training in the skills of warfare and the finer arts from some of the best teachers on Earth.

As a young man, Heracles mastered the teachings of:

- *Amphitryon*, his foster father, who taught him how to drive a chariot
- *Autolycus*, the notorious thief, who taught him boxing
- *Castor*, a renowned horseman, who tutored Heracles not only in combat strategy and cavalry tactics, but the art of fencing as well
- *Cheiron*, perhaps the only Centaur (half-human, half-horse) who had a reputa-tion for tenderness, refinement, and wisdom, who taught him manners, deco-rum, and other polite arts

♦ *Eumolpus*, founder of the *Eleusinian Mysteries*, who schooled the young hero in both singing and playing the lyre

♦ *Eurytus*, a renowned bowman, who taught him archery

♦ *Linus*, son of Ismenius (a river god), who introduced him to literature

 Logos _____

The **Eleusinian Mysteries** were the most renowned religious rites of the ancient world. The mysteries, developed in the town of Eleusis outside Athens, included rituals, purification rites, fasts, and dramatizations of the story of Demeter and Persephone (see Chapter 11). Participation in these mysteries guaranteed safe passage to and happiness in the next world. Exactly what was involved in these rites remains, well, a mystery, for severe penalties awaited any who revealed the details of the ceremony.

Linus also had the ill fate to substitute for Eumolpus in teaching Heracles the lyre. The two tutors differed in teaching methods, however, and when Heracles refused to heed his substitute's instruction, Linus made the mistake of striking his formidable student. Enraged, Heracles smashed his lyre over Linus's head, killing him with a single blow.

In his trial for murder, Heracles argued that he had merely responded in kind to his tutor's violence, and won acquittal. Yet Amphitryon, fearful of further incidents of violence, sent the young man to finish his training at a cattle farm in the country.

Heracles learned his lessons well. He soon became the best archer who ever lived, and rarely missed the mark when throwing a spear, too.

Having received the best training available, Heracles was outfitted for warfare by a half-dozen Olympian benefactors:

♦ Zeus offered an unbreakable shield forged by Hephaestus, the god of fire and patron of blacksmiths and artisans.

♦ Athena provided a helmet and coat of arms.

♦ Apollo gave him a bow and a quiver of eagle-feathered arrows.

♦ Hermes presented him with a sword.

♦ Hephaestus provided a golden breastplate and brass buskins (protective footwear).

♦ Poseidon, the creator of horses, entrusted him with a magnificent team of horses.

Divinely equipped and fully trained, Heracles was now ready to become the greatest hero of the ancient world. Yet the road to immortality would prove long and arduous.

Marriage, Madness, and Murder

Though Heracles had not yet accomplished much, King Thespius of Thespia recognized the young hero's potential. With an eye toward a future dynasty, he resolved that each of his 50 daughters would have a child by Heracles. In a single night, Heracles impregnated 49 of the 50 daughters with 51 sons (the eldest and youngest daughter had twins). One daughter refused to take part in this marathon of love-making, and she remained a virgin throughout her life, serving as a priestess in the temple of Heracles at Thespia. Many Greeks consider this feat of procreation the "13th labor" of Heracles, as formidable in its way as the 12 labors that followed it.

Mythed by a Mile

Some say that Thespius resorted to trickery to get Heracles to sire his grandchildren. Heracles remained a guest in Thespius's home for seven weeks. To make his guest's stay a happier one, Thespius hospitably offered his "eldest" daughter to lie with Heracles. Each night, however, the king sent a different daughter to Heracles' bed, and in this way accomplished his aim.

After attending to the daughters of Thespius, Heracles headed home to Thebes. Along the way, he met a group of Minyans, the noble clan that ruled the city of Orchomenus—and, at this time, Thebes as well. Several years earlier, a Theban had accidentally killed the king of Orchomenus. In retribution, the Minyans had forced Thebes to pay an annual tribute of 100 cattle.

The Minyans, on their way to collect this tribute, scoffed that the Thebans were lucky that Erginus, king of Orchomenus, had not cut off all of their ears, noses, and hands in punishment. Heracles immediately chopped off the messengers' ears, noses, and hands, hung these severed parts around their necks, and sent them back to Erginus.

Knowing Erginus would retaliate, Heracles quickly gathered together an army of Thebans. Led by Heracles, this army not only successfully defended Thebes and repelled the Minyans, but also killed Erginus and captured the city of Orchomenus.

Creon, king of Thebes, rewarded Heracles for his heroism by offering him his eldest daughter, Megara. But Hera's hostility toward Heracles had not waned; she would not allow him a happy life. The goddess drove Heracles mad, and he killed his children—and perhaps Megara—thinking they were either wild beasts or enemies of Thebes.

The Labors of Heracles

When his sanity returned, Heracles exiled himself from Thebes for his crime. He traveled to Delphi to ask the oracle how best to atone for his crime. The Pythia, the priestess of the oracle, instructed Heracles to go to Tiryns and perform any 10 labors devised for him by King Eurystheus. (This number would grow to 12 when Eurystheus later nit-picked about whether Heracles had truly completed 2 of the labors assigned to him.)

By successfully completing these labors, Heracles would not only pay for his crime, but also achieve immortality and take his place among the gods.

Reluctantly, Heracles agreed to submit to the will of the hated Eurystheus, to whom Hera had given the throne that Zeus had intended for Heracles.

Beastly Chores: The First Four Labors

When Heracles reported to Eurystheus at Tiryns, the king assigned him his first labor: the killing of the Nemean lion. This beast would provide a great challenge for the young hero, because its invulnerable skin could not be pierced with either stone or metal.

After traveling to Nemea, a region of the northeastern Peloponnesus, Heracles found his arrows, his sword, and his club useless, and so was forced to engage in hand-to-paw combat. After sealing off one entrance to the lion's two-mouthed cave, Heracles entered the other unarmed. He wrestled the beast to the ground, wrapped his mighty arms around it, and squeezed the lion until it choked to death.

Using the lion's own claws to cut off its skin, Heracles fashioned a cloak from its invulnerable hide and a helmet from its head. Returning triumphantly to Tiryns, he so frightened Eurystheus with this get-up that the king ordered him to leave all future trophies outside the city's gates. Eurystheus then had a large, bronze jar forged and buried it in the earth. Thereafter, whenever Heracles approached, the cowardly Eurystheus hid in this jar and had a messenger relay his next orders to the hero.

Eurystheus directed Heracles to kill the Lernaean Hydra (water snake) as his second labor. A child of the monsters Typhon and Echidna—whom Apollodorus credits with begetting the Sphinx and the Nemean lion as well—the Hydra had a huge dog-like body and many serpentine heads (some say as few as seven; others claim 10,000), one of which was immortal. The beast was so deadly that even its breath was poisonous.

Heracles arrived quickly in Lerna, a coastal town just south of Argos. The hero first tried a straightforward attack, holding his breath and hacking off the Hydra's heads with his sword or crushing them with his club. His attack only made the monster more deadly, for when one head was destroyed, two more grew in its place. Heracles ultimately defeated the beast by calling on his friend and charioteer Iolaus (the son of the hero's half-brother, Iphicles) to sear each new wound with burning branches. This checked the flow of blood and prevented the growing of new heads. Heracles then slew the beast by chopping off its immortal head and burying the still-hissing head under a rock.

Before returning to Tiryns, Heracles dipped his arrows in the poisonous blood of the Hydra. Thereafter, anyone wounded with one of these arrows would die.

Unfortunately, Eurystheus refused to credit him with accomplishing this labor since, although Heracles had defeated the Hydra, he had relied on the help of Iolaus to complete it. Eurystheus next commanded Heracles to capture the Erymanthian boar. This savage beast haunted Arcadia in central Peloponnesus near Mount Erymanthus, a mountain sacred to Artemis.

On his way to Arcadia, Heracles accepted the hospitality of a Centaur named Pholus. When Pholus offered the Centaurs' communal wine to his guest, the other Centaurs smelled the strong wine and went mad. Heracles killed many of the attacking Centaurs and drove the rest to a new home on Mount Malea, where their king Cheiron lived.

One of Heracles' arrows, however, passed through his intended victim and struck his old friend and teacher, Cheiron. Though Cheiron was immortal, the poisoned arrow brought so much pain that the king of the Centaurs wished he were dead. (The Titan Prometheus [see Chapter 2] later assumed the burden of Cheiron's immortality so that the Centaur could go to Hades.)

The poisonous arrows of Heracles soon claimed another of his friends as a victim. His kindly host Pholus was examining them when he dropped one on his foot and died instantly.

Heracles once again set out for Mount Erymanthus. There, he trapped the vicious boar in deep snow, captured it with chains, and brought it back alive.

For his fourth labor, Heracles was ordered to capture the Ceryneian hind alive. A wonderful deer with golden antlers and brass hoofs, this hind roamed the hills of Ceryneia between Arcadia and Achaea, in central

Mythed by a Mile

One version of this myth says that Heracles shot an arrow with such skill that it pierced both of the deer's forelegs, pinning them together without drawing a single drop of blood. Then he carried the hind back to Tiryns.

Peloponnesus. Because the hind was sacred to Artemis, the goddess of hunting, Heracles hoped to capture it unharmed.

Heracles pursued the deer for a full year. He then either netted the beast or seized it while it slept. While returning to Tiryns with the deer on his shoulders, Heracles met Artemis and Apollo. Artemis chastised Heracles, but let him pass with her sacred deer when he insisted that it was Eurystheus, the man who had ordered him to complete this task, who bore the blame for this insult.

> **What a Life!**
>
> A beautiful young man, Hylas was the son of Theiodamas, king of the Dryopes. Heracles killed Theiodamas when the king refused him the gift of an ox. Infatuated with the son of his victim, however, Heracles carried Hylas away with him, making the boy his servant and lover.

Heracles then took a sabbatical from his labors to join Jason on his quest for the Golden Fleece (see Chapter 14). The Argonauts asked him to be their captain, but Heracles properly deferred to Jason. Heracles quit the voyage before long, however. When the *Argo* (Jason's ship) stopped in Mysia, on the northwestern coast of Asia Minor, nymphs of the spring, infatuated with Heracles' squire and lover Hylas, dragged the boy down into the water. While Heracles searched in vain for Hylas, the *Argo* left without him.

Even More Beastly Chores: The Second Four Labors

Heracles once again returned to Tiryns. The fifth labor that Eurystheus assigned was to rid Lake Stymphalus in Arcadia of its vast flocks of man-eating birds. The crane-sized Stymphalian birds had claws, beaks, and wings of bronze. The voracious birds killed both men and beasts by showering them with bronze feathers and poisonous excrement.

With the assistance of Athena, who lent him a pair of bronze castanets forged by Hephaestus, Heracles drove the birds far away from Arcadia. The noise of the clattering castanets frightened the birds, who flew as one into the air. Heracles shot a great many of them, while the others quickly fled the scene.

Perhaps to humiliate Heracles, Eurystheus assigned as his sixth labor the noxious task of cleaning the stables of Augeas, king of Elis. The stables, which housed thousands of head of cattle, had not been cleaned for 30 years. The dung from these beasts had created a pestilence and made the pastures of the Peloponnesus infertile.

Heracles agreed to clean all the dung off the land in a single day. But first he arranged with Augeas for a payment of one tenth of his herd for doing the dirty job. He completed the task without soiling himself a bit by diverting the course of two rivers,

Alpheus and Peneus, to wash away the filth of nearly 100,000 cattle-years. The rivers not only swept away the dung from Augeas's stables, but cleaned the outlying pastures as well.

The More Things Change …

American tall tales featuring such frontier heroes as Paul Bunyan and Pecos Bill recall Heracles' heroic feats of strength. Just as Heracles changed the course of two rivers to clean Augeas's stables, the giant Paul Bunyan—with the help of his enormous blue ox, Babe—stretched and straightened the rivers of Minnesota to make it easier to send felled trees downstream. Similarly, some storytellers claim that Pecos Bill used a lasso to straighten out the Rio Grande. Such myths often help explain natural features of a region's geographical landscape.

Unfortunately, Heracles found himself in a double-bind. Augeas refused to pay what he had promised, insisting that Heracles already had a duty to perform this labor for Eurystheus. To make matters worse, Eurystheus refused to credit Heracles for this labor, contending that he had done it as a job for hire.

Perhaps tiring of how quickly Heracles had completed his first six labors, all of which had been confined to the Peloponnesus, Eurystheus began assigning him tasks that would send him far away from Tiryns.

The seventh labor sent Heracles to Crete to capture the Cretan bull, the father of the Minotaur by Pasiphaë, wife of King Minos (see Chapter 15). A beautiful yet terrifying beast, the Cretan bull spit flames and was ravaging the crops and orchards of Crete.

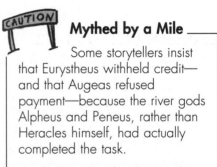

Mythed by a Mile

Some storytellers insist that Eurystheus withheld credit—and that Augeas refused payment—because the river gods Alpheus and Peneus, rather than Heracles himself, had actually completed the task.

Heracles captured the beast after a lengthy struggle. He brought it all the way back across the sea to Tiryns. After allowing Eurystheus to see it, Heracles set the magnificent beast free. The beast roamed to Marathon, where Theseus later captured it and sacrificed it to Athena (see Chapter 15).

Eurystheus next sent Heracles to Thrace, to capture the four man-eating mares of King Diomedes. The son of Ares, Diomedes fed his savage mares on the living human flesh of his naive guests. On his way to Thrace, Heracles enjoyed the hospitality of Admetus, king of Pherae in northeastern Greece. The perfect host, Admetus entertained his guest while hiding the fact that he was in mourning for his wife,

Read All About It

The story of Admetus and Alcestis—and the heroic intervention of Heracles—can be found in *Alcestis*, a drama by Euripides. The play paints a vivid portrait of Heracles' buffoonish side. What the big hero liked to do best was eat, drink, and make merry. But when he realized that he had been "living large" in a house of mourning, his shame motivated him to rescue Alcestis.

Alcestis. When Heracles discovered his host's secret, he rushed to Alcestis's tomb and attacked Thanatos (Death) before he could carry her off.

After rescuing Alcestis, Heracles continued on to Thrace. There he stole the king's horses and drove them to the sea. When Diomedes and his subjects pursued him, Heracles drove the bulk of them away, clubbed Diomedes, and fed him to his own horses.

Heracles then harnessed the untamed mares to Diomedes' chariot and drove them all the way back to Tiryns. Eurystheus consecrated the mares to Hera and set them free to roam on Mount Olympus, but wild beasts eventually tore the mares to pieces.

The Far Corners of the Earth: The Final Four Labors

For his ninth labor, Heracles was dispatched even farther northeast than Thrace. He set sail for the Thermodon River, which flowed through northeastern Asia Minor and emptied into the Black Sea. Eurystheus sent him there to obtain the golden girdle (a belt used to carry a sword) worn by Hippolyta, queen of the Amazons.

After meeting with Heracles, Hippolyta seemed more than willing to give him the girdle, perhaps as a love token. But Hera appeared in the guise of an Amazon and warned the others that Heracles planned to abduct their queen. When the women warriors attacked the ship, Heracles, thinking Hippolyta had betrayed him, killed her and took the girdle. He and his handful of companions then defeated the Amazon armies and headed back home with the prize.

What a Life!

The Amazons were a society ruled by women warriors, the daughters of Ares. Some say that to keep their men devoted to household chores, the Amazons broke the arms and legs of male infants, making them ill suited for either war or travel. Others insist that the Amazons killed all male infants. The Amazons may also have cut off their right breasts to eliminate any possible hindrance to drawing a bow or hurling a spear.

On his return voyage, Heracles stopped in Troy, where he found King Laomedon's daughter Hesione naked and chained to a rock, an offering intended to appease a sea monster that had ravaged the kingdom. After agreeing on a price for rescuing

Hesione (her hand in marriage and some magnificent mares that Zeus had given to Laomedon), Heracles leapt into the belly of the beast and after three days vanquished the monster. When Laomedon refused to honor his agreement, Heracles left, but vowed vengeance.

After Eurystheus presented the girdle to his daughter Admete, he sent Heracles to Spain, where the hero was directed to fetch the cattle of Geryon, a monster who had three upper bodies. Geryon owned a herd of beautiful red cattle, kept under the watchful eyes of Eurytion, a son of Ares, and the two-headed dog Orthrus, yet another monstrous child of Typhon and Echidna.

When Heracles reached the Strait of Gibraltar, he erected pillars on both sides (one in Europe, one in Africa) to mark the great distance he had traveled. Those pillars, still standing, are today called the Rock of Gibraltar (or Mount Calpe) and Morocco's Jebel Musa (or Mount Abyla).

> **CAUTION**
>
> **Mythed by a Mile**
>
> Some storytellers insist that Heracles himself cut the channel that separates the continents of Europe and Africa in order to gain access to the ocean. Others contend he narrowed the channel to prevent sea monsters from entering the Mediterranean.

Although both Orthrus and Eurytion attacked him as he approached the herds of cattle, Heracles killed both of them with his club. As he drove the cattle toward his ship—an enormous golden cup that Helius had lent him—Geryon tried to stop him, too. But Heracles shot a single arrow through all three of his bodies and made off with the herds.

Hampered in his travels by the cattle, Heracles endured a long return trip to Tiryns. In Liguria (near present-day Marseilles), Heracles killed two thieves who tried to steal the cattle. To avenge these deaths, the Ligurians mounted an attack so numerous that Heracles ran out of arrows and, left defenseless, was wounded. But Zeus sent a shower of stones and Heracles used them to defend himself and force the Ligurians to retreat.

Soon after, Heracles arrived at the site of the future city of Rome (though it was nothing but wilderness then). While Heracles slept, a cave-dwelling, three-headed giant named Cacus—a son of Hephaestus and Medusa—stole some of Geryon's cattle. Undaunted by the flames spewing from the giant's mouth, Heracles entered his cave the next morning and killed the giant with his bare hands. Heracles thanked the gods for his victory over Cacus by sacrificing some of his cattle on an altar that the Romans would later call the Ara Maxima ("Greatest Altar"). In Roman times, this altar stood in the middle of the great city, not far from the Forum.

Several days later, Geryon's finest bull broke away from the herd and swam from Italy to Sicily. Heracles pursued the beast and found it mingled among the herds of Eryx, a formidable boxer and wrestler. Eryx, who killed those he outfought, challenged Heracles to a match, wagering his island kingdom against the herd of cattle. Heracles killed Eryx by smashing him to the ground during their wrestling match.

After turning over the cattle to Eurystheus, Heracles had completed 10 labors. But denied credit for the second and fifth labors, he still had two more chores to perform. Eurystheus sent him to the westernmost part of the world, the Garden of the Hesperides, where he was to obtain three Golden Apples from the tree that Gaia had given her granddaughter on Hera's wedding day. The golden-fruited tree was tended by nymphs known as Hesperides and guarded by a vicious hundred-headed dragon, Ladon, the monstrous offspring of Typhon and Echidna. Over the garden towered the Titan Atlas, who bore the heavy burden of holding up the sky.

Heracles first had to find the garden. He seized the sea god Nereus, an oracle, and forced him to reveal the location of the garden—and how he might obtain the Golden Apples. Nereus urged Heracles to talk Atlas into plucking the fruit for him. So when Heracles arrived at Mount Atlas, he offered to relieve Atlas in return for this small favor. After Heracles shot an arrow over the garden walls and killed Ladon, Atlas eagerly accepted this chance to unload his burden.

When Atlas returned with the apples, however, he seemed most unwilling to resume his responsibility. Instead, he offered to take the apples to Eurystheus himself. Heracles agreed that this was a fine plan, but complained that his head ached under the weight of the heavens. He asked Atlas to hold up the sky for just one minute longer so that Heracles might place a cushion of some kind on his head. The gullible Titan agreed. But as soon as Atlas had the sky back on his shoulders, Heracles picked up the apples and walked off.

Again, Heracles had many adventures on the way home. In Libya, he met a giant named Antaeus, the son of Gaia and Poseidon, who liked to wrestle his guests to exhaustion and then kill them. As they fought, Heracles realized that every time Antaeus was thrown to the ground, he grew stronger, as his Mother Earth restored and revitalized him. Heracles therefore held the giant high in the air and crushed him to death in his arms.

Arriving at the Caucasus Mountains, Heracles found the Titan Prometheus, who had been chained to a cliff for 30,000 years. Heracles shot and killed the eagle that had daily feasted on Prometheus's liver. He then arranged for the wounded Centaur Cheiron—who begged for escape from the pain caused by Heracles' poisonous arrow—to take the Titan's place in the Underworld, and freed Prometheus from his chains.

When Heracles finally presented the Golden Apples to Eurystheus, the king immediately handed the fruit back to him. Since the sacred fruit belonged to Hera, they could not remain out of the garden. Heracles therefore turned them over to Athena, who returned the apples to the Hesperides.

Heracles had just one labor left. But Eurystheus had saved the most dangerous task for last: bringing Cerberus, the three-headed guard dog of Hades, up from the Underworld. While in the Underworld, Heracles freed his friend Theseus from the Chair of Forgetfulness (see Chapter 15). He also freed Ascalaphus, the gardener of Hades who had told of seeing Persephone eat the pomegranate seeds (see Chapter 11) and was imprisoned under a rock by Demeter.

When he told Hades why he had come, the God of the Underworld gave Heracles leave to take Cerberus—provided he use no weapons to do so. By wrapping his mighty hands around the Hell-hound's throat, Heracles subdued Cerberus and dragged the beast to Eurystheus. The king quickly told him to return the monster to Hades. With this, Heracles completed his service to Eurystheus—and ensured his own immortality.

Love and Death

Freed from his obligations to Eurystheus, Heracles set out to win a new bride. He defeated his former teacher Eurytus in an archery contest for the hand of his daughter, Iole. But Eurytus, perhaps recalling the madness of Heracles' youth, refused to honor the wager.

When Eurytus's son Iphitus later suspected Heracles of stealing his father's cattle to avenge this insult, the enraged Heracles threw the young man from a tower to his death. Tormented with bad dreams, Heracles sought guidance from the oracle at Delphi. When the Pythia refused to speak to him, Heracles threatened to raze Delphi and establish his own oracle. Apollo himself came down from Olympus to defend his oracle, engaging in a fierce battle with Heracles. Yet Zeus threw a thunderbolt between his sons and restored order and amicability.

Lydia, Oh Lydia, Oh Have You Seen Lydia?

The oracle advised Heracles to sell himself into slavery for a year and to turn the proceeds over to the heirs of Iphitus. Queen Omphale of Lydia (a land in western Asia Minor), though unaware of Heracles' identity, recognized his worth and quickly purchased him.

While faithfully serving Omphale for one year—or perhaps three—Heracles rid the country of bandits who preyed on its people. He also killed a huge serpent that had been destroying the citizens and crops of Lydia.

It pleased Omphale, according to some accounts, to have her hulking slave wear feminine clothes. Heracles spun thread and did other "woman's work." The sight of the massive hero in drag did not deter Omphale, who soon brought her slave—who fathered several children by her—into her bed. After finally discovering who was in her service, Omphale released Heracles and allowed him to return to Tiryns.

Vengeance Is Mine

Heracles set out to avenge himself on King Laomedon of Troy, who had reneged on the reward promised for saving his daughter Hesione. Heracles led a small army that easily conquered Troy. He killed Laomedon and all but one of his sons: Priam (see Chapter 16).

Telamon, the hero's most valiant ally, had actually been the first to enter the city in the attack on Troy. Enraged by this breach of protocol, Heracles almost killed Telamon—but the warrior saved himself by quickly building an altar to Heracles in honor of his victory. Heracles rewarded Telamon for this loyalty with the hand of Hesione.

When Heracles left Troy, Hera summoned a storm that blew his ships far off course. Zeus, furious at her constant persecution of his heroic son, hung Hera to the rafters by her wrists and attached anvils to her ankles. He then led Heracles back to Argos.

Before Heracles had embarked on another adventure, a band of giants attacked Mount Olympus. Hera grimly prophesied that no god could defeat these giants. The only one who could kill them was a lion-skinned mortal.

Zeus quickly sent Athena to summon Heracles to the battlefield at Phlegra. Heracles, outfitted in the Nemean lion's hide, single-handedly killed two giants—and dealt the death blows to all the other giants subdued by the gods. (For a more detailed account of this monumental battle, see Chapter 8.)

Having helped his father to victory in the gods' war against the giants, Heracles resumed his quest for vengeance against those who had wronged him. He marched on Elis, where King Augeas had refused to pay him for cleaning his stables. But Augeas had expected this attack, and his army defeated Heracles—who was weakened by illness—and his allies. Among those killed was Heracles' half-brother Iphicles.

Soon after suffering this rare defeat, Heracles mounted a second attack on Elis. This time he emerged victorious, killing Augeas and his sons.

Fatal Attraction: Deianira

Heracles finally settled in Calydon in central Greece, where he began courting Deianira, the daughter of King Oeneus and his wife Althaea. (If truth be told,

Dionysus was actually the beautiful Deianira's father.) Heracles' only rival for her hand was the river god Achelous. Achelous appeared sometimes in the form of a bull, sometimes a serpent, and sometimes a man with the head of a bull.

Heracles and Achelous began wrestling for Deianira. Achelous escaped one hold by turning into a serpent. When Heracles grabbed him by the throat, Achelous changed into a bull and charged. But Heracles grabbed the bull by the horns, breaking one of them off as he threw Achelous to the ground again. The river god slunk away in defeat.

Three years after Heracles married Deianira, the couple set out for Trachis, 80 miles northeast of Calydon. When they reached the river Evenus, Nessus—a Centaur who ferried travelers across the river for a small fee—offered to carry Deianira. Heracles agreed to hire the Centaur and began swimming across the river. But instead of following him, Nessus carried off Deianira and tried to rape her. Hearing his wife's screams, Heracles quickly let fly a poisoned arrow that killed the Centaur.

Before he died, however, Nessus feigned remorse. He gave Deianira his blood-stained shirt, claiming it would serve as a love charm to ensure her husband's fidelity. Deianira—who no doubt knew Heracles' reputation—accepted the tunic and stowed it away.

After settling in Trachis, Heracles set out on his final adventure: seeking vengeance against Eurytus for refusing to yield his daughter Iole after their archery contest. Arriving in Oechalia, Heracles easily defeated King Eurytus and his sons and captured Iole. Iole tried to commit suicide, but failed—and Heracles sent her to Trachis.

> **CAUTION** **Mythed by a Mile**
>
> Nessus may have told Deianira to gather up his spilled blood and semen and smear them on Heracles' shirt. Or, as Sophocles tells it in his tragedy *The Women of Trachis*, he may have given her some wool soaked in his tainted blood, urging her to weave it into a shirt for her husband.

To honor Zeus for securing victory in this final battle, Heracles began building an altar and preparing a sacrifice of bulls. He sent his messenger Lichas back to Trachis for a shirt more suitable to the occasion. Naive Deianira, jealous of the newly arrived Iole, sent the shirt smeared with Nessus's blood, hoping to win back his love.

As soon as Heracles put on the shirt, the Hydra's venom that had poisoned Nessus's blood began eating away at his skin. He tore the shirt from his body, but his flesh came off with it. Tormented, Heracles hurled Lichas into the sea, where he turned to stone. (Upon learning what she had done, Deianira killed herself.)

Logos

The name **"Heracles"** means "Glory of Hera." Although her stand-in, Eurystheus, seemed to cause most of Heracles' problems, Hera's glory lay in creating or initiating all the difficulties the hero ultimately surmounted. Heracles was a larger-than-life reminder of her husband's philandering—and the damage done to her own reputation. Heracles therefore served as Hera's glory (or fame) for both good and ill.

Though writhing with pain, Heracles told his son (by Deianira), Hyllus, to carry him to the top of Mount Oeta. He instructed his son to build a funeral pyre there and burn him alive. When the time came to light the fire, however, neither Hyllus nor any of his companions could do it.

At last, a shepherd ordered his son, Philoctetes, to light the pyre as Heracles had asked. In gratitude, Heracles presented the boy with his bow and the poisoned arrows that had led to his destruction.

The fire burned away the hero's mortality, while releasing the immortal part of him. Heracles ascended to Olympus, where his father warmly welcomed him. Even Hera at last reconciled with *Heracles*, allowing him to marry her daughter Hebe and regarding him thereafter as her own son.

The Least You Need to Know

- Zeus impersonated Amphitryon, husband of Alcmene, in order to conceive the hero Heracles. Hera's jealousy of Alcmene made Heracles an object of her hatred throughout his life.

- Driven mad by Hera, Heracles murdered his children and perhaps his first wife, Megara, as well. To atone for this crime—and to become an immortal on Mount Olympus—he undertook 12 labors determined by King Eurystheus of Tiryns.

- Heracles killed many monsters or monstrous animals: the Nemean lion, the Hydra, dozens of Stymphalian birds, a sea monster, Geryon and Orthrus, the dragon Ladon, and many giants.

- His labors required Heracles to capture alive many storied beasts: the Ceryneian hind, the Erymanthian boar, the Cretan bull, the mares of Diomedes, the cattle of Geryon, and Cerberus, the hound of Hades.

- Two of his labors involved obtaining prized objects: the girdle of the Amazon Hippolyta and the Golden Apples of the Hesperides. His most humiliating labor was to clean the stables of Augeas.

- The Centaur Nessus tricked Deianira, the hero's second wife. She unwittingly killed Heracles with a shirt soaked in the Centaur's blood, which had been poisoned by one of the hero's own arrows. Heracles then took his place among the gods on Olympus.

Chapter 14

Crimes of Passion: Jason, Medea, and the Argonauts

In This Chapter

- ◆ Jason's pursuit of the Golden Fleece
- ◆ The many adventures of the Argonauts during the quest
- ◆ Medea's crimes on Jason's behalf
- ◆ Jason's betrayal and Medea's revenge

The Argonauts, who sailed with Jason to obtain the legendary Golden Fleece, were the most storied assemblage of heroes prior to the Trojan War. Many of the Argonauts, children or grandchildren of the gods themselves, first displayed their heroism while serving on the ship called the *Argo*.

Like most mythical quests, the story of the Argonauts neither begins nor ends with the successful achievement of the goal. The pursuit of the Golden Fleece may provide the heart of the story, but the adventures shared by the steadfast crew in the course of acquiring the fleece and on the voyage home provide the body. This series of adventures offers the heroes a chance to demonstrate their character, skills, and heroism.

Jason, a young man who had a charming way with women but was otherwise unremarkable, may seem an odd choice to lead a band of the greatest, noblest, and most adventurous heroes on any quest. He was neither the cleverest nor bravest of men. He was not the most skilled hunter or bowman or even sailor. But Hera, Queen of the Gods, handpicked Jason for this mission precisely because of his allure to women. For Hera had ulterior motives—and to achieve her ends, she needed Jason to bring the powerful sorceress Medea back to Greece.

Assembling the Argonauts

Jason was the grandson of Tyro and her uncle Cretheus, whom she had married after killing her children by another uncle, Sisyphus (see Chapter 11). The eldest son of Tyro and Cretheus, Jason's father, Aeson, should have inherited the kingdom of Iolcus, a seaport in Thessaly (northeastern Greece), which Cretheus had founded. But Tyro had also had twin sons by the god Poseidon, and one of these twins, Pelias, had seized the throne.

Although Pelias had not harmed his half-brother, Aeson feared for his own life and that of his unborn son. So when his wife (either Polymede or Alcimede) gave birth to Jason, Aeson claimed the baby had died. He entrusted the boy to the care of Cheiron, the wisest of the Centaurs, who had also tutored Heracles.

The Other Shoe Drops: The Return of Jason

When he reached manhood, Jason traveled to Iolcus to retake the throne. Before he reached the city he came to the river Anaurus, where he met an old woman. The young hero gallantly carried the woman across the river on his shoulders. The extra weight caused him to lose one of his sandals, which got stuck in the mud of the river bed. Safely on the other side, he set the old woman down and sped off to Iolcus, where Pelias was hosting a festival in honor of his father, Poseidon.

What Jason didn't know was that the old woman was actually Hera in disguise. Hera hated Pelias, who never offered her sacrifices or showed her proper respect. What's more, he had committed the outrage of killing Tyro's cruel stepmother, Sidero, while the woman clung to the altar of Hera for sanctuary. The goddess was planning her revenge for these insults—and her plot would involve both Jason and the sorceress Medea.

Pelias soon heard of the one-sandaled man who had arrived in the city. This news frightened him, for an oracle had once warned Pelias that a man with one sandal, a descendant of Aeolus (the great-grandfather of both Aeson and Pelias), would cause his death. Without identifying himself, Pelias confronted Jason and demanded to know who he was. Jason answered truthfully, boldly announcing his intention to reclaim the throne either for himself or his father.

Pelias surely wanted to murder his nephew, but knew that such a crime against the laws of hospitality would incur the wrath of the gods. Looking for a way to dispose of Jason, Pelias decided to assign this young man an impossible task: obtaining the Golden Fleece from Colchis, a barbaric land on the eastern shore of the Black Sea.

Pelias no doubt thought that he would rid himself of Jason forever. So he identified himself and blithely promised to turn over the throne without a struggle if Jason succeeded in performing this task. Jason, bold and ambitious, saw this quest as his path to glory and so agreed to Pelias's request.

Golden Fleece? What Golden Fleece?

Some years earlier, Athamas (another brother of Cretheus and Sisyphus), the king of Orchomenus, had left his wife Nephele to marry Ino, a daughter of Cadmus. Hoping to improve the lot of her own children, Ino plotted the destruction of Nephele's son, Phrixus, and daughter, Helle (see Chapter 12). Ino damaged all of the seed grain in the kingdom. When the crops failed, messengers were sent to the Delphic oracle for guidance. Ino bribed the returning messengers to deliver a lie: Phrixus must be sacrificed!

> ### The More Things Change ...
>
> Tales of Greek parents sacrificing their children—for example, Phrixus, Pelops, and Iphigenia (see Chapter 16 for her story)—contrast sharply with tales of sacrifice from the Bible. The God of the Hebrews tested Abraham's faith, but spared Isaac when Abraham showed his willingness to sacrifice his own son. The sacrifices to Greek gods were never tests of faith, but instruments of vengeance: payback for some insult to a god's honor.

Athamas reluctantly agreed to heed the false oracle. But just as Athamas raised the knife over his son on the sacrificial altar, a golden, winged ram appeared. The ram carried away Phrixus and Helle on its back. En route to Aea, the capital of Colchis—a mythic kingdom on the eastern coast of the Black Sea—Helle fell off and drowned in the strait that connects the Aegean Sea to the Sea of Marmara. (The site, Hellespont, was named after her.) Phrixus safely reached Aea, where King Ae'tes—who distrusted and despised strangers—had been ordered by Zeus to welcome him.

Phrixus, who later married Aeëtes' daughter Chalciope, sacrificed the ram to Zeus, his rescuer. The Golden Fleece of this glorious ram he hung upon a tree in a sacred grove in Colchis. In this grove, a sleepless dragon had guarded the fleece ever since.

Help Wanted

After consulting the oracle at Delphi, Jason invited the most daring noblemen from all the cities of Greece to join him. The roster of those who heeded this call to adventure and potential glory included some of the greatest heroes in all of Greece. Many of the volunteers chosen to join Jason were children or later descendants of the gods themselves. Those who signed up included:

- Heracles, the son of Zeus, the mightiest of all heroes (see Chapter 13)

- Polydeuces (called Pollux by the Romans), the son of Zeus by Leda and an expert boxer

- Castor, the twin of Polydeuces (though his father was not Zeus, but Tyndareus, king of Sparta), who excelled at taming, training, and riding horses

- Euphemus, son of Poseidon, so swift that he could race across water without getting his feet wet

- Periclymenus, son (or grandson) of Poseidon, who could change his form at will during battle

- Nauplius, son (or later descendant) of Poseidon, an expert seaman

- Idas, son of Poseidon (though some deny this parentage), a boastful but strong ally

- Lynceus, the half-brother of Idas (son of Aphareus, king of Messenia), who possessed vision so keen he could see things under the surface of the earth

- Orpheus, son of Apollo, the most gifted of all musicians (see Chapter 11)

- Idmon, a son of Apollo and a famed prophet, who foresaw a successful quest and joined the crew though he knew he would die

- Augeas, son of Helius and king of Elis (see Chapter 13)

- Echion and Erytus, sons of Hermes

- Zetes and Calais, twin sons of Boreas (god of the North Wind), who flew on wings

Not all the Argonauts were of divine birth. Tiphys would serve as pilot of the *Argo*. The brothers Telamon and Peleus (the latter would marry the sea goddess Thetis and beget Achilles [see Chapter 17]) joined the crew. Meleager, the young prince of Calydon, eagerly came onboard. So did Jason's pious cousin Admetus. The promise of fame and glory even enticed another cousin—Acastus, the son of Jason's treacherous uncle Pelias—who defied his father's orders by sailing with the Argonauts.

Atalanta, the famed huntress, also volunteered for the quest. Jason, however, fearing the turmoil that might arise with a woman onboard, reluctantly refused her.

In Search of Adventure

Jason's crew named themselves the Argonauts after their magnificent ship, the *Argo*. Perhaps the first ship ever built, the *Argo* was assembled under the watchful eye of Athena, who taught humans the art of sailing the seas. The ship's beams came from Mount Pelion in Thessaly and included a talking beam from the oracular oaks of Dodona. This allowed the Argonauts to receive advice from their own ship during their long journey.

The launching of the *Argo* was such a marvelous sight that even the Nereids, sea goddesses, rose from the ocean's depths to wonder at this odd contrivance. It was here that Peleus met his future bride: the sea goddess Thetis (see Chapters 16 and 17).

After offering a traditional sacrifice to Apollo, the Argonauts set sail for Colchis.

The Island of Women

Midway across the northern Aegean Sea, the Argonauts arrived at the island of Lemnos. Years earlier, the women of Lemnos had failed to honor Aphrodite properly. To punish them, the goddess had given the women a noxious odor that drove their husbands away. The men of Lemnos had raided Thrace, brought home female captives, and begun having children with them.

The Lemnian wives, mad with jealousy, had killed the Thracian women and all Lemnian men except one. Loyal Hypsipyle, later Queen of Lemnos, could not kill her father, King Thoas. Instead, she hid him away and put him on a boat or chest that drifted safely to the island of Oenoe.

> **What a Life!**
>
> The Lemnian women, after discovering how Hypsipyle had saved her father, banished their queen to Nemea. There she became a slave to the Nemean king. Her sons by Jason remained on Lemnos, where one of them, Euneus, would later become the island's king.

By the time the Argonauts landed, the women of Lemnos had realized that they needed men, if only as breeders. So they welcomed the male visitors to their island—and into their bedchambers. Jason lay with Hypsipyle, and though he vowed fidelity, he soon abandoned her to continue on his quest.

The Argonauts might have stayed on Lemnos forever. But Heracles, who had remained aboard the *Argo*, sent a message questioning whether this was really the way they wanted to win glory for themselves. The Argonauts, shamed into returning to the ship, left behind an island of pregnant women. (Hypsipyle would give birth to twin sons.)

Surprise Attacks

The Argonauts next traveled to Samothrace, an island in the northern Aegean, at Orpheus's suggestion. There they became initiates in the Samothracian Mysteries, religious rites that they hoped would offer them further protection on their journey.

After passing through the Hellespont and entering the Sea of Marmara, the *Argo* stopped on an island where Cyzicus, king of the Dolione tribe, welcomed them. Most of the crew joined Cyzicus in ascending to the top of Mount Dindymus. But while they admired the view, a band of six-armed giants attacked the nearly defenseless ship. Fortunately, one of the guards left behind was Heracles. The son of Zeus alone shot several giants with his bow and arrows before the crew hurried back and killed the rest.

The next morning, the *Argo* again set sail. But the ship ran into a strong headwind and poor visibility. That night, not knowing what little progress they had made, they stopped on the shores of the very same island. Under the dim light of the moon, the Doliones—fearing that pirates had landed—engaged the Argonauts in a bloody battle that lasted throughout the night.

At dawn, the Argonauts sadly realized what they had done. Dozens of Doliones, including Cyzicus himself, lay dead on the beach. The Argonauts remained on the island to honor their fallen friends with proper funeral rites.

> **What a Life!**
>
> Heracles, who tended to hold a grudge, met up with Zetes and Calais again shortly after the *Argo* returned to Iolcus. There he killed the sons of Boreas for their disloyalty.

Once the crew set sail again, they were forced to stop in Mysia (northwestern Asia Minor) when Heracles broke his oar. Here Heracles parted ways with the Argonauts. While he and a fellow crew member, Polyphemus, searched for Heracles' young lover Hylas (see Chapter 13), the *Argo* left without them. When the crew noticed their absence, the brothers Zetes and Calais convinced them not to turn back—a decision seconded by the sea god Glaucus, who rose from the water to tell them that Zeus intended Heracles to complete his labors.

Winged Avengers and Clashing Rocks

Before reaching the Bosporus, the *Argo* stopped to rest once more. But Amycus, the brutal king of the Bebryces, challenged the Argonauts to choose a champion for a boxing match. (These matches usually ended with the death of Amycus's opponent.) Polydeuces, an expert boxer, nimbly avoided the powerful blows of Amycus and killed him with a shot to the ear.

The Argonauts then quickly repelled a retaliatory attack by Amycus's subjects. They appropriated many Bebrycian sheep for a feast before setting sail again.

At the southern end of the Bosporus, they stopped in Salmydessus, a land ruled by Phineus, whose wife was a sister of Zetes and Calais. They found the king starving, filthy, blind, and so weak he could hardly move. Zeus had sent the Harpies to punish Phineus, a prophet, for revealing too much about the future of the human race. The Harpies, noxious bird-women who doled out divine vengeance, would steal his food and pollute whatever they left behind with a horrible stench.

The Argonauts prepared some food for Phineas to set a trap for the Harpies, who immediately appeared, stole the food, and flew off. The winged sons of Boreas took off in hot pursuit. Zetes and Calais finally caught up to the Harpies and seized them. Just then, Iris—Zeus's messenger—descended from Olympus. If the twins spared the Harpies, Zeus promised that they would leave Phineus alone. Zetes and Calais reluctantly released the Harpies and returned to Salmydessus.

Phineus, who feasted for the first time in ages, was so grateful that he foretold some of what the future held for the Argonauts (though, mindful of Zeus's punishment, he did not tell everything). Most importantly, he offered invaluable advice on how to navigate the treacherous Clashing Rocks at the eastern end of the Bosporus: the entrance to the Black Sea. These two enormous floating islands, driven by the wind, crushed everything in their path as they smashed together without warning.

As the *Argo* neared the end of the Bosporus, the swift Euphemus released a dove that flew directly between the Clashing Rocks. Phineus had told them that if the dove could make it through the strait, the *Argo* could, too. The islands crashed together, but the dove lost only a few tail feathers. When the islands separated again, the 50 oarsmen rowed with all their might. Like the dove, the ship made it almost all the

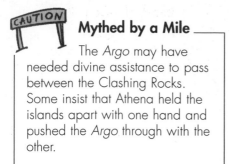

Mythed by a Mile

The *Argo* may have needed divine assistance to pass between the Clashing Rocks. Some insist that Athena held the islands apart with one hand and pushed the *Argo* through with the other.

way through, losing only an ornament from the stern. The Clashing Rocks parted once more and, with the spell broken, forever after remained apart.

Sailing along the southern coast of the Black Sea, the crew put in near the Acheron River. There, the seer Idmon was slain by a wild boar and the helmsman Tiphys died of illness. These were the first Argonauts to die. But Lycus, king of the Mariandyni, grateful to the Argonauts for having rid him of his enemies—Amycus and the Bebryces—offered to replace one of them with his own son, Dascylus.

Near an island sacred to Ares, a flock of birds—perhaps the same ones driven from Lake Stymphalus by Heracles—attacked the *Argo*, showering it with arrowlike feathers. Half the crew held their shields above their heads to form a protective roof while the other half continued rowing. Then, recalling the strategy of Heracles (see Chapter 13), the Argonauts landed on the island and began shouting and banging their swords on their shields. Alarmed and confused by the clatter, the birds rose as one and deserted the island.

As the Argonauts refreshed themselves on the island, four castaways approached them. The four identified themselves as the sons of Phrixus and Chalciope, the daughter of Ae'tes. While sailing to Orchomenus to claim the treasures Phrixus had inherited, they had become shipwrecked. Hoping the four might help persuade their grandfather to give up the Golden Fleece, Jason invited the sons of Phrixus to join his crew.

Witch Way to the Golden Fleece

The *Argo* soon entered the mouth of the River Phasis, where Aea, the capital of Colchis, lay. Now Aeëtes, the son of the sun (Helius), was so powerful that even the goddesses Hera and her ally Athena would need help to ensure that the Greeks escaped with the fleece—and their lives. Jason and his crew sought out Athena, who agreed to bribe Eros with a golden ball to wound the heart of Aeëtes' daughter, Medea. For if Medea, a powerful witch, would assist them, even to the point of betraying her father, Jason and the Argonauts might have a chance to win the Golden Fleece.

A priestess of the Underworld goddess Hecate, Medea was the first in Colchis to see the Argonauts. Smitten by Eros, she instantly became infatuated with Jason.

With this ace in the hole, Jason opted to try a diplomatic approach first. So he set out with Telamon, Augeas, and the sons of Phrixus for the magnificent palace that Hephaestus had built for Aeëtes.

Arriving at the palace, the sons of Phrixus introduced the three Argonauts and attempted to impress Aeëtes by telling him that Augeas, too, was a son of Helius and that Telamon descended from Zeus. Aeëtes would have none of it. He called them liars and accused them of plotting a coup against him. Jason insisted they did not want his throne, but only the fleece—and offered to do battle with the Sauromatians, Aeëtes' enemies, in exchange.

Read All About It _____

The tale of Jason's challenges—as well as the entire story of the voyage of *Argo*—can be found in *Argonautica*, an epic poem written by Apollonius of Rhodes during the third century B.C.E.

Aeëtes had been warned by an oracle of treachery from his own family. Since he had unshaking faith in his daughters' loyalty, Aeëtes suspected the betrayal would come from his grandchildren, now Jason's allies. So he refused Jason's offer, instead challenging him to pass a test of strength in order to win the fleece.

Like the test Pelias had set for Jason, this one too seemed impossible: He would have to harness a pair of fire-breathing bulls to a plow, sow a field with dragon's teeth, and then kill all the men who sprang from this seed. The ruthless king of Colchis doubted that Jason would survive even the first part of the test. He ordered his subjects to wait for Jason's death, then force the Argonauts—including his own grandsons—back to their ship and set it aflame.

The sons of Phrixus went to Chalciope, asking their mother to appeal to her much-younger sister Medea to help Jason achieve this dangerous task. Medea, already smitten with Jason, needed little convincing to help him survive her father's deadly test.

Jason and Medea met for the first time at dawn in the shrine of Hecate at Colchis. Jason, drunk with gratitude, promised to take Medea back to Iolcus, where he said her name would be honored forever.

Before undertaking the test, Jason anointed himself and his weapons with a magic drug that Medea had given him. With the drug protecting him from their flames, Jason forced the bulls to their knees and quickly harnessed them. Within a few hours he had sown the entire field with the teeth of the same dragon that Cadmus had slain in founding Thebes (see Chapter 12). Following Cadmus's example, Jason hurled an enormous stone in the middle of the sown men, which started them fighting amongst themselves. In the resulting confusion, Jason rushed in with his sword gleaming and started swinging. By nightfall, he had slain them all.

Aeëtes did not turn over the fleece as promised, but instead sulked back to his palace and plotted against the Greeks. Medea stole away to join the celebrations of Jason and the Argonauts. After hearing Jason vow to Hera that he would marry Medea when they returned to Greece, Medea led them to the grove of Ares. When the beautiful sorceress used her magic to cause the sleepless dragon to nap, Jason made off with the fleece. The fleeing lovers quickly set sail as soon as they reached the *Argo*.

Crime and Punishment: The Long Way Home

Learning of the theft, Aeëtes quickly sent his son Apsyrtus and a fleet of warships after them. Half the fleet headed for the Bosporus; the other half for the mouth of the Danube. Though the *Argo* had made for the Danube as well, Apsyrtus arrived there before them.

The Argonauts soon found themselves trapped: A Colchian ship guarded the entrance to the Danube River. They took refuge on an island sacred to Artemis, where they knew the Colchians would not dare launch an attack that might offend the goddess.

Am I My Brother's Keeper?

Sending him a message claiming she had been abducted, Medea then lured her brother to a meeting on the island, where Jason ambushed and killed him. The Argonauts killed everyone on Apsyrtus's ship and fled toward the Danube.

The *Argo* escaped the Colchians. But Zeus—furious at this brazen betrayal of Medea's brother—brewed up a storm. Zeus ordered Jason and Medea to seek purification for the murder from Medea's aunt, the famed sorceress Circe. But Circe lived on the island of Aeaea off the western coast of Italy—and the *Argo* lay in the Danube, cut off from any direct route to Aeaea. Rather than finding an outlet to the sea and sailing all the way around the southern coasts of Greece and Italy, the *Argo* boldly chose a circuitous—and highly improbable—route of inland rivers to somehow cross northern Greece and Italy. After making its way to the western Mediterranean, the ship sailed on to Aeaea.

Without asking any questions, Circe purified Jason and Medea with the blood of a pig and made sacrifices to both Zeus and the Erinyes (Furies). But when Circe learned who they were and how they had betrayed her brother, Aeëtes, and her nephew, Apsyrtus, she angrily chased them off the island.

> **CAUTION** **Mythed by a Mile**
>
> The crime might have been even worse. According to Apollodorus, Apsyrtus was just a child who ran away with his sister on the *Argo*. Medea and Jason killed the innocent boy, dismembered him, and tossed the body parts into the sea. This forced the Colchian ships to call off the chase in order to collect the body parts for burial.

Dangerous Waters

Jason and Medea were fortunate that Hera had not given up her plot to punish Pelias. The goddess ordered favorable winds from Aeolus, the keeper of the winds, and asked the sea goddess Thetis for help, too.

As they approached Anthemoessa, home of the Sirens, whose seductive singing had caused so many sailors to abandon their voyages and slowly waste away from hunger, Orpheus began to sing and play on his lyre as loudly as he could. By drowning out the seductive strains of the Sirens, Orpheus saved the Argonauts.

To reach the Ionian Sea, west of Greece, the *Argo* still had to navigate the narrow strait between the cliff of Scylla, a six-headed beast that preyed on sailors from a sea cave, and the whirlpool of the monster Charybdis. But Thetis secretly took the helm and steered them safely through.

The Nereids then safely skimmed the *Argo* over the surface of the water around Sicily. This prevented the violent currents from carrying them into the Wandering Rocks—moving rocks that destroyed ships attempting to pass among them.

After crossing the Ionian Sea, the Argonauts at last reached the Greek island of Drepane (probably what we call Corfu today). Here they met the other half of Aeëtes' fleet. The Colchians demanded the immediate return of Medea.

The Argonauts sought help from Queen Arete and King Alcinous, who agreed to prevent the separation of Jason and Medea—as long as the couple were married. The crew performed the marriage rites that very night in the sacred cave of Macris. The newlyweds slept that night in this cave, which was known forever after as Medea's Cave.

The next morning, King Alcinous informed the Colchians that he would not allow them to take Medea from her new husband. The Colchians, unwilling to challenge the King of Drepane and afraid to face the wrath of Aeëtes if they returned home empty-handed, received permission from Alcinous to settle there. Jason and Medea were free to go.

Dry-Docked

Just as the *Argo* reached the southern coast of Greece, an ill wind blew them all the way across the Mediterranean Sea to the Libyan coast. An enormous wave then deposited the ship far inland, leaving it stranded on the desert sands.

The Argonauts might have given up, but three nymphs appeared and issued a cryptic oracle: After seeing Poseidon's horses unyoked, they should repay their mother for carrying them so long in her womb. When a horse galloped out of the sea and raced across the desert, Jason solved the riddle. Their mother's womb was the *Argo*. So the Argonauts repaid the ship by carrying her on rollers across the desert for nine arduous days.

When they arrived at the saltwater Lake Tritonis, the Argonauts went out to search for fresh water. They found themselves in the Garden of the Hesperides, where the wailing nymphs informed them that after stealing their apples, Heracles had created a freshwater spring just the day before (see Chapter 13).

In trying to find Heracles, the Argonauts lost two more of their members. Canthus was killed by a shepherd after trying to steal some sheep. The seer Mopsus died from the bite of a deadly snake—one of those that had sprung up from the blood that dripped from Medusa's head as Perseus flew over Libya (see Chapter 10).

Logos

To the ancient Greeks, a **tripod** was a three-legged vessel used for heating coals, usually in preparation for a sacrifice to the gods. In essence, a tripod was a barbecue grill.

After returning to the *Argo*, the crew searched for days but could find no outlet from Tritonis to the sea. Orpheus suggested offering the gods his bronze *tripod*, a gift from his father Apollo. The god Triton responded, pushing the ship all the way to the Mediterranean along a route that the Argonauts never could have navigated themselves.

After the long journey across the sea, the Argonauts arrived at Crete. But the giant Talus prevented them from landing by hurling boulders at the ship. The last of the ancient race of bronze giants, Talus was invulnerable—except for one vein near his ankle. Medea used her sorcery to hypnotize the giant, who stumbled, banging his ankle against a sharp rock. The vein burst and Talus plummeted into the sea.

No Place Like Home?

Long before the *Argo* returned to Iolcus, rumors had spread that the ship and her crew had all been lost. Pelias, emboldened by this news, forced Jason's father Aeson to commit suicide by drinking bull's blood, a fatal toxin. Pelias killed Jason's young brother, Promachus, too. Jason's mother cursed Pelias, but then killed herself with a sword.

Jason correctly suspected that Pelias would renege on his promise to give up his throne. So the *Argo* docked outside the city, where Medea hatched a horrifying plot to seize the throne without a costly battle.

Medea disguised herself as a crone and entered the city. After claiming that Artemis had sent her to restore Pelias's youth, Medea slipped into a tent. She quickly emerged as the young and beautiful woman she really was, impressing Pelias so much that he agreed to submit to her promised "treatment."

The spell required the cooperation of Pelias's daughters, Medea insisted. Despite their loyalty to their father, however, the daughters of Pelias were reluctant to follow Medea's recipe: Chop up their father into pieces and stew them. Medea then made a show of slaying a ram, cutting it up, and putting the pieces into her cauldron. When the sorceress lifted out a frisky lamb, the apparent miracle convinced all but the eldest daughter, Alcestis. Her sisters killed Pelias and stewed his body parts—then wailed with despair when he failed to return.

With Pelias out of the way, the Argonauts easily took the city. Jason's shipmate Acastus, however, who succeeded his father in the throne, expelled the couple from Iolcus after learning of the treacherous way in which they had murdered his father. Or perhaps they left the city to accept an invitation for Medea to rule Corinth, where some say her father Aeëtes once reigned. In either case, the objective of the quest was never fulfilled.

> **Mythed by a Mile**
>
> Some say Aeson was still alive, though just barely, when Jason returned to Iolcus. But Medea restored his youth and vigor by slitting his throat, draining his blood, and filling his veins with a brew of magic herbs.

A Woman Scorned

Jason and Medea settled in Corinth, where they had two (or three) children and spent 10 happy years together. But Jason increasingly found Medea, whom the Corinthians feared and loathed, an embarrassment to him. He decided to divorce her.

When King Creon of Corinth offered the hand of his daughter Glauce (or Creusa), Jason eagerly accepted. Divorcing Medea and marrying Glauce would add to his own power and prestige as well as ensure the citizenship rights of his children. But his abandonment crushed Medea.

Beware of Colchians Bearing Gifts

Ditched, divorced, and then exiled by Creon—who had good reason to fear her sorcery—Medea took advantage of her final day in Corinth to send Glauce a robe and crown for her wedding. When the naive Glauce tried on the robe, which Medea had drenched in poison, it burst into flames. The fire consumed not only Glauce, but Creon, his entire family, and the palace of Corinth as well. Simply to hurt Jason further, Medea then killed their children. When she left Iolcus, Medea took their bodies with her, making it impossible for Jason even to bury them. The sorceress escaped Corinth on a chariot pulled by dragons, a gift from her grandfather, Helius.

The Aftermath of Tragedy

Medea fled to Athens, where she convinced King Aegeus, who had long been child-less, to marry her by promising him children. (Aethra, the daughter of King Pittheus of Troezen, was already pregnant with Aegeus's son Theseus, but Aegeus didn't know that.) Aegeus and Medea, who had a son named Medus, lived together in Athens for many years. However, when she tried to kill Theseus in order to clear a path to the throne for her own son, Medea and Medus were both exiled by Aegeus.

With nowhere else to go, Medea returned at last to her homeland of Colchis. There Medus—egged on by his mother—killed King Perses, who had dethroned his brother Aeëtes. Medus thus captured the throne for himself (or recaptured it for his grand-father if, as some accounts have it, Aeëtes was still alive). Nothing further is known of Medea.

As for Jason, he never again approached the glory of his younger days. Desolate in his grief, Jason died while revisiting his past glory: the wreckage of the *Argo* at Corinth. There, a beam from the rotten ship fell upon his head, ending his glory days forever.

The Least You Need to Know

- Jason assembled the most talented adventurers in Greece to help him acquire the Golden Fleece—and regain his father's throne in Iolcus from Pelias.

- Though the *Argo* met with many dangers—giants, warriors, and the hazards of the sea—almost all of the Argonauts survived their arduous quest.

- To help Jason win his glory, Medea committed horrible crimes. She murdered and dismembered her own brother and later tricked the daughters of Pelias into killing their own father.

- When Jason abandoned her, Medea murdered his new bride, his prospective father-in-law, and her own children.

- Jason's pursuit of the Golden Fleece and his marriage to Medea were engineered by Hera, who wanted to punish Pelias for refusing to honor her.

Lucky in War, Unlucky in Love: Theseus

In This Chapter

- How Theseus made the Isthmus of Corinth safe for travelers
- How Theseus navigated the Labyrinth to slay the Minotaur
- The tragic result of Phaedra's love
- The ill-conceived plan to marry the daughters of Zeus

Befitting Athens, a city renowned for its thinkers, Theseus, the chief hero of Athenian legends, was known more for his quick wit than his strength, and his brain rather than his brawn. The cleverness of Theseus made him—along with such heroes as Heracles, Perseus, and Odysseus—one of the great monster-slayers of classical mythology.

Theseus earned a reputation not only for his daring and intelligence, but also for his fairness. An early king of Athens, he was one of the first rulers to reform the government in the direction of democracy. As both a king and an adventurer, he defended the oppressed and consistently fought for the ideal of justice.

Who's Been Sleeping in My Bed?

Theseus came from good stock. On his mother's side, he descended from Pelops, the great king of Pisa, whom the gods had restored to life after his father Tantalus had tried to serve him to them in a stew (see Chapter 11). On his father's side, Theseus was the son of either a king (Aegeus) or a god (Poseidon).

King Aegeus of Athens had long wanted a child, but his efforts in two marriages had proved fruitless. He at last decided to consult the oracle at Delphi, where he received a cryptic instruction: Do not unloose the foot (in other words, spout) of your wine-skin until you return to Athens. Failing to appreciate this counsel as a sexual metaphor, Aegeus puzzled over its meaning, but could not decipher the riddle.

The More Things Change ...

Tales about the mythic adventures of Theseus, the greatest hero of Athens, became popular shortly after the vogue of stories about Heracles. The two myths explore similar themes and the heroes undertake similar heroic deeds, especially in their monster-slaying. The two heroes even cross paths several times. These parallels suggest that the Ionians (the racial group of Athenians) may have developed the mythic tales of Theseus to rival the Dorians' tale of Heracles.

Instead of returning directly to Athens, Aegeus headed for the small town of Troezen in Argolis. Aegeus hoped that Pittheus—the king of Troezen, who had a reputation for wisdom—could help. Pittheus, a son of Pelops, immediately understood the oracle. Yet he did not share his wisdom with Aegeus, for he had other plans for him.

That night, Pittheus filled Aegeus with drink and led him to the bed of his daughter Aethra. Later that same night, Poseidon lay down with Aethra, too—but neither Pittheus nor Aegeus knew of this coupling.

The next morning, Aegeus buried his sword and his sandals under a massive boulder near Troezen. He told Aethra that if she gave birth to his son and that boy grew strong enough to push aside the stone, she should send him with these items to Athens. In this way, Aegeus would recognize him as his son.

Aethra did have a son and named him Theseus. The boy soon demonstrated both strength and cleverness. As a young wrestler, Theseus is credited with transforming the sport from a contest of brute strength into an art that merged fighting skill with agility and quick wits.

At age 16, Theseus moved the stone, put on Aegeus's sandals and sword, and set off for Athens. He ignored his mother's and grandfather's advice to sail across the Saronic Gulf. Instead, he boldly chose the hazardous land route across the Isthmus of Corinth.

The More Things Change ...

The tale of Theseus retrieving his father's sword and sandals from under a stone in order to prove his paternity calls to mind the Arthurian legends of medieval England. Just as young Arthur demonstrated his worthiness to be king by drawing the sword Excalibur from the stone in which it had been buried for so many years, Theseus established himself as heir to the throne of Athens by drawing his father's sword (and sandals) out from under the rock. Both rites identify the heroes as inheritors of their dynasties.

Road Warrior

The dangers on the road from Troezen to Athens did not arise from the terrain, but rather from its inhabitants. Monsters—most of them human, but beastly nonetheless—preyed on any travelers unlucky enough to cross paths with them. Most of these highwaymen had devised horrifying ways to torture and dispose of their victims.

Theseus turned the tables on every one of these predators. Defeating them in battle or using his wits to trick them, he forced each to suffer the same fate they had meted out to their many victims.

Batter Up

In Epidaurus, on the coast of the Saronic Gulf, Theseus met up with Periphetes, nicknamed Corynetes (which means "Clubman"). Periphetes, a lame son of the lame god of metalworking and craftsmanship, Hephaestus, had the unpleasant habit of smashing his formidable iron (or bronze) club over the heads of strangers.

Using his quickness and agility, Theseus easily defeated the brute strength of Periphetes. After stripping the monster of his weapon, Theseus killed him with it. Thereafter the young hero carried the club—which no doubt had been forged by Hephaestus—as both a trophy and a weapon.

Up a Tree

As he approached the isthmus near Corinth, Theseus encountered Sinis, a notorious highwayman. Sinis had acquired the nickname of Pityocamptes ("Pine-Bender") because of the unique way in which he disposed of his victims. After robbing them, the mighty Sinis would bend two strong trees toward each other. After strapping the victim's arms to one tree and his legs to another, Sinis would let go. The trees, snapping back upright, would tear the victim to pieces. Theseus overpowered Sinis, strapped him to the bent trees, and let them fly.

After killing Sinis, Theseus caught sight of his beautiful daughter, Perigune. She turned and ran away, hiding herself in a patch of shrubs and asparagus. Approaching gently and speaking sweetly, Theseus convinced the young girl to come out of hiding. The two had a brief liaison, the outcome of which was a son, Melanippus.

Theseus had not gone much farther when a ferocious sow rushed out at him. This wild pig had long ravaged the town of Crommyon. Named Phaea after the old woman who bred or owned her, the beast was yet another monstrous offspring of Typhon and Echidna.

Theseus used both sword and spear to gore the beast, killing it with little difficulty.

Look Out Below

Moving along the southern coast of the isthmus, Theseus next encountered Sciron. Now, Sciron did not rob his victims; he merely killed them. Sciron sat blocking a particularly narrow path at the edge of a cliff that towered over the Saronic Gulf. He would stop any wayfarers foolish enough to travel this route and would request that they humble themselves by washing his feet as "payment" to pass him. When they bent down to do so, he would suddenly kick his victims off the cliff. In the waters below, a monstrous sea turtle waited to devour them.

Theseus agreed to wash Sciron's feet, but when he bent down, he hurled the foot bath at the murderer's head. Grabbing Sciron by the ankles, Theseus then hurled *him* into the water, where he became the last victim of the man-eating turtle.

Wanna Wrestle?

After completing his trek across the isthmus, Theseus arrived at Eleusis, a city ravaged by a monster named Cercyon. This brute challenged all wayfarers to wrestle with him.

Most of his opponents died while wrestling; those exhausted few who survived were immediately put to death. Once again, Theseus used wits, quickness, and agility—as well as his well-honed skill as a wrestler—to defeat brute strength. At the end of the match, Theseus lifted Cercyon up and smashed him to the ground, killing him instantly.

The Perfect Fit?

The final monster slain by Theseus on his way to Athens was named Procrustes. The father of Sinis the Pine-Bender, Procrustes at first appeared a kindly host. He would invite all travelers through Erineus to rest their weary bones in his home.

But after his guests fell asleep, Procrustes would torture them. He seemed obsessed with having all of his guests fit into his bed. If their legs or feet hung over the end of the bed, he would chop them off. If they were too short, he would attach weights to their arms and legs and stretch them to size—or he would hammer them out the way his father, Hephaestus, hammered out metal. As he had done with all the monsters that came before, Theseus used the torturer's own method to slay Procrustes.

A Lot of Bull

Having rid the isthmus and its surrounding regions of all monsters and highwaymen, Theseus finally arrived at Athens. The Athenians, who traditionally wore short tunics, at first ridiculed the stranger, calling him a girl because he wore a long robe. But Theseus, not taking kindly to having his masculinity questioned, silenced his critics by hurling two oxen higher than a roof.

King Aegeus, unaware that the stranger was his son, nonetheless welcomed him as the conqueror of the Isthmian terrors. The king arranged for a lavish banquet to celebrate the triumphs of the young hero. Aegeus, adhering to rules of hospitality, asked no questions of his guest; Theseus, in turn, offered no hint of who he was.

Maternal Instinct Gone Wild

The sorceress Medea, however, who had married Aegeus shortly after Theseus was born, recognized her stepson through sorcery. Medea seethed, seeing the young hero—rightly so—as a threat to the future reign of her own son, Medus (see Chapter 14). Her whispers soon made Aegeus suspicious of the stranger. (Aegeus was already wary of a possible uprising led by his rebellious brother, Pallas, who had an army of 50 sons.)

To rid himself of the stranger, Aegeus sent Theseus out to kill the Marathonian bull. Aegeus knew well the danger of the chore he had assigned this

> **What a Life!**
>
> The enormous Marathonian bull was the same one captured by Heracles in the course of his labors (see Chapter 13). After Heracles released what was then called the Cretan bull, it wandered to Marathon, a coastal plain 26 miles south of Athens, and roamed the countryside there, trampling fields and creating havoc. (This is the first occasion on which Theseus and Heracles cross paths.)

young hero. Years earlier, Aegeus had rid himself of Androgeus—an athletic champion and the son of King Minos of Crete—by asking him to perform the same task.

Bound by the laws of hospitality and his own thirst for adventure, Theseus could not refuse his host. Theseus went to *Marathon*, literally caught the bull by the horns, and forced it to the ground. Tying a rope around its neck, Theseus led the bull back to Athens and presented it to Aegeus to sacrifice. Aegeus was amazed at this feat of daring; Medea was enraged.

Logos

Our word **marathon** comes from the name of the Greek plain 26 miles south of Athens. Marathon footraces— today a standard 26 miles and 385 yards—commemorate the legendary run of a Greek soldier from Marathon to Athens to bring news of the Greek victory over Persian invaders in 490 B.C.E.

In a fury, Medea stirred deadly poison into a cup of wine and talked her husband into offering it to Theseus to toast his victory. But as Theseus reached for the cup, Aegeus suddenly recognized the sword hanging from his guest's belt. After a quick glance at the young man's sandals, Aegeus dashed the cup from Theseus's lips—and embraced him as his son.

Furious at the unmasking of this new heir to the throne, Pallas and his 50 sons openly rebelled. But Theseus, defending his own claim to the throne as well as his father's, killed many of the rebels and forced Pallas and his sons to flee the city. Medea and Medus also left Athens, banished by Aegeus for plotting to kill his son.

Birth of a Beast: The Minotaur

The happy reunion of Theseus and Aegeus did not last long. Eighteen years earlier, King Minos of Crete had attacked Athens to avenge the death of his son Androgeus. Athens, weakened by a plague, had succumbed to Minos or had averted the invasion by agreeing to pay a terrible price. Every nine years, Minos came to Athens to collect his awful payment: seven boys and seven virginal girls to be offered as food for the savage Minotaur. Now, the time came for the third tribute.

The Minotaur, a monster with a bull's head and a man's body, was the offspring of Minos's wife, Pasiphaë, and a handsome bull. At the beginning of Minos's reign, the king wanted to discourage any challenges to the throne by proving his divine right to rule Crete. He prayed to Poseidon to send him a sign: a bull, which he promised to sacrifice. When the beast emerged from the sea, Minos admired it so much that he substituted another for the sacrifice.

Poseidon avenged this insult by making Pasiphaë fall in love with the bull. The queen secretly petitioned Daedalus, a brilliant inventor, to help her consummate her love. Daedalus constructed a hollow wooden cow and covered it with cow hides. The fake cow was so convincing that it fooled the magnificent beast. Pasiphaë, who had hidden herself inside, conceived a monstrous child: the Minotaur.

Daedalus then designed the Labyrinth, a mazelike prison in which the Minotaur lived. No one—except Daedalus himself—had ever entered the Labyrinth and then found a way out.

No Way Out: The Maze and the Minotaur

Despite his father's protests, Theseus volunteered for the sacrifice to the Minotaur. He planned to kill the beast and thus end the tribute forever. Justifiably concerned about his son, Aegeus made Theseus promise that if he escaped death and was returning safely to Athens, he would signal his survival by replacing his ship's black sail with a white one.

On the voyage to Crete, Minos became enamored of Theseus's cousin (once removed) Periboea, the daughter of Megarian King Alcathous (a son of Pelops). Rushing to her assistance, Theseus provoked an argument with Minos in which each questioned the other's divine paternity. Minos prayed to his father (or, according to some, his grandfather) and Zeus answered with a show of thunder and lightning.

The Cretan king then tore off his signet ring, threw it into the sea, and dared Theseus to prove his paternity by retrieving it. Without hesitation, Theseus dived into the water, where dolphins led him to the home of the Nereids. The sea nymphs returned the ring to Theseus—and the sea goddess Thetis also gave him her jeweled crown, a wedding present from Aphrodite. Theseus swam back to the ship, triumphantly gave Minos his ring, and kept the crown himself.

When the shipload of Athenian sacrifices arrived in Crete, Ariadne—a daughter of Minos—became enamored with Theseus. She resolved to help him escape.

Ariadne gave Theseus a spool of thread and a sword. When Theseus entered the Labyrinth, he attached one end of the thread to the entrance. He then unraveled the ball as he explored the maze. Eventually, he found his way to the center of the maze, where he slew the Minotaur with the sword Ariadne had provided. Then he wound the thread back onto the ball, following its trail back to the entrance.

Loss and/or Abandonment

After escaping the Labyrinth, Ariadne, Theseus, and the other 13 Athenians battled their way back to the ship. Having put holes in the hull of the Cretan ships, the Athenians set sail. On the return voyage, Theseus stopped on the island of Dia, also called Naxos. While Ariadne slept, Theseus slipped away in his ship, abandoning the girl on the desert island.

Mythed by a Mile _____

Not all storytellers agreed that Theseus was such a cad. Some insisted that when the Athenians stopped at Dia, the god Dionysus appeared, stole Ariadne away from Theseus, and made her his bride. Still another version suggested that Ariadne, pregnant with the hero's child, stopped to rest on Cyprus, where a storm carried Theseus and the other Athenians away. Ariadne wasted away and died from her grief.

Ariadne awoke, saw the departing Athenian ships, and cursed Theseus. She called upon the gods to punish Theseus for neglecting her. Because he had forgotten his debt to Ariadne, the gods made him forget his promise to his father, too.

Neglecting to change the sails of his ship, Theseus sailed on to Athens. Aegeus, who had long been waiting for word of his son's fate, saw the black-sailed ship approaching the harbor, assumed Theseus was dead, and leaped from the cliffs to his death. The sea that claimed his body was thereafter named the Aegean Sea in his honor.

The triumphant return of Theseus was thus steeped in sorrow. His brief reunion with his father had come to a sudden and tragic end.

King Theseus Wants a Wife

With the death of Aegeus, Theseus assumed the throne of Athens. As king, Theseus used this "bully pulpit" to convince the independent demes (townships) surrounding Athens to join formally in an organized commonwealth. Pointing the way toward democracy, Theseus also ceded some of his own powers as king to this commonwealth.

The reign of Theseus was also marked by limited expansionism. He incorporated the city of Megara—once ruled by his uncle Nisus, but lost in a war with Crete—into the Athenian federation. He also established dominance over Eleusis by seating Hippothoon—like Theseus, a son of Poseidon (by Alope, daughter of the slain Cercyon)—on the throne. Through these actions, Theseus expanded the borders of the Athenian empire all the way across the isthmus to Corinth.

Attack of the Amazons: Antiope

Though his greatest acts of heroism already lay behind the young king, Theseus did not shy away from adventure after attaining the throne of Athens. Some say he joined the Argonauts in their quest for the Golden Fleece (see Chapter 14). If so, he did not distinguish himself in this adventure. He also took part in the Calydon boar hunt (see Chapter 17), though here too he failed to make a significant mark.

Theseus did contribute significantly to the victory of Heracles over the Amazons (see Chapter 13). Antiope, one of three Amazonian queens, fell in love with Theseus. Betraying her sisters, she obtained Queen Hippolyta's girdle for Heracles and escaped with her new lover.

The Amazons pursued Theseus and Antiope to Athens, where they engaged in a costly four-month battle. Hippolyta, defeated in battle, escaped to Megara, but died there.

> **CAUTION**
>
> **Mythed by a Mile**
>
> Naysayers insist that Theseus did little to help Heracles obtain the precious girdle, if indeed he accompanied Heracles at all. These stories insist that Theseus abducted Antiope, perhaps while with Heracles or during the course of an entirely separate adventure.

Antiope, whether as captive or consort, lived with Theseus long enough to give him a son, Hippolytus. The cause of her death, however, remains in dispute. Some say an Amazon warrior killed Antiope as she battled side by side with Theseus. Others hold that an Amazonian ally of hers, Penthesileia, accidentally shot her with an arrow while battling the other Amazons. Some even insist that Theseus himself killed Antiope when she attacked the guests at his wedding to Phaedra.

Forbidden Love: Phaedra

Phaedra was the sister of Ariadne. Their brother Deucalion, who succeeded their father Minos as king of Crete, apparently shrugged off the ill treatment of Ariadne. In reaching a peaceful resolution of the hostilities between Crete and Athens, Deucalion agreed to allow Theseus to marry Phaedra.

The king and his new queen had two sons: Acamas and Demophon. Theseus intended these sons to succeed him in ruling Athens. So he sent Hippolytus, his son by Antiope, to Troezen, where Theseus intended him one day to succeed Pittheus.

Seeing the birth of Acamas and Demophon as establishing a clear line of succession to the throne of Athens, Theseus's uncle Pallas attempted one last time to seize the kingdom. Theseus vanquished Pallas and his sons, killing them all. For this immoderate

196 Part 3: Everyone Needs a Hero

defense of his throne, Theseus condemned himself to one year in exile. With Phaedra at his side, Theseus headed to Troezen to join his son and his grandfather.

In Troezen, Phaedra fell deeply in love with her stepson. But Hippolytus had no interest in women, especially his stepmother. The young man scorned the rites of Aphrodite. A chaste virgin himself, he devoted himself to hunting and to worship of the virgin goddess Artemis.

Phaedra could not keep her love to herself. She revealed her love to her nurse, who in turn told Hippolytus—but only after getting the young man to swear an oath of secrecy. Hippolytus, disgusted, spurned his stepmother's love, but true to his word, remained silent.

Rejected, Phaedra hanged herself after writing a suicide note in which she accused Hippolytus of raping her. Theseus refused to listen to his son's version of the story. He not only banished Hippolytus, but called for his son's death by invoking one of three curses that his father Poseidon had once given him.

Read All About It

Hippolytus, a drama by Euripides, offers a detailed account of the tragic story of Hippolytus and Phaedra. The Roman playwright Seneca told a similar story in his *Phaedra*.

As Hippolytus rode away along the coast in his chariot, a bull rose out of the sea and spooked his horses. The horses upset the chariot and dragged Hippolytus, who had become tangled in the reins, to his death.

The goddess Artemis later appeared before Theseus. From her, he learned that his son had been innocent. Aphrodite had set the whole affair in motion to punish Hippolytus for neglecting her.

Midlife Crisis: The Abduction of Helen

Despite the tragic ends of his affairs with Ariadne, Antiope, and Phaedra, Theseus had not yet given up on finding a suitable wife. This time, he aimed a little higher. Instead of an Amazon queen (Antiope) or a granddaughter of Zeus (Ariadne and Phaedra), Theseus chose to pursue a daughter of Zeus: Helen, a princess of Sparta who would soon become famous for sparking the Trojan War (see Chapter 16).

In this folly, he was strongly influenced by his new friend Peirithous, king of the Lapithae, a rugged tribe who lived in Thessaly (northeastern Greece). The son of Zeus or Ixion, Peirithous met Theseus after stealing a herd of his cattle from Marathon. Peirithous wanted to test the already legendary courage and strength of Theseus. When the hero obligingly pursued Peirithous and caught up with him, the two admired each other so much that they set aside their fight and instead swore eternal friendship.

Theseus stood by his friend's side on the day Peirithous married Hippodameia. When the Centaurs—half-brothers of Peirithous—got drunk and tried to carry off all the women, including the bride, Theseus rushed to his friend's aid. The skirmish set off an all-out war between the Lapithae and the Centaurs. Theseus helped drive the Centaurs out of Thessaly.

Somehow, the two friends—perhaps due to their own divine parentage—got the notion that each should marry a daughter of Zeus. Now middle-aged, Theseus chose young Helen, the adopted daughter of King Tyndareus of Sparta and sister of Castor and Polydeuces. The two friends had little trouble abducting Helen, who was just 10 or 11, from Sparta. Theseus was then obliged to leave Helen with his mother Aethra in the town of Aphidnae in order to help Peirithous achieve his end of the bargain.

Peirithous made an even more foolish choice than Theseus had. He wanted to kidnap Persephone from the Underworld. The two heroes joined to undertake the perilous journey to the Underworld. To their surprise, Hades greeted them warmly and invited them to sit in stone chairs. Instantly, either their flesh grew fast to the stone or serpents or chains held them down. In any case, they could not get up again. What's worse, these Chairs of Forgetfulness stripped them of all memory of who they were and why they had come.

While performing his final labor, Heracles eventually rescued Theseus (see Chapter 13), but a sudden quaking of the ground dissuaded him from freeing Peirithous.

Brought back to the living, Theseus returned to Athens. There he learned that during his absence, the Dioscuri (Castor and Polydeuces) had sacked Aphidnae (and perhaps Athens as well), rescued their sister, and abducted and enslaved Aethra.

The Athenians were furious that Theseus had brought on this attack with his vainglorious abduction of Helen. Menestheus—whom Plutarch called a direct descendant of the great Athenian King Erechtheus—had stirred up resentment toward the absent Theseus. By the time he returned, the Athenians had ousted Theseus as king. Menestheus had assumed the throne—or had been placed there by the victorious Dioscuri.

Unable to wrest back the throne, Theseus took refuge on the Aegean island of Scyrus. Lycomedes, the king of the island, put on a show of welcoming Theseus. But secretly, the king envied his guest's fame and the reverence that his own people showed this stranger. Perhaps he feared that the Scyrians might replace him with his guest. Whatever his reasons, Lycomedes gave Theseus a shove while they were walking along a cliff (or maybe Theseus just "slipped"). The exiled hero plunged to his death.

Long after his death, the image of Theseus, fully armed, arose and helped Athenians to victory over the Persians in the Battle of Marathon (490 B.C.E.). When the Persian

Wars ended, the bones of Theseus were restored to Athens for burial. The renowned monster-slayer and great king of Athens finally reaped the well-deserved honors that his follies had for too long overshadowed.

The Least You Need to Know

- ◆ While traveling to Athens to meet his father, Theseus slew six predators who robbed, tortured, or killed anyone who passed through the Isthmus of Corinth.

- ◆ Theseus navigated the Labyrinth by unraveling a ball of thread and then rolling it back up again. At the maze's center, he killed the Minotaur.

- ◆ While ruling as king, Theseus attempted to introduce some democratic reforms to the Athenian government.

- ◆ Phaedra, Theseus's wife, fell in love with Hippolytus, his son. The affair ended tragically: Phaedra committed suicide and Theseus caused his son's death.

- ◆ Theseus chose wives and consorts unwisely. Ariadne he quickly abandoned; her sister Phaedra killed herself. Choosing Antiope brought an attack by the Amazons. Abducting Helen incurred the wrath of the Dioscuri.

Chapter 16

All's Not Fair in Love and War: The Fall of Troy

In This Chapter

- How Eris crashed the wedding party of Peleus and Thetis and sowed discord with the Golden Apple
- The 10 years of war that followed the abduction of Helen
- The heroes on both sides of the war between the Greeks and Trojans
- How an enormous wooden horse led to the fall of Troy
- The tragic returns of Agamemnon and the Greek troops

The most significant and renowned event in all of classical mythology, the Trojan War, destroyed thousands of valiant and not-so-valiant combatants and nearly a thousand ships. So many legendary figures died in the 10 long years of fighting (traditionally placed around 1200 B.C.E.) that the war and its aftermath brought the age of heroes to an end.

Though it comes to a tragic conclusion—a city destroyed forever, the best and the brightest lying bloody on the battlefield, hundreds more lost at sea—the story of the Trojan War is a rich one. Within its basic framework—an alliance of Greek cities attempting to win back Helen by defeating the impenetrable city of Troy—the story features countless acts of valor, deception, betrayal, treachery, loyalty, and compassion by the heroes on both sides. Through several centuries, countless Greek storytellers focused on one aspect or another of this grand tale as the fabric for their own mythmaking.

One Bad Apple Does Spoil the Bunch

The events that led to the Trojan War began long before the war itself did. The ingredients included a treacherous beauty contest, a prized apple, an oath to protect a marriage, a bribe of love, an unfaithful wife, and an impenetrable wall. Together, they added up to a war that would last for a decade.

Who's the Fairest of Them All?

The wedding of Peleus and Thetis (see Chapter 17) was a marriage made in heaven. Almost all the gods and goddesses attended Mount Pelion (in northeast Greece) for the wedding—for it was the rarest of occasions when a goddess married a mortal man. But Eris, the disagreeable goddess of discord, had not been invited. Angered at this slight, she tossed a Golden Apple, inscribed "For the Fairest," among the goddesses. Immediately Hera, Athena, and Aphrodite started to fight over the apple. Zeus ordered them to take their quarrel elsewhere, and instructed Hermes to lead the goddesses to Troy, a great walled city on the Aegean coast of Asia Minor.

To decide the matter, Zeus appointed Paris, a Trojan prince and reputedly the handsomest of mortal men. Paris thus found himself in the unenviable position of becoming the favorite of one goddess while incurring the wrath of the other two.

Rather than trust the prince's good judgment, all three goddesses attempted to bribe Paris. Hera promised him dominion over the whole world. Athena offered certain victory in every battle. Aphrodite merely offered the most beautiful woman in the world: Helen, a daughter of Zeus and a sister of the Dioscuri. Paris did not hesitate, quickly accepting the beauty and awarding the Golden Apple to the goddess of love.

But She's Already Married!

Unfortunately for Paris, Helen was married to the Greek king of Sparta, Menelaus. Helen was so beautiful that nearly every Greek prince—more than two dozen—had wooed her. Her foster father Tyndareus, fearing that those not chosen might react with violence, had made all her suitors stand on a slain horse and take a solemn oath. Each had sworn not only to abide by Helen's choice, but to punish anyone who might steal the bride away.

Helen had chosen Menelaus, brother of the wealthy Agamemnon, king of Mycenae (and husband of Helen's sister Clytemnestra). The couple had a daughter, Hermione, and perhaps a son or two as well. Before Paris set out some years later to claim his "prize," his brother and sister, the seers Helenus and Cassandra, warned him not to go after Helen.

Ignoring these naysayers, Paris left for Sparta. Helen's husband, King Menelaus, and her brothers, Castor and Polydeuces, warmly welcomed the Trojan prince and entertained him for nine days. Unaware of his guest's motives, Menelaus then left home to attend his grandfather's funeral. In his absence, Paris carried off Helen and a good deal of treasure from the palace as well. (Helen may or may not have gone willingly. Some storytellers insisted that she eagerly deserted her husband to join her handsome young lover. Others argued that Paris forcibly raped and abducted her.)

> **Mythed by a Mile**
>
> The playwright Euripides contended that Helen never made it to Troy. Hera, still angry at Paris for choosing Aphrodite as "the Fairest," spirited Helen away to Egypt and substituted a phantom fashioned from a cloud. Thus, the Greeks and Trojans waged war for 10 years over nothing more than a cloud.

The Face That Launched a Thousand Ships

Learning of Helen's disappearance, Menelaus asked his brother Agamemnon for help. Agamemnon, who would serve as commander in chief of the Greek forces, rounded up the former rivals for Helen's hand. Reminding them of their oath of allegiance, Menelaus demanded they join him in recovering Helen and punishing the Trojans.

Not all of the suitors were eager to fulfill their obligation to Menelaus after so many years had passed. Some bought their way out of their duty. Odysseus, the wily prince of Ithaca, feigned madness but was tricked into giving himself away (see Chapter 18). His ruse exposed, Odysseus reluctantly left his wife Penelope and his infant son Telemachus and joined the Greek forces.

Despite the few who seemed reluctant, the Greeks in time assembled quite a rescue force: more than 1,000 ships from over two dozen different Greek kingdoms. They gathered in Aulis, a Boeotian town on the strait that separated the mainland from the island of Euboea.

Which Way to Troy?

Unfavorable winds kept the fleet from setting out for Troy. Calchas, a soothsayer, blamed the ill winds on Agamemnon, whose boastful claim that he could hunt better than Artemis had offended that goddess. The soothsayer insisted that Agamemnon appease the goddess by sacrificing his daughter, Iphigenia. Odysseus and Diomedes brought her to Aulis under the pretext of her marrying Achilles (the son of Peleus and Thetis), but the beautiful young girl was instead offered to Artemis. (As told by Euripides in *Iphigenia in Tauris*, the goddess may have spared Iphigenia, substituting a deer and whisking the girl away to serve as her priestess in Tauris, the Crimean Peninsula on the Black Sea.)

Clytemnestra was furious at her husband. She refused to believe that a miracle had saved her daughter and despised Agamemnon from that day forward.

What a Life!
Priam was the only son of King Laomedon to survive Heracles' siege of Troy years earlier. After Heracles killed Laomedon and captured his daughter Hesione, he allowed her to buy the freedom of one prisoner. She chose her brother Podarces, who was renamed Priam.

Once the winds changed, the fleet set out. Since no one knew the way to Troy, however, the fleet landed to the south of Troy, in Mysia. Telephus—a son of Heracles and son-in-law of Priam, king of Troy—led a Mysian force that killed several of the Greeks. When Achilles—who would prove the greatest of all the Greek war heroes—wounded him, Telephus followed the Greeks back to Euboea, where he agreed to show the Greeks the way to Troy if Achilles cured him—but he refused to fight against his father-in-law's city (see Chapter 17).

After getting underway again, Philoctetes—who as a boy had inherited Heracles' bow and arrows in return for lighting his funeral pyre (see Chapter 13)—was bitten by a snake on an Aegean island. As one of Helen's ex-suitors, Philoctetes had brought seven shiploads of men to the service of Menelaus. But the stench of his wound and the sound of his agony caused his shipmates—at the urging of Odysseus—to abandon the renowned bowman on the island of Lemnos.

The Long Siege of Troy Begins

Before the Greek fleet landed at Troy (also called Ilium), Menelaus and the eloquent Odysseus went ahead to appeal to King Priam personally. Diplomacy might have prevailed, for Priam saw returning Helen and the Spartan gold as a way to avoid waging war with the impressive Greek fleet. But Priam's sons—he had 50, in addition to 12 daughters and at least 42 illegitimate children—called for war in defense of their brother. They would have killed Menelaus and Odysseus on the spot, but Antenor, Priam's most respected councilor, would not allow them to risk angering the gods by so blatantly violating the laws of hospitality.

An oracle had foretold that the first invader to set foot on Trojan soil would be the first Greek to die there. Only *Protesilaus*, commander of 40 ships from Thessaly, dared defy this oracle. Though he killed several Trojans in this first attack, Protesilaus was indeed the first Greek to fall.

Rather than mount a direct attack on the formidable fortress of Troy, the Greeks set out to destroy the surrounding towns and cities that supplied the city with both provisions and aid. The Greeks used their victories over these outlying regions not merely to cut off supplies to Troy, but to plunder food and provisions for their own armies.

In the course of this nine-year campaign to isolate Troy, the Greek conquerors committed many atrocities in the towns they seized. To satisfy their greed, they looted the surrounding towns of anything they could carry; to serve their lust, they raped and enslaved the women of Phrygia (the large area of Asia Minor in which Troy was situated).

Logos

The name **"Protesilaus"**— derived from "protos" (first) and "hallomai" (jump)—means "first to jump ashore." Unless his parents were seers, the meaning of the name suggests that mythmakers created the character simply in order to fit the story element.

Heroes of the Battlefield

Despite considerable bloodshed and the less-than-noble deeds of the victors, the war also allowed many Greeks—and many Trojans as well—to display their considerable heroism. Even the gods and goddesses got involved in the conflict. Though Zeus forbade the immortals from intervening, most nonetheless lined up on one side or the other:

- ◆ Aphrodite, chosen by Paris as the fairest of goddesses, naturally sided with the Trojans. So did Artemis and her brother Apollo.

- ◆ Hera and Athena, offended by the judgment of Paris, favored the Greeks, as did Poseidon, Hermes, and Hephaestus.

- ◆ Ares, who simply thirsted for battle and bloodshed, fought on both sides.

- ◆ Only Zeus, Hades, Demeter, and Hestia remained neutral throughout the war.

Among the mortals, heroic and tragic figures abounded. In addition to Paris, Menelaus, and Agamemnon, heroes of note were:

♦ *Achilles.* The greatest of Greek warriors, the nearly invulnerable Achilles killed countless Trojans in battle. Achilles proved irreplaceable on the battlefield. When Agamemnon stole away his concubine, Achilles was so offended that he quit the battlefield. The Greeks, who started to suffer serious losses, felt Achilles' absence keenly.

Patroclus, the squire, best friend, and lover of Achilles—horrified at the sight of Trojans attacking the beached Greek ships—asked to borrow Achilles' armor. Though he was no Achilles, Patroclus inflicted great damage on the Trojans. (For a more detailed account of the heroics of Achilles, see Chapter 17.)

Read All About It

Homer's epic, *The Iliad*, focuses on the events of 50 days near the end of the Trojan War, and ends just after the death of Hector. A more comprehensive summary of all 10 years can be found in books 3 through 5 of Apollodorus's *Epitome*.

♦ *Hector.* The eldest son of King Priam, Hector proved himself the mightiest of Trojan warriors. Noble and courageous, Hector repeatedly showed his mettle on the battlefield. It was he who killed the first Greek, Protesilaus. Late in the war, Hector insisted that Paris—who after nine years offered to give back the treasure, but still refused to give up Helen—meet Menelaus in one-on-one combat to decide the issue once and for all. This might have ended the war a year earlier—and at far less cost to the Trojans—but before Menelaus could kill him, Aphrodite spirited Paris away.

Hector also killed Patroclus, which proved his undoing. Achilles returned to the battlefield in a fury, killing dozens of Trojans, including Hector. After the Greeks returned the body, both sides called an 11-day truce in order to mourn the greatest of Trojan heroes.

♦ *Diomedes.* A hero of Argos, Diomedes—who led 80 ships from Argos and its surrounding cities—was second only to Achilles among Greek warriors. In addition to killing many Trojans, Diomedes even wounded two gods: Aphrodite and Ares. The war god, who never really distinguished himself in battle, suffered so badly from his wound that his screams equaled that of 10,000 men.

♦ *Odysseus.* Renowned for his cleverness, Odysseus often teamed up with the daring Diomedes—and not always purely for the greater good of the Greeks. For example, when the pair captured Dolon, a Trojan spying on the Greek camps, they forced him to reveal the layout of the Trojan camp—which no doubt helped the Greek troops—but also listened attentively when Dolon told them they would reap rich rewards if they captured Rhesus, king of Thrace—and then directed them to his camp. After killing the sniveling spy, Odysseus and Diomedes stole into the camp, killed Rhesus and 12 of his men in their sleep, and helped themselves to his valuable horses.

Odysseus and Diomedes also joined in a more heinous conspiracy: engineering the murder of Palamedes, who before the war had tricked Odysseus into revealing his sanity and therefore joining the Greek forces.

Odysseus nursed his hatred for Palamedes for many years. While camped outside of Troy, Odysseus buried some gold under the tent of Palamedes. He then forged a letter from Priam promising Palamedes gold if he betrayed the Greeks. When the letter and gold were "discovered," Agamemnon ordered the Greek troops to stone the "traitor" to death. (For more of the adventures of Odysseus, see Chapter 18.)

◆ *Ajax of Salamis.* The son of Periboea and Telamon, who had captured Troy with Heracles more than a generation earlier, Ajax led 12 ships from Salamis. The tallest of all the warriors, Ajax was an imposing figure on the battlefield. At one point, he met Hector in one-on-one combat and fought to a draw. After the fight, the two combatants showed their respect for each other by exchanging gifts: Ajax gave Hector his belt, while the Trojan gave him a sword.

◆ *Teucer.* Another son of Telamon (by Hesione), Teucer was the best of all Greek archers—at least until the Greeks summoned Philoctetes. He often fought from behind the shield of his half-brother Ajax. Teucer would dart out to the side, shoot an arrow or two, then quickly duck back behind the shield. If Zeus had not broken his bowstring, Teucer would have slain Hector long before Achilles did.

◆ *Ajax of Locris.* The leader of 40 ships from Locris, the "lesser" Ajax was adept with a spear and second only to Achilles in swiftness. He became an inseparable ally of Ajax of Salamis, often fighting side by side with the "greater" Ajax.

◆ *Aeneas.* A Trojan prince, related to Priam but not one of his sons, Aeneas fought with valor. When he was wounded, his mother Aphrodite quickly rescued him (though Diomedes wounded her), and Artemis and Leto healed him. One of the few fighters on the Trojan side to survive the war, Aeneas led several other survivors to a new home in Italy, where the Romans claimed him as the ancestor of their first emperors (see Chapter 22).

The Final Battles: The Tenth Year of the War

After nine long years, the Greeks had seized, ransacked, and looted innumerable towns, but had come no closer to penetrating the impregnable walls of Ilium. The tenth and final year would prove costly to both sides—but only one side would emerge victorious.

The End of Achilles

For a time, it looked as if Troy had gained the upper hand. Just when they needed it the most, the Trojans received reinforcements from foreign lands. Penthesileia, queen of the Amazons, was the first to arrive. Years earlier, King Priam had purified her after she had accidentally killed another Amazon queen, Antiope (see Chapter 15). To repay this favor, she fought alongside the Trojans, inflicting great damage on the Greek troops, until Achilles killed her.

Memnon, the king of Ethiopia, next joined the Trojans, bringing with him a formidable army of thousands. Memnon and his army killed many Greeks, including Antilochus, the young and brave son of Nestor. Nestor, the king of Pylos, who had led 90 ships and offered sage counsel to the Greeks, challenged Memnon to meet him on the field of battle so that he could avenge the death of his son. When Memnon refused, citing Nestor's venerable age, Achilles offered to take the old man's place. Memnon accepted the challenge—and also died at the hands of Achilles.

Paris, who had instigated the war, had never demonstrated a great deal of skill in combat. Though his arrows occasionally hit their targets, the wounds he caused never proved fatal. But in the tenth year of the war, with Apollo guiding his bow, Paris shot an arrow that soared over the walls of Troy, pierced Achilles in the heel—the only vulnerable part of his body—and killed the great warrior.

Though still under heavy fire, Ajax of Salamis carried the body of Achilles off the battlefield, while Odysseus defended him against the Trojan attack. After burying Achilles, Odysseus and Ajax both claimed the right to wear Achilles' armor, which the god Hephaestus had forged.

When the Greek leaders judged Odysseus the most deserving recipient, Ajax went mad. He slaughtered the Greeks' herds of livestock, thinking they were the Greek generals who had insulted him. Once his sanity was restored, Ajax—deeply ashamed—killed himself by falling on the sword he had won from Hector.

A Recipe for Winning the War

After Achilles' death, Odysseus captured the Trojan seer Helenus, brother of Paris. The Greeks persuaded him to tell them the fate of the siege on the city. Helenus revealed that Troy would fall to the Greeks only if the following conditions were met:

♦ Achilles' son, Neoptolemus, joined the fighting.

♦ The Greeks used the bow and arrows of Heracles.

♦ One of the bones of Agamemnon's grandfather, Pelops, was brought to Troy.

♦ The Palladium, an ancient wooden statue of Athena, was stolen from the Trojan citadel called the Pergamum.

Odysseus and Diomedes first went all the way back to the island of Scyrus to recruit *Neoptolemus.* The son quickly donned his father's armor to join the Greeks. In battle, he would prove a champion almost as bold, ruthless, and daunting as his father.

On their way back to Troy, the three stopped at Lemnos, where Philoctetes—cruelly abandoned nine years earlier—had survived by shooting and eating birds. Regarded as the greatest archer in Greece since the death of Heracles, Philoctetes still possessed the hero's bow and arrows. Philoctetes wanted to kill the Greeks, especially Odysseus, whom he had long cursed for his part in the abandonment. Despite his resistance, the archer finally succumbed to persuasion—and the appearance of the spirit of Heracles, who told him it was his duty to fight on the side of the Greeks.

The four returned to Troy, where they found that the people of Elis had gladly sent their fellow Greeks a shoulder blade of Pelops. That left only the Palladium. Under cover of night, Odysseus and Diomedes slipped into Troy and stole the statue, which they carried to the Greek fleet.

Their scavenger hunt immediately began to yield results. Machaon or his brother

> **What a Life!**
>
> When Ilus, founder of Ilium (Troy), arrived on the site where he would build the great walled city, he prayed to Zeus for a sign. The carved, wooden statue of Athena suddenly fell down from the sky and landed in front of Ilus's tent. His prayers answered, Ilus quickly placed the Palladium in the Trojan citadel, where it had protected the city from that day forward.

> **Logos**
>
> The son of the quintessential warrior Achilles, **Neoptolemus** has a name that means "new war."

Podaleirius—grandsons of Apollo and sons of Asclepius, a mortal who had been deified as a god of healing—cured the wound of Philoctetes, who then mortally wounded Paris with one of Heracles' poisoned arrows.

Beware of Greeks Bearing Gifts!

Despite losing virtually all of its greatest champions, Troy still would not fall. The city's walls, built by Apollo and Poseidon, were impenetrable.

Odysseus came up with an ingenious plan to get inside the city. With Athena's help, Epeius, an artisan, constructed an enormous wooden horse. Led by Odysseus, a small army of the boldest Greek warriors hid themselves inside. The Greek fleet then sailed away—but only as far as the far side of the offshore island Tenedos.

When the Trojans found the horse, which had an inscription dedicating it to Athena, some wanted to burn it or push it off a cliff. But others argued that if they brought it inside the city walls and used it to replace the stolen Palladium, the horse would bring them luck. The prophets Cassandra and Laocoön explicitly warned the Trojans that Greek troops were hidden inside the horse—but of course no one believed them.

> **What a Life!**
>
> Cassandra, a priestess of Apollo, had spurned the lustful advances of the god who had taught her prophecy. Apollo punished Cassandra by having all of her prophecies disbelieved. The gift of prophecy, coupled with the curse of disbelief, tormented her all of her days.

Laocoön underscored his warning by hurling his spear at the wooden horse. At that moment, two sea serpents rose out of the sea and attacked Laocoön's sons. The serpents killed the boys and Laocoön, who rushed to his children's defense. Though Athena sent these serpents to shut him up for good and thereby bring about the destruction of Troy, the Trojans who witnessed this horrifying tragedy assumed that the priest was being punished for desecrating the wooden horse.

With the Trojans already inclined to bring the wooden horse inside the city, the Greek Sinon—perhaps a son of the cunning Sisyphus—gave them the last push they needed. The Trojans found him outside the Trojan walls, with his arms tied and his clothes torn to shreds. Apparently enraged at his comrades, Sinon claimed that he had escaped being sacrificed to Athena, who had become angry at the Greeks for stealing the Palladium. The Greeks, Sinon added, had built the enormous horse to appease the goddess—and had designed it so that it would not fit through the city's gates because they knew that placing it in the citadel would bring the Trojans victory. Harming it, Sinon warned, would turn the wrath of Athena on the Trojans.

Persuaded by Sinon's lies, the Trojans breached their own city's walls in order to secure the wooden horse. That night, Helen—suspicious of treachery—walked around the horse and, mimicking the voices of their wives, called out the names of some of the most renowned Greek warriors. But Odysseus kept the men quiet.

After the Trojans had fallen into bed following a drunken celebration of their impending victory, Sinon freed the Greek warriors and sent a beacon to the Greek fleet, which quickly returned. Those inside opened the gates and the Greeks seized the city in a single bloody night.

The Agony of Defeat

In sacking Troy, the Greeks treated the Trojans cruelly and ruthlessly. They committed atrocities that offended both men and gods:

- Neoptolemus slaughtered Priam after dragging him from the sacred altar of Zeus.

- Ajax of Locris raped Cassandra at the shrine of Athena, and in doing so may have knocked down the statue of the goddess. This sacrilege offended even Odysseus, who called on the Greeks to stone Ajax in order to appease the goddess. But the Greeks did not dare, for Ajax clung to the shrine of the very goddess he had affronted.

- Neoptolemus, obeying the ghost of his father, sacrificed Polyxena, Priam's daughter, on the grave of Achilles (who may have wanted the girl to join him in the Underworld).

- Neoptolemus or Odysseus threw Astyanax, the infant son of Hector, to his death from the walls of the city—thus ending the line of Priam forever.

After Menelaus killed Deiphobus—who had forced Helen to marry him after the death of his brother Paris—Helen pleaded for mercy. Menelaus had been determined to kill her for her unfaithfulness—an act that after 10 years both Greeks and Trojans would have applauded. But when faced with her beauty and tears, Menelaus relented and ultimately forgave her.

The End of Heroes

The war cost nearly all the Trojan warriors their lives and destroyed Troy itself, which never recovered from the ransacking, pillaging, and murder done by the victors. But the war also cost Greece dearly. After a decade of battle, few of its warriors returned home alive—and many of these wandered for years before finding their way home.

Welcome Home?

To avenge the crime committed at her shrine, Athena—with the assistance of Poseidon—destroyed most of the Greek fleet on their return voyage. Many of those few who survived the savage seas met their deaths on the rocky shores of Euboea. Nauplius, the aggrieved father of Palamedes, wanted revenge for the conspiracy that had resulted in his son's murder. As the Greek ships, fighting off a storm, approached Euboea, Nauplius lit a huge bonfire. This false beacon lured many of the ships to crash against the rocks. Those sailors who managed to swim to shore were swiftly dispatched by Nauplius.

Of the more than 1,000 ships that sailed from Greece 10 years earlier, less than 100 embarked on the return journey. And most of these were lost before they arrived home.

Those who survived both the war and the arduous trip home did not receive a warm welcome. Among the prominent Greeks who survived:

♦ Both Diomedes of Argos and King Idomeneus of Crete returned home to discover they had been cuckolded. (According to some storytellers, Nauplius influenced both wives to stray.) Both were eventually banished from their homelands and settled in Italy.

Read All About It

The saga of Agamemnon figured prominently in the works of the great Greek tragedians. Three surviving plays by Aeschylus— *Agamemnon, The Libation Bearers,* and *The Eumenides*— are known collectively as the *Oresteia.* In addition, four plays by Euripides—*Iphigenia in Aulis, Orestes, Electra,* and *Iphigenia in Tauris*—as well as *Electra* by Sophocles, focus on the children of Agamemnon.

♦ Philoctetes left Greece to find a new home in Italy.

♦ Odysseus wandered for 10 years before returning home to faithful Penelope (see Chapter 18).

♦ Telamon, who had come to the conclusion that his surviving son, Teucer, had participated in the Greeks' ill treatment that had led Ajax (his other son) to kill himself, refused to allow Teucer to land in Salamis.

♦ Nestor peacefully resumed the throne of Pylos— the only Greek to reach home without incident.

◆ Neoptolemus, warned by his grandmother Thetis against the dangers that awaited those who went by sea, took a long overland route, but eventually arrived in Greece.

◆ Storms drove the ship carrying Menelaus and Helen far off course. The couple spent considerable time in Crete, Libya, Phoenicia, Cyprus, and Egypt. Though stranded, Menelaus amassed even greater wealth during his time in Egypt and the coastal lands of North Africa. By the time he and Helen returned home and resumed the rule of Sparta, several years had passed.

The House of Blood: Agamemnon's Return

By the time Agamemnon returned to Mycenae, Clytemnestra—still incensed at her husband's sacrifice of their daughter Iphigenia—had taken a lover. To add to the insult, Clytemnestra had chosen her husband's cousin Aegisthus, the son of Agamemnon's estranged uncle, Thyestes.

Many years earlier, Agamemnon's father, Atreus, had been betrayed by both his brother Thyestes and his wife Aerope, who had entered into an adulterous affair. In exacting his revenge, Atreus took a page from his grandfather Tantalus (see Chapter 11). Atreus killed his brother's children, cooked them, and served them to their father. After cruelly showing Thyestes the heads and hands of his children, Atreus banished his brother—who cursed the House of Atreus—from Mycenae.

An oracle later told Thyestes that he could avenge his children's deaths by conceiving a child with his sole surviving daughter, Pelopia. Aegisthus, the product of this union, would indeed become the instrument for his father's revenge on the House of Atreus.

In Agamemnon's absence, Aegisthus had used his influence over Clytemnestra to rule Mycenae. So he watched carefully for his rival's return. That very day, while Agamemnon was bathing after his long journey home, Clytemnestra pinned him down with his robes and hacked him to pieces with an axe. Clytemnestra also killed the seer Cassandra, whom Agamemnon had brought home as a slave.

Electra, a daughter of Agamemnon and Clytemnestra, sent her younger brother Orestes to Phocis (a region of central Greece on the other side of the Gulf of Corinth) to protect him.

Logos

The **Erinyes,** called the Furies by the Romans, were vengeful female spirits who punished mortals who had committed crimes against their own family members. In *The Eumenides* of Aeschylus, these violent, punishing goddesses also became patrons of Athenian fertility and safety.

Eight years later, Orestes, now a young man, returned to avenge his father's death. Ordered by Apollo and egged on by Electra, Orestes killed both his mother and her lover.

Orestes was sentenced to death for this crime—though the sentence was later reduced to one year's banishment. Worse than being exiled was the relentless torture inflicted by the *Erinyes*, who drove Orestes mad.

Beset by the Erinyes, Orestes traveled to Delphi to seek help from the god who had told him to commit this crime. Apollo sent the tormented boy to Athens. Tried on the Areopagus for matricide, Orestes was acquitted when Athena cast the decisive vote in his favor. This verdict offered some satisfaction to the Erinyes, who eased up on their persecution of Orestes.

Cured of his madness, Orestes claimed his father's throne in Mycenae. He later conquered Arcadia and—as Tyndareus's grandson—succeeded to the throne of Sparta. This consolidation of power made him the most powerful monarch in the Peloponnesus.

Hermione, the daughter of Helen and Menelaus, had been promised to the boy Orestes before the war. But near the end of the war, Menelaus had also promised her to Neoptolemus. Orestes fumed when he found that Neoptolemus had married his intended. Eventually, Orestes killed him or had him killed. At last, he married Hermione and lived to a grand old age.

The Least You Need to Know

- Eris, the goddess of discord, sowed the seeds of war by throwing a Golden Apple among the goddesses, which was to belong to the fairest among them. Paris was selected by Zeus to decide who was the most beautiful. He chose Aphrodite, who had bribed him with Helen.

- Because all the princes of Greece had sworn to defend the marriage of Helen and Menelaus, more than two dozen Greek kingdoms united to attack Troy after Paris abducted Helen.

- After a decade of fighting, the Trojans breached their own city walls to bring in the wooden horse filled with Greek soldiers.

- Clytemnestra killed her husband, the war hero Agamemnon, and was later killed by her son Orestes.

17

Achilles: The Angry Young Hero

In This Chapter

◆ Peleus and Thetis: A marriage literally made in heaven

◆ How Thetis made her son Achilles invulnerable (well, almost)

◆ The mightiest of the Greeks

◆ Why Achilles quit the war

◆ The return of Achilles—and his death on the battlefield

Of all the heroes who fought in the 10-year Trojan War, none approached the greatness of Achilles. A bold and ruthless warrior, Achilles showed his courage and skill on the battlefield countless times. He alone killed multitudes of Trojans, as well as their most fierce allies.

The perfect hero on the battlefield, Achilles was not without flaws. His brashness led him to ignore the advice and counsel of others. His tremendous pride caused him at one point to abandon his Greek comrades and quit the war because he felt insulted. His explosive anger and bloodlust led him to desecrate the body of his most heroic adversary.

As it turned out, Achilles—who seemed unbeatable whether in one-on-one combat or in the middle of a bloody battlefield—was not invulnerable either. Guided by the hand of Apollo, an arrow pierced *Achilles' heel*—the one spot where he could be killed. His death demonstrated for the ages that even the greatest of heroes was vulnerable.

How to Create an (Almost) Invulnerable Hero

The creation of the ancient world's greatest war hero did not happen by accident or chance. The gods brought his parents together. His mother made him nearly invulnerable. His tutors trained him in martial skills with an eye to his future glory. And the greatest princes of Greece recruited him while he was still a boy.

Logos

Even today, when we refer to a specific flaw that causes the mighty to fall, we use a term that harkens back to the death of Greece's greatest war hero: We call this weakness a person's **Achilles' heel.**

What a Life!

Aegina was named after the river god Asopus's daughter, whom Zeus had abducted and brought to the uninhabited island. (Zeus consigned Sisyphus to eternal torment for telling Asopus who had taken his daughter.) Aeacus, son of Zeus and Aegina, grew up alone on the island. When he prayed for company, his father Zeus transformed the island's ants into men and women whom Aeacus named the Myrmidons— the "ant-men."

A Lover, Not a Fighter: His Father Peleus

Achilles was the son of Peleus, the king of Phthia, a city in Thessaly (northeastern Greece), and Thetis, a goddess of the sea. As young men, Peleus and his brother Telamon—sons of Aeacus, king of the island of Aegina—killed their half-brother Phocus. Though they had murdered Phocus at the behest of their mother, Aeacus banished both Peleus and Telamon from the island.

Telamon migrated to the island of Salamis, where he later became king. Peleus headed for Thessaly, where Eurytion, the king of Phthia, welcomed him. Eurytion performed the rites necessary to purify Peleus of his brother's murder and offered his guest the hand of his daughter, Antigone. Peleus settled there for a time, but his life in Phthia ended when he accidentally killed his father-in-law Eurytion with an errant toss of his spear during the Calydon boar hunt.

Peleus took refuge in Iolcus, where his fellow Argonaut, Acastus, had succeeded Pelias to the throne (see Chapter 14). Acastus purified his friend of the accidental killing, and invited him to remain in Iolcus.

Unfortunately, Astydameia, Acastus's wife, fell in love with Peleus. When he spurned her advances, Astydameia claimed that Peleus had violated her.

Acastus could not commit the impiety of killing a man he had recently purified, but he was incensed by his friend's alleged betrayal. So he worked out a plan of indirectly causing Peleus's death.

What a Life!

King Oeneus of Calydon once forgot to include Artemis when he sacrificed the first fruits of the harvest. To avenge this insult, the goddess sent down a wild boar to ravage the countryside, destroy the crops, and kill both people and animals. The Calydon boar hunt brought together some great heroes: Peleus and Telamon, Castor and Polydeuces, Theseus and Peirithous, Jason, the huntress Atalanta, and Meleager, who finally killed the beast.

Acastus invited Peleus to join him and his nobles in a hunting contest. Peleus returned from the hunt apparently empty-handed, but he silenced the laughter of the other hunters by pulling the tongues of his kills out of his pouch. By not taking the time to drag the animals back to camp, he had easily won the contest.

Exhausted, Peleus fell asleep. Under the cover of night, Acastus stole his sword, hid it under a dung heap, and abandoned Peleus, hoping that the barbarous Centaurs would find him and kill him. The half-human beasts might have done so, but Cheiron—the wise and civilized Centaur who made his home on Mount Pelion—found him first. Cheiron saved Peleus and returned his sword.

Peleus—accompanied by Jason, Castor, and Polydeuces—later returned to Iolcus with an army. He killed Astydameia for her treachery and had his army march between the pieces of her severed body.

A Marriage Made in Heaven

Thetis, like the other 49 Nereids, was a daughter of the old sea god Nereus and the sea goddess Doris. Zeus had courted Thetis, who had once helped rescue him from a rebellion by Poseidon, Hera, and Athena (see Chapter 6). But the ruler of the gods lost interest in the sea nymph when he learned from Prometheus that the son she would bear would become greater than his father. Remembering that he had over-thrown his own father to become king of the gods and fearful of suffering the same fate himself, Zeus decided that Thetis should not marry any god. Instead, she would become the rare goddess who married a mortal. Zeus chose Peleus, who had inherited the throne of Phthia from his father-in-law Eurytion. (Antigone, Peleus's first wife, had killed herself when Astydameia's lies raised doubt about her husband's fidelity.)

Cheiron, king of the Centaurs, soon sent his friend Peleus to Thetis's favorite grotto. Cheiron told Peleus that if he could hold on to the sea goddess through all her transformations, she would become his bride. Peleus found Thetis, wrapped his arms around her, and refused to let go. Though she changed into fire, water, a lioness, a snake, and a cuttlefish, Peleus held on tight. Finally, the sea goddess yielded, consenting to be his wife.

All the gods and goddesses attended this legendary wedding. The gods, already honoring the couple with their presence, added to the honor with presents. Thetis received a magnificent jeweled crown from Aphrodite. To Peleus, the gods brought two immortal horses, Xanthus and Balius.

Unfortunately, Eris, the only goddess not invited to the wedding, tried to crash the party. When she was still refused admittance, she used the Golden Apple—and the rivalry it sparked among three goddesses—to sow the discord that would more than a decade later lead to the 10-year Trojan War (see Chapter 16).

Don't Try This at Home!

Thetis—a minor goddess perhaps, but still a goddess—was not content to have a mere mortal as a son. So when her child, Achilles, was born, she set about to make him an immortal. Heracles, you'll recall, burned off his mortality on a funeral pyre, while the immortal part of him ascended to Mount Olympus. Thetis hoped to do the same for her son. So she anointed him with ambrosia by day and set him on the coals at night. Peleus saw his son on the coals one night and quickly pulled him off. Thetis, insulted by her husband's lack of faith in her, abandoned both Peleus and her son and returned to the sea.

Mythed by a Mile

Mythmakers do not agree on just how Thetis made her son immortal. Some say the goddess dipped the baby in the river Styx, which burned the mortal life away from him and made him nearly immortal—except for the heel by which Thetis held him. Others insist that Thetis had already given birth to several children before Achilles was born. To test their mortality, she dipped each child into a pot of boiling water, but none had survived the test. When Peleus saw his wife trying this test with Achilles, he pulled his child from the pot not even realizing that the boy had passed the test—again except for the heel by which Thetis held him.

Hey, This Kid's Got Potential!

Now a single father, Peleus gave the boy to his old friend Cheiron—renowned for his breeding, wisdom, and teaching abilities—to rear. It was Cheiron who gave the boy his name, Achilles. Cheiron taught him both the polite arts and the manly arts. Even in early childhood, Achilles showed great promise. Indeed, he ran so fast that he could chase down a deer. To build the boy's courage and strength, Cheiron fed him the intestines of wild animals. Before Achilles left Pelion, Cheiron cut down one of the mountain's great ash trees and shaped it into Achilles' spear.

While still a boy, Achilles returned to his father's home in Phthia. There Phoenix, king of the Dolopians and a friend of Peleus, took over the boy's training.

What a Life!
Phoenix had fled his homeland of Ormenium to escape his father's wrath. His mother, insanely jealous of her husband's concubine, had convinced Phoenix to seduce her rival. When his father discovered this betrayal, he cursed Phoenix, asking the Furies to deny him children. Though Phoenix considered killing his father, he chose to leave his homeland instead. Peleus gave Phoenix refuge and made him king of the Dolopians (a tribe in Thessaly).

While studying under Phoenix, Achilles met Patroclus, the son of Menoetius. Both father and son had taken refuge in Phthia (where Peleus was an exceedingly kind-hearted host). Patroclus, it seems, had killed a playmate in an argument over a game of dice in Opus, their native city. After Peleus purified the boy of the killing, Patroclus—several years older than Achilles—became the younger boy's squire. Before long they became friends and, in later years, lovers.

The renowned seer Calchas also recognized Achilles' potential. When the son of Peleus was just nine years old, Calchas prophesied that the Greeks would never take Troy without him.

The More Things Change ...
Although Homer never presented Achilles and Patroclus as lovers, most tale tellers by the fifth century B.C.E. did. Male homosexuality played a much more significant social role in fifth-century Athens than it had earlier. Male social and political connections sometimes included a sexual component, but this did not necessarily imply an exclusive homosexual orientation. Male citizens also had a social obligation to marry and father legitimate children.

Draft Dodging? Try Dressing in Drag

Thetis, however, knew that her son was fated to die if he fought in the Trojan War. So in an attempt to keep him from joining Menelaus in the campaign to recover Helen, the goddess disguised Achilles as a girl and sent him to the Aegean island of Scyrus. Called by the feminine name of Pyrrha, Achilles lived among the daughters of King Lycomedes (yes, the same Lycomedes who killed Theseus [see Chapter 15]).

Placing a handsome and virile teenage boy—even one disguised as a girl—in the same bedroom as several pretty teenage girls had predictable results. Shortly after Achilles left the island, Deidameia, one of Lycomedes' daughters, gave birth to a son. She named the boy Pyrrhus, in honor of the "girl" who fathered him. (After Achilles' death, Phoenix renamed the boy—who would contribute greatly to the Greek victory—Neoptolemus.)

When Odysseus came to Scyrus to enlist Achilles for the war effort, Lycomedes claimed that the boy was not there. But the wily Odysseus knew a lie when he heard one, and he devised a scheme to get Achilles to reveal himself.

Odysseus laid a spear and a shield down on the porch next to a handful of baubles and trinkets. He invited all the "king's daughters" to play with the pretty jewels. While the girls played, the ship's trumpeter—acting under Odysseus's orders—sounded a martial call, indicating that they were under attack. The trick worked. As soon as the horn blew, Achilles alone dropped the baubles, seized the sword and shield, and stripped off his feminine clothes. Gotcha!

To War!

With Phoenix's help, Odysseus persuaded Achilles to help the Greek cause even though he had been far too young to have been one of Helen's suitors.

Thetis tried to persuade her son to forsake the Greeks. She confided in him that if he remained at home in Phthia, he would have a long, safe, and comfortable life. But if he journeyed to Troy, he would have a short, dangerous, and glorious one. A hero through and through, Achilles did not hesitate to choose the glory.

Odysseus and Achilles soon joined the fleet in Aulis. There Achilles, still a very young man, was appointed an admiral in Agamemnon's fleet. Achilles would lead an army of Myrmidons, the "ant-people" who had migrated to Phthia with Peleus when his father banished him from Aegina. (Peleus, who was too old to join his son in battle, bestowed upon Achilles his golden armor, which Hephaestus himself had forged, and the glorious horses the gods had given him at his wedding.) After the sacrifice of Agamemnon's daughter, Iphigenia, Achilles and the Greeks headed east across the Aegean Sea.

A Curious Cure

After crossing the Aegean, the Greek fleet mistakenly landed at Mysia, where they found themselves under attack. The repelling force was led by Telephus, the son of Heracles and Auge and the husband of Paris's sister Astyoche. The Mysian troops forced the Greek armies to retreat to their ships, but not before Achilles wounded Telephus in the thigh.

The Greeks withdrew and returned home. But Telephus, who had learned from an oracle that only the one who had wounded him could heal him, followed the fleet all the way back to Euboea.

Achilles did not know the first thing about healing, but Odysseus divined that "the one who wounded" Telephus was not Achilles himself, but rather his spear. So Achilles cured Telephus by scraping some rust from the spearhead into the wound—but only after securing the Mysian's promise to show them the way to Troy.

First Blood: The Early Battles

Before attacking Troy, the Greeks first sacked the offshore island of Tenedos. Ignoring his mother's warnings, the son of Thetis killed King Tenes—a son of Apollo—who had tried to prevent the invaders from landing by pelting them with heavy stones. Apollo was not at all pleased; the god would eventually help to kill Achilles.

Achilles established himself as a force to be reckoned with in the very first attack on Troy. Achilles battled with Cycnus, the king of Colonae (and foster father of Tenes). Poseidon, his father, had made Cycnus totally invulnerable to weapons. Finding his spear, sword, and arrows all useless, Achilles strangled Cycnus with the thongs of his own helmet. As Cycnus died, his father Poseidon transformed his body into a swan.

Achilles then led the forces that conquered 12 Phrygian cities by sea and 11 more by land. Everywhere the Greeks battled, Achilles seemed to make his mighty presence felt. In the Hypoplacian Thebes, the warrior killed King Eëtion, the father of Hector's wife Andromache, and his seven sons in a single day. Achilles honored the king and his prowess by awarding him a full funeral and burial in his armor. But he held the queen, Hector's mother-in-law, for ransom.

In an attack on Mount Ida, Achilles drove the Trojan leader Aeneas from his home and forced him to take refuge in the nearby city of Lyrnessus. Apollo later urged Aeneas to challenge Achilles once again. But Poseidon—pointing toward the Trojan's greater destiny as the founder of the Roman race—safely removed him from the battle. (For more on Aeneas, see Chapter 22.)

More than any other Greek warrior, Achilles tormented and terrorized the 50 sons of the Trojan King Priam. He ambushed and killed Troilus. He captured Isus and Antiphus while they were tending sheep on Mount Ida. Priam paid a ransom for their return only to see them both killed in battle by Agamemnon.

Achilles also captured Lycaon, another son of Priam, while the boy was cutting fig shoots to make rims for his chariot wheels. He sold the boy as a slave to King Euneus of Lemnos in return for a silver mixing bowl. Lycaon was later ransomed by a friend and returned to the war. But just 12 days after regaining his freedom, Lycaon was killed in battle by Achilles, who ignored the young man's pleas for mercy.

Never Insult Your Greatest Warrior

In the Greek attack on Lyrnessus, Achilles killed two sons of King Evenus: Mynes and Epistrophus. He also abducted a young beauty named Briseis to serve as his concubine after killing her parents, three brothers, and husband.

Read All About It

Achilles is the hero of Homer's epic *The Iliad,* which tells of events from the abduction of Briseis until the death of Achilles. The epic begins, "Sing, goddess, the anger of Achilles, son of Peleus." His anger at both Trojans and Greeks dominates the epic, which depicts Achilles as a bloodthirsty fighting machine. In the final book, however, Achilles reveals his humanity. Touched by the grief of his greatest enemy's father, he softens his wrath and returns the body of Hector to Priam.

Meanwhile, Agamemnon enslaved a concubine of his own on the island of Chryse: Chryseis, daughter of the island's priest of Apollo. But her father persuaded that god to send a pestilence on the Greeks. Both animals and men began dying in and around the Greek camp.

Though Agamemnon preferred her charms to those of any other woman, the Greek commander in chief—urged by the seer Calchas and pressured by the other Greek generals—was forced to give Chryseis back to end the pestilence.

To compensate for his loss, Agamemnon appropriated Briseis from Achilles. Grossly offended, Achilles vowed to remain in his tent and refused to fight—or to allow his troops to fight—any longer in Agamemnon's army.

Thetis, who had kept a close watch on her son since the day he left Scyrus to join the Greek armies, petitioned Zeus to deny the Greeks any victories until they begged Achilles to return to them. Zeus agreed, and the Greeks began suffering serious setbacks. Hector, commander of the Trojan forces, led an assault that pushed the Greeks all the way back to their beached ships, then nearly set fire to the entire fleet.

Agamemnon sent Odysseus, Achilles' brave cousin Ajax (a son of Telamon), and his old tutor Phoenix to plead with Achilles to rejoin the Greek force. They offered Achilles not only the return of Briseis, but an enormous amount of treasure as well. Achilles still refused. Phoenix remained with his ward while Odysseus and Ajax returned to the Greek camp with the bad news.

The Final Battles

Though Achilles himself would not fight, he agreed to lend his armor to his squire, friend, and lover Patroclus, who was inspired to join the battle. Patroclus performed valiantly, but soon died at the hands of Hector.

I Have Not Yet Begun to Fight

Stung by the loss of Patroclus, Achilles finally returned to battle. (At the request of Thetis, who had reared Hephaestus after Hera had thrown him out of Mount Olympus, the god of artisans forged new armor for Achilles.)

Achilles cut through the battlefield in a fury. He savagely killed dozens of Trojans and tossed them into the river Scamander. Finding his waters choked with the mighty warrior's victims, the river god rose up against Achilles. Scamander flooded the plain where Achilles fought, but Hephaestus saved the hero from drowning by drying up the river with a single, tremendous flame.

Though Hector tried to compel the Trojans to stand their ground, Achilles almost single-handedly forced the Trojan troops to retreat inside the walls of their city. Hector alone came out to challenge Achilles on the battlefield. Achilles chased and finally slew the Trojan hero, then desecrated Hector's body, dragging the corpse behind his chariot and circling the walls of Troy three times. Only after both Priam and Thetis appealed to him did Achilles give up the body for burial.

> **What a Life!**
>
> When Patroclus died, the immortal horses that had pulled his chariot—Xanthus and Balius—wept. Zeus, observing their mourning, rued the day he placed them among the miserable race of men. When Achilles resumed his place in the chariot, Xanthus—given the power of speech by Hera—warned him of his impending death. But Achilles would not hear it, and the Furies silenced Xanthus forever.

Love Among the Ruins

Though his fury died down somewhat after the death of Hector, Achilles remained a formidable warrior until his death. When Penthesileia, the Amazon queen, arrived and fought valiantly on the side of the Trojans, it was Achilles who defeated her. As she died, however, Penthesileia looked into the eyes of her killer. In that moment, Achilles fell in love with her. The Amazon queen was so beautiful that Achilles wept as he stripped her corpse of her armor.

The impulsive murder of Thersites—who mocked the hero's feelings toward his victim—forced Achilles to take leave from the fighting. He traveled to Lesbos, where he made sacrifices to Apollo, Artemis, and Leto before Odysseus purified him.

Upon his return to the battlefield, Achilles killed Memnon, the king of Ethiopia and nephew of Priam, who had come to aid the Trojans with an army of thousands.

Achilles, the mightiest of all Greek warriors, achieved no more victories on the battlefield. From inside the walls of Troy, Paris—with the considerable assistance of Apollo, the archer god—shot an arrow that pierced the hero's vulnerable heel.

The Greeks constructed a funeral pyre to honor their fallen hero. After his corpse had been burned, Thetis and her 49 sisters (the Nereids) arose from the sea. After collecting her son's ashes in a golden urn, she mixed them with the ashes of Achilles' slain friend and lover, Patroclus, and disappeared back into the sea.

The Least You Need to Know

- Achilles was the son of Peleus, a mortal, and Thetis, a sea goddess, whose wedding party sparked the Trojan War.

- Thetis burned away most of Achilles' mortality, but never finished the job, leaving his heel vulnerable.

- Thetis tried to keep her son from participating in the Trojan War by dressing him in girl's clothing, but Odysseus tricked Achilles into revealing himself.

- Achilles became the greatest warrior in Greek mythology, killing dozens of Trojans and their allies during the 10-year Trojan War.

- Achilles left the Greek army when Agamemnon wounded his pride. He returned in a fury, though, after his squire Patroclus was killed by the Trojan Hector.

- Paris, with Apollo guiding his bow, shot Achilles in the heel and killed him.

Take the Long Way Home: Odysseus

In This Chapter

- ◆ How Odysseus, a suitor of Helen, won Penelope instead
- ◆ The hero's big mistake: blinding the Cyclops
- ◆ Facing dangers on land and at sea during 10 years of wandering
- ◆ Long layovers with Circe and Calypso
- ◆ The sole survivor home at last: slaying the suitors and reuniting with the faithful Penelope

Returning home to Greece from the Trojan War was no pleasure cruise. Indeed, very few of the Greek warriors made it home at all. Most of the returning ships were destroyed at sea. Even among those that remained intact, most arrived home only after being blown considerably off course, suffering delays that lasted up to several years (see Chapter 16).

But of all the returning Greek heroes of the Trojan War, none took a more tortuous route than Odysseus. After 10 years of war, the king of

Ithaca wandered the Mediterranean and its coastal lands for another 10 years before finally arriving home. When he got there, Odysseus didn't like what he found: a house full of "noble" men, each hoping to win his wife Penelope—and his fortune—for himself.

Is This the Stuff Heroes Are Made Of?

Odysseus came from a long line of thieves, tricksters, and scoundrels. His mother was Anticleia, daughter of the notorious cattle thief Autolycus. Odysseus's father in name was King Laertes of Ithaca. Yet a rumor spread that Anticleia was already pregnant when she married Laertes. Odysseus's real father may have been the infamous rogue Sisyphus, who seduced Anticleia to punish her father for stealing his cattle (see Chapter 11).

Odysseus's grandfather Autolycus had a great influence on the young boy. Asked by his daughter to name her child, Autolycus called the boy "Odysseus," meaning "giver and receiver of pain"—in memory of all the misery Autolycus had caused and suffered in his roguish days. When he reached manhood, Odysseus began his travels with a trip to his grandfather. While hunting with the sons of Autolycus, a boar gored him in the thigh with its tusk, giving Odysseus a scar that he would bear for the rest of his life.

As a young man, Odysseus became friends with Iphitus, a son of Eurytus, the famed archer who had taught young Heracles how to draw a bow. Iphitus honored Odysseus with the gift of his father's bow, which Odysseus prized so highly that he refused to use it to hunt or to fight—with one notable exception some 30 years later.

Choosing Wisely

When the time came for Helen to choose a husband, Odysseus was the only one of her many suitors not to bring gifts. Strongly suspecting that Helen would choose the wealth of Menelaus over the assets of all other men, Odysseus instead turned his attention to her cousin Penelope. So when Helen's father Tyndareus worried that the rejected suitors would do harm to the chosen one, Odysseus suggested that all the suitors take an oath to protect the interests of whomever she chose. In return for this ingenious solution, Tyndareus put in a good word about Odysseus to his brother Icarius, Penelope's father. As it turned out,

Mythed by a Mile

Some storytellers insist that Odysseus won the right to marry Penelope through an athletic contest (a foot race). Icarius, they say, offered Penelope's hand in marriage as the prize.

Odysseus made the right choice. Helen, who abandoned her husband, went down in legend as the most faithless of wives, while Penelope, who waited 20 years for Odysseus to return, earned fame as the most faithful wife of all.

Though Icarius consented to the marriage of Penelope and Odysseus, he wanted the couple to remain in Sparta with him. But the prince of Ithaca refused. As Odysseus drove off with her in his chariot, Icarius ran behind begging his daughter not to leave him. Penelope answered by raising her veil to cover her face, modestly indicating that she would go with her new husband. Icarius, left in the dust, later erected a shrine to modesty at that site.

Draft Dodging? Try Feigning Insanity

When Helen ran off to Troy with Paris, Odysseus was bound by his oath to help Menelaus recover her. Yet he was happily married to Penelope and had no desire to leave his wife and their new baby: a son named Telemachus.

Odysseus feigned madness in an attempt to avoid the war. When Palamedes came to recruit him, he found Odysseus, apparently insane and oblivious, guiding a plough hitched with a donkey and an ox and sowing salt in a field. But Palamedes suspected trickery, and proved it by placing the infant Telemachus in front of the draft animals and plow. When Odysseus turned the plow to avoid his son, his sanity was revealed.

Despite his reluctance, Odysseus became the most loyal of all of Agamemnon's troops. On the battlefield, Odysseus—who led 12 shiploads of men from Ithaca and the sur-rounding islands—demonstrated courage to the point of fearlessness. Even more so, however, he employed eloquence and wiles to defeat his enemies. It was Odysseus who:

- Saw through Achilles' disguise and tricked him into giving himself away.

- Lured Iphigenia to Aulis under the false pretense of wedding her to Achilles.

- Manufactured false evidence to frame Palamedes as a traitor (a trick that led the Greeks to kill him).

- Persuaded the Greek generals to award him, rather than Ajax, the armor of Achilles.

- Devised the trick of all tricks, a ploy that would have made his crafty grandfather Autolycus and his wily father Sisyphus proud: the Trojan Horse. (See Chapter 16 for more on the wartime exploits of Odysseus.)

It seems clear that without the deviousness and powers of persuasion of Odysseus, the Greeks would never have won the war.

Going Home So Soon? Not Bloody Likely

Like so many of the Greek soldiers, however, Odysseus had a difficult time getting home. His long journey began when he quickly crossed the Hellespont from Troy to the peninsula known as the land of the Bistones (a Thracian tribe). Odysseus brought with him as his slave Hecuba, the wife of Priam. Near the end of the war, Hecuba had sent her youngest son Polydorus and a shipment of gold to the Thracian King Polymestor, a Trojan ally. Now she hoped to recover them both.

Sadly, Hecuba discovered that Polymestor had murdered Polydorus and stolen the gold. Hecuba avenged her son's death by luring the king into her tent, blinding him, and killing his two infant sons. Turning into a dog with eyes of fire, Hecuba then dived into the sea.

> **The More Things Change …**
>
> Mythic journeys in which a hero learns of the world abroad and returns home wiser, though sometimes sadder, appear in many different ages and cultures. These include: the Babylonian epic of *Gilgamesh* (see Chapter 3), Dante's *Divine Comedy*, the quest for the Holy Grail, *Huckleberry Finn*, and *The Wizard of Oz*.

What Are We Doing Here?

Odysseus continued on, moving westward along the coast of Thrace to the Ciconian city of Ismarus. He and the crew members of his 12 ships sacked the city, sparing only Maron, a priest of Apollo, who gratefully bestowed upon them fine wine and other gifts. Despite Odysseus's warning, his crews celebrated their victory for too long. The main force of Ciconians descended upon them and drove them out to sea. Six benches of rowers from each of Odysseus's 12 ships were lost. (Each bench held two or three men.)

The dozen ships sailed the Aegean uneventfully. Soon they reached Cape Malea, the southernmost point of the Peloponnesus, and prepared to sail north to Ithaca. But nine days of foul winds drove them all the way across the Mediterranean to Libya. When three men, sent inland to scout the territory, failed to return, Odysseus went after them himself.

Odysseus soon found a tribe of natives who offered him the yellow-orange fruit of the lotus. Yet he saw the effect the fruit had produced in his scouts: The three men had entirely forgotten their mission and had no further ambition but to continue eating this fruit. Odysseus dragged the three away from the Lotus-Eaters and brought them back to the ships.

My, What a Big Eye You Have!

Odysseus next put in at a wooded island (perhaps Sicily). Unknown to Odysseus and his men, the savage, one-eyed giants known as Cyclopes lived here.

With a dozen men, Odysseus climbed to a cave where they found a bounty of cheese, lambs, and kids. Though the crew wanted to take these spoils and run, Odysseus ordered them to wait and see who lived there. A giant Cyclops named Polyphemus returned with his flocks at dusk, trapping everyone inside by closing off the entrance to his cave with a massive boulder.

What a Life!

A seer named Telemus had once warned Polyphemus that a man named Odysseus would blind him. But Polyphemus was too heartbroken to pay attention to this oracle. The grotesque Cyclops had loved the sea nymph Galatea, but she only had eyes for the handsome human youth Acis. Polyphemus crushed his rival under a giant rock. But Galatea only hated him more after this murder, while Acis—in answer to her prayers— was changed into a river god.

Odysseus appealed for kindness under the laws of hospitality. But Polyphemus, who recognized neither gods nor laws, demonstrated his idea of hospitality by devouring two of Odysseus's men. Odysseus kept his wits about him. He knew he should not kill the Cyclops because only Polyphemus was strong enough to reopen the cave's mouth. So he plotted their escape throughout the night.

When morning came, Polyphemus ate two more Greeks, then left to tend to his flocks—but not until he had again closed off the entrance to the cave with the giant boulder. The Cyclops returned that night and devoured two more men.

Odysseus, who cleverly introduced himself to the Cyclops as "Nobody" (Outis), filled his host with Maron's delicious wine that night. When the giant passed out in a drunken stupor, Odysseus drove a heated stake through his eye. Polyphemus roared with pain, which brought his fellow Cyclopes running to the entrance of his cave. But when they asked what was wrong, Polyphemus screamed, "Nobody has blinded me! Nobody is killing me!" The Cyclopes, simultaneously relieved and annoyed by this news, told him to be quiet and go back to sleep.

The next morning, Polyphemus shoved the boulder aside, but blocked the entrance with his own body, hoping to catch the remaining seven men as they tried to leave. But during the night, Odysseus had tied himself and his men to the undersides of rams in the ogre's flock. As Polyphemus sent the animals out to graze, he stroked each on its back to make sure it was indeed a sheep. But because he failed to stroke their underbellies, the Cyclops never discovered their passengers. Once safely outside, Odysseus and his men quickly led the flocks to their ship.

The Poseidon Adventures

After the ships had left the shore, Odysseus shouted taunts at the giant, proudly revealing his true name. Polyphemus now recalled the prophecy of Telemus. Though he could not punish his tormenters himself, the Cyclops prayed to his father Poseidon for vengeance. Poseidon, who hated Odysseus from that day forward, would plague Odysseus again and again, transforming his return to Ithaca into a long, lonely, and costly journey.

Good Host, Bad Host

Fair winds carried the ships to Aeolia, a mythical floating island, where King Aeolus, keeper of the winds, welcomed them kindly, offering his weary guests a month of feasts and entertainment. Aeolus tied up all but the gentle west wind in an ox-hide bag as a gift to Odysseus. The free wind carried them within sight of Ithaca in just 10 days.

Odysseus, happy to be almost home, slept soundly that night. But his curious crew wondered what treasure Aeolus had given their captain, and opened the bag to see for themselves. The rush of winds they released carried them all the way back to Aeolia. Aeolus, recognizing the handiwork of the gods in this twist of fate, turned them away, refusing to help again.

A week's rowing brought them to a harbor walled in by high cliffs. Odysseus alone kept his ship outside the harbor; the other 11 ships entered its narrow mouth.

Three scouts sent to explore the land met an apparently kind giantess who invited them into a palace to meet her father, Antiphates, king of the Laestrygonians. The king eagerly welcomed them—and immediately devoured one of his guests. The other two escaped and ran back to the harbor.

The More Things Change ...

Many of the fantastic elements in the story of Odysseus seem more akin to the fairy tales of the Brothers Grimm than to the lofty legends of Greek gods and heroes. The foul-tempered Cyclops is not unlike the troll who blocks the Billy-Goats Gruff or the giant who chases Jack down the beanstalk. In the tale of Aeolus, we see that "curiosity killed the cat"—a common theme found in folk tales from Pandora to Goldilocks.

Odysseus immediately put his ship out to sea. But the Laestrygonians hurled boulders down upon the 11 ships trapped in the harbor. As the ships sank, the giant cannibals speared the crew like fish and carried them home for supper.

Pigging Out

Devastated by the loss of his men, Odysseus—now with just the one flagship—sailed for many weeks until he reached the island of Aeaea off the western coast of Italy. By now wary of unfamiliar places, the crew split into two groups of 22 men and drew lots. One group, led by the ship's first mate Eurylochus, had the bad luck to be chosen to explore the island. In the middle of a forest, the scouting crew came upon the house of the sorceress Circe, the daughter of Helius and Perse (a daughter of Oceanus). They were greeted by packs of apparently tame wolves and lions.

When Circe invited the scouts inside for a feast, only the suspicious Eurylochus remained outside. After waiting much longer than any feast should take, Eurylochus ran back to the ship and told Odysseus what had happened.

Odysseus immediately set out alone to try to save his men. Before he reached the house, however, he met Hermes, the divine helper of travelers in distress. The god told Odysseus that Circe had used her sorcery to transform his crewmen into swine. Hermes gave Odysseus a magical herb that he called *moly*, which would work as an antidote to Circe's drugs, then disappeared into the woods.

Odysseus sat down to a feast in Circe's hut. When her tricks failed to turn him into a beast, he drew his sword upon her. After being forced to swear an oath to the gods that she would try no more to harm him, Circe changed the swine back into men.

Circe became Odysseus's mistress, and the nymphs who attended her entertained and served Odysseus and his crew for a full year.

When at last Odysseus resolved to leave, Circe advised her lover to seek out the counsel of Teiresias, the famed Theban soothsayer. Unfortunately, Teiresias was dead. Odysseus and his crew would have to travel to the edge of the Underworld to speak to him. But Circe promised to conjure up a favorable wind to carry them there.

The night before they left, Elpenor—the crew's youngest member—got drunk and fell asleep on Circe's roof. Still groggy the next morning, he tumbled off the roof and broke his neck. But the crew hurried away without giving a proper burial.

A Ghost of a Chance

The ship sailed to the land where the sun never shines. When they came on foot to the juncture of the Underworld rivers Acheron, Periphlegethon, and Cocytus, the rivers that formed the boundaries of Hades, Odysseus dug a pit to honor Hades and Persephone. Into this pit he poured milk and honey, wine, water, and the blood that flowed from the sacrifice of a young ram and a black ewe provided by Circe.

From the pit arose a swarm of ghosts. As Circe had advised, Odysseus stood over the pit with his sword drawn to ensure that Teiresias got the first drink.

First Elpenor appeared, begging his captain for a proper funeral, which Odysseus promised him. Odysseus was shocked and saddened next to see his own mother, Anticleia, who had died of grief during her son's long absence—or had killed herself upon hearing a false report that he had died. Though it pained him to do so, Odysseus refused both of these shades a drink.

The ghost of Teiresias finally appeared carrying a golden staff. After drinking gratefully from Odysseus's libations, Teiresias foretold that Poseidon's wrath would continue to torment the crew on their long journey home. Despite hardships, however, Odysseus and all his men would arrive home safely—as long as neither he nor his crewmen laid a hand on the immortal herds of cattle or flocks of sheep tended by the daughters of Helius on the island of Thrinacia. Teiresias also told him to expect to find many suitors courting his wife and foretold further wanderings even after his reunion with Penelope.

Once Teiresias had drunk his fill, the other shades stopped to drink from the pit. Anticleia told Odysseus that Penelope had not lost hope. Agamemnon, recounting his own murder (see Chapter 16), warned Odysseus to disguise himself until he discovered what dangers awaited him at home. Odysseus cheered Achilles with news of the heroics of his son, Neoptolemus, in the final battles of the Trojan War.

Odysseus saw Ajax, too, but the mighty warrior, still angry at Odysseus for winning the armor of Achilles, turned his back on him. Heracles—or the shade of his mortal life—sympathized with Odysseus's endless wanderings. Finally, the hordes became so thick that Odysseus fled back to his ship.

Returning to Aeaea, Odysseus and his crew cremated the body of Elpenor, buried his ashes, and planted the young man's oar in the mound of earth over his grave. Circe offered advice about the dangers still in store for Odysseus and his crew: the Sirens and either the Wandering Rocks or the strait between Scylla and Charybdis. She, too, warned him against harming the herds of Helius.

Eeek! Sea Monsters!

Approaching Anthemoessa, the island of the Sirens, Odysseus had his crew members fill their ears with beeswax and had himself bound tightly to the mast. This allowed him alone to hear the intoxicating song of the Sirens—the bird-women whose seductive singing had caused so many sailors to forget their purpose, abandoning all activity to listen to their song until they died of starvation.

Upon hearing their rapturous song, Odysseus cried out for release, but his crew steadfastly refused. The Sirens, distraught that any sailor might hear their song yet not succumb, threw themselves into the sea and were heard no more.

Unaware that the *Argo*'s safe passage through the Wandering Rocks had stilled them forever (see Chapter 14), Odysseus headed instead for the narrow Strait of Messina that separates Sicily from Italy. On the western side of the northern entrance to this strait, the mighty whirlpool Charybdis sucked down all the water around it three times a day—then later belched it out again. Above the roar of the whirlpool, Odysseus ordered his men to row with all their might under the cliff along the opposite side of the strait. To avoid raising alarm, he neglected to warn them about Scylla: the long-necked, six-headed beast that lived in a cave on that cliff.

> ### The More Things Change ...
>
> The way in which Odysseus resists the deadly pleasure of the Sirens recalls his own forbearance among the Lotus-Eaters. Odysseus not only faces the challenge of conquering giants and ogres in his quest to return to Penelope. The hero must also deny himself the delights of the lotus, Circe, the Sirens, and later Calypso—or he will never make it home.

Odysseus stood ready to defend his crew from the monster. But the roar of Charybdis made him turn his head for a moment, and in that instant the monster snatched six screaming men—one in each mouth—from their oars.

> ### What a Life!
>
> Scylla was once a beautiful but aloof maiden, the beloved of Glaucus, a sea god. Glaucus asked Circe to prepare a potion to cause Scylla to fall in love with him. Circe, herself enamored with Glaucus, attempted to seduce him, but the sea god could think only of Scylla. So instead of a love potion, the jealous sorceress gave Glaucus a potion that transformed his beloved into a grotesque monster.

Don't Have a Cow

The crew emerged from their harrowing trip through the strait exhausted, scared, angry, and upset. So when Odysseus ordered his crew to row past the island of

Thrinacia (perhaps Sicily) without stopping, the men nearly mutinied. In the face of their resistance, Odysseus acquiesced to their obvious need for a rest.

Before landing, Odysseus reminded them that Circe had provided them with plenty of food and ordered them not to eat anything from the island. For here grazed the immortal animals of Helius—seven herds of 50 cattle and seven flocks of 50 sheep—that both Teiresias and Circe had warned them not to touch.

For a full month after they landed, a strong south wind blew. Unable to depart without being carried back to Scylla and Charybdis, the crew remained on Thrinacia. Food stores grew thin. The men started fishing and hunting game, but with little success. Finally, while Odysseus slept, Eurylochus ordered some men to kill some of the cattle that grazed so tantalizingly nearby.

Odysseus was horrified. So were Phaëthusa and Lampetia, the daughters of Helius who tended the animals. When Lampetia told their father, Helius demanded that the gods punish the criminals. He threatened to light up Tartarus if the gods did not heed his demand. So after the crew set sail again, Zeus sent a violent storm that tore the ship apart and killed everyone onboard—save Odysseus himself.

Clinging to the floating mast and keel, Odysseus drifted helplessly. At daybreak, he found himself once again at the edge of the rushing whirlpool of Charybdis. For an entire day, Odysseus clung to the branch of a fig tree that overhung the whirlpool. At dusk, when Charybdis spit up the raft, Odysseus dropped down and paddled as hard as he could. For nine more days he drifted before washing up on the island of Ogygia.

The Hard Life of a Love Slave

Calypso, the daughter of Atlas, was smitten with Odysseus, and wanted him to remain forever with her in her cave on Ogygia. She offered not only herself, but immortality and eternal youth as well. But Odysseus refused her. Oh, sure, he slept with her, dined on fine food, and worked not a single day during the seven years (that's right, seven) he remained on the island—but he didn't want to stay there forever. He longed to return home to Penelope, and spent his days staring forlornly at the sea.

Meanwhile, on Mount Olympus, Athena took advantage of an absence by Poseidon to plead Odysseus's case with Zeus. After his many years of suffering and countless sacrifices to the gods, Odysseus deserved divine assistance. Zeus agreed, and sent Hermes to Ogygia to order Calypso to let Odysseus go. Calypso reluctantly complied, lending him materials to build a boat, filling it with provisions, and creating a breeze to carry him on his way.

Upon returning to Olympus, Poseidon—furious that his brother Zeus had helped his enemy—sent a storm that destroyed Odysseus's tiny boat. But the sea goddess Leucothea—once the mortal Ino, loving aunt of Dionysus and unloving stepmother of Phrixus and Helle (see Chapter 12)—saved him. She gave Odysseus her veil to buoy and protect him and told him to swim with all his might. Two days later, he arrived at the island of Scheria. Tossing the veil back into the sea, he collapsed from exhaustion.

Odysseus awoke to the delighted cries of girls playing ball: Nausicaa, a Phaeacian princess, and her servants were entertaining themselves while waiting for their laundry to dry on the shore. Nausicaa fed and clothed the castaway and brought him to meet her father. Approaching as a suppliant, Odysseus was welcomed to the court of Alcinous, a wise and generous king with a reputation for saving shipwrecked sailors. The king promised to have Odysseus taken safely to Ithaca—unless he wanted to stay and marry Nausicaa. Odysseus graciously declined.

Read All About It

Homer's epic poem *The Odyssey* detailed all of the wanderings of Odysseus as the hero tried to get home to Ithaca—and Penelope. The poem went on to narrate the hero's violent homecoming and ultimate reunion with his son, his father, and of course, his wife.

Hi, Honey, I'm Home!

Once onboard the Phaeacian ship, Odysseus fell so deeply asleep that the sailors did not have the heart to wake him when they arrived at Ithaca. They simply laid him on the shore, piled up gifts from Alcinous next to him, and returned homeward. (They never made it. Poseidon turned the ship to stone as they approached their harbor.)

Odysseus awoke completely disoriented, but Athena appeared and reassured him that he was at last in Ithaca. Ten years after setting out from Troy—and 20 years after leaving Ithaca—he had finally come home. Yet Athena warned Odysseus that the crowds of lords and princes who were courting Penelope in an attempt to gain his wealth would not be pleased to see him. If he returned to the palace alone, they would surely kill him. So the goddess disguised Odysseus as an aged beggar.

Reports of My Death Have Been Greatly Exaggerated

Odysseus went first to the hut of his loyal swineherd Eumaeus. Odysseus learned from Eumaeus that his father Laertes—due to grief over his wife's death, his son's presumed death, and his inability to rid the palace of the freeloading suitors—had become increasingly feeble, quit the palace, dressed in rags, and lived in a small hut.

Odysseus's son Telemachus—an infant when Odysseus left for Troy but now fully grown—stopped by the hut, but regarded his father as a stranger. Though he offered the old man food and clothing, Telemachus regretted that he could not invite the stranger to stay in the palace. The young man doubted that he had the strength to defend his guest from the all-but-certain abuse of his mother's suitors.

When Eumaeus left the hut, Odysseus revealed himself to his son. Tears of joy cascaded from the eyes of both father and son. But they quickly set aside the happiness of their reunion to plot their revenge against Penelope's suitors.

Still in disguise, Odysseus entered the banquet hall of his palace and began begging food. All the lords and princes gave him tidbits except the arrogant Antinous, who tossed a stool at him. When a beggar named Irus, attempting to protect his territory, threatened the old stranger, the suitors, ever eager for some excitement, arranged a boxing match. Odysseus knocked the man out with a single blow.

What a Life!

Penelope had warded off her suitors for years by telling them that she would choose a new husband only after she had completed knitting a shroud for her father-in-law, Laertes. Every day, she made a show of working hard at the loom. But at night, she carefully unraveled everything she had woven during the day. A disloyal servant gave away her trick, and the suitors forced her to finish the shroud.

Soon Penelope entered the hall and reproached the suitors for their boorishness and for living off her husband's wealth. Odysseus watched her with silent admiration and adoration, but did not want to reveal himself until he had rid the palace of her suitors. That night, while the suitors slept, Odysseus and Telemachus removed all the suitors' spears to the cellar storeroom.

Odysseus also arranged a meeting with Penelope that night under the pretext of having news of her husband. The stranger, claiming he had once entertained her husband, assured her that Odysseus would be home soon. Penelope wanted to believe this stranger, but replied that it would have to be very soon. Odysseus himself had instructed her to choose a second husband if he did not return from Troy, and she could not delay the decision any longer. She planned to hold a test of strength and skill—her husband's old trick of shooting an arrow through the hollow throats of 12 ax heads set in a straight line—to determine who would be her next husband.

Penelope bid the stranger goodnight and told her nurse, Eurycleia, to take good care of him. Eurycleia, who had nursed Odysseus as a boy, washed his feet that night. She gasped when she recognized the scar the boar had left on his thigh, but Odysseus urged her to keep his secret.

No Contest

The next day, Penelope brought out Odysseus's old bow, announced the rules of the contest, and offered herself as the prize. Yet try as they might, not one of the suitors could even string the bow, much less shoot an arrow through the axes. When the disguised Odysseus asked to take up the challenge, Penelope, despite the suitors' protests, consented to the request before retiring to her bed chamber.

Philoetius, a cowherd to whom Odysseus had revealed his identity, locked the door of the hall behind her. Odysseus strung the bow and sent an arrow through the axes.

In an instant, he turned the bow on the suitors, shooting Antinous and Eurymachus, while Telemachus killed Amphinomus with his spear. A bloody battle followed—pitting Odysseus, his son, and two servants against the many suitors. The four killed all the suitors, sparing only a herald, Medon, and a bard, Phemius, who despite their loyalty to him had been forced to serve the suitors.

Telemachus forced a dozen female servants who had become mistresses to the suitors to carry the corpses out of the hall. He then hanged the mistresses in the courtyard. Melanthius—Odysseus's goatherd and the brother of Melantho, one of the 12 mistresses—whose betrayal included bringing the suitors their weapons once the battle broke out, was mutilated and left to die in the courtyard.

Penelope disbelieved the good news of her husband's return, even after Odysseus came and stood before her. Penelope—a perfect match for her devious husband—then used trickery to find out whether this man truly was her husband. In his presence, Penelope ordered her servants to move their marriage bed out of their bedroom and make it up for this guest. Odysseus, who had carefully crafted their bed using an ancient olive tree—still rooted in the soil—as one of the bedposts, became enraged, thinking that someone must have sawed the bedpost. Hearing this secret of their bedchamber, Penelope embraced Odysseus as her husband, home at last. After 20 years of pure loyalty in his absence, Penelope's name now epitomized fidelity.

Eupeithes, the father of Antinous, urged the nobles of Ithaca to rise up against their king, who had returned only to kill all their sons. (Eupeithes gave no weight to the fact that Odysseus had saved his life years earlier.) Laertes, who had recovered his dignity when reunited with his son, threw the first spear, killing Eupeithes.

Another bloodbath might have followed, but Athena put a stop to the fighting with a scream that caused the Ithacan nobles to run away in terror. Odysseus began to pursue them, but Zeus stopped him by hurling a thunderbolt before him. Athena, taking the form of Mentor, a wise and respected Ithacan, then brokered a peace.

Many years later, Telegonus, a son of Odysseus and Circe, came searching for his father at Circe's request. Not knowing he had landed on Ithaca, Telegonus and his crew began raiding the island for food. When the aged Odysseus and Telemachus came out to defend Ithaca, Telegonus—who had never met his father—killed the old man with a spear dipped in the poison of a stingray.

Upon discovering who the killer was, Odysseus's family forgave him. Telemachus, Telegonus, and Penelope transported Odysseus's body to Aeaea and buried him there. Odysseus's wanderings became complete when Penelope married her stepson, Telegonus, while Telemachus married Circe. The sorceress gave them all immortality.

The Least You Need to Know

- After the 10-year Trojan War, Odysseus spent 10 years trying to get home.

- In blinding Poseidon's son Polyphemus, a Cyclops, by plunging a hot stake in his single eye, Odysseus earned the wrath of the sea god. Poseidon resolved to make the rest of Odysseus's trip long and costly.

- Odysseus set out from Troy with 12 fully manned ships. The giant Laestrygonians destroyed 11 ships and devoured their crews. Zeus destroyed the final ship to punish the crew for stealing cattle from Helius. Odysseus alone survived.

- Back in Ithaca, Odysseus killed a host of suitors who had lived off his wealth for years while waiting for Penelope to choose one of them as her second husband.

- Penelope remained faithful to her husband throughout his 20-year absence.

Not in Our Stars: Tragic Heroes and Their Fates

In This Chapter

- ◆ Echo's unrequited love for Narcissus

- ◆ Tereus's treachery toward Procne and Philomela

- ◆ How jealousy destroyed Cephalus and Procris

- ◆ How the ingenuity of Daedalus cost him his son Icarus

- ◆ How Phaëthon nearly destroyed the world by borrowing his father's chariot of the sun

Though classical mythology revolves around the tales of such great heroes as Theseus, Heracles, Achilles, and Odysseus, more human-sized heroes had adventures no less amazing than theirs. Mythmakers also told tales of great tragedy on a human scale: tales of lovers spurned or torn apart by jealousy, of sons who tragically disobeyed their fathers, of ambitious young men whose reach exceeded their grasp, and of the treachery of husbands toward their in-laws.

Most of these tales are on the short side: Tragedy generally strikes down these heroes and heroines in the prime of their lives. But whether cut down by their own pride, jealousy, or folly or by their presumptuous attempts to avoid their destiny, these tragic heroes and heroines have gripping stories to tell that are worthy of the gods.

He Loves Me, He Loves Me Not

No matter how commonly it occurs, unrequited love invariably causes pain and sometimes leads to tragedy. The small scale of a tragedy such as the story of Echo and Narcissus makes it even more personal for readers and listeners. We may find it difficult to picture ourselves as mighty warriors or monster-slayers or even ship-bound adventurers, but all of us can imagine—or recall—the pain of a love unreturned.

No Voice of Her Own

Echo, a nymph of Mount Helicon, served for many years as an attendant to Hera. An incessant talker, Echo couldn't stop herself from prattling on and on. Zeus, always on the prowl for young nymphs, saw that Echo could serve his own philandering purposes. When Zeus invited her sisters to Mount Olympus, Echo would distract his wife's attention with her endless and often amusing chatter, allowing the nymphs to escape Hera's notice as they crept in and out of her husband's bed. When Zeus visited one of the nymphs and Hera went looking for him, Echo would stall her long enough for the couple to uncouple.

Hera, ever jealous (and with good reason), exploded when she learned of Echo's role in her husband's infidelities. The goddess devised a cruel punishment for someone as talkative as Echo: She stole the nymph's ability to speak independently. Echo could never again start a conversation; she could only repeat senselessly what others had just said.

My Eyes Adored You

One day in the country, Echo caught sight of a gorgeous young man who was out hunting. She followed him, longing to speak to him, but the poor thing couldn't say a word.

Who was this handsome hunter who so captivated Echo? It was Narcissus, the son of Cephissus, a river god, and Liriope, a nymph. Narcissus, stunningly beautiful, was a cold, aloof, and heartless young man. Indeed, he was so proud of his beauty and infatuated with his own virtues that, though he was only 16, he had already scorned the romantic advances of dozens of prospective lovers, male and female.

Echo followed Narcissus quietly and at a distance. Despite her intense longing, she couldn't speak to him. Narcissus, who had become separated from his hunting party, soon wondered how far astray he had gone. Looking around him, Narcissus cried, "Is anyone here?"

"Here!" Echo replied.

Narcissus couldn't see anyone, but called out, "Let us come together!"

"Let us come together!" Echo enthusiastically agreed. She rushed out of hiding and threw open her arms to embrace him. But Narcissus rudely pushed her away.

"Don't touch me!" he cried. "I would sooner die than let you make love to me!"

"Make love to me!" Echo plaintively cried, but Narcissus had already turned away.

Spurned by Narcissus, Echo wasted away, unable to sleep or eat as she pined away for her unrequited love. Her body shriveled and eventually turned to stone. Only Echo's voice remained, haunting the mountains—as it still does today.

Mirror, Mirror, on the Wall

Echo would have revenge of sorts. For Narcissus, too, would die of unrequited love. One of his male suitors, cruelly rejected, prayed to the gods that Narcissus, too, experience the pain of love unreturned. Nemesis, goddess of vengeance, heard this plea and agreed that this young man's *hubris* deserved punishment.

The goddess arranged for Narcissus—exhausted and parched from the hunt—to stop and quench his thirst at a pool on Mount Helicon. The waters of this pool had never been disturbed by birds or animals or even leaves falling from the trees. As he knelt over the water and bent down to scoop up some water, Narcissus caught sight of his reflection. The image he saw was so beautiful that he fell in love at first sight.

Try as he might, Narcissus could not consummate his love. Every time he reached out to embrace or kiss his own image, his love seemed to want to return his embrace or offer him a kiss. But the mirror image disintegrated whenever he disturbed that surface of the water. So close to touching but never able to touch, Narcissus pined away for his own image.

Logos

The Greeks used the term **hubris** to describe extreme arrogance and pride. The trait of hubris suggested impiety, for it raised a mortal—if only in his own eyes—to an almost divine level. Because it manifested scorn toward human limitations, hubris was almost always punished by the gods.

Although Narcissus realized he could never hold his love, neither could he tear himself away. He stretched out on the grass by the pool and never lifted his gaze from his reflection. Though Narcissus knew he was dying, he regretted only that his love would die, too. At the same time, he drew comfort from the knowledge that this torture soon would end and that they would die together.

What a Life!

Sixteen years earlier, Liriope had asked a young seer named Teiresias whether her son Narcissus would have a long life. Teiresias replied, "Yes, if he never knows himself." Liriope, the seer's first client, scoffed at this apparently ridiculous prophecy. Yet the eventual fulfillment of this cryptic remark helped secure the reputation of Teiresias, who became the most famed soothsayer in ancient Greece (see Chapters 12 and 18).

Narcissus lay there in his rapture. Just before he died of starvation and unrequited love, he cried out, "Beloved in vain, farewell." From the mountains, Echo called, "Beloved in vain, farewell."

Upon his death, Narcissus was transformed into the flower that today still bears his name.

Switchblade Sisters

Both Echo and Narcissus remain solitary tragic figures, cursed with loneliness and tormented by a love they can never have. But even those bound by a powerful love—for instance, the bonds between sisters, between a husband and wife, between a father and son—can suffer tragedies. Love, it seems, does not always offer protection against tragedy. Indeed, love can actually lead to tragedy.

The sisters Procne and Philomela loved each other so much they could not bear the separation that came when Procne married. Yet their desire to reunite led only to tragedy. When they finally overcame the obstacles placed in their path by Procne's husband Tereus, the sisters bonded once more—in a quest for vengeance.

Sister Act

Pandion, king of Athens, and Labdacus, king of Thebes, couldn't agree on the border between these two territories. When they went to war, Pandion called upon Tereus—a son of Ares and the ruler of Daulis, a city in Phocis not far from Delphi—for assistance. With the help of Tereus, Pandion defeated and killed Labdacus.

In gratitude, Pandion offered his daughter Procne as a bride to Tereus. Procne and Tereus made a home in Daulis, where they had a son, Itys. But after five years, Procne confessed to her husband that she felt a little homesick. If only she could visit her sister Philomela or have her sister visit them, she would never ask anything of him again.

Tereus honored his wife's request and sailed across the Gulf of Corinth to Athens to fetch her sister. But sadly, Tereus became infatuated with Philomela. He found her beauty, grace, charms, and enchanting voice impossible to resist. He kept his feelings hidden, however. So with her father's blessing, the predatory Tereus took the innocent Philomela away with him to Daulis.

No sooner had they arrived than Tereus stole Philomela away to a deserted cabin in the woods and brutally raped the virgin. Fearful that she might escape and tell Procne or Pandion—and angry that the anguished girl was calling on the gods to punish him—Tereus chopped off Philomela's tongue. Again and again he raped her, then imprisoned her in the ramshackle cabin.

Dinner—and Vengeance—Is Served

Philomela spent a year in the cabin, but used her time well. She cleverly wove her tale of woe into a robe and sent it to Procne. Procne figured out the message, raced to the cabin, freed her sister, and joined with her in a plot to avenge her husband's wickedness.

> **Mythed by a Mile** _____
>
> In a slightly different version of this tale, Tereus—smitten with Philomela—hid *Procne* away in a cabin and informed Pandion that his daughter had died. Though tormented by the loss of his daughter, Pandion nonetheless thought to ease the supposed widower's anguish by offering Tereus his other daughter, Philomela, to take Procne's place. Tereus seduced Philomela even before the wedding could take place. In this version, Tereus cut out *Procne's* tongue and locked her up in the slave's quarters. But the abused wife wove a message into Philomela's bridal robe that read, "Procne is among the slaves." Philomela then freed her sister and the two sought vengeance against Tereus.

The two sisters came up with a grisly plot. Procne slaughtered her young son—the image of his father—slitting his throat and, with Philomela's help, carving him into pieces. The sisters boiled and roasted the body and had him served to Tereus as a special feast.

Just as Thyestes had enjoyed a meal of his children served by his brother Atreus (see Chapter 16), Tereus stuffed himself with the flesh of his son, relishing every bite. After the king announced he could eat no more, Philomela sprang into the banquet hall and tossed the head of Itys onto the table in front of him.

Realizing that he had just feasted on his own son, Tereus went mad with rage. Drawing his sword, he chased the sisters out of the palace. He might have killed them both, but all three were suddenly transformed by the gods into birds: Procne became a swallow; Philomela, a nightingale; and Tereus, a hoopoe (a small crested bird commonly found in southern Europe). The people of Phocis claim that fear of Tereus has kept the nightingale from singing or the swallow from nesting in Daulis ever since.

Mutual Mistrust: The High Cost of Jealousy

Pandion died of grief over his lost daughters, leaving his son Erechtheus to rule Athens. Erechtheus had many daughters of his own. But sadly, one of them, Procris, suffered a fate as tragic as those of her aunts.

A Test of Fidelity

Procris married Cephalus, a prince of Phocis, and the couple were deliriously happy together—but only for a couple of months. One day while Cephalus was hunting, Eos, the goddess of dawn, became enamored with him and carried him away. After she had her way with him, the goddess kept Cephalus with her for some time. Cephalus did not resist her advances, but he dreamed and spoke only of his beloved Procris. Finally, the annoyed goddess sent him home, but angrily warned him that he would one day regret having married Procris.

The words of Eos sowed distrust in Cephalus's heart. He began to wonder what she had meant. Had his wife remained faithful to him? After all, Eos had kept him away for quite a while. Could Procris have strayed?

Unable to silence his doubts, Cephalus decided to test his wife's honor and love for him. With the help of Eos, he disguised himself so thoroughly that even Procris would not recognize him. Approaching his own home as a stranger, Cephalus began courting his wife. Procris repeatedly turned the "stranger" away, explaining that her heart, body, and soul were all pledged to one man.

Finding gifts and words unpersuasive, the disguised Cephalus offered her a fortune to lie with him. When he doubled his offer, Procris hesitated, if only for a moment. But Cephalus seized on that moment, revealing himself and shaming his wife.

Mythed by a Mile _____

Apollodorus paints quite a different picture of Procris as a faithless wife. She first allowed herself to be seduced by a man named Pteleon, who bribed her with a golden crown. Fearful of what Cephalus might do when he found out, Procris fled to Crete, where Minos also seduced her. Minos, rather than Artemis, gave Procris the relentless hound and the infallible spear—as bribes to get her into his bed. The wrath of Pasiphaë, Minos's wife, now seemed more threatening than her husband's anger. So Procris fled Crete, too. Returning to her husband, she presented him the rewards of her shame—the hound and the spear—as a peace offering. Only then did the couple reconcile and live happily together.

Procris, hurt by her husband's distrust and ashamed that she had even considered succumbing to temptation, fled their home to devote herself to Artemis, the virgin goddess of hunting. Left on his own, Cephalus realized that he had wronged his wife. He sought her out, apologized, confessed his own indiscretion with Eos, and pleaded with her to return. Moved to compassion, the loving Procris reconciled with her husband. Returning home, she brought gifts from Artemis: Laelaps, a hound that never failed to catch its prey, and a spear that always hit its mark. The couple spent many more happy years together.

The Spy Who Loved Him

One day, a gossip came running from the woods to tell Procris that her husband had betrayed her. This rumor-monger overheard Cephalus, after a hunt, tenderly calling out the name Aura. What's more, Cephalus had been heard whispering words of praise to Aura for "her sweet breath" and the joy he felt when it touched his skin.

Jealous and wounded by this news, Procris collapsed with grief. Torn between trust and distrust, she refused to believe the story without further proof—but then she set out to gather that proof. The next morning, Procris trailed her husband, trying to catch him in the act (while all the time hoping she wouldn't).

After a long day's hunt, Procris too heard her husband calling out to Aura. When she sighed with anguish and crept closer to get a better look, Cephalus heard her rustling in the bushes. "A beast!" he thought, letting his unerring spear fly into the thicket.

Hearing his wife's cry, Cephalus raced to the bushes and found her bloodied body, his spear piercing her breast. As Cephalus tried to save her, Procris begged her husband, if he loved her at all, never to let Aura into their bedroom. Too late, Cephalus recognized the misunderstanding that had led them to this fate. Through his tears, he explained that he had merely been calling for a breeze (aura) to cool him after his exhausting hunt. Procris smiled weakly with relief, but died in her husband's arms moments later.

The Limits of Craftsmanship

Daedalus, the most renowned inventor of ancient Greece, also suffered from deadly jealousy. An ingenious artist and artisan, Daedalus was credited with inventing the wedge, the axe, the level, and sails, among other items. After learning smithcraft from the goddess Athena, he forged the sword of Peleus, which Achilles later wielded in battle. A masterful sculptor, Daedalus once carved a monument to Heracles so realistic that Heracles himself attacked it with a stone, thinking it was one of his enemies.

Yet his skill and his fame didn't stop Daedalus from envying the skills of others. And perhaps his greatest invention would lead only to tragedy.

Towering Ambition

Daedalus gained his greatest fame in the service of King Minos of Crete, but he was an Athenian by birth. Indeed, most storytellers claim that he was a direct descendent of Erechtheus, the fabled king of Athens (son of Pandion and father of Procris).

While still living in Athens, Daedalus took as an apprentice his nephew, Talos, the son of his sister. Just 12 years old, the boy showed great promise as an artisan—too great, as it turned out. Inspired by seeing the jagged spine of a fish, Talos invented the saw (though Daedalus claimed this invention as his own). The boy also invented the potter's wheel and the drafter's compass (the kind used to draw circles).

His nephew's inventiveness and skill drove Daedalus (who was no slouch in these departments himself) mad with jealousy. Unable to bear the possibility that the student might surpass the teacher, Daedalus lured his nephew to the roof of the temple of Athena and shoved him over the edge. After stuffing his nephew's body into a bag, Daedalus attempted to carry it off for a secret burial, but the bloodstains on the bag gave him away.

When his sister learned that Daedalus had murdered her son, she hanged herself. Daedalus, who either fled before the trial or was tried and banished for the murder, was forced to become an exile from his homeland.

Fly Like an Eagle, Drop Like a Stone

Daedalus ended up on Crete, where both King Minos and Queen Pasiphaë put his ingenuity to work. For Pasiphaë, he built the fake cow that allowed her to satisfy her lust for a gorgeous white bull given to Minos by Poseidon. For Minos, Daedalus designed the Labyrinth—a building with a maze of passageways so intricate it was virtually inescapable—to house the shameful offspring of that union: the Minotaur (see Chapter 15).

Minos soon imprisoned Daedalus and his son Icarus in the Labyrinth, too—to punish the inventor for the device that allowed Pasiphaë to mate with the bull. Yet Daedalus and his son escaped the inescapable prison. Three millennia before the Wright brothers took to the air, Daedalus made wings of feathers and wax for himself and his son. As both father and son escaped the Labyrinth, soaring upward on their wings, onlookers must have thought they were witnessing gods.

Despite his father's warnings to fly neither too low (because the sea spray might soak the wings) nor too high (because the sun might melt the wax), Icarus grew heady and soared ever closer to the sun. As the wax melted, the boy's wings fell apart. Icarus plunged down into the sea south of Samos—a body of water now called the Icarian Sea.

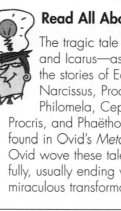

Read All About It

The tragic tale of Daedalus and Icarus—as well as the stories of Echo and Narcissus, Procne and Philomela, Cephalus and Procris, and Phaëthon—can be found in Ovid's *Metamorphoses*. Ovid wove these tales beautifully, usually ending with some miraculous transformation.

Daedalus, who had lost sight of his son, began calling for him. Hearing no answer, he desperately searched the surface of the water. But all he could see were scattered feathers.

Heracles later found the body of Icarus washed ashore on a small eastern Aegean island. Heracles buried him on the island, which became known as Icaria.

The Shell Game

A broken man, Daedalus took refuge on Sicily as a guest of Cocalus, king of Camicus. There, he endeared himself to the king's daughters by making scores of beautiful and innovative toys.

King Minos, however, would not give up his campaign of vengeance against Daedalus. He sailed throughout the Mediterranean Sea, stopping at every port to offer a handsome reward to anyone who could thread a string through a spiral seashell. When Cocalus accepted the challenge and, the next morning, handed Minos a threaded shell, Minos knew he had found the refuge of Daedalus. (Daedalus accomplished the task by tying a thread to an ant and luring it through the seashell with honey.)

When Minos demanded that Cocalus surrender Daedalus, the king reluctantly promised to do so—but only after that night's feast. Cocalus ordered his daughters to attend to their honored guest in his bath prior to the feast. They took care of him all right: They poured pots and pots of boiling water over Minos, killing him instantly.

Daedalus, freed of all obligations—but at such a high cost—lived out the rest of his lonely days on Sicily.

Dad, Can I Borrow Your Car?

Icarus was not the only young man of myth whose towering ambition led to a tragic end. Phaëthon, too, soared high—only to be brought crashing down to Earth. Unlike the fall of Icarus, however, the fall of Phaëthon nearly destroyed the entire planet.

Son of the Sun

Clymene, an Oceanid married to King Merops of Egypt, gave birth to a son, Phaëthon. Yet she insisted the boy's father was not her husband, but Helius, the god of the sun. Though he had never even met Helius, Phaëthon, a proud young man, never doubted his mother's tale—and boasted of his parentage to any who would listen.

One day, a friend accused Phaëthon of foolishness for believing his mother's fairy tale about his father. Stung by this insult, Phaëthon ran to his mother, demanding some proof of his parentage. Clymene swore that she had told the truth and advised her son to silence these new doubts by going to the royal palace of the sun and asking his father directly. Phaëthon traveled to the far east, whence his father set out in his chariot every morning. Helius, the all-seeing, called out to his son as he approached. When Phaëthon asked if the sun god was truly his father, Helius embraced the boy and assured him that his mother had spoken the truth.

Although reassured, Phaëthon still wanted proof that he could show to those on Earth who doubted his parentage. So Helius swore by Styx (a name that no god invoked lightly) to grant him any boon he might want.

No sooner had this oath been spoken than Phaëthon asked his father for permission to drive the chariot of the sun. Helius tried desperately to dissuade his son. He warned that none of the other gods and goddesses of Olympus—not even Zeus—had the power to control the winged horses that pulled the chariot of the sun. But Phaëthon would not listen to reason. He wanted nothing except to drive the golden chariot. Reluctantly, Helius honored his oath.

What a Life!
The sisters of Phaëthon followed Clymene as she wandered the earth searching for her son's body. When they found his bones on the banks of a foreign river, Clymene collapsed with sorrow and her daughters stood on the spot weeping for four months. Rooted to the ground where they stood, the girls were transformed into poplar trees and their tears into amber jewels.

Hold Your Horses

Phaëthon climbed into the chariot and picked up the reins. The four magnificent horses, feeling a lighter, more uncertain hand at the reins, shot up into the sky. Phaëthon, soaring much too high, almost immediately panicked. Scared out of his wits, the boy dropped the reins. The horses, free to run their own course, first bolted too high and then plunged down toward the earth. The scorching heat of the sun dried up rivers, burned mountains and trees, and destroyed cities. The intensity of the heat also reportedly darkened the skins of equatorial peoples. Phaëthon saw the earth burning, but could do nothing to stop it. The Earth petitioned Zeus to end this miserable suffering, which threatened not only her, but also his brother Poseidon's oceans and Zeus's own skies. After calling together Helius and all the gods and goddesses to explain that the runaway chariot would destroy everything if he did not stop it, Zeus hurled a thunderbolt down upon the chariot, killing Phaëthon instantly. The horses broke free from the chariot as the burning Phaëthon, trailing fire like a shooting star, fell from the heavens.

The Least You Need to Know

- Echo loved Narcissus, but Narcissus loved only himself. She wasted away for unrequited love of him. He wasted away for unrequited love of his own reflection in a pool.

- Tereus raped his sister-in-law, Philomela, and cut out her tongue to prevent her from talking. Philomela and her sister Procne avenged these crimes by feeding Tereus his son for supper. The gods turned all three into birds.

♦ Cephalus doubted his wife's faithfulness—and lost her through his jealousy. After reconciling, Procris doubted him—and lost her life when Cephalus accidentally speared her.

♦ Daedalus killed his nephew because he was jealous of the boy's talents. His own son Icarus died when, using wings Daedalus had fashioned from feathers and wax, he flew too close to the sun and they melted.

♦ To prove his parentage, Phaëthon borrowed the chariot of the sun from his father, Helius, but crashed it, burning much of the world. Zeus restored order by killing Phaëthon with a lightning bolt.

Part 4

Friends, Romans, Countrymen

The Romans borrowed heavily from the Greeks in creating their own mythology. But the Romans had deities and heroes of their own, too. The ancient peoples of Italy had a host of nature spirits and other divinities that watched over them, while the greatest of the Roman heroes were the founders of its culture. Aeneas, a military hero in the Trojan War, traveled to Italy to found the Roman race. Fourteen generations later, Romulus and Remus, descendants of Aeneas, founded the city that became the seat of a mighty empire: Rome.

By linking themselves with gods and goddesses and the mythic heroes of the past, the Romans and their rulers glorified themselves, establishing a divine mandate to rule an ever-expanding share of the Western world.

Chapter 20

When in Rome, Worship as the Romans Worship

In This Chapter

- ◆ The relationship between Romans and their deities
- ◆ How the Greek gods and goddesses joined native Latin deities to become the Roman pantheon
- ◆ How to get on the good side of Roman gods and goddesses
- ◆ Everyday life in Rome: a ritual for every occasion
- ◆ The lares, penates, and other household gods of Rome

What made the greatness that was Rome? If you asked this question to the citizens (or wives or slaves) of ancient Rome, they would not hesitate to answer: the gods and goddesses who smiled down upon them and their empire.

The Roman Empire quickly rose to become the greatest power the Western World had ever seen. As any right-thinking Roman would tell you, however, they could not have done it on their own. The Romans believed that success in any endeavor—whether giving birth to a child, feeding a family, raising crops, defending a city, conquering neighboring tribes, or giving birth to an empire—depended upon the cooperation of the gods and goddesses.

Through their devotion and worship—their prayers, their rituals, and their sacrifices—the Romans hoped to secure the cooperation and even complicity of their deities in achieving their goals. Or, at the very least, they hoped to persuade the deities not to stand in the way of their success.

A *Practical* Guide to Roman Mythology

Like most ancient pantheistic religions, the primitive religions of the Latin tribes of Italy—and the Roman religions that followed them—were based on a belief in the existence of natural and supernatural forces open to the persuasion of prayer and sacrifice. The entire basis of Roman religious practice—for individuals, groups, and the state as a whole—was to use the right words and demonstrate the proper devotion needed to win the gods' and goddesses' favor.

This was not a religion of sin, redemption, and salvation. This was a religion of utilitarian practicality. This was not a religion of morals and self-improvement, but a religion of health and prosperity. The Romans and their gods were very concerned with success and the happiness it might bring.

Roman worshippers focused on the pragmatic, practical aspects of everyday life. Through both daily and "special occasion" rituals, the Romans called upon the gods and goddesses to protect them from everyday dangers, to help them in their struggle for subsistence and survival, to safeguard their harvests, and to guard them in warfare.

Greek Immigrants: The Gods of Olympus Arrive in Rome

As the Empire expanded, Roman mythology and religious practices—rooted in the native Latin tribes' worship of nature spirits and ancestral spirits—would take on aspects of the beliefs and rituals of the Etruscans of northern Italy, the Celts of Northwestern Europe, and the Phoenicians and Egyptians of North Africa. But no one had a greater influence on the mythology of Rome than the Greeks.

Roman mythology was expansive and inclusive—absorbing and incorporating outside influences—precisely because the Roman people judged the effectiveness of their prayers and rituals by results. If an appeal to a known or native deity failed to achieve the desired outcome, why not try an appeal to an unknown or foreign god? After all, in a religion that already featured so many deities, what's a few more gods and goddesses?

Without sacrificing any of their old deities (the ancestral and nature spirits of the Latins), the Romans consistently added new members to their pantheon. Although ties between Greece and Rome had been strong for four centuries, Rome had completely dominated Greece politically by 146 B.C.E. The absorption of Greek culture, which had already made its influence felt on Rome, accelerated with this conquest. Greek art, for example, with its depiction of gods and goddesses as idealized human forms, gradually took the place of the simple clay gods of the early Latins.

> **⚠ CAUTION**
>
> ### Mythed by a Mile _____
>
> Ovid offered a much simpler explanation of how the Romans came to adopt Greek mythology as their own. In *Fasti*, he wrote, "Aeneas from the flames of Ilium brought his gods into our land …." Undoubtedly, this story contains at least a grain of truth. The Greek and Trojan immigrants who settled Rome and conquered the native Latins did arrive on Italy's shores with their own set of religious beliefs.

The mythology of the Greeks was similarly incorporated. Originally, the Latins did not have much of a mythology of their own. What mattered to the ancient people of Italy was not the lives, loves, and other adventures of their gods and goddesses, but the practical impact of these deities on their day-to-day existence—the way that the divine manifested itself in their personal lives. They looked to deities not for personalities, stories, or moral instruction, but for the divine gesture (in the form of good or bad outcomes) in response to their rituals or prayers.

As a result of the Latin people's pragmatic relationship to their deities, they gave less attention to their gods' and goddesses' genealogies, histories, and mythical deeds. In such a void, the Greek myths—so powerful in both storytelling and character portrayal—attached themselves to ancient native beliefs. So strong was the Greek influence that by the Augustan Age, the mythology of Rome represented a fusion of Greek and primitive Latin stories.

Pick a God, Any God

Through this fusion of cultures, the Romans acquired a host of deities that played a part in their everyday worship. In addition to the "naturalized" Olympians—the Pantheon of gods and goddesses imported from Greece to Rome—the Romans paid homage to ancient sylvan deities of flowers (Flora), fruit (Pomona), and other aspects of the natural world. In the home, they worshipped the god of doors (Janus), the goddess of the hearth (Vesta), and even the goddess of bread-baking (Fornax). In various stages of life, they sought the blessing or assistance of the goddess of childbirth (Juno Lucina or Carmenta), the goddess of youth (Juventas), the god of healing (Apollo or Aesculapius), or the goddess of death (Libitina). (For an exploration of the characters and aspects of these major and minor deities, see Chapter 21.) Every natural phenomenon, every activity of daily or civic life, every profession or trade had its own patron god or goddess.

The Romans believed in the supreme importance to their own lives and happiness of maintaining a good relationship with their deities. Not a day went by without invoking the name of several different deities for help and sustenance.

Logos

Our word piety, meaning devotion to god, comes directly from the Latin word **pietas**. Yet in our usage, the word has come to indicate primarily religious faith and feeling. To the Romans, however, pietas reached beyond what we would call religious feeling and included a sense of one's obligations to family and to friends and, importantly, to the state.

Gods in the Balance

For the Romans, the success of every aspect of life depended upon maintaining *pax deorum*—the peace of the gods. Sustaining a peaceful relationship with the gods insured that everything in the life of an individual, a family, a group, or a state would remain in balance.

For this reason, the Romans, both individually and collectively, tried to earn the goodwill of the deities through their *pietas*—their proper behavior toward gods and goddesses, family, district, and country. They sought the cooperation of the gods in their own endeavors by taking active steps to maintain the right relationship with the gods—primarily through prayer and sacrifice.

Say a Little Prayer for Me

The Romans believed that no single god or goddess had charge over everything. Instead, each deity had his or her own sphere of influence, his or her own dominion, his or her own function:

♦ Every town had a patron deity: Rome revered Mars; Ostia, Vulcan; Veii, Juno; and Falerii, Minerva.

♦ Every profession had a patron deity: Merchants owed thanks to Mercury; farmers to Ceres; soldiers to Mars; and artisans to Minerva.

♦ Every growing thing had a patron deity: Flora watched over flowers; Ceres over grain; Pomona over orchards; Diana over wild animals; Pales over cattle herds; and Faunus over flocks.

For the Roman, reverence for the gods involved knowing which deity to implore, invoke, or placate on every occasion or at every juncture of one's day or one's life.

Fortunately, most Roman deities were approachable. They would listen to the prayers of their petitioners—but only if they were called by the right name. You needed to know exactly whom to ask for what you wanted. (Romans who felt at all unsure that they had invoked the correct deity would often follow up a specific invocation with the fail-safe strategy of calling upon all other gods of heaven, of Earth, and of the Underworld.)

In petitioning the gods and goddesses, Romans seldom prayed for excessive rewards or favors for themselves. Rather, they prayed for continued good fortune, peace, and the protection and enjoyment of what they already had or for divine support in actions they planned to undertake.

Even then, Romans understood that prayers and rituals alone could not guarantee the success of their endeavors. Petitioners also needed to take the initiative, accompanying their prayers with appropriate actions in pursuit of their ends.

The Rituals of Everyday Life

Since every moment of life took place in the presence of a deity, almost any action undertaken by an individual, a group, or the state was a religious act. As such, nearly every action demanded certain rituals to ensure success. Individual Roman citizens scrupulously performed the proper rituals for:

- Waking
- Preparing a meal
- Eating a meal
- Leaving home
- Returning home
- Embarking upon business ventures
- Planting seeds
- Harvesting crops
- Going to bed
- Conceiving a child
- Giving birth

- Healing from injury or illness
- Dying
- Burying the dead

In addition, the state would perform rituals for:

- Maintaining peace
- Going to war
- Promoting a good harvest
- Protecting the economy
- Marking the changing seasons of the calendar

In short, virtually every aspect of life had its own accompanying ritual. Every May, for example, farmers would parade a bull, sheep, and pig three times around their fields. They would then sacrifice the animals to Ceres, the goddess of growth, or to Mars, the god of strength. This procession—called a *lustratio*—protected the crops from damage during the growing season. The ritual would create a kind of magic circle that enclosed a sacred space. (The state conducted a similar procession—followed by an animal sacrifice—in order to protect troops before they set out for battle.)

Roman rituals aimed to achieve one of three goals:

- Thanking (or paying back a promise to) a deity for a divine favor
- Averting the threat of a deity's anger—in other words, warding off ill fortune by staying in a god's or goddess' good graces
- Placating the gods or goddesses, attempting to appease wrath already unleashed (through floods, famines, plagues, and so on)

Most individual and state rituals involved some sort of *sacrifice*. The Romans believed that such gifts helped sustain or renew the vitality of the gods and goddesses. By keeping them strong and able to function effectively in their special roles, the Romans actually served their own interests. For a strong deity can better fulfill any special requests the petitioner has.

Certain rules governed the carrying out of rituals. For example, the Romans sacrificed white animals to upper deities and black animals to Underworld deities. And the organs that seemed most vital—especially the heart, liver, and kidneys—were offered exclusively to the gods.

The civic rituals of Rome were the annual festivals. Each festival—and there were around a hundred—honored a specific deity. The civic rites that celebrated gods and goddesses, like those performed by individuals, culminated in a sacrifice intended to keep the deity vigorous.

Every Home a Temple

As if deities of heaven, Earth, and the Underworld (described in detail in Chapter 21) were not enough, every Roman household had its own set of more personal gods. (The city of Rome, metaphorically the "household" of all its citizens, had its own sets of these gods, too.) These household and ancestral gods had a special interest in the members of their own households. They served as guardians of the household and all of its inhabitants.

Bless This House: The Lares

Every Roman family had its own lares, household gods who represented the deified spirits of its dead ancestors. Often represented as a youth carrying a drinking horn and cup, the lares originated either as spirits of a family's founding ancestors or as fertility spirits who brought prosperity by watching over the family fields. Every family had its own lar or lares, as did the state, principal crossroads, and adjacent neighborhoods of the city of Rome.

Every home had a *lararium*, a shrine for making offerings of incense or wine to the family lares. Romans prayed to their lares, their penates, and the goddess Vesta every day. Following a death in the home, a family would remain in mourning for eight days before making a sacrifice to the household lares—now joined by the recently deceased.

> **CAUTION** **Mythed by a Mile**
>
> Vergil tells a different tale about the origin of the lares. In the *Aeneid*, he relates how Aeneas brought both lares and penates with him from Troy to Italy (see Chapter 22).

What's in the Pantry? The Penates

Every household also its own penates, Roman gods of the storeroom or pantry. The penates had the responsibility to watch over the family's larder or storehouse. Since they guarded the storeroom, the penates were regarded—along with Vesta—as protectors of the overall welfare of the household. Every family honored its penates at meals and on special occasions.

The state of Rome—considered the metaphorical "king's family"—had its own penates, too: the *penates publici*. Rome's shrine of Vesta featured a storehouse to hold elements needed in civic rituals as well as statuettes that represented the penates who guarded Rome.

Spirits Everywhere

The lares and penates were the primary spirits who inhabited the world of the Romans. But the Romans saw spirits everywhere around them.

The Roman spirits of the dead were called *manes*. The manes usually inhabited the Underworld, but occasionally they emerged in the surface world. At such times, the living needed to perform rituals to propitiate them. Of particular importance to every family were its ancestral ghosts or manes known as *parentes*. Once a year, every family would conduct special rites intended to appease the parentes and send them safely back under the ground for another year.

Rome also had its *daemons*. These ancient spirits presided over persons, places, private counsels, secret intentions, and society.

Finally, every person, creature, or thing had within it an inherent spirit, its *genius*, which served essentially as a guardian spirit. Originally, geniuses were personifications of the reproductive powers of the male and female heads of households. But the concept of genius was later extended to mean the divine counterpart of any individual (human or animal) or thing. Still later, the concept was extended to include the spirit of groups and places—buildings, monuments, or the entire state of Rome.

The Least You Need to Know

- The Romans believed that their deities played a part—or *could* play a part—in every aspect of their daily lives.

- The openness of the Romans to the gods and goddesses of the Greeks and other cultures stemmed from their essential practicality. If their own deities failed to deliver success, the Romans felt it only made sense to try other deities.

- The Romans used prayer, sacrifice, and other rituals to maintain *pax deorum*, keeping the gods and goddesses happy and well nourished.

- The Romans developed rituals for every occasion, both personal and civic. They believed success in life depended upon the proper completion of these rituals.

- Each Roman household had its own minor gods. The most important of these were the lares, the ancestral gods of the household, and the penates, the gods of the pantry.

Chapter 21

Meet the New Boss(es), Same as the Old Boss(es): The Gods and Goddesses of Rome

In This Chapter

- The seven greatest gods and goddesses of Rome
- Profiles of these five "naturalized" Olympians and two native Roman gods
- The lesser role played by other Olympian immigrants
- Other Greek immigrants: the minor deities
- Nature spirits: the ancient Latin deities

So who were the gods and goddesses who received the honor of daily Roman rituals and sacrifices? Who were the gods to whom the Romans offered up their prayers?

If you know anything about our solar system, many of the names will sound familiar: Jupiter, Saturn, Mars, Venus, Mercury, Neptune, and

Pluto. Over the centuries, many of these have come to be identified with Greek counterparts that share certain identifying characteristics. Jupiter is the Roman Zeus; Mars is Ares; Venus is Aphrodite; Mercury is Hermes.

But the Italians had their own deities long before those gods and goddesses began absorbing the traits of the Olympians. Mars, for example, was primarily a god of agriculture before taking on the warlike aspects of the Greek Ares. In addition, the Romans worshipped many deities who had no counterpart whatsoever in Greek mythology.

The Magnificent Seven

Of all these gods and goddesses, Rome—with its Seven Hills—worshipped seven of them above all: Saturn, Jupiter, Juno, Vesta, Janus, Mars, and Venus. So put on your best clothes and sacrifice your finest cow. It's time to meet the great gods and goddesses of Rome.

Read All About It

The most complete depiction of the Roman gods (and the rituals performed in their honor) is found in Ovid's *Fasti*, a half-finished poetic treatment of the Roman calendar and its festivals. In the poem, various gods and goddesses reveal a lot about themselves in explaining to Ovid the origins of certain festival rites and other rituals.

Logos

The name **Saturn** is so ancient that its origin is uncertain, but our best guess is that it comes from the same root as the Latin word "satum," which means sown with seeds.

The Great Civilizer: Saturn

Originally the ancient Italian god of fertility, especially agriculture and sowing, *Saturn* (in Latin, *Saturnus*) came to be identified with the Greek Cronus, father of the Olympians. Yet Saturn held much more importance for the Romans than Cronus ever did for the Greeks. Unlike the story of Cronus, the Roman myth of Saturn had no violence attached to it. Like Cronus, Saturn carried a sickle—but in his case it functions not so much as a weapon (Cronus, you'll remember, castrated his father), but as a tool of agriculture.

Like Cronus, Saturn was dethroned by his son, Jupiter (in a Roman adaptation of the Greek tale). Seeking revenge, Saturn incited the Titans to attack. Consulting an oracle, Saturn learned that he would defeat the gods if he burned the entrails of a wondrous bull born of Terra Mater (Gaia, or Mother Earth). Saturn quickly had this bull, whose hind portions were a serpent, sacrificed, but just as the entrails were to be put on the fire, Jupiter commanded the birds to steal them away. Jupiter rewarded the kite, the bird that brought the entrails to him, with a heavenly constellation.

After Jupiter forced him out of the celestial realms, Saturn wandered the world before arriving in a ship at the Tuscan River. The exiled god landed in *Latium*, where he received a warm welcome from the Tuscan natives. Often called the first king of Latium, Saturn introduced the agricultural arts—and thereby civilization—to Italy. In *Metamorphoses*, Ovid depicted Saturn's reign as a golden age—a time of peace and eternal spring, when the earth gave forth its abundance without need of a plow and the rivers flowed with milk and honey. The people did not need laws or punishment, for everyone cherished justice and right. With no ships, no war, and no soldiers, all the people during Saturn's reign lived free of fear.

The Romans established a lineage between the great civilizer of Italy and the Roman kings. Saturn's great-great-granddaughter Lavinia would marry Aeneas (see Chapter 22). Due to the influence of the Greeks, the Romans often worshipped Saturn along with the agricultural goddess Ops (associated with Cronus's wife Rhea). Originally, however, the Italians worshipped him with an obscure earth goddess named Lua.

The Roman calendar year ended with a winter festival in the god's honor known as the Saturnalia. (The god also gave his name to the end of the week, Saturday.) A holiday of peace and goodwill, the Saturnalia represented a return to the golden age. One intriguing aspect of this holiday was that slaves were given the privileges of freedom and masters waited on their slaves at meals.

By Jove, It's Jupiter!

The chief god of the Romans was *Jupiter*, the god of the sky, who threw thunderbolts as his chief weapons. Identified with the Greek god Zeus, Jupiter was held in highest esteem in Rome, too. His temple on the Capitoline Hill honors Jupiter as the "Best and Greatest" (*Optimus Maximus*).

> ### What a Life!
>
> Terra Mater, also called Tellus or simply Terra, was—like the Greek Gaia—both the earth and the Roman goddess of the earth. Terra was associated with both fertility (earth's fruitfulness) and the dead (earth's cargo). The latter connection led the Romans to worship her along with Pluto and the spirits of the dead.

> ### Logos
>
> The name **Latium** comes from the Latin word *latens*, which means "hiding." This identifies Latium as the place where Saturn hid from his son, Jupiter.

> ### Logos
>
> **Jupiter** represents the contraction of two Latin words, *dies* ("day") and *pater* ("father"). Thus "Jupiter" was also called by his uncontracted form, "Dies-piter," a name that highlights the two most important aspects of the god: his association with the sky and his role as father of the gods.

Jupiter, also called Jove, was regarded as a patron god of Rome. In invoking the god, a Roman would often indicate which aspect of the god was wanted by appending a suffix to his name. Jupiter Lucretius, for example, controlled light, while Jupiter Fulgar wielded lightning and Jupiter Elicius brought rainfall.

Marrying Money: The Goddess Juno

The Roman goddess of marriage, Juno—the wife of Jupiter—loved brides, according to Ovid. Identified with the Greek Hera, Juno was the patroness of women from birth to death. Like her husband's, her name, a feminine form or feminine counterpart of "Jupiter," was often invoked with a suffix that indicated her function. Thus, Juno Lucina served as the guardian of childbirth (though some Romans saw Lucina as a distinct goddess of childbirth, a daughter of Juno rather than Juno herself), while Juno Moneta, interestingly enough, governed finances. (The Roman mint was situated in Juno's temple on the Capitoline Hill.)

Juno played an important role in the propagation of the Roman race. After the Romans and the Sabine tribes merged (see Chapter 23), the women found that they could not give birth. The future of Rome seemed dire. But the Roman husbands and their Sabine wives visited the sacred grove of Juno Lucina. The goddess appeared and commanded the sacrifice of a male goat. After the sacrifice, the women submitted to having their backs beaten with thongs cut from the goat's hide. Ten months later, all the women gave birth, assuring the survival of the Roman race.

The Romans honored her importance by naming the fourth (later the sixth) month of the calendar after her: June. (Juventas [known as Hebe to the Greeks]—the goddess of youth, daughter of Juno, and wife of Hercules [Heracles]—also claimed the month as her own.)

Like a Virgin: Vesta

Although her Greek counterpart (Hestia) remained only a household goddess, the Roman goddess Vesta—guardian of the hearth and its fire and patroness of all household activities—played an important role in both private and public life in Rome. The first of all deities invoked at festivals, Vesta played a central role in the individual and civic lives of all Romans. Vesta protected all the essential elements of family and domestic life. What's more, by extension she was the guardian of the community and the state (the larger family of Rome).

Although a virgin goddess, Vesta was worshipped as a metaphorical mother of the city of Rome. In founding the city of Rome, Romulus invoked only three deities by name. Vesta was one of them. (The others were Jupiter and Mars.)

The Romans built few public shrines for Vesta, because she did not need them: Her shrine was every fire and hearth. She did have one major shrine: the public hearth of Rome. There, the Vestal Virgins—six unmarried, chaste priestesses—attended to its sacred and undying flame. (This practice, which probably predates any of her temples, was no doubt a matter of practicality: In a culture with no matches or lighters, keeping a fire going is much more convenient than having to restart one by rubbing two sticks together.)

What a Life!

No honor for a young Roman girl was greater than to be chosen as a Vestal Virgin. Since the goddess herself had refused to marry either of her suitors—Neptune (Poseidon) and Apollo—and had instead remained a virgin, the Vestal Virgins likewise remained unmarried and chaste. Although very few Vestals failed to remain chaste, those who tasted the pleasures of the flesh paid a severe penalty: They were buried alive.

Training, performing sacred duties, and teaching initiates each lasted 10 years. After 30 years of service, the Virgins were free to leave—and even marry and bear children.

Eyes in the Back of His Head: Janus

One of the few Roman gods who had no Greek counterpart at all was Janus—the god of doors and gates. This may not sound like a very important deity, but few gods or goddesses received the number of honors given to Janus. For Janus also presided over all beginnings and endings (which are symbolic doorways) as well as sowing (the beginning of crops).

What a Life!

Ovid told the story of a nymph named Cranae, a sister of Apollo, born in the ancient grove of Alernus near the Tiber River, who chased wild beasts with darts. The beautiful nymph was chased, too—by many suitors. Yet she remained chaste by insisting that, though she wanted nothing more than to yield herself, doing so in the bright sun would bring her too much shame. Instead, she invited them to find a dark cave where they might go together. When the suitor took the lead, Cranae would follow for a short way before hiding herself in the bushes.

Janus beheld Cranae in the grove one day and fell in love. Though she tried the same trick on Janus that had fooled so many suitors before him, this time it did not work. Since Janus could see behind him, when she tried to hide, he caught her in his embrace and had his way with her. In gratitude, he made Cranae (whom Ovid may have confused with Cardea) goddess of the hinge.

Represented as having two faces in opposite directions—like a door, which faces both in and out—Janus alone of all the gods saw behind his back. The eternally vigilant god held a staff in his right hand and a key in his left.

All doors and gates—as well as all beginnings—were sacred to Janus. The Romans sought the god's blessing at the start of every day, month, and year, and also at the start of any new venture or endeavor. Indeed, when Julius Caesar added two months to the beginning of what had been a ten-month calendar, he named the first after the god of beginnings: "January."

Whenever a Roman conducted a sacrifice to another deity, they would begin by first offering incense and wine to Janus, who guards access to the other gods, even Jupiter himself.

Originally Janus served as a guardian of peace. Rome's temple of Janus carried enormous political significance. During times of war the doors were kept open, while in times of peace they were closed. At the end of the long and bloody civil wars, Augustus Caesar dramatically closed the doors of this temple, signifying that Rome was finally at peace.

War and Peace: Mars

Unlike his Greek counterpart, Ares, Mars had contradictory responsibilities, for he was both the god of agriculture and the god of war. Sometimes called Mavors (Mars is a contraction), Mars—as an agricultural deity who protected everything that grows—was worshipped above all other gods by the Latins and other early peoples of Italy long before the foundation of Rome. Revered in Latium as the patron of the sword, Mars became *the* special god of Rome just as Athena was the special goddess of Athens.

Originally just a god of agriculture, Mars promoted the growth of fruits and grains, vines and trees. He kept shepherds and cattle safe and could help stave off bad weather or disease that might threaten a farm. Renowned as Mars Silvanus (his name in an agricultural context), he was the farmer's chief protector. But as the early Romans became more powerful and militarily aggressive, Mars Gradivus (his name in a military context) assumed more warlike functions—and thus became associated with the Greek god Ares. In addition, the Romans gave Mars the responsibility for seeing that the rule of law was observed and for keeping the peace.

In Roman mythology, Mars was not a son of Jupiter and Juno (as Ares had been a son of Zeus and Hera), but of Juno alone, who conceived him through parthenogenesis. Juno was upset that Jupiter had not needed her in order to conceive Minerva (see the birth of Athena in Chapter 7). Juno wept openly before Flora, the goddess of flowers. Sharing the cause of her misery, Juno wondered aloud why, if Jupiter could do it, she couldn't. A look came over Flora's face that made Juno suspect that she might be able to help, so she pleaded for Flora's assistance. After Juno swore by Styx that Jupiter would never find out who had helped her, Flora touched her bosom with a special flower. Juno immediately became pregnant and later gave birth to Mars.

What a Life!

Mars fell in love, not with Venus (Aphrodite) as the Greeks would have you believe, but with Minerva (Athena). He consulted the aged goddess Anna Perenna—a personification of both the year (Anna) and the endless procession of years (Perenna) for help. Anna Perenna agreed to represent him in his courtship of Minerva. After many appeals and repeated delays, Anna came to Mars with good news: Minerva had at last consented to marry him. After preparing a bridal chamber, Mars went to claim his bride, who had hidden her face under a modest veil. But when the god lifted the veil to kiss her, he found the crone, Anna herself. All the goddesses had a good laugh at Mars's expense.

The city of Rome revered Mars over all other gods because he was the father (by Rhea Silvia) of Romulus, the founder of the city. He had also saved young Romulus and his twin brother, Remus, when their uncle had thrown them into the Tiber River in an attempt to kill them (see Chapter 22).

During the age of Augustus, worship of Mars became more prominent. Saluting the god as the father of the city's founder, Augustus bestowed upon the god a new title, *Mars Ultor* ("Mars the Avenger"). In this role, the god had a unique importance for Augustus—a man whose adoptive father (Julius Caesar) had been murdered.

Love Makes the World Go Around: Venus

Originally a minor fertility goddess—specifically, ruling over the fertility of gardens—Venus later took on attributes of the Greek love goddess Aphrodite.

The Romans revered Venus as the mother of the Roman race. Augustus, and before him Julius Caesar, claimed ancestry from Venus through Iulus, the son of Aeneas and grandson of Venus.

The Romans treated Venus, as the mother of all Rome, with great veneration. In *Fasti*, Ovid credits her with the creation of all the (minor) gods, too numerous to name. In addition to giving birth to the Roman race, Venus—through her dominion over love—inspires every species to remain in existence. For this reason, Ovid hails her as owning "a kingdom second to that of no god."

Ye Gods! Lesser Deities of the Romans

Although no gods or goddesses commanded more reverence than the seven described above, the Romans did worship many other deities. Some of these were Olympians imported from Greece, others holdovers—primarily nature deities—from the early Italian ancestors of the Romans.

New to the Neighborhood: The Other Olympians

Of the seven gods and goddesses held in highest esteem by the Romans during the Augustan Age, five were identified with Olympians: Jupiter (Zeus), Juno (Hera), Vesta (Hestia), Mars (Ares), and Venus (Aphrodite). But what about the other Olympian immigrants? What happened to them?

Diana, an ancient Latin or Sabine goddess of fertility and a patroness of wild things and of birth (both human and animal), took on the attributes of Artemis, the Greek goddess of hunting. Like Artemis, Diana also became associated with the moon. The Romans regarded Diana as the patron goddess of the city's plebeian class, most of whom had Latin or Sabine ancestry.

Apollo was the only Olympian who did not need to change his name when he emigrated from Greece—although the Romans sometimes called him *Sol* (Latin for "sun"). The god of prophecy and healing, among other arts, Apollo was seldom celebrated in Rome before the time of Augustus. But Augustus claimed that Apollo had appeared to him at a critical moment at the battle of Actium—the decisive victory in 31 B.C.E. that made Augustus the unchallenged ruler of the Roman Empire—and ensured his success. From that moment, Augustus regarded Apollo as his patron god.

In Apollo, Augustus saw more than a god of healing. He saw a god who brought both peace and civilization. What better deity for an emperor who believed that under his rule Rome would progress toward a new order?

> **What a Life!**
>
> The priest of Diana in her sacred grove at Nemi was known as the King of the Grove. Job requirements: The King of the Grove must be a runaway slave. The application process: A job seeker gained the position of King of the Grove by slaying his predecessor in single combat. Tenure: The King of the Grove held on to his job only until his successor killed him.

Ceres, the Roman goddess of agriculture, was an important deity to the farmers of Rome. Identified with the Greek Demeter, Ceres ruled over processes of growth. Grain (especially corn), fruits, flowers, harvest, and the earth and its fertility—all lay in the domain of Ceres. Ovid credits Ceres with being the first to invite man to eat more useful food than acorns. Ceres tamed the bulls and yoked them to the plow, which turned the soil and revealed the richness of the earth. Ovid added that Ceres was a goddess who delighted in peace.

Liber, an ancient Roman god of fertility often called Father Liber, eventually came to be identified with the Greek Bacchus (Dionysus), the god of wine. This may in fact have been a case of mistaken identity, since the original Italian deity had much less in common with Bacchus than he did with the Greek Iacchus—an obscure deity honored along with his companions, Demeter and Persephone, at the Eleusinian mysteries (see Chapter 13). Liber was similarly worshipped in Rome together with Ceres (Demeter) and Libera, an ancient Roman fertility goddess sometimes identified with Persephone.

Whether misidentified or not, once identified with Bacchus, stories about Father Liber—who also discovered honey—portrayed him as the god of the vine.

Mythed by a Mile

Ovid told a wonderful story about how Father Liber met his bride. Ariadne, the princess of Crete—abandoned by the Greek hero Theseus on the island of Dia after helping him escape from the Minotaur (see Chapter 15)—was later betrothed to Bacchus (Liber). After his pilgrimage to introduce wine to far eastern lands (see Chapter 9), Liber returned with a captive girl from India. Seeing the girl, Ariadne began wailing about her fate—doubly betrayed by each of her fiancés. She bemoaned the infidelity of men and wondered how Bacchus could throw away her love and break his promises to her.

Liber stole up behind her and, after hearing every word she said, passionately embraced her and kissed her tears away. The god of wine carried her up to heaven and shared his name with her: Libera. Presenting Ariadne with a crown that Vulcan had given to Venus and Venus in turn to Liber, Liber transformed the nine jewels of the crown into fires, which you can see in the stars even today.

Minerva was the Roman goddess of arts and crafts and the intelligence needed for them. As Romans identified her with the Greek goddess Athena, Minerva also took on the mantle of the goddess of warfare. For the pragmatic Romans, her rule over practical arts meant that Minerva controlled the fortunes of most industries.

Neptune, the chief Roman sea god, held little importance in the early days of Rome, since the early Romans were not seafarers. Yet when later identified with the powerful and majestic Greek god Poseidon, his stature grew greatly in the eyes of the Romans.

Mercury, the Roman god of merchants, cheats, and thieves, took on the qualities of the Greek god Hermes. Mercury ruled over the success of all business transactions in Rome. (The roguish god took a special delight in business transactions that combined selling, cheating, and thievery.) To honor his role as the patron of astronomy, the first planet was named after him.

What a Life!

Lara, a Naiad (water nymph), could never hold her tongue. When she told Juno that Jupiter was in love with her sister, a nymph named Juturna, the god of thunder punished her by making her mute. Jupiter then commanded Mercury to escort the blabbermouth to the Underworld. While escorting her, however, Mercury fell in love with her. Lara and Mercury became the parents of Rome's twin Lares, the public guardians of the city.

Vulcan, an ancient Italian god of uncontrolled fire—for example, the volcanoes that bear his name—shared a strong resemblance to the Greek god Hephaestus. Vulcan mimicked his Greek counterpart, becoming the Roman god of fire, metalworking, and other craftspeople who used fire for the good of humankind. Also called Mulciber—which means "He of the Gentle Touch"—Vulcan had an important role in Roman "history" as the father of Servius Tullius, the legendary sixth king of Rome (see Chapter 23).

Pluto, also called Orcus, was the Roman god of the Underworld. His name derives from the Greek word *ploutos*, meaning "wealth," an appellation that refers to the wealth of the earth's fertile soil. Pluto, of course, came to be identified with the Greek god Hades. Just as the Greeks sometimes referred to Hades as Aidoneus because they feared speaking the god's true name, the Romans sometimes referred to Pluto as Dis. (Dis is a contraction of Dives, the Latin translation of the Greek word, ploutos.)

Greeks in Togas: The Lesser Deities Go Roman

The Romans imported other characters from Greek mythology besides the Olympians. In incorporating these characters, some heroes and some minor gods or goddesses, into their own mythology, the Romans often increased their stature. Of course, the assimilation process frequently required the immigrants to change their names.

Of all the non-Olympians brought to Rome, none received greater honors than the hero Heracles. Renamed Hercules by the Romans, the deified son of Jupiter was turned into a local god. You may remember that Hercules defeated the giant Cacus, who had stolen some of the cattle of Geryon, on the future site of Rome (see Chapter 13). Killing the vicious thief who had terrorized the region made him a local hero.

The site where Hercules sacrificed one of the cattle to thank Jupiter for his victory became the Ara Maxima, the "Greatest Altar" near the Roman Forum. There, a group of public slaves looked after his worship.

What a Life!

The keeper of Hercules's temple at Rome once challenged the god himself to a dice contest. When Hercules won, the temple servant paid off his bet by locking Larentia, the most beautiful prostitute in the city, along with an abundant feast, in the sanctuary. After satisfying all of his appetites, Hercules released Larentia, advising her to court the next man she met. She did so, becoming the wife of a wealthy Etruscan who left her all his money. In turn, Larentia, upon her own death, bequeathed the money to the people of Rome.

Another refugee from Greek mythology who washed up on the shores of Italy was a goddess of sea travel whom the Romans called Mater Matuta. This "White Goddess"—often invoked by sailors in distress—was identified with the Greek Leucothea, a minor sea goddess. (Born as Ino, daughter of Theban king Cadmus, Leucothea leaped into the sea with her son Melicertes after trying to kill Phrixus and Helle [see Chapter 12].) Mater Matuta received credit for nursing Liber (Bacchus) in his youth.

Asclepius, the mortal son of Apollo, also emigrated to Italy, where his name was Latinized to Aesculapius and he was deified as a god of healing and medicine. Jupiter had thrown a thunderbolt that killed Aesculapius to punish him for using his healing powers to raise Hippolytus (see Chapter 15) from the dead. Yet Aesculapius himself was raised from the dead and arrived at Rome in the form of a huge snake during a deadly plague. Aesculapius cured the plague and the Romans forever after worshipped him—and the snake—as the god of healing.

What a Life!

After Aesculapius raised him from the dead, Hippolytus—who had spurned his stepmother Phaedra's love out of devotion to the virgin goddess Artemis (Diana)—was brought by Diana to Aricia, the center of her worship near Rome. There he became a minor Roman god called Virbius, the Twice-Born Man, and served as a consort of Diana.

Last but not least of the minor Greek gods who moved to Rome was Eros, whom the Romans called Amor or Cupid. In Rome, however, Amor changed not only his name, but his character. Where the Greek Eros was a primordial creature revered as a mature and distinguished personification of love, the Roman Cupid was the roguish, frivolous son of Venus—a mischievous boy god. The Roman version proved more durable, for when we now think of Cupid, we envision the archer whose gold-tipped arrows made even the gods fall in love.

What a Life!

One of the most touching, wrenching myths of love is the Roman story of Cupid and Psyche. Psyche, a breathtakingly beautiful mortal, became so renowned for her beauty that people began to neglect the shrines of Venus. The angry goddess sent her son Cupid to avenge her, but the winged god of love secretly married Psyche instead. Fearing for his bride's safety, however, Cupid kept his identity a mystery, appearing in Psyche's bedchamber only under a cover of complete darkness.

Egged on by her sisters, Psyche lit a lamp she had hidden by her bedside one night. Though she instantly fell in love with her husband, Cupid—stung by this betrayal—flew away. After enduring a series of torments inflicted on her by Venus, who literally sent the girl to hell and back, Psyche ultimately reconciled with Cupid, Zeus made her immortal, they had a child named Voluptas (Pleasure) ... and they lived happily ever after.

[handwritten margin note: to encourage someone to do something risky]

Everything Old Becomes New Again: The Ancient Italian Deities

Just because they embraced the new deities of the Greeks, the Romans did not abandon the gods and goddesses of their own history. The deities of the ancient Latins and other Italians remained objects of worship throughout the history of the Roman Empire.

What a Life!

Originally a nymph named Chloris, the future goddess Flora was ravaged by Zephyr (a personification of the west wind). According to Ovid, Zephyr then made her his wife and gave her the gift of eternal youth—perpetual spring—and dominion over the world's flowers.

Fauna, an ancient Roman goddess, had power over fertility, nature, farming, and animals. Known as *Bona Dea* ("Good Goddess") or *Bona Mater* ("Good Mother"), Fauna was worshipped exclusively by women. Said to be either the wife or daughter of Faunus, the sylvan god of flocks, Fauna had a reputation for chastity. Indeed, after her marriage, no man but her husband ever set eyes on her.

Flora, the ancient Roman goddess of flowers, fertility, gardens, and love, was responsible for the flowering of all things. In addition, her dominions included tilled fields (crops, vines, olive and fruit trees) and the flowering of sex. Her act of scattering seeds brought color to a formerly monochromatic world. The Romans also revered her for helping Juno conceive Mars, who in turn fathered Romulus and Remus.

Vertumnus was another Roman god of fertility, given charge over change: the changing seasons, the changes in vegetation, and the turning year. Perhaps originally an Etruscan deity, Vertumnus himself had the ability to change. He could assume any shape—becoming a girl, a charioteer, a hunter, a drunk—at will. The Romans offered the first fruits of the season—for example, newly ripened grapes or early corn—to Vertumnus.

What a Life!

Pomona, a shy Latin nymph who became the Roman goddess of fruit trees and gardens, lived modestly and chastely in her orchard. She spurned all suitors, including Vertumnus. But Vertumnus would not give up that easily. To woo Pomona, he assumed a series of guises—a reaper, a haymaker, a ploughman, a fisher, a soldier. Having no luck, he finally disguised himself as an old woman. In this form, Vertumnus eloquently pleaded his case and then finally revealed himself in his true form. Pomona relented and married him.

Faunus, a sylvan god of prophecy, also had influence over the fertility of both flocks and crops. Often identified with the Greek demigod Pan, Faunus was the grandson of Saturn and the son of Picus (a woodland demigod in the form of a woodpecker who was sacred to Mars). Faunus held a unique place in Roman mythology as the reputed father (by a water nymph named Marica) of Latinus, the king of Latium, whose daughter would wed Aeneas and found the Roman race (see Chapter 22).

What a Life!

Once upon a time, Faunus saw the Lydian Queen Omphale walking with her slave-for-a-year, Hercules (see Chapter 15), and instantly fell in love with her. He followed the couple to a cave, where they feasted and then fell asleep in separate beds. (They were remaining pure in order to celebrate a festival of Liber, the god of wine, the next day.)

Faunus waited until midnight and then stole into the pitch-black cave. Groping his way toward the sleeping couple, he felt the rough lion skin cloak of Hercules and quickly moved to the other bed. Feeling silken garments, Faunus brushed them aside and prepared to mount his conquest. Without warning, he found himself hurtling across the cave, thrown off by the mighty Hercules. Omphale, you may recall, was fond of dressing Hercules up in her own garments—and she had been sleeping under his cloak.

After this humiliating episode, Faunus insisted that his worshippers come naked to his rites—free of all deceptive garments.

Bit Players: Minor Italian Deities

The ancient Italians had many other gods and goddesses whom the Romans still revered during the Age of Augustus. They include:

- Ops, the goddess of plenty or of the harvest (often identified with the Greek Rhea)

- Silvanus, a god of agriculture, especially of the woods

- Pales, a deity of flocks and of shepherds (though it remains uncertain whether Pales was male or female—or even a pair of twins)

- Bellona, the goddess of war

- Fortuna, the goddess of fate, chance, good luck, and prosperity

- Carmenta, a goddess of healing and the future—or of childbirth

- The Camenae, goddesses of prophecy and healing—or fountain nymphs later identified with the Greek muses

- Fornax, the goddess of bread-baking

Surviving stories about these minor deities are sadly few and far between, so honors to them will need to be limited to the above invocations of their names and functions.

The Least You Need to Know

- The most important deities to Romans were Saturn, Jupiter, Juno, Vesta, Janus, Mars, and Venus.

- Of these seven, only two—Saturn and Janus—remained uniquely Roman, and even Saturn took on some of the aspects of the Greek Cronus. The other five major deities absorbed most aspects of their Greek counterparts.

- The other Olympian deities played far less significant roles in the mythology of Rome than they had in that of Greece.

- The Romans deified a number of Greek mortals, including Hercules, Mater Matuta, Asculapius, and Virbius.

- The ancient Latin gods and goddesses who retained importance in Roman mythology were primarily such deities of fertility as Flora, Fauna, Pomona, Vertumnus, and Faunus.

Chapter 22

All Roads Lead to Rome: The Odyssey of Aeneas

In This Chapter

- ◆ Aphrodite's wooing of Anchises
- ◆ Aeneas's battles in the Trojan War—and his escape from the sack of Troy
- ◆ The tragic love affair between Aeneas and Dido, queen of Carthage
- ◆ What Aeneas saw in his visit to the Underworld
- ◆ The conquest of Latium and the founding of the Roman race

The Romans borrowed so much of their own mythology from Greek sources that it seems fitting that they appropriated one of the heroes of the Trojan War as the progenitor of their civilization. Yet demonstrating a characteristic ambivalence toward Greece, the Romans chose an enemy of the Greeks, a Trojan hero, as the founder of their race: Aeneas.

In telling the story of Aeneas, the Romans not only highlighted a character drawn from Greek tales, they also employed a format that Greeks would find familiar: a series of adventures challenging a hero in pursuit of a distant goal—in other words, an odyssey.

Read All About It

The many adventures of Aeneas can be found in the greatest epic poem of the Augustan age, Vergil's *Aeneid*. The first six books of the *Aeneid*, comparable to Homer's *Odyssey*, detail the hero's wanderings. The second six books, comparable to Homer's *Iliad*, describe the war between

In many ways, the adventures of Aeneas parallel those of Odysseus (see Chapter 18):

◆ Each hero began his odyssey at the end of the Trojan War, and each headed off across the Hellespont to the site of Polydorus's murder.

◆ Odysseus and Aeneas both had to overcome obstacles placed in their paths by a divine force.

◆ Both heroes found romance along the way, but abandoned their loves to continue their quest.

◆ Each hero traveled to the Underworld in search of guidance.

Despite the similarities, one significant difference set these heroes apart. Odysseus weathered all challenges in order to get home, where his wife and son awaited his return. Aeneas was a hero without a home; his quest was to establish a new home for himself and his fellow Trojans.

A Born Hero

Like Heracles, Achilles, Theseus, Perseus, and many other heroes of classical mythology, Aeneas seemed destined for greatness from the moment of his conception. Aeneas, like these heroes, was born of a union between the human and the divine; in his blood, mortality and immortality intermingled. How could he have become anything but a hero?

The Son Also Rises

Anchises, the father of Aeneas, was an heir to the throne of Dardania. Both his mother and his father were direct descendants of Tros (the famous king who gave his name to Troy). Once the most powerful city in Phrygia, Dardania—located at the foot of Mount Ida—had long since been overshadowed in importance by the younger city of Troy.

Anchises was an extraordinarily handsome young man with a certain degree of dash and daring. As a youth, Anchises had stolen the famous horses of his uncle, King Laomedon of Troy, to stud for his own mares. Zeus had presented these magnificent animals to Laomedon or his grandfather Tros, in exchange for the Trojan prince Ganymede, whom the god had abducted to serve as his cupbearer and, most likely, his lover as well. Laomedon had once promised these same horses to Heracles in return for saving Hesione, but after his daughter was safe, he had refused to part with them (see Chapter 13).

Anchises was tending his cattle herds on Mount Ida one day when the goddess Aphrodite spotted him. Some say that Zeus had tired of the mockery Aphrodite heaped on the gods after using her powers to make them fall in love with mortals. This time, he determined, *she* would become enamored with a mortal and *he* would laugh at *her* folly. In any case, whether pro-pelled by a divine force or her own urges, the goddess did indeed fall in love at first sight of this beautiful young man.

Appearing before Anchises, Aphrodite asked him to lie with her. But Anchises feared that making love to the goddess would sap him of all his manhood—or worse, kill him. So Aphrodite adopted a ruse, returning disguised as the mor-tal daughter of Otreus, a Phrygian king. Only after the couple had conceived Aeneas did Aphrodite reveal her true identity to Anchises.

Read All About It

The story of Aphrodite's seduction of Anchises and the conception of Aeneas comes not from *The Aeneid*, but from *The Homeric Hymn to Aphrodite* (#5), which was written hun-dreds of years before Rome rose to power.

Aphrodite, who was indeed embarrassed at having made love to a mere mortal, com-manded Anchises to keep the child's parentage a secret. He was to tell anyone who asked that one of the nymphs was Aeneas's mother. Unfortunately, Anchises blurted out the truth after getting drunk one evening. To punish him, Zeus hurled a thunder-bolt that crippled Anchises. The moral of the story: Never embarrass a goddess.

Born on Mount Ida, Aeneas was reared by the nymphs who frequented that moun-tain. Brought to Anchises when he was five years old, Aeneas remained in his father's care thereafter. As so many other heroes had before him, Aeneas received his educa-tion from Cheiron, the wise king of the Centaurs. Aphrodite, though she had no direct hand in his upbringing, watched over Aeneas constantly throughout his youth and later during his adventures in both Troy and Italy.

The Good Soldier

During the Trojan War, Aeneas served well under the supreme commander of the Trojan armies: Hector, prince of Troy. As leader of the Dardanian troops, Aeneas may have resented his subordinate position—as well as the domination of the younger city

Ilium over his native Dardania. Nonetheless, he fought valiantly to defend the interests of Troy (see Chapter 16).

Like all the combatants, however, Aeneas suffered serious setbacks during the course of the 10-year war. Achilles, the greatest of Greek warriors, forced Aeneas and his troops to flee Mount Ida and take refuge in the city of Lyrnessus. Aeneas later received a wound that might have proved fatal had not his mother and Apollo quickly removed him from the field of battle. The goddess Artemis and her mother, the goddess Leto, healed him.

In the final years of the war, Apollo incited Aeneas to challenge Achilles directly. But Poseidon removed Aeneas from this battle to protect his greater destiny as the future leader of "Troy." As it turned out, however, his greater destiny did not lie in leading Troy (which never recovered from the devastation it suffered during the war), but rather in founding an entirely new race of people.

The Bitter End

When, after a decade of war, the Greeks finally sacked Troy, Aeneas, who realized he could no longer defend the burning city, deserted Troy. Some say he was spooked into leaving by the omen of sea serpents killing Laocoön when the prophet tried to warn the Trojans not to bring the wooden horse into Ilium (see Chapter 16).

In any case, Aeneas was one of just a handful of Trojan males to escape death or capture in the sack of Troy. Carrying his father Anchises on his back, Aeneas, accompanied by his son Ascanius (who would be called Iulus in Italy), returned briefly to Mount Ida.

His first wife, Creusa—a daughter of Priam and Hecuba—was less fortunate. Earlier, she had been captured by the Greeks, but Aphrodite—with the assistance of Cybele, a Phrygian mother goddess—had saved her daughter-in-law from enslavement. During the escape from Troy, however, Creusa became separated from Aeneas and neither he nor her son Ascanius ever saw her alive again. She was presumed dead. (Her ghost appeared to Aeneas, urging him to flee the dying city.)

A Man Without a Country

From Mount Ida, Aeneas led 20 shiploads of Trojans in search of a new home. Eventually, he and a small band of survivors would settle in Italy, where the Romans would later claim him as their ancestor. But just as it took Odysseus 10 years to find his way home, it would prove nearly as long and difficult a journey for Aeneas to find his way to Italy.

Are You My Mother(land)?

Aeneas and the Trojans left Mount Ida in early summer, intending to found a city in Thrace, a vast region between the Black and Aegean Seas. With this plan in mind, Aeneas and the Trojan survivors stopped first just across the Hellespont in the land of the Bistones. Had they settled there, the Roman race might never have been founded.

But while gathering cornel and myrtle boughs from an unmarked grave mound, they could not help but notice that the boughs were bleeding. Worse still, the voice of Aeneas's brother-in-law Polydorus, the murdered son of Hecuba and Priam (see Chapter 18), suddenly called out to them. Quickly changing their plans, the Trojans offered sacrifices to the dead and swiftly abandoned Thrace.

Aeneas next stopped on the island of Delos, the reputed birthplace of Apollo and Artemis. The king of this Aegean island, an old friend of Anchises named Anius, was a prophet, a priest, and son of Apollo. Calling on his gift of prophecy to help Anchises, Anius urged him to seek out his "ancient mother."

Anchises interpreted this ambiguous prophecy to mean Crete, home of his ancestor Teucer, the first ruler of Dardania. So the Trojans traveled next to Crete, where they unfortunately suffered from famine. At this point, the penates of Aeneas and Anchises, which they had brought with them from Troy, clarified the prophecy of Anius. The penates advised them to make their home not in the homeland of Teucer, but rather in the homeland of Dardanus: Italy.

What a Life!

Dardanus, a son of Zeus and son-in-law of Teucer, was regarded as the first ancestor of the Trojan race. Dardanus, the Romans insist, was born in Italy. As a young man, he traveled to Phrygia and married Bateia (called the Mother of the Trojan race), the daughter of Teucer. At the foot of Mount Ida, he founded the city of Dardania. When Teucer died, the new king named the entire region (Dardania) after himself.

Islands in the Storm

Setting out for Italy, the Trojans met with a storm that drove their ships back through the Ionian Sea, forcing them to seek refuge on the Strophades Islands, west of the Peloponnesus. Here Zetes and Calais had overtaken, but spared, the Harpies—the foul bird-women who had served as the instruments of Zeus's vengeance on Phineus, king of Salmydessus (see Chapter 14).

The Harpies—whose metallic wings proved impenetrable to Trojan swords—harassed and plundered the Trojans during their stay on the islands. They stole food and befouled what they left behind. They also warned of many dangers Aeneas and his crews would face before building their new city in Italy.

Heading north along the Adriatic coast of Greece, Aeneas next stopped in Buthrotum, a port opposite the island of Corcyra in Epeirus, a somewhat uncivilized coastal region of Greece. The seer Helenus—the son of Priam who had revealed to the Greeks the conditions that would lead to their victory over Troy—had founded and still ruled Buthrotum.

Helenus foretold that Aeneas would found the Roman race. The seer told Aeneas that he would know where to settle when he saw a white sow suckling 30 white piglets. Helenus offered directions that helped the fleet cross the Ionian Sea and arrive safely on Sicily, the vast island southwest of the Italian peninsula.

In Drepanum, a town in western Sicily, the aged Anchises died. With great ceremony, Aeneas honored his father by burying him on Mount Eryx—the Sicilian mountain named after another son of Aphrodite, whom Heracles had slain in a wrestling match (see Chapter 13).

Juno Acts as Matchmaker

Meanwhile, Juno (Hera) observed the progress of Aeneas and the Trojans with increasing displeasure. Juno hated Aeneas and the Trojans for several reasons:

◆ The goddess had not forgotten that Venus (Aphrodite), the mother of Aeneas, had won the Golden Apple as "the fairest" of the goddesses (see Chapter 16).

◆ Nor had she forgotten that a Trojan prince (Paris) had awarded this honor to her.

◆ She had foreknowledge that the descendants of Aeneas would destroy her favorite city, Carthage.

◆ She had never been favorably disposed toward the Trojan race, since it had descended from a coupling of Jupiter (Zeus) and one of his mistresses, Electra.

What a Life!

Zeus had abducted Electra—one of the Pleiades, daughters of Atlas—and brought her to Olympus. Though she had clung to the sacred Palladium (a wooden statue of Athena), Zeus had hurled the sacred image from heaven and had his way with her. (The statue landed on Earth at the feet of Ilus, who founded Troy on that exact spot.) This coupling resulted in the conception of Dardanus, father of the Trojan race.

The seething Juno ordered Aeolus, keeper of the winds, to destroy the Trojan fleet. Neptune (Poseidon), however, who jealously guarded his authority over the sea, calmed the waters and ruined her plans for destruction. Though saved from the wrath of the storm (and Juno), the Trojan ships were blown far off-course—to the coast of North Africa.

Aeneas and his crews landed safely in Carthage, a city on the Libyan coast. Queen Dido, the city's founder, received Aeneas warmly. Cupid (Eros) exercised a powerful influence on Dido's reception. At his mother Venus's request, Cupid disguised himself as the son of Aeneas and caused Dido to fall in love with the Trojan leader.

What a Life!

Dido's brother Pygmalion, king of the Phoenician city of Tyre, had secretly murdered her husband Sychaeus, a priest of Hercules (Heracles), in the hope that he would find the priest's hidden fortune. But Sychaeus's ghost had appeared to Dido in a dream and warned her of her brother's treachery. After disclosing the location of his hidden money, the vision of Sychaeus advised her to leave Tyre. Pygmalion thus reaped no rewards for his foul deed—and Dido brought a fortune when she founded Carthage.

Aeneas eagerly returned Dido's love. Indeed, he became so enraptured that Mercury (Hermes) came down from Olympus twice to remind him of his destiny in Italy. After a year with Dido, Aeneas finally, regretfully, resumed his course. Dido was so distraught at the separation that she cursed the Trojans and killed herself with her own sword.

After crossing the Mediterranean, Aeneas and his crews stopped once more on Sicily. There they remained as guests of King Acestes of Eryx, who was holding funeral games for Anchises. (As a descendant of Venus's son Eryx, Acestes was distantly related to Aeneas.)

By this point, Aeneas and the Trojan refugees had been traveling for seven years already. Many had reached their limit. So while most of the passengers and crew were celebrating their shore leave, the Trojan mothers—influenced by Juno—set fire to some of Aeneas's ships. These women hoped that destroying the ships would force Aeneas and the other Trojans to abandon their destiny and remain on this hospitable island.

This stratagem succeeded in part. The ships that escaped destruction could no longer carry all of the Trojans. So Aeneas allowed the older crew members and others who wanted to quit to remain on Sicily. These Trojan exiles founded Acesta—a city named after their kind host. The rest, however, continued on toward Italy.

Veni, Vidi, Vici

More than seven years after leaving Mount Ida, Aeneas and his followers finally arrived in Italy. They first docked at Cumae, just north of present-day Naples. Aeneas and the Trojans were now ready to meet their destiny: the founding of a new race. But where should they settle?

Passport to the Underworld

Aeneas had come to Cumae at the behest of his father's ghost, who had appeared in a vision. But Anchises had not told him why. Needing further guidance, Aeneas visited the Cumaean Sibyl, a prophetess who lived in a cave that had a hundred different openings. He asked her to guide him through the Underworld to seek out his father.

What a Life!

Perhaps the most famous prophetess in all of classical mythology, the Cumaean Sibyl had gained her longevity and the power of prophecy from Apollo. The god, who desperately wanted the Sibyl, offered her an extra year of life for every grain of sand she could hold in her hand. Unfortunately, she neglected to ask that her youth and beauty remain undiminished.

When Apollo offered the Sibyl continued youth in return for becoming his mistress, she refused. So she grew more aged and decrepit with each passing year—and she would live for a thousand years!

The Sibyl agreed to serve as his guide. Before she would leave, however, she directed Aeneas to visit a nearby wood and pluck a magical golden bough. This bough was sacred to Proserpine (Persephone), the Queen of the Underworld.

The Sibyl led Aeneas to the edge of the river Styx, which flowed nine times around the borders of Hades. There they met the souls of the unburied dead—forbidden by Charon, the ferryman, to cross into Hades. (Those not properly buried—those denied funeral rites and lacking a coin [an obol] in their mouth to pay Charon's fare—were doomed to wander the shore of the Styx for 100 years before gaining passage.)

Among the unburied dead, Aeneas recognized Palinurus, the helmsman of his flagship. Palinurus had fallen asleep at the tiller and been swept overboard by a wave. By swimming for four days, he had reached the shores of Italy, but barbarians had murdered him and left him unburied. Aeneas promised to find and bury his body so that Palinurus could continue his journey.

Seeing the golden bough, Charon regarded this gift for Proserpine as a passport to the Underworld. So he gave Aeneas and the Sibyl free passage across the Styx.

In the Underworld, Aeneas again met Dido. Aeneas tried to speak to her, but she refused to answer him and turned back to her husband Sychaeus.

Aeneas found Anchises in the Elysian Fields—the place reserved for mortals who, favored by the gods, are made immortal after their death: such heroes as Achilles, Cadmus, and Peleus. In the Elysian Fields, the sun always shines and the immortals devote their time to music, sport, feasting, and other pleasurable activities.

Anchises predicted that Aeneas's descendants would found Rome and establish a long line of kings. Finally, Anchises showed Aeneas a group of souls waiting to be reborn as Romans. With his destiny laid out for him, Aeneas returned to the upper world and set sail once more.

Arrival of a Rival

Arriving at the Tiber River, Aeneas and the Trojans set anchor for the last time in a land called Latium. This vast region, which stretched to the south of where Rome would soon be founded, was ruled by the aged King Latinus. Latinus had an impressive lineage. The son of Faunus (a sylvan god) and Marica (a nymph), Latinus was a great-grandson of Saturn, the god of time and fertility who had first introduced agriculture and civilization to Latium as the region's first ruler.

Latinus had learned from oracles that Lavinia, his daughter, would marry a foreign prince. So the king welcomed the ambassadors sent ahead by Aeneas. Indeed, even before meeting him, Latinus intimated that Aeneas would marry his daughter. What could possibly go wrong?

Juno once more brewed trouble for Aeneas. The goddess summoned Alecto, one of the Furies, to stir up hostilities between the Latins and the Trojans. Alecto first raised the hackles of Amata, Lavinia's mother, and her nephew Turnus, the young king of the neighboring Rutulians who inhabited the city of Ardea. With Amata's encouragement, Turnus had been wooing Lavinia for years. Turnus—who still had his aunt's favor as Lavinia's suitor—was not about to step aside for some stranger.

The More Things Change ...

Just like the Trojan War, which was sparked by a foreigner who came to Greece and stole a woman, the wars in Latium revolved around a romantic rivalry. Turnus saw Aeneas as playing the role of Paris, the eastern prince come to steal the local girl.

This Means War

Reluctant to declare war on his wife's nephew, Latinus instead abdicated his rule, leaving the throne of Latium empty.

Turnus began recruiting allies for the fight to come:

♦ Aventinus, a son of Hercules (Heracles) and a priestess named Rhea

♦ Camilla, the Amazon-like queen of the Volscian tribe, a swift and valiant virgin warrior dedicated to the service of Diana (Artemis)

♦ Mezentius, a former Etruscan king expelled for torturing and killing his subjects

♦ Juturna, Turnus's nymph or demigoddess sister, who masqueraded as his charioteer in order to help him

> **What a Life!**
>
> Evander was the son of Mercury and an Arcadian nymph named Carmenta. Before the Trojan War, he had led a group of settlers from Arcadia—a mountainous region of the Greek Peloponnesus—to the banks of the Tiber. There, on the future site of Rome, he had founded a city he called Pallanteum.

> **What a Life!**
>
> In bringing together Turnus, Diomedes, Mezentius, Cybele, and Aeneas, Vergil demonstrates just what an eclectic hodgepodge Roman mythology was. The Latin prince, the Greek war hero, the cruel Etruscan king, the Phrygian mother-goddess, and the Trojan exile—all contributed to the story of the founding of the Roman race.

Turnus also attempted to enlist his brother-in-law Diomedes, the exiled Greek hero who had once wounded Aeneas during the Trojan War. Diomedes, who had founded the city of Argyripa in Apulia, turned Turnus down. Since wounding Venus (Aphrodite) at Troy, Diomedes had suffered from an unending string of troubles—and was not eager to court any more by opposing the son of that goddess.

Aeneas, too, began rounding up allies to stand with him in battle:

♦ Pallas, prince of the nearby city of Pallanteum, sent with troops by his aged father Evander, who had befriended Aeneas

♦ The Etruscans, tribal people from the coastal regions north of the Tiber, who hated Mezentius for his cruelty

Early in the conflict, Rutulian troops set fire to the remaining Trojan ships. Since the ships had been made from the pine trees of Mount Ida, however, a country sacred to Cybele (a Phrygian mother-goddess), she transformed them into sea nymphs, and they dived down into the sea.

Among the major combatants, Pallas died at the hands of Turnus, who took the Arcadian's belt as a trophy. Aeneas killed both Mezentius and his son Lausus. Camilla was ambushed and killed during a battle in which the Volscians suffered heavy casualties.

At one point, Aeneas and Turnus agreed to end the bloody war by meeting in one-on-one combat. Juno, however, did not like Turnus's chances and so incited the Latins to break the truce. Following a Trojan attack on Ardea, false rumors spread that Turnus had died. Amata, his aunt and prospective mother-in-law, killed herself upon hearing this news.

Once again, the two principals warily agreed to meet in single combat. This time, Juno did not interfere. Critically wounded in the battle, Turnus begged Aeneas to carry him to his aged father, Daunus, the former king of Apulia, before he died. Aeneas almost relented, but became incensed when he spotted the belt of his ally Pallas boldly displayed on Turnus's armor. With one last blow, he slew Turnus, ending the war over Latium.

Friends, Romans, Countrymen

Aeneas brokered a peace with the conquered Latins. Under the agreement, the Trojans gave up their name and adopted the Latin language, while the Latins accepted the rule of the Trojans and began to worship the Trojan penates and lares.

Aeneas soon married Lavinia, the daughter of Latinus, who later gave birth to a son, Silvius, the first child born into the new Roman race. As the new king of Latium, Aeneas founded the city of Lavinium, which he named after his wife. As Lavinium grew, it absorbed neighboring Laurentum—the city once ruled by Latinus.

Iulus, the Trojan son of Aeneas originally named Ascanius, succeeded his father as ruler of Latium. Iulus established a family reign that would last as many as a dozen generations.

Descendants of the Julian House (named after Iulus) would include Julius Caesar and Augustus Caesar. It would remain the ruling house of Rome for the next four centuries.

At Venus's request, Jupiter granted Aeneas immortality. Venus bade the river god Numicius to carry Aeneas's body to the sea and purify him with his waters. As his mortality washed away, Aeneas—anointed by his mother—became a minor god, whom the Romans called Indiges.

The Least You Need to Know

- Aeneas was the offspring of Aphrodite's secret liaison with Anchises, king of Dardania (near Troy).

- After fighting valiantly in the Trojan War and escaping the sack of Ilium, Aeneas led 20 shiploads of men in a search for a new home.

- Aeneas and Queen Dido of Carthage fell deeply in love. When Aeneas—prodded by Mercury—left Carthage to fulfill his destiny, Dido killed herself in despair.

- The Sibyl, a truly ancient prophetess, led Aeneas—who carried a golden bough sacred to Proserpine—in a journey to the Underworld to seek his father's counsel.

- Aeneas won over or conquered the tribes inhabiting Latium. The new race that commingled Trojans and Latins would later be called the Romans.

Chapter 23

Rome Wasn't Built in a Day

In This Chapter

- ◆ The miraculous survival of Romulus and Remus
- ◆ How Romulus and Remus fought over the founding of Rome
- ◆ The rape of the Sabine women and war with the Sabines
- ◆ The seven kings of Rome
- ◆ The rape of Lucretia and the formation of the republic

Under the leadership of Aeneas and then Iulus, Lavinium grew so prosperous that Iulus founded a second city, Alba Longa. Situated farther inland than Lavinium, this city supplanted Lavinium as the capital of the race that combined Latins and Trojans in Italy. Alba Longa would remain the chief city of the Romans throughout the reigns of 12 kings, all descended from Iulus (and, of course, Aeneas).

Double Visionaries: Romulus and Remus

For 12 generations, the throne of Alba Longa passed peacefully from ruler to ruler with neither conflict nor challenge. But the unlucky thirteenth king, Numitor, did not fare so well. During the eighth century B.C.E.,

Numitor enjoyed only a brief reign in Alba Longa before his treacherous brother Amulius deposed him.

Whether in deference to Numitor's popularity among the citizens of Alba Longa or in fear of divine reprisal, Amulius did not risk killing Numitor himself. But after driving his brother from the throne of Alba Longa, Amulius took steps to ensure that no heirs of Numitor would ever challenge him and his descendants for the throne—or so he thought.

Dancing with Wolves

Upon seizing the throne, Amulius quickly eliminated his potential challengers by killing both of his nephews, the sons of Numitor. As for Numitor's daughter, Rhea Silvia, the usurper appointed her as a Vestal Virgin. As a professional virgin, of course, Rhea Silvia (who was also called Ilia) was unlikely to get pregnant and bear any future heirs who might interrupt a line of kings descended from Amulius.

Amulius had not taken into account the infatuation of Mars—the god of farming as well as war—with Rhea Silvia. Mars seduced or raped the Vestal Virgin and with her conceived twin sons. When Rhea Silvia gave birth to Romulus and Remus nine months later, Amulius confronted her, wanting to know how a Vestal Virgin managed to get pregnant. Upon hearing her claim that Mars had fathered her two children, Amulius angrily imprisoned her. Rhea Silvia was never seen again.

Logos

The **Tiber River** was called the Alba or Albula during the time of the Trojan settlement in Italy—and for seven generations beyond. But King Tiberinus, a descendant of Aeneas and Iulus—and a forebear of Romulus and Remus—drowned in the river, and the name was changed in his honor.

Romulus and Remus were still infants when their granduncle Amulius squeezed them into a basket and tossed the brothers into the *Tiber River*. Exposed to the dangers of both the waters and the wildlife, the twins seemed doomed to a very brief life.

The basket of babies eventually washed ashore on the banks of the river. The boys were saved from starving by their father, Mars, who sent them two creatures sacred to him: a wolf and a woodpecker. The she-wolf found the twins and, demonstrating a powerful maternal instinct, suckled the children and sheltered them in her home in the forest. After they had been weaned, a woodpecker fed the twins.

What a Life!

The woodpecker, Picus, was a prophetic bird who attended Mars. Once a mortal, Picus was a son of Saturn and later grandfather of Latinus, the king who welcomed Aeneas to Latium. Picus was engaged to a nymph named Canens, a beautiful nymph whose singing tamed wild beasts and stopped rivers. When Circe fell in love with him, Picus repeatedly rejected her. Insulted and enraged, Circe punished Picus by turning him into a woodpecker. Canens wasted away from grief over her lost love.

Having lived for some time under the protection of the she-wolf and the woodpecker, Romulus and Remus were discovered in the forest by Faustulus, the king's chief shepherd. Although he suspected their true identities, Faustulus defied the authorities by sheltering and concealing the children. The shepherd and his wife Acca Larentia reared the twins in their own home, feeding, educating, and caring for them as if the boys were their own children.

Mythed by a Mile _____

The identity of Acca Larentia remains somewhat of a mystery. Some say she was the wife of Faustulus. Some say that before she married Faustulus, she was an ancient Roman goddess, also called simply Larentia, whose original functions are obscure and unknown. (One of the annual festivals in Rome was called the Larentalia.) Most intriguingly, still others suggest that Larentia was herself the she-wolf who suckled the twins, Romulus and Remus. (The Latin word *lupa*, which means "she-wolf," was also a slang term for "prostitute.")

The Lost Generation Returns

Under the tutelage of Faustulus and Acca Larentia, Romulus and Remus grew up to become bold, strong men. They showed no fear of the wild animals that roamed the region. Nor did they run from the robbers who preyed on the area's inhabitants. Impressed with their courage and strength, the shepherds who tended their flocks on the hills outside Alba Longa came to regard this fearless pair as their leaders.

One afternoon, the twins got into a fight with Numitor's shepherds over a game they had been playing. The shepherds accused the boys of stealing some sheep that had gone missing. Although Romulus got away, the shepherds seized Remus and brought the young man (who remained unaware of his true parentage) before Numitor for punishment.

Remus made a powerful impression on the old man. Indeed, Numitor began wondering whether this handsome young stranger and the brother he had mentioned might be his long-lost grandchildren—given up for dead so many years ago.

Meanwhile, back in the forest, Faustulus—concerned about Remus's capture—had decided to reveal the details of the twins' early life to Romulus. After explaining how he had found them, Faustulus suggested that the boys might be the lost sons of Rhea Silvia.

Both grandsons soon reunited with their grandfather. Together, the three plotted to avenge the deaths of Numitor's sons—as well as the dastardly plot against Romulus and Remus in their infancy. Backed by a loyal band of shepherds, the twins stormed the palace of Alba Longa. Following a brief battle, they killed the tyrant who had usurped their grandfather's throne. In this way, Romulus and Remus restored Numitor to power.

Sibling Rivalry Is for the Birds

Romulus and Remus were not satisfied with merely restoring their grandfather to the throne and awaiting their turn to succeed him. Instead, they ambitiously set out to establish their own city at the site on the Tiber where they had washed ashore as infants.

Unfortunately, neither would concede any authority to the other. Each wanted to name the city and build it according to his own design. In addition, each had his own followers among the shepherds and other citizens of Alba Longa.

Since they could not agree on any of the details, Romulus and Remus decided to let the gods determine who would rule. How would they know who had won the gods' favor? A contest, of course. But any competition that called for the two to match skills, wills, wits, or intellect would be biased toward one or the other brother. So they decided on a game of chance: Whoever first saw a flight of vultures would have the final say on all matters regarding their new city.

Instead of settling the issue, however, the contest only increased the tension between the brothers. Remus positioned himself on the Aventine, one of the seven hills of Rome. Overlooking the Tiber, he quickly spotted six vultures. But Romulus, positioned on a nearby hill, the Palatine, saw 12 of the birds almost immediately afterward. Each claimed victory:

Mythed by a Mile

Another version of the story has Romulus winning the contest outright. But after Romulus had laid out the city, Remus brazenly insulted him by jumping over the new wall of the city, demonstrating how easily Romulus's fortifications could be overcome. To avenge this effrontery, Romulus or one of his men killed Remus.

Remus because he had seen the vultures first, Romulus because he had seen a full dozen. When a skirmish broke out among the two groups of followers, Remus was killed in the fighting.

The More Things Change ...

Fratricide, the killing of brother by brother, provided the mythical foundation upon which Rome was founded. Greek mythology had a similar story of fratricide and civic order: the tale of Eteocles and Polyneices, the twin sons of Oedipus who slew each other before the seven gates of Thebes in their struggle for political power. The notion that Rome arose out of the blood of fratricide had a particular resonance for Romans of the first century B.C.E. (the period when this myth was recorded), for at that time Rome was being torn apart by a protracted and bloody civil war.

Did Romulus honor his slain brother by naming the new city after Remus? Of course not. He named the city after himself: Rome. And the city's founder became its first king.

If You Can't Come to Rome, Rome Will Come to You

The new city of Rome attracted many male immigrants: a haphazard collection of vagabonds, outlaws, fugitives, and refugees. Despite the questionable character of many of its new inhabitants, the city flourished. Like an American frontier town, Rome was rough and ready, inhabited by those who couldn't fit in anywhere else. The city's reputation as a place where anything might happen then attracted even more vagabonds.

Personals: SM Seeks SF × 100

Yet the city had a problem. Virtually no women had settled there. Romulus, visionary leader that he was, knew that a city needs more than men in order to survive more than a generation. Rome needed women—and quickly.

At first, Romulus attempted to court wives from neighboring cities. But most outsiders refused to let their daughters marry Romans, whom they regarded as scurrilous rogues. The Etruscans, a wealthy and sophisticated people whose kingdom was north of Rome, looked down upon the Roman band of vagrants and wastrels. (The other surrounding cities, far less successful than the Etruscans, may also have been motivated by envy, denying the newly powerful Rome wives in the hope that the city would soon fail.)

Finding it impossible to secure wives by honorable means, Romulus came up with a more violent and treacherous scheme. Romulus invited neighbors such as the Sabines—a group of powerful ancient tribes—to join the Romans in a huge festival. Yet the invitation was a cruel deception. Once the guests were trapped inside the walls of Rome, the Romans swiftly set upon them, killing or injuring the men and boys and abducting and *raping* the women and girls.

The Sabine men who escaped—maimed fathers, husbands, and brothers—headed to their home in the mountains northeast of Rome to regroup and gather reinforcements. Led by their king, Titus Tatius, the Sabines waged war on Rome. They demanded the return of their daughters, wives, and sisters.

Tatius secretly offered Tarpeia, the daughter of a Roman commander, anything she wanted if she would open the gates of the Roman citadel for the Sabines. Tarpeia named her price for betraying Rome: what each soldier wore on his left arm. By this, Tarpeia meant the gold bracelets worn by all Sabine men—and Tatius agreed to her demand. But after gaining access to the city, Tatius ripped the shield off his left arm and tossed it on top of the girl. The other Sabine men followed suit, crushing Tarpeia under the weight of their shields.

Though the Sabine avengers might have sacked and burned the breached city, Rome escaped destruction only by winning support from an unlikely quarter. The Sabine women themselves defended their new husbands. Persuading their families that they were happy in their new married lives, the Sabine women ended the brief war.

Finally adopting a more diplomatic approach, Romulus proposed to Tatius that the Romans and Sabines combine their populations to form a single tribe. Though power would (of course) remain centralized in Rome, Tatius and Romulus would share the rule equally. Tatius accepted the offer and the two peoples became one. The Sabines—ancestors of later generations of Roman patricians—did indeed have a powerful position in Roman government.

Logos

Our word "**rape**" comes from the Latin "rapere," meaning "to seize or snatch." Wife-stealing was not an uncommon practice in the ancient world—and the ancient "rapist," as this etymology suggests, sometimes sought a much more permanent relationship with his victim than that which we now associate with the term.

What a Life!

Not long after the Sabines joined with the Romans, Tatius was murdered in a quarrel unrelated to any struggle over the throne. Romulus, content to have sole rule over both the Romans and the Sabines, did nothing to avenge the death of his co-ruler.

Imperialist Rome

After uniting with the Sabines, Romulus continued to expand the boundaries of Rome. He conquered several outlying cities, taking advantage of local resistance to Roman rule along the Tiber River as an excuse to crush the opposition and install his own puppet governments. In a short time, Rome had become so powerful that not even the mighty Etruscans along the northwestern coast of Italy would risk war with the city.

An excellent military commander, Romulus assumed full authority over the growing Roman kingdom. Though resented somewhat by the *patricians*, he was very popular with the commoners and ruled Rome for nearly four decades.

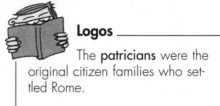

Logos

The **patricians** were the original citizen families who settled Rome.

The death of Romulus was shrouded in mystery. While inspecting troops on the Campus Martius—playing fields dedicated to Mars and devoted to such sports as boxing, wrestling, discus and javelin throwing, horse riding, and chariot races—a storm appeared out of nowhere and Romulus disappeared, engulfed by low-lying clouds. The storm quickly dissipated, but Romulus was nowhere to be found.

The gods must have lifted him up to heaven—or so the senators who had stood near enough to touch him insisted. A rumor quickly spread, however, that the resentful patrician senators, veiled by the clouds, had murdered Romulus, tearing him limb from limb and scattering the pieces in the strong winds.

Nonetheless, the commoners and soldiers who had always revered Romulus readily accepted the notion of his divinity. From that day forward, they worshipped the son of Mars as Quirinus, a minor god of war, and built temples in his honor.

Rome Rules!

Roman mythology holds that Romulus, the founder of Rome, was only the first of seven kings of the ancient city. The mythical age of kings, which lasted about two-and-a-half centuries, would see great expansion of Roman territory and influence. Several of these kings were ruthless and/or brilliant military leaders; others

Read All About It

The legends of the early kings of Rome have come to us almost exclusively through Livy's history of Rome, a monumental work that combined legend and history.

were wise and just legislators. But all—with the exception of the seventh and last king of the city—contributed to the greatness that was Rome.

Long Live the Kings

Romulus was succeeded by Numa Pompilius, the son-in-law of the murdered Titus Tatius. The first Sabine king of Rome, Numa was renowned for his wisdom and piety. In his 43 years on the throne, Numa established legal practices and religious observances that survived for centuries. He established a rule of law and order and kept the peace with his neighbors.

The More Things Change ...
Numa, called "The Lawgiver," resembled two real leaders of Greek cities: Lycurgus of Sparta and Solon of Athens. All three were revered as lawgivers during the early periods of cities that would soon become great. All three also became the subjects of legends. The pattern of a great military leader (Romulus) giving way to a great political and civic theoretician (Numa) was also repeated in the early (real-life) history of the United States, where Thomas Jefferson assumed the presidency shortly after the founding president, George Washington.

Following the death of his wife Tatia, Numa claimed to draw his wisdom from Egeria, a nymph of Diana's grove at Aricia. Numa and Egeria would meet in a secluded woodland hideaway frequented by nymphs. There he received wise counsel and warm kisses. Numa courted and ultimately married the nymph.

As queen, the sage Egeria proposed many new laws and approved all written laws before they were instituted. When Numa died, Egeria, heartbroken, fled back to Aricia and dissolved into tears. Her mistress Diana took pity on her and transformed her into a natural spring.

The militant Tullus Hostilius next assumed the throne. Disdaining Numa's love of law as a weakness, Tullus kept the Roman armies busy. Tullus doubled Rome's population by conquering Alba Longa and forcing its people to migrate to the capital. He also waged war against the few Sabine tribes that had not joined the Romans under Romulus—as well as the Sabine tribes that wanted to withdraw after Tullus took the throne.

Tullus ruled Rome for 32 years. In his final year, Rome suffered a devastating plague and the king began wasting away from illness. When he received word of ominous portents, Tullus—who had given little thought to honoring the gods during better times—attempted to appease Jupiter with hollow religious rites. The god's answer: too little, too late. Tullus was struck by lightning and died.

What a Life!

Beset by a lightning storm the likes of which had never been seen, King Numa sought the help of the nymph Egeria. She told him how he could capture Picus and Faunus, who would be able to teach him a ritual to calm the thunderbolt. She led him to a spring, where he sacrificed a sheep and laid out bowls of wine. When Picus and Faunus arrived to slake their thirst, they helped themselves to the wine and sank into a deep sleep. When they awoke, they found that Numa had shackled them tightly. If Numa would release them, they promised to call down Jupiter.

Though awestruck by Jupiter's appearance, Numa stuck to his purpose, asking how to atone and avert the god's great weapon. The king of the gods ordered him to cut off a head. "Of an onion?" asked Numa. "No, of a man," Jupiter replied. "His hair then," Numa bargained. "No, a life," the god insisted. "Very well, then, a fish's life," Numa replied. Laughing at Numa's quick wit, Jupiter agreed to the bargain—and the next day sent down from heaven a special shield—the *ancile*. Thereafter, the Romans used an onion, human hair, and fish in a ritual to calm a thunderbolt.

The fourth king of Rome was Ancus Marcius, a grandson of Numa Pompilius. Ancus expanded the Roman kingdom farther south and west—into Latium and all the way to the edge of the sea. He founded Ostia, establishing it as Rome's port at the mouth of the Tiber.

I Just Can't Wait to Be King

The fifth king of Rome was an outsider, the first of three generations of Etruscan rulers: Lucius Tarquinius Priscus. His Greek father, Demaratus, had been exiled from Corinth and had taken up residence and married in Tarquinia, an Etruscan city. Tanaquil, the wife of Tarquinius, persuaded her husband to emigrate from Tarquinia to Rome. An ambitious woman, Tanaquil knew that despite their great wealth, they would never elevate their status among the Etruscans.

Once in Rome, Tarquinius insinuated himself into the good graces of the king, Ancus Marcius. When Ancus died, Tarquinius won a popular election to succeed him as king. No sooner had he risen to the throne than Tarquinius—a shrewd politician—elevated 100 of his friends and followers to the rank of senator, thereby solidifying his power.

During his 38 years in power, Tarquinius expanded the Roman dominion even farther. He conquered the Sabines yet again and also secured Roman rule over all the ancient Latin cities and towns.

Near the middle of his reign, Tarquinius, at the urging of his wife Tanaquil, began taking a special interest in a small boy named Servius Tullius. Tanaquil knew that Servius—the son of one of her servants, a captive Latin woman—was destined for greatness. One night, she had seen the boy sleeping unharmed and tranquil as flames danced around his head. With this omen in mind, Tanaquil and Tarquinius reared Servius as if he were their own. When Servius reached adulthood, they gave him the hand of their daughter in marriage.

The sons of Ancus rightly feared that Tarquinius was grooming his son-in-law as his successor—a position they coveted for themselves. So they hired assassins to kill the king.

When she heard of her husband's death, Tanaquil quickly put on a brave face and announced falsely that her husband had merely been injured in the attack. Until he recovered, Tanaquil claimed, he had installed Servius Tullius as the acting regent. Through this stratagem, Tanaquil gave Servius the time he needed to apprehend the murderers. When the hit men confessed, Servius forced into exile those who had hired them: the sons of Ancus. In this way, Tanaquil ensured that her husband's chosen successor did indeed gain the throne of Rome.

What a Life!

In a vain attempt to win over the two sons of Tarquinius, Servius had arranged for each to marry one of his daughters. Unfortunately, the pairs were poorly matched. Tullia, the vicious and ruthless daughter of Servius, was paired with the gentle son of Tarquinius, while the sweet daughter was wedded to the cruelly ambitious son, Lucius. Tullia recognized in her brother-in-law a kindred spirit and convinced Lucius to murder his wife. After she murdered her husband, Tullia and Lucius married each other.

The sixth king of Rome, Servius was beloved and admired by his people due to his excellence as both a legislator and a warrior. In his 44 years on the throne, Servius introduced significant changes in the Roman constitution, many of them favoring the common people (the plebeians). He thus earned the resentment of the city's patricians despite his well-deserved reputation for fairness.

The noble and popular Servius—like his foster father, Tarquinius—died at the hands of assassins. His own daughter Tullia, moved to violence by her ambition, prodded her husband, Lucius Tarquinius *Superbus* (a son of Tarquinius Priscus), to kill her father.

One day, Lucius brazenly seated himself on the throne. The aged Servius protested this insolence, but Lucius threw the old man down the steps of the senate house. As Servius wandered the streets of Rome in a daze, Lucius's cronies caught up to him and finished the job. Finally Tullia, riding home in her chariot, wantonly drove the horses directly over her father's corpse.

Logos

Superbus, Latin for "arrogant," was not a term that Lucius Tarquinius would have applied to himself. Later Roman historians labeled him Superbus to highlight the sin of Rome's last king. When Octavian became the sole ruler of Rome in the first century B.C.E., he considered many titles (for example, Father of the Fatherland or High Priest) before settling on "Augustus Caesar." One title he never considered, however, was "Rex" ("King"), for the arrogance of Lucius Tarquinius Superbus had soured Romans on "kings" forever.

Et Tu, Junius Brutus?

Treacherous and tyrannical, Lucius Tarquinius Superbus ruled with an iron fist for 25 years. Never seeking the consent of the senate or the people, Lucius held the throne by force alone. But he was ultimately undone by the sins of his son, Sextus.

Sextus Tarquinius and his friends got drunk one night and started bragging about their wives. They decided to see whose wife was most virtuous. Visiting each of their homes in turn, the men found all of their wives feasting or wasting time. Only Lucretia, the wife of Lucius Tarquinius Collatinus, was found dutifully weaving at her loom, spinning cloth in the company of her servants.

What a Life!

The Cumaean Sibyl (see Chapter 22), a great prophetess, had written down the oracles of her thousand-year life in the Sibylline Books. Tarquinius Superbus wanted to buy these nine books and keep them for Rome to consult in national emergencies (plagues, droughts, etc.). But when the Sibyl named her price—an exorbitant amount—Tarquinius refused. The Sibyl promptly burned three of the books and offered him six for the same price. Still unsatisfied, she burned three more. At last, Tarquinius relented. He paid the full price she had originally asked, but received only three books. These books were preserved in the Roman temple of Capitoline Jupiter until a fire destroyed them early in the first century B.C.E.

The virtue of Lucretia fired the lust of Sextus, who longed to corrupt it. Several nights later he returned to Lucretia's home alone. Lucretia politely received her husband's friend, served him dinner, and offered him a room for the night. Later in the evening, he entered her bedchamber and asked her for sexual favors. When she refused him, Sextus threatened to tell Collatinus that he had found Lucretia in bed with one of her slaves and had killed them both. Fearing the dishonor that this would bring on her family, Lucretia reluctantly consented to Sextus's sexual demands.

After Sextus had satisfied his lust, he left. When Collatinus came home, Lucretia related this horrifying tale to both her husband and her father. Despite his outrage, Collatinus assured Lucretia that she was not to blame. Yet after securing their oaths—and that of her husband's friend, Lucius Junius Brutus—to avenge her honor and her life, Lucretia plunged a dagger into her heart. With her dying words, she explained that she never wanted any other woman to be able to excuse her own lack of chastity by pointing to Lucretia's example.

Lucius Junius Brutus used this cruel crime as an excuse to lead a successful revolt against the second Tarquinius. Junius and the rebels killed Sextus, then overthrew his father, the tyrant Lucius, and drove him from the city. The expulsion of Tarquinius (the younger) brought an end to the reign of kings in Rome.

Junius abolished the monarchy and installed a republican government, with himself and Collatinus as the first two consuls (leaders). But the people no longer trusted any Tarquins, even one who had led them in their rebellion against the monarchy. The Romans banished all members of the Tarquin family, including Lucius Tarquinius Collatinus, who resigned his authority and went into exile in Lavinium.

Though the Etruscans periodically attempted to conquer the city and reestablish a throne for themselves for several more generations, each attack was successfully repelled by the Romans. Rome continued to renounce monarchy and embrace republicanism. Governmental power would rest in the hands of senators and other elected officials until the days of Augustus Caesar.

The Least You Need to Know

- When their grand-uncle tried to kill Romulus and Remus by throwing them in the Tiber River, the god Mars saved his sons by sending a she-wolf and a woodpecker to care for them.

- Romulus and Remus fought over who would have more authority in the founding of Rome. Remus was killed in this struggle for power.

- Unable to attract women to Rome, the Romans under Romulus abducted and raped women from the Sabine tribes.

- Under Romulus and six successive kings, Rome became a great power by annexing neighboring towns and conquering adjacent territories.

- The rape of Lucretia by the king's son led to the overthrow of the monarchy and the creation of the Roman Republic.

Glossary of Terms

aegis   1. A protective garment either carried on the arm or worn over the shoulder. 2. The shield of a warrior.

aetiology   The study of "first causes," a frequent subject of myths.

ambrosia   The food of the gods.

Argo   The ship manned by Jason and the Argonauts on their quest for the Golden Fleece.

autochthony   The spontaneous creation of an individual or tribe from soil; birth from the earth.

bas relief   A sculpted panel in which the design is raised very slightly from the background panel.

buskins   Protective footwear.

chorus   In Greek dramas, the group of dancers set in front of the proscenium who commented on the play's events through song and dance.

cithara   A musical instrument resembling a large lute.

daemons   Ancient Roman spirits who presided over persons, places, private counsels, and society.

demes   Townships, districts, or villages in ancient Greece.

Eleusinian Mysteries   The most widespread of the mystery religions, with practices including fasting, purification, and other rites, and a dramatization of the tale of Demeter and Persephone.

evoe!   An exclamation of joy cried out by Dionysian worshippers.

genius   A Roman guardian spirit, inherent within every person, creature, or thing; the divine counterpart of any individual (human or animal) or thing.

girdle   A belt used to carry the sword of a warrior.

Golden Apples   The fruit of the legendary tree that Rhea gave her daughter Hera on the day of her wedding to Zeus. The tree was planted in the Garden of the Hesperides.

Golden Bough   A branch from a magical tree that grew near Cumae, which Aeneas offered Proserpine in order to gain access to the Underworld.

Golden Fleece   The sheepskin from the legendary ram that saved Phrixus from sacrifice at the hands of his father Athamas. The fleece was later sought after by Jason and the Argonauts.

Great Dionysia   A celebration that became the setting for an annual playwriting contest during the fifth century B.C.E.

hubris   The sin of arrogance or excessive pride, which caused many tragic downfalls since the gods almost always punished it.

Labyrinth   The impossible-to-navigate maze that served as the home of the monstrous Minotaur in Crete.

lares   Minor Roman household gods, often considered ancestral spirits or spirits of fertility.

lustratio   A Roman ritual, often consisting of parading on the perimeter of a space and then sacrificing one or more animals, intended to create a sacred space that protects everyone and everything inside it.

maenads   Female followers and attendants of Dionysus.

manes   Roman spirits of the dead, who usually inhabit the Underworld, but occasionally come to the surface world.

me   The set of preordained decrees that determined the development of Sumerian political, cultural, and religious institutions.

moly   A magical flower used by Odysseus to ward off the magic spells of Circe the sorceress.

mystery religions   Cults devoted to Demeter, Dionysus, or Orpheus that used rituals, feasts, and dances to achieve spiritual fulfillment.

nectar   The drink of the gods.

nymph   Semi-divine female spirits of nature who typically inhabit a body of water, a tree, or a mountain.

obol   An ancient Greek coin placed in the mouths of corpses to pay the fare of Charon, ferryman of the dead.

oracle   1. A priest or priestess who received divine knowledge, often regarding future events. 2. The often cryptic or ambiguous prophecy or hidden knowledge received by such a medium.

parentes   Roman ancestral ghosts; the spirits of a family's deceased relatives.

parthenogenesis   Creation of new life that does not depend upon the coupling of both genders, but comes from one gender alone.

patricians   The original citizen families who settled Rome; aristocratic descendants of the Sabine tribe.

pax deorum   Literally "the peace of the gods," a peaceful relationship with the gods that insured that the life of an individual, a family, a group, or a state would remain in balance.

penates   Roman household gods of the pantry or storeroom, protectors of a home's inhabitants.

pietas   The proper behavior of Romans, both individually and collectively, toward gods, family, district, and country.

plebeians   The common people of ancient Rome.

rhapsode   A traveling poet of ancient Greece who went from town to town entertaining the local people with his tales.

sacrifice   A sacred ritual intended to make a place, time, or thing holy through the observation of certain religious rites and customs; in ancient practice, often a communal barbecue.

sparagmos   The ritualized dismemberment of a live animal, one of the rites of Dionysus.

spartoi   Men sown from the earth by scattering the teeth of a dragon.

syrinx   The pipes of Pan, a flute made of reeds tied together in a row, named after the nymph who was transformed into reeds to escape Pan's pursuits.

Tartarus   Lowest region of the Underworld.

thyrsus   A ceremonial pole, wrapped in live ivy and grapevines and topped with a pine cone, carried by Dionysian worshippers.

tripod   A three-legged container used to burn coals for a sacrifice—in essence, an ancient barbecue grill.

Trojan War   The 10-year war between the walled city of Troy and a united force drawn from all the kingdoms of Greece. Begun when the Trojan prince Paris abducted the Spartan queen Helen, the war ended with the complete destruction of Troy.

Underworld   Land of the dead souls, ruled by Hades.

Vestal Virgins   Priestesses of ancient Rome who dedicated at least 30 years to serving Vesta, the goddess of hearth and home; like the goddess herself, they were expected to remain virgins while serving her.

Wandering Rocks   Moving rocks in the sea around Sicily that destroyed countless ships before the *Argo*, borne by the Nereids, passed through safely, thereby arresting their movement.

Who's Who in Classical Mythology

Acamas (ACK a mahs): Son of Theseus and Phaedra.

Acastus (uh KASS tuss): King of Iolcus; son of Pelias who joined his cousin Jason on the *Argo*; banished Jason and Medea from Iolcus after they murdered his father; husband of Astydameia; father of Sterope.

Acca Larentia (ACK uh luh REN shi uh): Wife of Faustulus; concealed Romulus and Remus, raising the twins as if they were her own children; may also have been the she-wolf who suckled the young twins.

Acestes (a SESS teez): King of Eryx on Sicily when visited by Aeneas; held funeral games for Aeneas's father Anchises.

Achelous (ack uh LO us): River god who fought Heracles for the hand of Deianira.

Achilles (a KILL eez): Greatest Greek hero of the Trojan War; son of Peleus and Thetis.

Acis (AY sis): Human beloved by Galatea, crushed under a rock by his rival, the Cyclops Polyphemus.

Acoetes (uh SEE teez): Helmsman of a Tyrrhenian pirate ship that kidnapped Dionysus; only crew member to recognize Dionysus as a god and urge kindness; only crew member spared Dionysus's wrath.

Acrisius (a KRISS i us): King of Argos; brother of hated Proetus; husband of Aganippe; father of Danaë; accidentally killed by his grandson, Perseus.

Actaeon (ack TEE on): Hunter turned into a stag and killed by his own hounds after seeing Artemis bathing; son of Aristaeus and Autonoe; brother of Macris; grandson of Cadmus.

Adad (uh DAD): Sumerian storm god who gave Gilgamesh courage.

Admete (ad MEE tuh; ad MEE tee): Daughter of Euystheus; recipient of Hippolyta's girdle, the ninth labor of Heracles.

Admetus (ad MEE tuss): Husband of Alcestis, who volunteered to die in his place.

Adonis (uh DON iss): Beautiful son of Cinyras and his daughter Smyrna; loved by both Aphrodite and Persephone; killed by Ares in the form of a wild boar.

Adrasteia (ad rass TEE a; ad rass TY a): Cretan nymph who cared for Zeus in his infancy.

Adrastus (uh DRASS tuss): King of Argos whose daughter married Polyneices, son of Oedipus.

Aeacus (EE a kuss): First king of Aegina; son of Zeus and Aegina; his father relieved his loneliness by transforming the island's ants into people (the Myrmidons); father of Peleus, Telamon, and Phocus.

Aeëtes (ee EE teez): King of Colchis; son of Helius and Perse; brother of Circe and Pasiphaë; holder of the Golden Fleece until his daughter Medea helped Jason steal it.

Aegeus (EE jyoos; EE jee us): King of Athens; brother of Pallas; foster father (or father) of Theseus; father (by Medea) of Medus; exiled Medea and Medus when he discovered their plot to kill Theseus; killed himself grieving over mistaken belief that Theseus had died.

Aegina (ee JIE nuh): Daughter of river god Asopus abducted by Zeus; mother of Aeacus.

Aegipan (EE jee pan): A god of shepherds, forests, wildlife, and fertility; perhaps one and the same as Pan.

Aegisthus (ee JISS thuss): Son of Thyestes; lover of Clytemnestra, with whom he conspired to murder her husband, Agamemnon, upon his return from the Trojan War.

Aeneas (ee NEE us): Trojan prince who traveled to Italy and founded the Roman race; son of Aphrodite and Anchises; in Troy, husband of Creusa; in Italy, husband of Lavinia; in Carthage, lover of Dido; father (by Creusa) of Ascanius (called Iulus in

Italy) and (by Lavinia) of Silvius; when King Latinus abdicated the throne of Latium, he battled with Turnus and his allies, who challenged his right to the throne; after his victory, he founded the city of Lavinium.

Aeolus (EE oh luss): 1. Keeper of the winds. 2. King of Thessaly; father of Sisyphus, Salmoneus, Cretheus, and Athamas.

Aerope (ay ER oh pee): Wife of Atreus who committed adultery with her husband's brother Thyestes; mother of Agamemnon and Menelaus.

Aeschylus (ESS kuh luss): Greek tragedian of the fifth century B.C.E.

Aesculapius (ess kyoo LAY pi us): Minor god of healing and medicine; son of Apollo (in Greek, Asclepius); father of Machaon and Podaleirius; killed by Zeus, brought back to life, and deified in Rome.

Aeson (EE son): Son of Cretheus and Tyro; half-brother of Pelias, who usurped the throne of Iolcus from him; husband of Alcimede (or Polymede); father of Jason and Promachus.

Aether (EE ther): Personification of the upper air or sky; son of Nyx and Erebus.

Aethra (EE thra): Daughter of Pittheus; mother of Theseus (by Aegeus or Poseidon); abducted and enslaved by Castor and Polydeuces when they rescued Helen, whom Theseus had abducted.

Agamemnon (ag uh MEM non): King of Mycenae and Argos; Greek commander in chief during the Trojan War; son of Atreus and Aerope; brother of Menelaus; father of Iphigenia, Orestes, and Electra; sacrificed Iphigenia to get the Greek fleet moving; murdered after the war by his wife Clytemnestra.

Aganippe (ag uh NIP ee): Wife of Acrisius; mother of Danaë.

Agave (uh GAY vee): Daughter of Cadmus and Harmonia; sister of Semele, Autonoe, Ion, and Polydorus; wife of Echion; mother of Pentheus; driven mad by Dionysus, she tore her son into pieces.

Agenor (uh JEE nor): Fiancé of Andromeda killed by Perseus; more commonly called Phineus.

Aglaia (uh GLEE a): One of the three Graces; personification of beauty; daughter of Zeus and Eurynome; sister of Euphrosyne and Thalia.

Agrius (AG ri us): A Giant, brother of Thoas, beaten to death by the Fates in the war between the Giants and the Olympians.

Ahareus (uh HAR ee us): King of Messenia; father of Lynceus, an Argonaut.

Aias (AY us): Greek name for Ajax.

Ajax of Locris (AY jacks): Greek warrior during Trojan War; brought ruin upon victorious Greeks by offending Athena when he tore Cassandra away from the shrine of the goddess and raped her.

Ajax of Salamis (AY jacks): Greek warrior during Trojan War; son of Telamon and Periboea; the "Greater Ajax"; half-brother of Teucer; went mad and killed himself after losing contest with Odysseus for the armor of fallen Achilles.

Alcaeus (al SEE us): Son of Perseus and Andromeda; brother of Electryon and Sthenelus; father of Amphitryon; grandfather of Heracles.

Alcathous (al KATH oh us): King of Megara; son of Pelops; father of Theseus's cousin Periboea.

Alcestis (al SESS tiss): Wife of Admetus who offered to die in her husband's place; only daughter of Pelias who did not take part when Medea tricked her sisters into killing their father.

Alcimede (al SIM uh dee): Daughter of Phylacus and Clymene; according to some accounts, wife of Aeson and mother of Jason and Promachus; killed herself after Pelias killed Promachus.

Alcinous (al SIN oh us): King of Phaeacians on island of Scheria (Drepane) famed as a savior of shipwrecked sailors; husband of Arete; father of Nausicaa.

Alcippe (al SIP pee): Daughter of Ares whom Halirrhothius raped or attempted to rape.

Alcmene (alk MEE nee): Daughter of Electryon and Anaxo; mother of Heracles (by Zeus) and Iphicles (by her husband Amphitryon).

Alcyoneus (al SY oh nyoos): One of the Giants killed by Heracles in the war between the Giants and the Olympians.

Alecto (uh LECK toe): One of the three Erinyes (Furies).

Alope (al OH pee): Daughter of Cercyon; mother (by Poseidon) of Hippothoon.

Althaea (al THEE uh): Wife of Oeneus, king of Calydon; mother (by Dionysus) of Deianira and (by Oeneus) of Meleager.

Amaltheia (am al THEE uh): Goat nymph who nursed the infant Zeus with her own milk.

Amata (uh MAY tuh): Mother of Lavinia; wife of Latinus; ally of her nephew Turnus in battle against Aeneas; killed herself upon hearing a false rumor of Turnus's death.

Amazons (AM uh zonz): A tribe of women warriors.

Amor (AY mor): Roman personification of love (in Greek, Eros).

Amphinomus (am FIN uh muss): One of Penelope's suitors; killed by Telemachus.

Amphion (am FIE on): King of Thebes; husband of Niobe.

Amphitrite (am fi TRY tee): Sea goddess; a Nereid, wife of Poseidon; mother (by Poseidon) of Triton, Rhode, and Benthesicyme.

Amphitryon (am FIT ri on): Son of Alcaeus; husband of Alcmene; forced into exile from Argos after accidentally killing his father-in-law, Electryon; foster father of Heracles; father of Iphicles.

Amulius (a MYOO li us): King of Alba Longa who usurped the throne of his brother Numitor, killed his nephews, and made his niece, Rhea Silvia, a Vestal Virgin; when she managed to get pregnant anyway (by Mars), he imprisoned her and tossed her twin sons in the Tiber River; these twins, Romulus and Remus, later killed him.

Amycus (AM i kuss): King of the Bebryces, a warlike Mysian tribe; vicious boxer who challenged and killed all wayfarers; killed by the Argonaut Polydeuces.

An (AHN): Sumerian sky god; son of Nammu; mated with his sister Ki to create the great gods of Sumer.

Anchises (an KIE seez): Father of Aeneas (by Aphrodite); crippled by Zeus for revealing the identity of his son's mother; when Troy fell, Aeneas carried him away on his back; died before they could reach Italy; his ghost appeared to Aeneas, foreseeing that his son's descendants would found Rome and serve as kings of the Roman empire.

Ancus Marcius (ANG kuss MAR shuss): Fourth king of Rome; grandson of Numa Pompilius; founded port city of Ostia.

Androgeus (an DRO ji us): Son of Minos and Pasiphaë; brother of Ariadne, Deucalion, and Phaedra; killed while trying to capture or kill the Marathonian bull.

Andromache (an DROM uh kee): Wife of Hector; daughter of Eetion; mother of Astyanax; enslaved by Neoptolemus after the Trojan War.

Andromeda (an DROM uh duh): Wife of Perseus, who saved her from a sea monster; daughter of Cassiopeia and Cepheus, king of Ethiopia; mother of Perses, Electryon, Alcaeus, Sthenelus, and three other children.

Anius (AY nih uss): King of Delos; prophet and priest of Apollo; father of three magical daughters, Elais, Spermo, and Oino, who could turn anything they touched to oil, corn, or wine.

Anna Perenna (AN uh Per EN uh): Roman personification of both the year and the endless procession of years.

Anshar (AN shar): Father (by Kishar) of Babylonian sky god Anu; son of Apsu and Tiamat.

Antaeus (an TEE us): Giant son of Gaia and Poseidon; crushed to death by Heracles in a wrestling match.

Antenor (an TEE nor): Wisest of counselors to King Priam of Troy.

Anticleia (an ti KLEE uh): Mother (by Sisyphus or Laertes) of Odysseus; daughter of Autolycus, seduced by Sisyphus to avenge her father's theft of Sisyphus's cattle; killed herself when wrongly convinced her son would never return from the Trojan War.

Antigone (an TIG uh nee): 1. Daughter (by Jocasta) and sister of King Oedipus of Thebes; accompanied her father into exile, wandering with him until his death; buried alive by her uncle Creon after performing funeral rites for her brother Polyneices (or married Creon's son Haemon, but later committed suicide when her son was sentenced to death by Creon). 2. First wife of Peleus; daughter of King Eurytion of Phthia; committed suicide when tricked into doubting her husband's love.

Antilochus (an TILL uh kuss): Greek warrior in the Trojan War; son of Nestor; slain by Memnon.

Antinous (an TIN oh us): One of Penelope's suitors; son of Eupeithes; killed by Odysseus.

Antiope (an TIE uh pee): Amazon queen carried away by Theseus; sister of Hippolyta; mother (by Theseus) of Hippolytus; killed in battle with other Amazons, accidentally by Penthesileia, or by Theseus himself.

Antiphates (an TIFF uh teez): King of the Laestrygonians, a tribe of giant cannibals who destroyed all but one of Odysseus's ships.

Antiphus (AN ti fuss): A son of Priam and Hecuba; captured by Achilles during Trojan War; regained freedom when Priam paid a large ransom; later killed by Agamemnon.

Anu (A noo): Babylonian sky god; father of Ea and Ishtar; son of Anshar and Kishar.

Aphrodite (af roe DIE tee): Goddess of love; born of the sea foam that carried Uranus's severed genitals; unhappily wed to Hephaestus; mother (by Anchises) of Aeneas, (by Dionysus) of Priapus, (by Hermes) of Hermaphroditus, and (by Ares) of Phobus, Deimus, and Harmonia.

Apollo (uh POL oh): God of fine arts, medicine, music, poetry, and eloquence; son of Zeus and Leto; brother of Artemis; sometimes called Phoebus Apollo, just Phoebus (usually when linking him to the sun), or (by the Romans) Sol.

Apollodorus (uh pol uh DOE russ): Greek mythographer, probably of the first or second century C.E.

Apollonius Rhodius (ap uh LOE ni us ROE di us): A Greek poet of the second century B.C.E.

Apsu (AP soo): Babylonian father of all things, the primeval sweetwater ocean; husband of Tiamat; while attempting to destroy his progeny, killed by his great-grandson Ea.

Apsyrtus (ap SER tuss): Son of Aeëtes, king of Colchis; killed by his sister Medea, who was escaping with Jason and the Golden Fleece.

Ares (AY reez; AIR eez): God of war; son of Zeus and Hera; brother of Hebe and Eileithyia; lover of Aphrodite; father (by Aphrodite) of Phobus (Panic), Deimus (Fear), and Harmonia.

Arete (uh REE tee): Wife of Alcinous, king of the Phaeacians on the island of Scheria (Drepane); mother of Nausicaa.

Arges (AR jeez): One of the Cyclopes; son of Gaia and Uranus; brother of Brontes and Steropes; forgers of thunder and lightning for Zeus.

Argonauts (AR guh nawts): The crew of the *Argo*, led by Jason.

Ariadne (ar i AD nee): Daughter of Pasiphaë and King Minos of Crete; sister of Androgeus, Deucalion, and Phaedra; helped Theseus escape the Labyrinth; deserted on island of Naxos (Dia), where she married Dionysus; mother (by Dionysus) of Thoas, Staphylus, Phanus, and Oenopion.

Arion (uh RYE un): Remarkably swift horse; offspring of Demeter and Poseidon, who mated as horses.

Aristaeus (a riss TEE us): Beekeeper who chased Eurydice, who stepped on a poisonous snake and died; son of Apollo; husband of Autonoe; father of Actaeon and Macris.

Aristogeiton (a riss tuh GYE tun): Lover of Harmodius; the two killed Hipparchus, brother of King Hippias of Athens, and were in turn killed by Hippias.

Aristophanes (a riss TOFF uh neez): Greek writer of comedies during the late fifth century B.C.E.

Artemis (AR tuh miss): Virgin goddess of hunting and the moon; daughter of Zeus and Leto; sister of Apollo.

Ascalaphus (ass KAL uh fuss): Gardener for Hades who saw Persephone eating pomegranate seeds; transformed into an owl or buried under a rock by Demeter for telling; freed by Heracles.

Ascanius (ass KAY ni us): Original (Trojan) name of Iulus.

Asclepius (ass KLEE pi us): *See* Aesculapius.

Ashur (ASH er): Highest god of the Assyrians.

Astarte (ass TAR tee): Great goddess of the Egyptians, Ugarits, and Hittites; the supreme goddess of sexual love, fertility, and war.

Asteria (ass TEE ri a): Daughter of Titans Coeus and Phoebe; sister of Leto; mother (by Perses) of Hecate.

Astraeus (ass TREE us): Father (by Eos) of the winds, Zephyrus, Boreas, and Notus; son of the Titan Crius and Eurybia; brother of Perses and Pallas.

Astyanax (ass TIE uh naks): Infant son of Hector and Andromache killed at end of Trojan War by Odysseus or Neoptolemus.

Astydameia (ass ti duh MEE uh): Wife of Acastus who falsely claimed that Peleus had violated her; her lies caused Antigone, Peleus's wife, to kill herself; mother (by Acastus) of Sterope; later killed by Peleus.

Astyoche (ass tie OH kee): Wife of Telephus; daughter of Priam and Hecuba.

Atalanta (at uh LAN tuh): Huntress who became a heroine of the Calydonian boar hunt; turned down when she offered to join the crew of the *Argo*.

Athamas (ATH uh muss): King of Thebes; son of Aeolus; husband of Nephele and later Ino; father (by Nephele) of Phrixus and Helle and (by Ino) of Learchus and Melicertes.

Athena (uh THEE nuh): Virgin goddess of wisdom, practical arts, and war; daughter of Zeus and Metis, born fully grown out of her father's head.

Atlas (AT luss): A Titan; son of Iapetus and Clymene; brother of Prometheus; after commanding the Titans in their war against the Olympians, forced to hold up the heavens on his shoulders.

Atreus (AY tree us): Father (by Aerope) of Agamemnon and Menelaus; son of Pelops and Hippodameia; brother of Thyestes; he killed, cooked, and served his brother's children to avenge Thyestes' adultery with Aerope.

Atropos (AT roe poss): One of the three Moirai (Fates); sister of Clotho and Lachesis; holder of the shears that cut the thread of life.

Auge (AW jee): Mother (by Heracles) of Telephus.

Augeas (aw JEE us): King of Elis; crew member on the *Argo*; owner of Augean stables cleaned by Heracles as his sixth labor; later killed by Heracles for refusing to pay for the job.

Aurora (uh ROE ra): Roman goddess of dawn (in Greek, Eos).

Autolycus (aw TOL i kuss): Famous thief; son of Hermes (by Chione); caught stealing cattle by Sisyphus; father of Anticleia; taught Heracles how to wrestle.

Autonoe (aw TON oh ee): Daughter of Cadmus and Harmonia; sister of Agave, Ion, Semele, and Polydorus; mother (by Aristaeus) of Actaeon and Macris.

Aventinus (av en TIE nuss): Latin ally of Turnus in war against Aeneas and the Trojans; son of Heracles.

Bacchants (BACK ents): Worshippers of Dionysus whose wild, ecstatic rites shocked more traditional Greeks.

Bacchus (BACK us): *See* Dionysus.

Balius (BAY li us): One of two immortal horses that the gods gave Peleus when he married Thetis; they wept at the death of Patroclus and warned Achilles of impending death.

Bateia (buh TIE uh): Daughter of Teucer; wife of Dardanus; called the "Mother of the Trojan Race."

Battus (BAT us): Old man turned to stone by Hermes for revealing the secret (though only to Hermes himself in disguise) that Hermes had stolen Apollo's cows.

Bellona (beh LOE nuh): Roman goddess of war.

Beroe (beh ROE ee): Nurse to Semele; Hera may have assumed this disguise in order to talk Semele into demanding to see Zeus in his full glory, a demand that would kill Semele.

Bia (BYE uh): Personification of force; son of Styx and Pallas; brother of Zelus, Nike, and Cratus; he and his brothers became constant companions of Zeus.

Bias (BYE us): Brother of the seer Melampus who gained one third of the kingdom of Argos when his brother cured Argive women of madness.

Boreas (BOE ree us): The North Wind; offspring of Eos and Astraeus; father of winged sons Zetes and Calais.

Briareus (bry ER i us): One of three Hundred-Handed Giants, the first beings born through procreation; son of Gaia and Uranus; brother of Cottus and Gyges; helped Cronus defeat Uranus and later helped Zeus defeat Cronus.

Briseis (brih SEE iss): Young beauty abducted by Achilles to serve as his concubine after he killed her husband, brothers, and parents; stolen away by Agamemnon, who had been forced to give up his own concubine; this insult caused Achilles to quit the war for a time.

Brontes (BRON teez): One of the Cyclopes; son of Gaia and Uranus; brother of Steropes and Arges; forgers of thunder and lightning for Zeus.

Broteas (BROE ti us): Son of Tantalus and Dione; brother of Niobe and Pelops; driven mad by Artemis for refusing to honor her, he fatally threw himself into a fire.

Buphagus (byoo FAY gus): Son of Iapetus shot by Artemis when he tried to rape her.

Busiris (byoo SIE riss): King of Egypt; a son of Poseidon; annually sacrificed strangers to Zeus; killed by Heracles, who ended the practice.

Cacus (KAY kuss): Three-headed, flame-spitting giant; son of Hephaestus and Medusa; beaten to death by Heracles after trying to steal some of Geryon's cattle.

Cadmus (KAD muss): Founder and king of Thebes; brother of Europa; served Ares to atone for killing the god's favorite dragon; father (by Ares' daughter Harmonia) of Ino, Semele, Agave, Autonoe, and Polydorus; one of the few Theban men to accept his grandson Dionysus as a god.

Calais (KAL ay iss): A crew member on the *Argo*; winged son of Boreas; twin brother of Zetes; convinced crew not to turn back to retrieve Heracles, who had been left behind; chased Harpies away from brother-in-law Phineus; killed by Heracles after returning to Iolcus.

Calchas (KAL kuss): Soothsayer who told Agamemnon he would have to sacrifice his daughter Iphigenia in order to appease Artemis and allow the Greek ships to set sail at the beginning of the Trojan War.

Calliope (kuh LIE uh pee): One of the nine Muses; generally considered the Muse of epic or heroic poetry; daughter of Zeus and Mnemosyne.

Callisto (kuh LISS toe): An attendant to Artemis; ravished by Zeus, who disguised himself as Artemis to get close to her; transformed into a bear by Zeus to hide her from Hera, but shot and killed by Artemis.

Calypso (kuh LIP so): Daughter of Atlas who offered Odysseus immortality and eternal youth if he would remain with her on the island of Ogygia; after seven years, Hermes brought word from Zeus that she would have to let him go.

Camenae (kuh MEE nee): Roman goddesses of prophecy and healing or fountain nymphs, later identified with the Greek Muses, and hence with the arts.

Camilla (kuh MILL uh): Amazon leader of the Volscian tribe; ally of Turnus in his war against Aeneas; ambushed and killed in combat.

Campe (KAM pee): Jailer of Tartarus; killed by Zeus when he freed the Hundred-Handed Giants and the Cyclopes.

Canens (KAN enz): Nymph with a beautiful singing voice engaged to Picus before jealous Circe turned him into a woodpecker and she wasted away from grief.

Canthus (KAN thuss): A crew member on the *Argo*; killed by a shepherd near Lake Tritonis after he tried to steal some sheep.

Cardea (kar DEE uh): A minor Roman goddess of hinges (according to Ovid).

Carmenta (kar MEN tuh): 1. A Roman goddess of healing and the future or of childbirth. 2. A nymph; mother (by Hermes) of Evander.

Cassandra (kuh SAN druh): Famed seer who warned the Trojans not to bring the Wooden Horse within the walls of Troy; Apollo punished her for rejecting his advances by giving her the gift of prophecy coupled with the curse that no one would ever believe her; daughter of Priam and Hecuba; sister of Helenus, Paris, and many others; at the war's end, raped by Ajax of Locris at the site of Athena's shrine; enslaved by Agamemnon and then murdered by his wife, Clytemnestra.

Cassiopeia (kass i oh PEE uh): Wife of Cepheus; mother of Andromeda; offended Poseidon by favorably comparing her own beauty to that of the Nereids, the god's attendants; Poseidon sent a sea monster that Perseus later killed.

Castor (KAS ter): Crew member on the *Argo*; an expert rider; son of Leda and Tyndareus; brother of Polydeuces, Helen, and Clytemnestra; taught Heracles fencing and military strategy and tactics; helped rescue Helen after Theseus had carried her away.

Cecrops (SEE krops): King of Athens whose daughters Athena entrusted with the care of the infant Erichthonius.

Celeus (SEE li us): King of Eleusis; father (by Meteneira) of Demophon; to reward his kindness, Demeter taught him her secret rites, which became known as the Eleusinian Mysteries.

Centaurs (SEN torz): Race of creatures, half men and half horses; offspring of Ixion and a cloud in the shape of Hera; driven by Theseus and Peirithous out of their original homeland of Thessaly; later forced to Mount Melea by Heracles.

Cephalus (SEF uh luss): Prince of Phocis; a hunter; abducted and kept by Eos; father (by Eos) of Phaëthon; after Eos released him, he unwisely tested the depth of his wife's fidelity, driving her away from him, though they later reconciled; while hunting, he heard a rustling and threw his unerring spear, which pierced the heart of his wife, who had been jealously spying on him.

Cepheus (SEE fee us): King of Ethiopia; husband of Cassiopeia; father of Andromeda; brother of Phineus or Agenor.

Cephissus (suh FISS us): A river god; father (by Liriope) of Narcissus.

Cerberus (SER buh rus): Three-headed watchdog who stood guard at the gate of the Underworld; offspring of Echidna and Typhon.

Cercyon (SER si on): Inhospitable host who wrestled his guests to death or killed them after the match had exhausted them; killed when Theseus smashed him to the ground during a match; father of Alope.

Ceres (SEE reez): Roman agricultural goddess of the harvest and fertility, especially growth processes and grain (in Greek, Demeter).

Ceryneian hind (ser i NEE an HIND): Magnificent deer with golden antlers and brass hoofs; captured alive by Heracles as his fourth labor.

Ceto (SEE toe): A sea monster; daughter of Gaia and Pontus; sister of Nereus, Phorcys, Thaumas, and Eurybia; mother (by Phorcys) of the Graeae and the Gorgons; also mother of Echidna.

Chalciope (kal SIE oh pee): Daughter of King Aeëtes of Colchis; wife of Phrixus; mother of four sons rescued by Jason after a shipwreck; her sons joined with Jason and returned to Colchis.

Chaos (KAY oss): A personification of what existed before the Creation of the Universe; to Hesiod, an enormous chasm; to Ovid, shapeless, ever-changing matter.

Charon (KAR un; KAY run): Ferryman of the Underworld; carried the dead across the river Styx.

Charybdis (kuh RIB diss): Monstrous whirlpool in the Strait of Messina; three times a day it sucked down all the water around it, only to belch it up again later.

Cheiron (KY ron): A wise, gentle, refined, and immortal Centaur; teacher of many heroes, including Heracles, Jason, Peleus, and Achilles; accidentally wounded by one of Heracles' poisoned arrows, he suffered agonizing pain until Prometheus assumed his immortality, allowing him to go to the Underworld.

Chloris (KLOE riss): A nymph, the wife of Zephyr, who made her the Roman goddess Flora.

Chrysaor (KRIS ay or; kry SAY or): Giant warrior; son of Medusa and Poseidon; brother of Pegasus.

Chryseis (kry SEE iss): Daughter of the priest of Apollo on the island of Chryse; abducted by Agamemnon to serve as his concubine; when, at her father's request, Apollo sent a pestilence down on the Greeks, Agamemnon reluctantly returned her to her home.

Chrysippus (kri SIP pus): Illegitimate son of Pelops; abducted by Laius, who wanted the boy to be his sexual plaything; killed himself from shame.

Cinyras (SIN i russ): King of Cyrus who boasted that his daughter's beauty exceeded Aphrodite's; the goddess made his daughter, Smyrna, fall in love with him; father (by Smyrna) of Adonis.

Circe (SER see): Famed sorceress who turned half of Odysseus's crew into swine; daughter of Helius and Perse; sister of Aeëtes and Pasiphaë; mother (by Odysseus) of Telegonus; later wife of Telemachus.

Clio (KLY oh; KLEE oh): One of the nine Muses; generally considered the Muse of history; daughter of Zeus and Mnemosyne.

Clotho (KLOH tho): One of the three Moirai (Fates); sister of Lachesis and Atropos; responsible for spinning the thread of mortal lives.

Clymene (KLIM uh nee): An Oceanid; mother (by Iapetus) of Prometheus, Atlas, Menoetius, and Epimetheus and (by Helius) of Phaëthon. Wife of Merops, king of Egypt.

Clytemnestra (kly tem NESS tra): Daughter of Leda and Tyndareus; sister of Helen, Castor, and Polydeuces; wife of Agamemnon; mother of Iphigenia, Orestes, and Electra; never forgave her husband for sacrificing Iphigenia to free the Greek ships going to the Trojan War; plotted with her lover, Aegisthus, to kill Agamemnon upon his return; also killed the enslaved Trojan seer Cassandra; Orestes killed her to avenge his father's murder.

Clytie (KLY ti ee): A nymph; jealous lover of Helius; orchestrated demise of his new lover Leucothoe and hated by Helius for it; wasted away and turned into heliotrope flower.

Clytius (KLY ti us): A Giant burned to death by Hecate during the war between the Giants and the Olympians.

Cocalus (KO kuh luss; KOCK uh luss): King of Camicus on Sicily; after fleeing Crete, Daedalus took refuge in his palace, where he invented toys that entertained the king's daughters; when King Minos of Crete demanded that he surrender Daedalus to him, the king's daughters killed Minos by pouring gallons of boiling water over him.

Coeus (SEE us): One of the original Titans; son of Gaia and Uranus; father (by Phoebe) of Leto and Asteria.

Corynetes (kor i NEE teez): Nickname of Periphetes.

Cottus (KOT us): One of three Hundred-Handed Giants, the first beings born through procreation; son of Gaia and Uranus; brother of Briareus and Gyges; helped Cronus defeat Uranus and later helped Zeus defeat Cronus.

Cranae (KRAY nee): A nymph whom Janus loved and made the Roman goddess of hinges.

Cratus (KRAY tuss): Personification of strength; son of Styx and Pallas; brother of Zelus, Nike, and Bia; he and his brothers became constant companions of Zeus.

Creon (KREE on): 1. King of Thebes after the deaths of Eteocles and Polyneices; brother of Jocasta; father of Haemon and Megara, who later married Heracles. 2. King of Corinth; father of Glauce (or Creusa); burned to death when the robe that jealous Medea gave his daughter burst into flames and destroyed the palace.

Cretan bull (KREE ten BULL): Fire-spitting bull; father (by Pasiphaë) of the Minotaur; captured by Heracles as his seventh labor; released, it wandered to Marathon (*see* Marathonian bull).

Cretheus (KREE thyoos): Founder and king of Iolcus; son of King Aeolus of Thessaly; brother of Sisyphus, Salmoneus, and Athamas; father (by his niece Tyro) of Aeson.

Creusa (kree YOO suh): 1. First wife of Aeneas; daughter of Priam and Hecuba; captured by the Greeks during the Trojan War, but saved from enslavement by Aphrodite and Cybele; when Troy fell, she became separated from Aeneas as they fled and was never seen again. 2. Name sometimes given for Glauce, daughter of King Creon of Corinth, who was murdered by Medea.

Crius (KRY us): One of the original Titans; son of Gaia and Uranus; father (by Eurybia) of Astraeus.

Cronus (KRO nus): King of the Titans; son of Gaia and Uranus; castrated his father to set the Titans free; father (by Rhea) of six Olympians: Hestia, Demeter, Hera, Hades, Poseidon, and Zeus; imprisoned in Tartarus by the victorious Olympians.

Cupid (KYOO pid): Roman personification of love as a roguish boy god (in Greek, Eros); son of Venus and Mercury; husband of Psyche; father of Voluptas.

Cybele (SIB i lee): Phrygian mother goddess who cured Dionysus of the madness inflicted by jealous Hera and initiated him in her religious rites, which he would adapt for his own worship.

Cyclopes (sie KLO peez): 1. Brontes, Steropes, and Arges; one-eyed giants; sons of Gaia and Uranus; became forgers of Zeus's thunder and lightning and Poseidon's trident. 2. One-eyed, man-eating giants; sons of Poseidon.

Cycnus (SICK nuss): King of Colonae; son of Poseidon made invulnerable to weapons; killed by Achilles, who strangled him with the thongs of his own helmet; after death, turned into a swan.

Cyllene (si LEE nee): Nymph who nursed the infant Hermes in an Arcadian cave.

Cymopoleia (sie moe puh LEE uh): A daughter of Zeus; given by her father to Briareus in gratitude for helping defeat the Titans.

Cyzicus (SIZZ i kuss): King of the Dolione tribe; welcomed Argonauts to his island; later killed in attack by the Argonauts, who had left in a fog and unknowingly returned to the same island, where they were mistaken as enemies.

Daedalus (DED uh luss; DEE duh luss): Brilliant inventor; killed his talented nephew and apprentice, Talus; exiled from Athens, moved on to Crete, where he devised the hollow cow that allowed Pasiphaë to mate with a bull and the Labyrinth that housed their monstrous offspring, the Minotaur; father of Icarus; imprisoned in the Labyrinth with his son, he constructed wings of wax and feathers and escaped (though his son flew too high and died when his wings melted); took refuge in palace of Cocalus on Sicily.

Damastes (duh MASS teez): Monstrous host who stretched or mutilated his guests so that they would fit in his guest bed; son of Hephaestus; father of Sinis; slain by Theseus in the same manner he killed his own guests; also called Polypemon.

Damkina (dam KEE nuh): Wife of Babylonian high god Ea; mother of Marduk.

Danaë (DAN ay ee): Daughter of Acrisius and Aganippe; mother (by Zeus) of Perseus, who later rescued her from the lecherous Polydectes.

Danaus (DAN ay us): A king of Argos.

Daphne (DAFF nee): Mountain nymph pursued by Apollo; turned into a laurel bush to avoid his embrace.

Dardanus (DAR duh nuss): First ancestor of the Trojan race; king and founder of Dardania; son of Zeus and the Pleiad Electra; husband of Bateia.

Dascylus (DASS ki luss): Son of Lycus, king of the Mariandyni; joined the crew of the *Argo* just before they reached Colchis.

Daunus (DOE nuss): King of Apulia; father of Turnus and Juturna.

Deianira (dee uh NIE ra): Wife of Heracles; daughter of Althaea and Dionysus (or Oeneus); killed Heracles when she unwittingly sent him a cloak soaked in the poisonous blood of the Hydra.

Deidameia (dee duh MY uh): Daughter of Lycomedes; mother (by Achilles) of Pyrrhus (Neoptolemus).

Deimus (DEE muss): Personification of fear; son of Ares and Aphrodite; brother of Phobus and Harmonia.

Deiphobus (DEE if uh bus): Son of Priam and Hecuba who forced Helen to marry him after the death of his brother Paris near the end of the Trojan War; killed by Helen's husband, Menelaus.

Delphinus (dell FIE nuss): Messenger who persuaded Amphitrite to marry Poseidon.

Delphyne (dell FIE nee): Dragon charged by Typhon with guarding the sinews cut from Zeus's hands and feet.

Demaratus (dem uh RAH tuss): Greek father of Lucius Tarquinius Priscus, fifth king of Rome; exiled from Corinth, he moved to the Etruscan city of Tarquinia, married, and fathered Tarquinius.

Demeter (dee MEE ter): Goddess of fertility and the harvest; daughter of Rhea and Cronus; sister of Hestia, Hera, Poseidon, Hades, and Zeus; mother (by Zeus) of Kore (Persephone) and Iacchus; mother (by Poseidon) of Despoena and Arion; also mother (by Iasion) of Plutus.

Demophon (DEM oh fon; DEE muh fon): 1. A king of Eleusis; son of Celeus and Meteneira. 2. A son of Theseus and Phaedra.

Despoena (des poe EE nuh): A nymph; daughter of Poseidon and Demeter.

Deucalion (doo KAY li on): 1. A son of Prometheus; husband of Pyrrha; warned by his father, built a boat that survived the great flood; with Pyrrha, repopulated the earth by throwing stones that turned into people. 2. King of Crete; son of Minos and Pasiphaë; brother of Ariadne, Androgeus, and Phaedra.

Diana (die AN uh): Roman goddess of hunting and the moon (in Greek, Artemis); began as an ancient Latin or Sabine goddess of fertility and a patroness of wild animals and of birth (both human and animal).

Dictys (DICK tiss): King of Seriphus; originally a poor fisher who rescued and cared for Danaë and Perseus; brother of King Polydectes; protected Danaë in Perseus's absence; rewarded for his kindness with the throne after Perseus killed Polydectes.

Dido (DIE doe): Founder and queen of Carthage; widow of Sychaeus; sister of Pygmalion; fell in love with Aeneas, who eagerly returned her love, lingering a year before—prodded by Mercury—he resumed his journey to Italy; despairing over his departure, she cursed the Trojans and killed herself with her own sword.

Dike (DIE kee): Personification of justice; one of the Horae (Seasons); daughter of Zeus and Themis; sister of Eunomia and Eirene.

Diomedes (die oh MEE deez): 1. King of Thrace; son of Ares; fed his mares human flesh; Heracles clubbed him to death, fed him to his own horses, and then took the horses away as his eighth labor. 2. King of Aetolia during the Trojan War; among the Greeks, his daring and skill as a warrior were exceeded only by those of Achilles; frequent companion of and conspirator with Odysseus; banished from his homeland after the war, he settled in Italy, where he founded the city of Argyripa.

Dione (die OH nee): One of the Pleiades; daughter of Atlas and Pleione; wife of Tantalus, king of Sipylus; mother of Niobe, Broteas, and Pelops.

Dionysus (die oh NIE suss): God of wine, grapes, and revelry; son of Zeus and Semele; also called Bacchus and Bromius; wandered the world spreading his own worship; persecuted for introducing newly ecstatic religious rites; husband of Ariadne; father (by Ariadne) of Thoas, Staphylus, Phanus, and Oenopion, and (by Aphrodite) of Priapus.

Dioscuri (die us KYOO rye): The twins (of different fathers) Castor and Polydeuces, sons of Leda and Tyndareus and Leda and Zeus, respectively.

Discordia (dis KOR di uh): Roman goddess of discord or personification of strife (in Greek, Eris).

Dolon (DOE lon): Trojan spy captured, forced to reveal Trojan secrets, and then killed by Odysseus and Diomedes.

Doris (DOE riss; DOR iss): An Oceanid; daughter of Oceanus and Tethys; mother (by Nereus) of the 50 Nereids.

Dryads (DRY adz): Tree-dwelling wood nymphs.

Dryope (DRY uh pee): A nymph; the mother (by Hermes) of Pan.

Dryops (DRY ops): A son of Apollo; grandfather of Pan.

Dumuzi (doo MOO zee): Sumerian god of fertility; husband of Ishtar; took wife's place in Underworld for six months per year, causing the seasons to change.

Ea (AY uh): 1. Babylonian master of all gods; son of Anu; husband of Damkina; father of Marduk; used magic to defeat great-grandfather Apsu and seize power; killed

Kingu, creating human race from his blood; also called Nudimmud or Enki.
2. Sumerian god of wisdom.

Echidna (ee KID nuh): Mother of all monsters; mother (by Typhon) of the Lernean Hydra, the Sphinx, the Nemean lion, the hundred-headed dragon Ladon, and the two-headed dog Orthrus.

Echion (ee KIE on): 1. Herald for the *Argo;* son of Hermes. 2. One of the five Spartoi who survived the initial attack by Cadmus; husband of Cadmus's daughter Agave; father of Pentheus.

Echo (ECK oh): A nymph, once an attendant to Hera; her incessant chatter distracted Hera's attention from Zeus's infidelities with other nymphs; punished by making her unable to speak except to repeat what another had said; when Narcissus rejected her love, she wasted away, leaving only her echoing voice.

Eetion (ee ET i on): King of Hypoplacian Thebes near Troy; father of Andromache; he and seven sons were slain by Achilles.

Egeria (ee JER i uh): A wise nymph of Diana; adviser and second wife of Numa Pompilius; dissolved in tears when her husband died; Diana transformed her into a natural spring.

Eileithyia (eye lie THIGH uh): A goddess of childbirth; daughter of Zeus and Hera; sister of Ares and Hebe.

Eirene (eye REE nee): Personification of peace; one of the Horae (Seasons); daughter of Zeus and Themis; sister of Eunomia and Dike.

Elais (el AY iss): Daughter of Anius; sister of Spermo and Oino; could turn anything she touched to oil; kidnapped by the Greek forces on their way to the Trojan War; Dionysus turned the sisters into doves to allow them to escape.

Electra (e LEK truh): 1. Daughter of Agamemnon and Clytemnestra; sister of Iphigenia and Orestes; protected young Orestes by sending him away after their mother murdered their father; urged him, when grown, to avenge the murder by killing their mother. 2. One of the Pleiades (daughters of Atlas); mother (by Zeus) of Dardanus. 3. An Oceanid; daughter of Oceanus and Tethys; mother (by Thaumas) of Iris.

Electryon (e LEK tri on): King of Argos; son of Perseus and Andromeda; brother of Alcaeus and Sthenelus; father of Alcmene; grandfather of Heracles; accidentally killed by his son-in-law Amphitryon.

Elpenor (el PEE nor): Youngest crew member on Odysseus's flagship; got drunk and fell off the roof of Circe's house, killing himself; his ghost later appeared and asked Odysseus for a proper burial, a request that Odysseus granted.

Enceladus (en SELL uh dus): A Giant crushed by Athena during the war between the giants and the Olympians.

Endymion (en DIM i on): King of Elis; lover of Selene and father of her 50 daughters; given the opportunity to determine his own fate, vainly chose eternal youth and beauty at the price of eternal sleep.

Enki (EN kee): 1. Sumerian god of wisdom. 2. Another name for Ea.

Enkidu (en KEE doo): Best friend of Sumerian hero Gilgamesh; tormented and driven to death by great goddess Ishtar after helping Gilgamesh kill the Bull of Heaven.

Enlil (en LEEL): Sumerian ruler of all gods; god of vegetation, cattle, agricultural tools, and the art of civilization; son of An and Ki.

Eos (EE oss): Goddess of the dawn; daughter of Hyperion and Theia; sister of Helius and Selene; mother (by Astraeus) of Eosphorus (the Dawnstar) and Zephyrus, Boreas, and Notus (the three winds); also mother (by Tithonus) of Memnon and Emathion and (by Cephalus) Phaëthon.

Eosphorus (ee OSS fuh russ): The Dawnstar; offspring of Eos and Astraeus.

Epeius (e PEE us): Artisan who built the Wooden Horse that led to Greek victory in the Trojan War.

Ephialtes (eff i AL teez): 1. Giant son of Poseidon; twin brother of Otus; trapped Ares in a jar for a year; after pursuing Hera, tricked by Artemis or Apollo into killing Otus, who killed him. 2. Giant killed by arrows of both Apollo and Heracles during the war between the Giants and the Olympians.

Epicasta (ep i KASS tuh): Name some storytellers gave to Jocasta.

Epimetheus (ep i MEE thee us): Brother of Prometheus, Atlas, and Menoetius; son of Iapetus and Clymene; received Pandora as a "gift" from the Olympians.

Epistrophus (ep i STROH fuss): Son of King Evenus of Lyrnessus; brother of Mynes and Marpessa; he and Mynes killed by Achilles.

Erato (ER uh toe): One of the nine Muses; generally considered the Muse of love poetry and marriage songs; daughter of Zeus and Mnemosyne.

Erebus (ER uh bus): Personification of the darkness of the Underworld; son of Chaos; father (by Nyx) of Hemera and Aether.

Erechtheus (ee REK thee us): Renowned early king of Athens; son of Pandion; brother of Procne and Philomela; father of Procris.

Ereshkigal (eh RESH ki gol): Sumerian ruler of the Underworld; sister of Inanna.

Erginus (er JIE nuss): King of Orchomenus; demanded an annual tribute of 100 cattle from Thebes; Heracles ended this practice; killed by Heracles.

Erichthonius (er ik THOE ni us): King of Athens; son of Hephaestus, who spilled his seed on Athena, who wiped it off and threw it to the ground, unwittingly fertilizing Gaia; reared by Athena; reportedly had a snake's tail instead of legs.

Erigone (ee RIG uh nee): Daughter of Icarius, who introduced wine to Athens; possibly a lover of Dionysus; hanged herself in despair after discovering her murdered father's body.

Erinyes (ee RIN i eez): Alecto, Tisiphone, and Megara; the Furies; three sisters who avenge perjury and crimes against one's family; daughters of Gaia bred from the blood dripping to the earth from Uranus's severed genitals.

Eris (ER iss; EE riss): Goddess of discord; personification of strife; daughter of Nyx.

Eros (ER oss; EE ross): Personification of love; a primeval being considered the creative force behind the Universe; according to the Orphic cult, the first being to emerge from the egg conceived by Nyx and the Wind.

Erymanthian boar (er i MAN thi un BORE): Savage wild boar captured alive by Heracles as his third labor.

Erysichthon (er i SICK thon): Mortal who offended Demeter by cutting down trees sacred to her; punished with insatiable hunger, he ultimately ate his own flesh and died.

Erytus (ER i tuss): A crew member on the *Argo*; son of Hermes.

Eryx (ER iks): A boxer and wrestler who challenged Heracles to a match; Heracles killed him by smashing him to the ground.

Eteocles (ee TEE oh kleez): King of Thebes; son of Oedipus; brother of Polyneices, Antigone, and Ismene; after agreeing to rule Thebes jointly after their father's exile, he refused to give up the throne to Polyneices; the struggle led to the war of the Seven Against Thebes, in which the brothers killed each other.

Eumaeus (yoo MEE us): Swineherd loyal to Odysseus, even in his absence; the first Ithacan Odysseus contacted upon his return home.

Eumenides (yoo MEN i deez): Originally the Erinyes (Furies) avenging the murder of Clytemnestra by her son Orestes, they became patron deities of Athens.

Eumolpus (yoo MOL pus): Founder of the Eleusinian Mysteries; taught Heracles singing and playing the lyre.

Euneus (YOO ni us): King of Lemnos who bought Lycaon, a son of Paris and Hecuba, from Achilles, then sold him back to the Trojans for a huge ransom.

Eunomia (yoo NOH mi uh): Personification of law and order; one of the Horae (Seasons); daughter of Zeus and Themis; sister of Dike and Eirene.

Eupeithes (yoo PIE theez): Father of Antinous once saved by Odysseus; fomented rebellion among Ithacan nobles after Odysseus returned and killed all their sons; killed by Laertes.

Euphemus (YOO fuh muss): A crew member on the *Argo*; swift son of Poseidon.

Euphrosyne (yoo FROSS i nee): One of the three Graces; daughter of Zeus and Eurynome; sister of Aglaia and Thalia.

Euripides (yoo RIP i deez): Greek tragedian of the fifth century B.C.E.

Europa (yoo ROE puh): Sister of Cadmus abducted by Zeus, who took the form of an enchanting white bull; mother (by Zeus) of Minos, Sarpedon, and Rhadamanthus.

Euryale (yoo RYE uh lee): One of the immortal Gorgons; sister of Stheno and Medusa.

Eurybia (yoo ri BEE uh; yoo RIB i uh): A daughter of Gaia and Pontus; sister of Nereus, Phorcys, Thaumas, and Ceto; mother (by Crius) of Astraeus.

Eurycleia (yoo ri KLEE uh; yoo ri KLY uh): Odysseus's nurse, who saw through his disguise when she washed his feet and recognized his scar.

Eurydice (yoo RID i see): 1. Beloved wife of Orpheus who, fleeing the amorous advances of Aristaeus, stepped on a poisonous snake and died; Orpheus tried to retrieve her from the Underworld, but failed. 2. Daughter of Lacedaemon and, according to some accounts, the wife of Acrisius and mother of Danaë.

Eurylochus (yoo RILL uh kuss): First mate on Odysseus's flagship; led the scouting party that Circe turned into swine; later made the fatal decision to kill some of Helius's cattle.

Eurymachus (yoo RIM uh kuss): One of Penelope's suitors; slain by Odysseus.

Eurynome (yoo RIN uh me): 1. According to Pelasgian (early Greek immigrants from Asia Minor) myth, the Goddess of All Things, who created the universe by laying the Universal Egg. 2. An Oceanid (daughter of Oceanus and Tethys) who rescued and reared Hephaestus after he was thrown from Olympus; mother (by Zeus) of the three Graces: Aglaia, Euphrosyne, and Thalia.

Eurystheus (yoo RISS thee us): King of Mycenae and Tiryns; assigned the labors that Heracles had to perform to atone for killing Megara and her children; son of Sthenelus and Nicippe; father of Admete.

Eurytion (yoo RIT i on): 1. King of Phthia; purified Peleus of the murder of his half-brother Phocus; offered him the hand of his daughter, Antigone; accidentally killed by Peleus during the Calydonian boar hunt. 2. A son of Ares who guarded the cattle of Geryon; clubbed to death by Heracles.

Eurytus (YOO ri tuss): 1. An excellent bowman; father of Iole and Iphitus; he taught archery to Heracles; later refused to allow Heracles to marry his daughter, but Heracles took her away anyway. 2. Giant beaten to death by Dionysus during the war between the Giants and the Olympians.

Euterpe (yoo TER pee): One of the nine Muses; generally considered the Muse of music and lyric poetry; daughter of Zeus and Mnemosyne.

Evander (ee VAN der): Led settlers from Arcadia in Greece to the banks of the Tiber, where they founded Pallanteum; son of Hermes and Carmenta; father of Pallas.

Evenus (ee VEE nuss): King of Lyrnessus; son of Ares; father of Marpessa, Mynes, and Epistrophus.

Fauna (FAW nuh; FOE nuh): Ancient Roman goddess with power over fertility, nature, farming, and animals; also called Bona Dea ("Good Goddess") or Bona Mater ("Good Mother"); wife (or daughter) of Faunus.

Faunus (FAW nuss): Roman god of prophecy, fields, shepherds, and their flocks (in Greek, Pan); grandson of Saturn; son of Picus; husband (or father) of Fauna; reputed father (by Marica) of Latinus, king of Latium.

Faustulus (FOWS tyoo luss): Chief shepherd of the king of Alba Longa; husband of Acca Larentia; concealed Romulus and Remus, raising the twins as if they were his own children.

Flora (FLOE ruh): A Roman goddess of flowers, fertility, gardens, and love who helped Juno conceive Mars without a mate.

Fornax (FOR naks): A Roman goddess of bread-baking.

Fortuna (for TYOO nuh): A Roman goddess of fate, chance, good luck, and prosperity.

Furies (FYOO reez): *See* Enrinyes.

Gaia (GAY uh; GUY uh): The Earth; mother (by herself) of Uranus and Pontus; mother (by Uranus) of the Hundred-Handed Giants, the Cyclopes, and the Titans.

Galatea (gal uh TEE uh): Sea nymph loved by the Cyclops Polyphemus, but in love with the mortal Acis.

Ganymede (gan i MEE dee): A beautiful prince of Troy abducted by Zeus to serve as the god's cupbearer and lover.

Geryon (jee RYE on; GER ee on): A monster with three heads, three torsos, and six hands; as his tenth labor, Heracles killed him with a single arrow, then made off with his herds of beautiful red cattle.

Geshtinanna (gesh ti NON nuh): Sumerian goddess of the grapevine; sister of Dumuzi; alternated time in Underworld with Dumuzi every six months.

Gilgamesh (GILL guh mesh): Sumerian king of Uruk; the first hero in literature, said to be one-third human and two-thirds god; son of goddess Ninsun and mortal Lugalbanda.

Glauce (GLAU see): Daughter of King Creon of Corinth; betrothed to Jason, she died when a poisoned robe sent by Jason's first wife Medea burst into flames; sometimes called Creusa.

Glaucus (GLAU kuss): 1. King of Ephyra (later Corinth); son of Sisyphus and Merope; brother of Ornytion and Sinon; after losing a chariot race, eaten by his own flesh-eating mares. 2. A minor sea god who loved the maiden Scylla; he asked Circe for a love potion, but the jealous sorceress turned Scylla into a grotesque monster instead.

Gorgons (GORE gonz): Three serpent-haired daughters of Ceto and Phorcys; Euryale, Stheno, and Medusa; so hideous that anyone who looked upon them turned to stone.

Graeae (GREE ee): Three ancient witches ("gray women"), sisters of the Gorgons; gray-haired since birth, the three sisters shared just one eye and one tooth among them; Perseus forced them to reveal the lair of the Gorgons.

Gration (GRA ti on): Giant shot and killed by Artemis during the war between the Giants and the Olympians.

Gyges (JIE jeez): One of three Hundred-Handed Giants, the first beings born through procreation; son of Gaia and Uranus; brother of Briareus and Cottus; helped Cronus defeat Uranus and later helped Zeus defeat Cronus.

Hades (HAY deez): Lord of the Underworld; brother of Zeus, Poseidon, Hestia, Demeter, and Hera; abductor and later husband of Persephone.

Haemon (HEE mon): Son of Creon; either devoured by the Sphinx or much later disobeyed his father's orders to bury Antigone alive, instead marrying her; when Creon discovered their son and sentenced him to death, he and his wife both committed suicide.

Halirrhothius (hal i ROE thi us): A son of Poseidon; attempted to rape Alcippe, daughter of Ares; Ares killed him, then became the first defendant tried—and acquitted—for murder.

Hamadryads (ham uh DRY adz): Wood nymphs who inhabit oak trees.

Harmodius (har MOE di us): Young Athenian man with whom King Hippias became infatuated; fearing sexual violence, he and his lover, Aristogeiton, set out to kill the king, but killed his brother, Hipparchus, instead; the uproar that followed Hippias's execution of the two lovers helped usher in Athenian democracy.

Harmonia (har MOE ni uh): Daughter of Ares and Aphrodite; sister of Deimus and Phobus; wife of Cadmus, king of Thebes; mother (by Cadmus) of Ino, Semele, Agave, Autonoe, and Polydorus.

Harpies (HAR peez): Noxious bird-women who meted out divine vengeance; spared by Argonauts Zetes and Calais when Zeus promised they would leave their brother-in-law Phineus alone.

Hebe (HEE bee): A daughter of Zeus and Hera; a perpetually youthful beauty; the goddess of youth; sister of Ares and Eileithyia; wife of Heracles after he ascended to Olympus.

Hecate (HECK uh tee): Dark goddess of sorcery; attendant to Persephone; originally a powerful and benevolent goddess; daughter of Perses and Asteria.

Hector (HECK ter): Commander of the Trojan forces and mightiest of Trojan warriors; eldest son of Priam and Hecuba; husband of Andromache; father of Astyanax; killed by Achilles, who dragged the corpse behind his chariot.

Hecuba (HECK yoo buh): Wife of Priam, king of Troy during the Trojan War; mother of many children, including Hector, Paris, Helenus, Cassandra, Antiphus, Troilus, Isus, Lycaon, Astyoche, Creusa, Polydorus, and Polyxena; enslaved by Odysseus at the end of the war; avenged the murder of Polydorus by blinding his killer, Polymestor, and killing his two infant sons; then turned into a fire-eyed dog and dived into the sea.

Helen (HELL un): The most beautiful woman in the world; daughter of Zeus and Leda; sister of Clytemnestra, Castor, and Polydeuces; wife of Menelaus, king of Sparta; mother (by Menelaus) of Hermione; abducted by Theseus, leading to his downfall; later abducted by or ran off with Paris, Prince of Troy, setting off the 10-year Trojan War; returned to Sparta with Menelaus after the war.

Helenus (HELL uh nuss): Famed Trojan seer who warned his brother Paris not to capture Helen and later told the Greeks how they could win the Trojan War; brother of Cassandra and many others; the only one of the 50 sons of Priam and Hecuba to survive the war; later founded and ruled Buthrotum and foretold that Aeneas would found the Roman race.

Helius (HEE li us): God of the sun; son of Hyperion and Theia; brother of Selene and Eos; father (by Clymene) of Phaëthon.

Helle (HELL ee): Daughter of Athamas and Nephele; sister of Phrixus; when a golden, winged ram saved Phrixus from sacrifice, she flew away on its back, too; she fell into the sea at the spot now known as the Hellespont.

Hemera (HEE mer uh): Personification of day; daughter of Nyx and Erebus.

Hephaestus (hee FESS tuss): Lame god of smithing, metalworking, and craftsmanship; son of Hera (by herself); craftsman to the gods; cuckolded husband of Aphrodite.

Hera (HEE ruh; HAIR uh): Goddess of marriage and childbirth; daughter of Rhea and Cronus; sister of Hestia, Demeter, Poseidon, Hades, and Zeus; mother (by herself) of Hephaestus; mother (by her husband Zeus) of Ares, Hebe, and Eileithyia; jealous tormenter of Zeus's many mistresses and bastard children.

Heracles (HER uh kleez): Greatest hero of classical myth; son of Zeus and Alcmene; half-brother of Iphicles; husband of Megara; killed Megara and their children under the influence of madness inflicted by Hera, who persecuted him throughout his life on Earth; to atone for his crime, forced to work for Eurystheus, who assigned him ten difficult labors (which soon grew to twelve due to the pickiness of Eurystheus in granting credit for labors done); killed many monsters and giants and captured many fabled beasts; after completing these labors, sought vengeance against those who had wronged him along the way; also turned the tide in the war between the Olympians and the Giants; later husband of Deianira; father of more than 50 children by Megara, Auge, Deianira, Omphale, and the 49 daughters of Thespius; tricked by Nessus, jealous Deianira sent him a poisoned shirt thinking it had a potion that would guarantee eternal love; his mortal life ended, but he nonetheless rose to Olympus; married Hera's daughter Hebe on Olympus.

Hercules (HER kyoo leez): Roman name for Heracles.

Hermaphroditus (her maff roe DIE tuss): A double-sexed child, the offspring of Hermes and Aphrodite.

Hermes (HER meez): Messenger of the gods; one of the Olympians; son of Zeus and Maia; patron god of travelers, merchants, rogues, and thieves; also guided dead souls to the Underworld.

Hermione (her MY oh nee): Daughter of Helen and Menelaus; promised to both Orestes and Neoptolemus; she first married Neoptolemus; after Orestes had Neoptolemus killed, she married Orestes.

Herodotus (huh ROD uh tuss): A Greek historian of the fifth century B.C.E.

Hesiod (HESS i ud; HEE si ud): Greek poet of the eighth century B.C.E.

Hesione (heh SIE oh nee): Daughter of King Laomedon of Troy; Heracles saved her from a sea monster, but her father then reneged on his promise to let the hero marry her; years later, Heracles killed Laomedon, captured her, and offered her hand to his friend and ally Telamon.

Hesperides (hess PER i deez): Nymphs who watched over Hera's garden, in which the Golden Apple tree stood.

Hestia (HESS ti uh): Virginal goddess of the hearth, home, and community; first-born child of Rhea and Cronus; sister of Demeter, Hera, Poseidon, Hades, and Zeus.

Hipparchus (hip PARK us): Brother of King Hippias of Athens; killed by Athenian lovers Harmodius and Aristogeiton.

Hippias (HIP pi us): King of Athens who became enamored with a young man named Harmodius; had Harmodius and his lover Aristogeiton killed after they murdered his brother, Hipparchus; ensuing scandal toppled the tyranny and ushered in democracy in Athens.

Hippodameia (hip uh duh MY uh): 1. Daughter of King Oenomaus of Pisa; sister of Leucippus; wife of Pelops; mother of Pittheus, Atreus, and Thyestes. 2. Daughter of Butes; wife of Peirithous.

Hippolyta (hi POL i tuh): Queen of the Amazons; daughter of Ares; killed by Heracles to obtain her golden girdle, his ninth labor.

Hippolytus (hi POL i tuss): 1. Virginal hunter who worshipped Artemis; son of Theseus and Antiope; rejected the amorous advances of his stepmother Phaedra; accused of raping Phaedra, he was unjustly banished and cursed by his father; caught in the reins and dragged to his death when the horses pulling his chariot were startled when a bull sent by Poseidon rose out of the sea. 2. Giant killed by Hermes during the war between the Giants and the Olympians.

Hippothoon (hih POTH oh on): King of Eleusis; son of Poseidon and Alope; placed on the throne by Theseus.

Homer (HOE mer): A Greek poet of about the eighth century B.C.E.

Horace (HOR iss; HOR us): A Roman poet and satirist during the Augustan Age.

Horae (HOE ree): Personification of the seasons; three sisters, children of Zeus and Themis: Eunomia, Dike, and Eirene.

Humbaba (hum BAH buh): Evil Sumerian giant who breathed fire; killed by Gilgamesh and Enkidu.

Hundred-Handed Giants (HUN dred HAN ded JIE ents): Cottus, Briareus, and Gyges; the first beings born through procreation; sons of Gaia and Uranus; helped Cronus defeat Uranus and later helped Zeus defeat Cronus.

Hyacinthus (hie uh SIN thuss): Beautiful young man wooed by Apollo; accidentally killed by Apollo (or deliberately by the West Wind) with a discus; his blood yielded the first hyacinth.

Hydra (HIE druh): See Lernean Hydra.

Hylas (HIE luss): Squire and lover of Heracles; dragged down into the water by spring nymphs on Mysia who became infatuated with him.

Hyllus (HILL us): Son of Heracles and Deianira who built his father's funeral pyre but could not light it.

Hymen (HIE mun): A late classical god of marriage.

Hyperion (hie PEER i un): An ancient god of the sun; one of the original Titans; son of Gaia and Uranus; father (by Theia) of Helius, Selene, and Eos.

Hypnos (HIP noss): Personification of sleep; son of Nyx.

Hypsipyle (hip SIP i lee): Queen of Lemnos; daughter of Thoas; spared her father when Lemnian women killed all other men on the island; mother of twin sons by Jason; banished to Nemea after discovery that Thoas was still alive; enslaved by the Nemean king.

Iacchus (EYE ack us): Son of Zeus and Demeter; brother of Kore (Persephone).

Iapetus (eye AP uh tuss): One of the original Titans; son of Gaia and Uranus; father (by Clymene) of Prometheus, Atlas, Menoetius, and Epimetheus.

Iasion (eye AY si un): Father (by Demeter) of Plutus; killed by Zeus after making love to Demeter.

Icarius (eye KER i us): 1. Citizen of Athens chosen by Dionysus to learn grape cultivation and introduce wine to Athens; father of Erigone; beaten to death by Athenian farmers who thought he had poisoned them. 2. Brother of Tyndareus; father of Penelope; urged his daughter and her new husband, Odysseus, to remain in Sparta; nonetheless, Penelope left for Ithaca with Odysseus.

Icarus (ICK uh russ): Son of Daedalus; imprisoned in the Labyrinth, they escaped using wings of wax and feathers; ignoring his father's warnings, he flew too high and the sun melted his wings, causing him to plunge to his death in the sea below.

Idas (EYE duss): A crew member on the *Argo*; boastful son of Poseidon; half-brother of Lynceus; husband of Marpessa (who chose him over Apollo).

Idmon (ID mon): Famed prophet and crew member on the *Argo*; son of Apollo; joined Jason though he knew he would die on the journey; killed by a wild boar before reaching Colchis.

Idomeneus (eye DOM uh nyoos): King of Crete during the Trojan War; banished from his homeland after the war and settled in Italy.

Ilia (ILL i uh): Name sometimes given to Rhea Silvia.

Ilus (EYE luss): Founder of Ilium (Troy).

Inanna (i NON nuh): Sumerian great goddess, the supreme goddess of sexual love, fertility, and war.

Indiges (IN di jeez): Minor god; formerly Aeneas, who had his mortality washed away.

Ino (EYE noh): Daughter of Cadmus and Harmonia; sister of Semele, Agave, Autonoe, and Polydorus; wife of Athamas, king of Thebes; mother of Learchus and Melicertes; plotted to kill her stepchildren, Phrixus and Helle; cared for Dionysus in his youth; driven mad by jealous Hera, boiled Melicertes and jumped with him into the sea, becoming the minor sea goddess Leucothea.

Io (EYE oh): 1. Mortal mistress of Zeus transformed into a cow to hide her from Hera; unfooled, Hera sent a gadfly to sting her and force her to wander the world. 2. Cretan nymph who cared for Zeus in his infancy.

Iolaus (eye oh LAY us): Friend, nephew, and charioteer of Heracles; son of Iphicles; helped Heracles defeat the Lernean Hydra.

Iole (EYE oh lee): Daughter of Eurytus; brother of Iphitus; Heracles defeated Eurytus in an archery contest for her hand, but Eurytus refused to let her marry him; years later, though by then married, Heracles captured her and sent her to his home in Trachis.

Iphicles (IF i kleez): Son of Amphitryon and Alcmene; half-brother of Heracles; father of Iolaus; killed in his brother's attack on King Augeas of Elis.

Iphigenia (if i juh NIE uh): Daughter of Agamemnon and Clytemnestra; sister of Orestes and Electra; sacrificed by her father to appease Artemis and allow the Greek ships to set sail at the beginning of the Trojan War.

Iphitus (IF i tuss): Son of Eurytus; brother of Iole; either Heracles threw him from a tower for suspecting the hero of stealing his father's cattle or he much later became good friends with Odysseus and presented him with his father's prized bow.

Iris (EYE riss): Goddess of the rainbow and messenger of the gods, especially Zeus and Hera; daughter of Thaumas and the Oceanid Electra.

Irus (EYE russ): Beggar in the palace of Ithaca; he threatened Odysseus, who was disguised as a beggar, but Odysseus knocked him out with a single blow.

Ishtar (ISH tar): Great goddess of the Akkadians of Mesopotamia; the supreme goddess of sexual love, fertility, and war.

Ismene (iss MEE nee): Daughter of Oedipus and Jocasta; sister of Eteocles, Polyneices, and Antigone.

Ismenius (iss MEE ni us): A river god; father of Linus.

Isus (EYE suss): A son of Priam and Hecuba; captured by Achilles during Trojan War; regained freedom when Priam paid a large ransom; later killed by Agamemnon.

Itys (EYE tuss; IT us): Son of Procne and Tereus; to avenge her husband's rape of her sister, Procne killed the boy, cooked him, and served him to Tereus for supper.

Iulus (eye YOO luss): King of Latium and founding king of Alba Longa; son of Aeneas and Creusa; in Troy, originally called Ascanius; established line of kings that lasted 13 generations.

Ixion (ick ZYE un; ick SIE un): Thessalian king who attempted to seduce Hera; Zeus substituted a cloud in her shape; father (by the cloud) of the race of Centaurs; eternally tormented in the Underworld, where he was strapped to a fiery wheel that turned endlessly.

Janus (JAY nuss): Roman god of doorways, porter of heaven, and guardian of all gates; also god of beginnings and endings and of sowing.

Jason (JAY sun): Leader of the *Argo* on a quest for the Golden Fleece; son of Aeson and Alcimede (or Polymede); brother of Promachus; obtained the fleece with the help of Medea, daughter of Aeëtes, king of Colchis; husband of Medea; exiled to Corinth after killing uncle Pelias, king of Colchis; when he abandoned Medea for Glauce (or Creusa), Medea killed their children and his new bride; he died when a beam from the *Argo* fell on his head.

Jocasta (joe KASS tuh): Daughter of Menoeceus; sister of Creon; wife of Laius, king of Thebes; mother (by Laius) of Oedipus and (by Oedipus) of Eteocles, Polyneices, Antigone, and Ismene; hanged herself when she learned she had married her own son (or after her sons by Oedipus killed each other); sometimes called Epicasta.

Junius Brutus, Lucius (LOO shuss JOO ni us BROO tus): First republican leader of Rome; friend of Lucius Tarquinius Collatinus; helped orchestrate the overthrow of Rome's last king, Lucius Tarquinius Superbus, after the king's son, Sextus Tarquinius, brutally raped Collatinus's wife Lucretia; installed a republican government and ruled as praetor, jointly with Collatinus at first, but after Collatinus's exile, on his own.

Juno (JOO noh): Roman goddess of marriage and childbirth and patroness of all women (in Greek, Hera); wife of Jupiter; mother (by herself) of Mars and (by Jupiter) of Juventas and perhaps Lucina; as Juno Lucina, guardian of childbirth; as Juno Moneta, guardian of Rome's finances.

Jupiter (JOO pi ter): Roman ruler of the gods and god of thunder and lightning and of the sky (in Greek, Zeus); also called Jove; son of Saturn; husband of Juno; father of Hercules and many deities; as Jupiter Lucretius, lord of light; as Jupiter Fulgar, wielder of lightning; as Jupiter Elicius, bringer of rainfall.

Juturna (JOO ter nuh): 1. Daughter of Daunus; sister of Turnus; served as his charioteer. 2. Nymph loved by Jupiter; sister of Lara.

Juventas (joo VEN tus): Roman goddess of youth (in Greek, Hebe); daughter of Jupiter and Juno; wife of Hercules; perhaps sister of Lucina.

Keres (KEE reez): Female death-spirits who collected corpses.

Ki (KEE): Sumerian earth goddess; daughter of Nammu; mated with her brother An to create the great gods of Sumer.

Kingu (KIN goo): Military leader of rebellious Babylonian gods; mate of Tiamat; killed by Ea, who created human race from his blood.

Kishar (KEE shar): Mother (by Anshar) of Babylonian sky god Anu; daughter of Apsu and Tiamat.

Kore (KOE ree): Daughter of Zeus and Demeter; called Persephone after Hades abducted her and made her Queen of the Underworld.

Labdacus (LAB duh kuss): 1. King of Thebes; son of Polydorus and Nycteus; killed by King Pandion of Athens over a border dispute.

Lacedaemon (lass uh DEE mon): King and founder of Lacedaemon and its capital, Sparta; son of Zeus and the Pleiad Taygete; husband of Sparta.

Lachesis (LACK uh siss): One of the three Moirai (Fates); sister of Clotho and Atropos; responsible for measuring out the span of each mortal life.

Ladon (LAY don): Hundred-headed dragon that guarded the Golden Apple tree in the Garden of the Hesperides; offspring of Typhon and Echidna; shot by Heracles in performing his eleventh labor.

Laelaps (LEE laps): Hound that never failed to catch its prey; given to Cephalus as a gift from Artemis when Procris reconciled with him.

Laertes (lay ER teez): King of Ithaca; husband of Anticleia; father (or foster father) of Odysseus; neglected himself while grieving over his wife's suicide and his son's presumed death; recovered when his son returned after 20 years.

Laius (LAY us): King of Thebes; forced from Thebes as a boy, welcomed into the home of Pelops and Hippodameia; abducted Pelops's illegitimate son Chrysippus when he returned to Thebes to reclaim the throne; husband of Jocasta; father of Oedipus; unknowingly killed by his son.

Lampetie (lam PEE shi ee): Daughter of Helius who, with her sister Phaëthusa, tended their father's cattle on the island of Thrinacia.

Laocoön (lay OCK oh on): Trojan priest of Apollo who warned against bringing the Wooden Horse within the walls of Troy; he and his two sons were then killed by two sea serpents, which the Trojans took as a sign that he was wrong about the Wooden Horse.

Laomedon (lay OM uh don): King of Troy; brother of Tithonus; father of Hesione and Priam (Podarces); killed by Heracles after refusing to pay agreed-upon reward for rescuing Hesione.

Lara (LAR uh): Mother (by Mercury) of Rome's twin Lares; talkative Naiad; sister of Juturna.

Larentia (luh REN shi uh; law REN shi uh): 1. Ancient Roman goddess of unknown function. 2. Prostitute for whom Hercules found a wealthy Etruscan husband; benefactor of Rome. *See also* Acca Larentia.

Latinus (luh TIE nuss): King of Latium; son of Faunus and Marica; great-grandson of Saturn; husband of Amata; father of Lavinia; welcomed Aeneas, his prospective son-in-law, to Italy; abdicated the throne, leading to war between the Latins and the Trojans.

Latona (luh TOE nuh): Roman name for Leto.

Lausus (LAW suss): Son of Mezentius; killed by Aeneas during his war with Turnus.

Lavinia (luh VIN i uh): Daughter of Latinus and Amata; wooed by her cousin Turnus; wife of Aeneas; mother of Silvius.

Learchus (lee AR kuss): Son of Athamas and Ino; brother of Melicertes; killed by his father who, driven mad by Hera, thought his son was a deer or a lion cub and shot him.

Leda (LEE duh): Queen of Sparta; mother (by Zeus) of Helen and Polydeuces; mother (by Tyndareus) of Castor and Clytemnestra.

Lernean Hydra (LER nee un HIE druh): Monster with a huge dog-like body and many serpentine heads; offspring of Echidna and Typhon; killed by Heracles as his second labor.

Leto (LEE toe): Daughter of Phoebe and Coeus; sister of Asteria; mother (by Zeus) of Artemis and Apollo.

Leuce (LOO see): Nymph transformed into a poplar tree by Persephone to thwart Hades' attempts to seduce her.

Leucippus (loo SIP us): Son of King Oenomaus of Pisa who disguised himself as a girl to remain close to his beloved Daphne; ripped to shreds by nymphs when Apollo exposed him.

Leucothea (loo KOTH ee uh): Minor sea deity; formerly Ino, who was transformed when she leapt into the sea with her son Melicertes.

Leucothoe (lu KOTH oh ee): Mortal beloved by Helius; daughter of King Orchamus of Persia; buried alive by her father when he learned of the affair; turned into a frankincense bush by Helius.

Liber (LIE ber): Roman god of wine and revelry (in Greek, Dionysus); often called Father Liber; originally an ancient Italian god of fertility, perhaps mistakenly associated with Bacchus instead of Iacchus; husband of Libera.

Libera (LIE ber uh): Ancient Italian fertility goddess sometimes identified with Persephone; wife of Liber; perhaps originally called Ariadne, daughter of King Minos of Crete.

Lichas (LIE kuss): Herald of Heracles; unknowingly brought Heracles the poisoned shirt that would kill him; dying, Heracles hurled him into the sea, where he turned to stone.

Linus (LIE nuss): Son of Ismenius; taught literature to Heracles; while substituting as the hero's lyre teacher, he swatted his pupil; Heracles struck back, killing him instantly.

Liriope (ler EYE uh pee): A nymph; mother (by Cephissus) of Narcissus.

Livy (LIV ee): A Roman historian during the Augustan Age.

Lotus-Eaters (LOE tuss EE terz): Indolent tribe of northern Africa encountered by Odysseus and his crew members; eating the lotus fruit robbed all partakers of any ambition or initiative.

Lua (LYOO uh): Ancient Italian earth goddess; perhaps the original wife of Saturn.

Lucina (lyoo SIE nuh): Roman goddess of childbirth (in Greek, Eileithyia); perhaps daughter of Juno and Jupiter; perhaps merely an aspect of Juno's (Juno Lucina).

Lucretia (loo KREE shuh): Wife of Lucius Tarquinius Collatinus; brutally raped by Sextus Tarquinius, son of Roman king Lucius Tarquinius Superbus; after telling her husband to avenge her honor and her life, she killed herself.

Lugalbanda (loo gol BAHN duh): Mortal father (by the goddess Ninsun) of Sumerian hero Gilgamesh.

Lycaon (lie KAY on): 1. King of Arcadia; father of 50 sons; offended Zeus by attempting to serve him human flesh in a stew; transformed by Zeus into a wolf. 2. Son of Priam and Hecuba captured by Achilles and sold to Euneus; ransomed by a friend, he returned to battle only to be slain by Achilles.

Lycomedes (lie koe MEE deez): King of Scyrus who killed Theseus by pushing him off a cliff; hid Achilles among his daughters in an unsuccessful attempt to keep him out of the Trojan War; father of Deidameia and many other daughters.

Lycurgus (lie KER gus): King of Thrace's Edonian tribe; drove Dionysus and his followers out of his kingdom; to avenge this insult, Dionysus drove him mad, causing him to slaughter his wife and children; to restore fertility to their land, the Edonians killed him, throwing him among man-eating horses.

Lycus (LIE kuss): King of the Mariandyni, a tribe on the coast of the Black Sea; father of Dascylus; offered his son as a crew member on the *Argo* in gratitude for Argonauts vanquishing his enemies, the warlike Bebryces.

Lynceus (LIN syoos): A crew member on the *Argo*; keen-eyed son of Ahareus, king of Messenia; half-brother of Idas.

Machaon (muh KAY on): Son of Asclepius, god of healing, and grandson of Apollo; brother of Podaleirius; cured the wound of Philoctetes near the end of the Trojan War.

Macris (MACK riss): Daughter of Autonoe and Aristaeus; sister of Actaeon.

Maera (MEE ruh): Dog extremely loyal to its master, Icarius, who introduced wine to Athens; killed itself by jumping into the well where it found its master's murdered body.

Maia (MY uh): One of the Pleiades (daughters of Atlas); mother (by Zeus) of Hermes.

Marathonian bull (mar uh THOE ni un BULL): Bull captured by Heracles and released near Tiryns; wandered to Marathon, where it remained for many years; killed

Androgeus, whom Aegeus had sent to kill the marauding beast; captured alive by Theseus, who brought the beast back for Aegeus to sacrifice. *See also* Cretan bull.

Marduk (mar DOOK): Highest god of the Babylonians; god of storms and creator of the Universe; son of Ea and Damkina; led gods in war against Tiamat and Kingu.

Marica (MAR i kuh): A water nymph; mother (by Faunus) of Latinus.

Maron (MAY ron): Ciconian priest of Apollo spared by Odysseus when his crews sacked the city of Ismarus; he thanked them with fine wine and other gifts.

Marpessa (mar PESS uh): Daughter of Evenus; wooed by both Apollo and Idas, she chose the mortal Idas because she feared the god's love would fade as she aged.

Mars (MARZ): Roman god of agriculture and of war (in Greek, Ares); protector of farmers and soldiers; originally called Mavors; son of Juno (by herself); father (by Rhea Silvia) and protector of Romulus and Remus.

Marsyas (MAR sie us): Satyr who played Athena's flute in musical contest against Apollo (playing the lyre); skinned alive by Apollo after losing the contest.

Mater Matuta (MAY ter muh TYOO tuh): Roman goddess of sea travel (in Greek, Leucothea) who nursed Liber in his youth.

Medea (mee DEE uh): Powerful sorceress and priestess of Hecate; daughter of Aeëtes; sister of Chalciope and Apsyrtus; helped Jason obtain the Golden Fleece and later married him; killed Apsyrtus and tricked daughters of Pelias into murdering their father; abandoned by Jason, she murdered his children and his new bride; fled to Athens; married King Aegeus; bore him a son, Medus; banished after trying to engineer death of Theseus; returned to Colchis.

Medon (MEE don): A herald in the palace of Ithaca forced to serve Penelope's suitors; spared by Odysseus upon his return.

Medus (MEE duss): Son of Aegeus and Medea; exiled by Aegeus when Medea plotted to kill Theseus; killed King Perses of Colchis to reclaim the throne for his grandfather Aeëtes—or to claim it for himself.

Medusa (muh DOO suh): One of the three Gorgons, whose gaze turned creatures to stone; mortal, unlike her sisters Euryale and Stheno; beheaded by Perseus, who then used her head as a weapon; mother (by Poseidon) of Pegasus and Chrysaor.

Megapenthes (meg uh PEN theez): King of Tiryns and later Argos; only son of Proetus; nephew of Acrisius; traded kingdoms (Tiryns for Argos) with Perseus after the hero accidentally killed his grandfather Acrisius.

Megara (MEG uh ruh): 1. First wife of Heracles; daughter of Creon; sister of Haemon; she and her children were killed by Heracles after Hera drove him mad. 2. One of the three Erinyes (Furies).

Melampus (muh LAM puss): Great seer who cured women of Argos of madness inflicted upon them by Dionysus; his payment was one third of the kingdom for himself and one third for his brother Bias.

Melanippus (mel uh NIP us): Son of Theseus and Perigune.

Melanthius (muh LAN thi us): Goatherd who betrayed Odysseus by bringing Penelope's suitors their weapons; brother of Melantho; mutilated and left in the courtyard of the Ithacan palace to die.

Melantho (muh LAN thoe): Servant in the palace of Ithaca who became the mistress of one of Penelope's suitors; sister of Melanthius; hanged (along with 11 other mistresses) by Odysseus.

Meleager (mel ee AY jer): Hero who killed the boar in the Calydonian boar hunt; son of Oeneus, king of Calydon, and Althaea; half-brother of Deianira; crew member on the *Argo*.

Meliae (MEE li ee): Ash tree nymphs.

Melicertes (mel i SER teez): Son of Athamas and Ino; brother of Learchus; driven mad by Hera, his mother plunged him in a boiling cauldron, then leapt with him into the sea; he then became Palaemon, a minor sea deity.

Melpomene (mel POM i nee): One of the nine Muses; generally considered the Muse of tragedy; daughter of Zeus and Mnemosyne.

Memnon (MEM non): King of Ethiopia; son of Eos and Tithonus; brought thousands of troops to Troy to support the Trojans; slain by Achilles in one-on-one combat.

Menelaus (men uh LAY us): King of Sparta; son of Atreus and Aerope; brother of Agamemnon; husband of Helen; father of Hermione; when Paris carried Helen off to Troy, Menelaus called on her former suitors to join him in bringing her back; after winning the 10-year Trojan War, he forgave Helen and brought her back to Sparta.

Menestheus (muh NESS thyoos): King of Athens; assumed the throne, or was placed there by the Dioscuri, while Theseus was trapped in the Underworld.

Menoeceus (muh NEE syoos): Father of Creon and Jocasta; descendant of the Spartoi and of Cadmus; threw himself from the walls of Thebes in an attempt to save the city from a plague.

Menoetius (muh NEE shi us): 1. Brother of Prometheus, Atlas, and Epimetheus; son of Iapetus and Clymene. 2. Father of Patroclus; fled from Opus to Phthia with his son after Patroclus killed a playmate during an argument over a game of dice; given refuge by Peleus, whose son Achilles became best friends with Patroclus.

Mentor (MEN tor): A wise and respected Ithacan elder; Athena took on his form to negotiate peace between King Odysseus and the Ithacan nobles whose sons he had killed.

Mercury (MER kyoo ree): Roman god of travelers, merchants, cheats, thieves, and astronomy; also, messenger of the gods (in Greek, Hermes); father (by a Naiad, Lara) of Rome's twin Lares.

Merope (MER oh pee): 1. Only one of the Pleiades to marry a mortal; daughter of Atlas and Pleione; wife of Sisyphus; mother of Glaucus, Ornytion, and Sinon; helped her husband escape death by refusing him proper burial, giving him an excuse to return to Earth. 2. Queen of Corinth; wife of Polybus; adoptive mother of Oedipus; more commonly called Periboea.

Merops (MER ops): King of Egypt; husband of Clymene; foster father of Phaëthon.

Meteneira (met uh NEE ruh): Queen of Eleusis; mother (by King Celeus) of Demophon.

Metis (MEE tiss): A wise Oceanid, daughter of Oceanus and Tethys; the first lover of Zeus; swallowed by Zeus before she could give birth to their child, Athena; continued to advise Zeus from within his belly.

Mezentius (muh ZEN shi us): Etruscan king expelled for torturing and killing his own subjects; ally of Turnus in his war against Aeneas; Aeneas killed him and his son Lausus in combat.

Midas (MY duss): King of the Mygdonian tribe in Phrygia or Mysia; Dionysus, to reward him for his kindness to the god's friend and follower Silenus, offered him any wish; Midas wanted everything he touched to turn to gold; gave up this power when he found he could no longer eat.

Mimas (MY muss): Giant killed by Hephaestus (or Ares) in the war between the Giants and the Olympians.

Minerva (mi NER vuh): Roman goddess of the practical arts and crafts and the intelligence needed for them; goddess of wisdom and war (in Greek, Athena).

Minos (MY noss): King of Crete; son of Zeus and Europa; husband of Pasiphaë; father (by Pasiphaë) of Androgeus, Ariadne, Deucalion, and Phaedra; demanded

Athens send seven boys and seven girls every nine years to feed the terrible Minotaur; killed by the daughters of Cocalus to prevent him from taking Daedalus away from them (during his bath, they poured pots of boiling water over him).

Minotaur (MIN uh tor): Monstrous offspring of Pasiphaë and a magnificent bull; had a bull's head and a man's body; housed in the nearly inescapable Labyrinth; slain by Theseus.

Minthe (MIN thee): Nymph transformed by Persephone into a mint plant to keep her from her husband Hades.

Minyas (MIN i us): King of Orchomenus; when his daughters refused to accept Dionysus as a god, Dionysus drove them mad, causing them to rip apart one of their children, then turned them into bats.

Mnemosyne (nee MOZ i nee): One of the original Titans; daughter of Gaia and Uranus; mother (by Zeus) of the nine Muses.

Moirai (MOY rye): The three Fates—Clotho, Lachesis, and Atropos—responsible for determining the length and course of mortal lives.

Mopsus (MOP suss): A seer and member of the *Argo* crew; killed by a snakebite near Lake Tritonis.

Moros (MORE oss): Personification of doom; a child of Nyx.

Mummu (MUM moo): Babylonian primeval rising mist; son of Apsu and Tiamat; imprisoned by Ea for backing Apsu's plan to destroy him.

Muses (MYOO zez): Nine goddesses who inspired artists; daughters of Zeus and Mnemosyne; named Clio, Euterpe, Thalia, Melpomene, Terpsichore, Erato, Polyhymnia, Urania, and Calliope.

Mylitta (MY lit tuh): Assyrian great goddess, the supreme goddess of sexual love, fertility, and war.

Mynes (MY neez): Son of King Evenus of Lyrnessus; brother of Epistrophus and Marpessa; he and Epistrophus both killed by Achilles.

Myrtilus (MER ti luss): Swiftest of all charioteers; son of Hermes; bribed by Pelops, he killed his master, King Oenomaus of Pisa; Pelops reneged on his promise of half the kingdom and a night with Oenomaus's daughter Hippodameia; murdered by Pelops.

Naiads (NY adz; NAY adz): Water nymphs found in springs, rivers, lakes, fountains, or brooks.

Nammu (NAM moo): Sumerian goddess of the primeval sea; mother of Ki and An (earth and sky).

Narcissus (nar SISS us): Beautiful young man who rejected the love of Echo—and of all others; the son of Cephissus and Liriope; punished by Nemesis for his coldness by making him fall in love with his own reflection in a pool of water; he wasted away from a love he could never consummate, turning into a flower (the narcissus).

Nauplius (NAW pli us): A crew member on the *Argo*; son of Poseidon.

Nausicaa (naw SICK ay uh): Daughter of Alcinous and Arete who found Odysseus on the shores of Scheria, fed and clothed him, and arranged for his return home to Ithaca.

Nemean Lion (ne MEE un LIE un): Enormous lion with tough skin, invulnerable to swords or arrows; Heracles squeezed the lion to death as his first labor, then used its own claws to skin it and fashion a cloak for himself.

Nemesis (NEM uh siss): A goddess of retribution; daughter of Nyx.

Neoptolemus (nee op TOL uh muss): Bold and ruthless son of Achilles and Deidameia; after his father's death, recruited by the Greeks to take his place and ensure Greek victory in the Trojan War; after the war, married Hermione; killed by Orestes, to whom she had also been promised; originally named Pyrrhus.

Nephele (NEF uh lee): First wife of Athamas, king of Orchomenus; mother of Phrixus and Helle.

Neptune (NEP tyoon): Chief Roman god of the sea (in Greek, Poseidon).

Nereids (NEE ri idz): Sea nymphs, the 50 daughters of Nereus and Doris; among the better known were Thetis and Amphitrite.

Nereus (NEE ri us; NEERYOOS): A god of the sea; son of Gaia and Pontus; father (by Doris) of 50 daughters, the Nereids; also called the Old Man or Old Man of the Sea.

Nessus (NESS us): A Centaur who charged travelers to carry them across the River Evenus; while trying to rape Deianira, mortally wounded by Heracles with one of his poisoned arrows; while dying, tricked Deianira into accepting his blood-stained shirt as a charm to ensure Heracles' undying love; the shirt would kill Heracles.

Nestor (NESS tor): King of Pylus; father of Antilochus; challenged his son's killer, Memnon, to one-on-one combat, but Memnon refused to fight the old man; Achilles took his place and killed Memnon.

Nicippe (nie SIP ee): 1. Wife of Sthenelus; mother of Eurystheus. 2. A priestess of Demeter.

Nicostratus (ni KOSS truh tuss): According to some accounts, the son of Menelaus and Helen and brother of Hermione.

Nike (NIE kee): Personification of victory; son of Styx and Pallas; brother of Zelus, Cratus, and Bia; he and his brothers became constant companions of Zeus.

Ninshubur (NIN shoo ber): Trusted aide of Sumerian great goddess Inanna.

Ninsun (nin SOON): Wise Sumerian goddess; wife of mortal Lugalbanda; mother of Gilgamesh.

Nintu (NIN too): Sumerian Mother Goddess; creator of human race.

Niobe (NIE oh bee): Daughter of Tantalus; boasted of having more and better children than Leto; Leto's children, Artemis and Apollo, killed her children; she wept eternally, even after turning to stone.

Nisus (NIE suss): King of Megara; brother of Pallas and Aegeus; uncle of Theseus.

Notus (NOH tuss): The South Wind; offspring of Eos and Astraeus.

Nudimmud (NOO dim mud): Another name for Ea.

Numa Pompilius (NOO muh pom PILL i us): Second king of Rome; successor to Romulus; first Sabine king of Rome; husband of Tatia and, after her death, of Egeria, a wise nymph.

Numicius (noo MI shuss): River god who washed Aeneas's body out to sea, purifying him and preparing for his ascent to godhood (as Indiges).

Numitor (NOO mi tor): Unlucky thirteenth king of Alba Longa; deposed by his treacherous brother Amulius, who killed his sons and made his daughter, Rhea Silvia, a Vestal Virgin; restored to power by his grandsons, Romulus and Remus.

Nycteus (NICK tyoos): Wife of Polydorus; mother of Labdacus.

Nymphs (NIMFS): Minor female divinities; beautiful, youthful, amorous spirits of nature; often served as attendants to gods or goddesses.

Nyx (NIKS): Personification of night; daughter of Chaos; mother (by Erebus) of Hemera and Aether; mother (by herself) of Moros, Thanatos, Hypnos, Nemesis, Eris, the Keres, and the Moirai; in Orphic myth, the mother (by the Wind) of the Egg of all creation.

Oceanids (oh see AN idz): The 3,000 daughters of Oceanus and Tethys.

Oceanus (oh SEE uh nuss): Ancient god of the primordial river that circled earth; first-born of the original Titans; son of Gaia and Uranus; father (by Tethys) of the world's rivers and the Oceanids.

Ocresia (oh KREE see uh): Mother (by Vulcan) of Servius Tullius, sixth king of ancient Rome; slave of Tanaquil, the wife of Lucius Tarquinius Priscus, Tullius's predecessor.

Odysseus (oh DISS i us): King of Ithaca; wandering hero who, following the 10-year Trojan War, spent another ten years trying to get home to Ithaca; only survivor of the 12 ships he commanded; renowned for trickery, eloquence, and courage; son of Anticleia and either Laertes or Sisyphus; grandson of Autolycus; husband of Penelope; father (by Penelope) of Telemachus and (by Circe) of Telegonus; when he finally got home, he and Telemachus killed all of Penelope's suitors, who had been living off his wealth for years; later killed by Telegonus, who didn't recognize his own father.

Oedipus (ED i pus; EE di pus): King of Thebes; solver of the riddle of the Sphinx; son of Laius and Jocasta; exposed on a mountain by his father, he grew up in the care of Polybus and Periboea of Corinth; unknowingly murdered his real father and married his mother; father (by Jocasta) of Eteocles, Polyneices, Antigone, and Ismene; blinded himself when he realized what he had done; exiled from Thebes, he wandered with Antigone to Colonus, outside Athens, and died.

Oeneus (EE nyoos): King of Calydon who offended Artemis by forgetting to include her in a harvest sacrifice; organized the Calydonian boar hunt, involving the greatest heroes of the age, to rid his land of the beast sent by Artemis in punishment; husband of Althaea; father of Meleager and stepfather of Deianira, his wife's child by Dionysus.

Oenomaus (ee nom AY us): King of Pisa; father of Hippodameia and Leucippus; killed in an "accident" staged by his charioteer Myrtilus, who had been bribed by Pelops.

Oenopion (ee NOH pi on): King of Chios; son of Dionysus and Ariadne; brother of Thoas, Staphylus, and Phanus.

Oino (OH ee no): Daughter of Anius; sister of Spermo and Elais; could turn anything she touched to wine; kidnapped by the Greek forces on their way to the Trojan War; Dionysus turned the sisters into doves to allow them to escape.

Olympians (oh LIM pi enz): The 12 great gods: Zeus, Poseidon, Hera, Hestia or Dionysus, Demeter, Athena, Aphrodite, Hephaestus, Ares, Artemis, Apollo, and Hermes; Hades, though sometimes called an Olympian, kept to himself in the Underworld.

Omphale (OM fuh lee): Queen of Lydia; purchased Heracles as a slave and later invited him into her bed; mother of several children by him.

Ophion (oh FIE on): According to Pelasgian myth, a primeval serpent created by Eurynome; father of all creation, who mated with Eurynome and hatched the Universal Egg she laid.

Ops (OPS): Roman goddess of plenty or of the harvest (in Greek, Rhea); sometimes regarded as wife of Saturn.

Orchamus (or KAY muss): King of Persia; father of Leucothoe who buried her alive when he learned of her affair with Helius.

Orcus (OAR kuss): See Pluto.

Oreads (OH ri adz): Nymphs of mountains and grottoes.

Orestes (oh RESS teez): King of Argos, Arcadia, and Sparta; son of Agamemnon and Clytemnestra; brother of Iphigenia and Electra; avenged his father's murder by killing his mother; exiled for a year for the crime and beset by the Furies of his mother; returned to claim the throne; married Hermione after killing her first husband, Neoptolemus.

Orion (oh RYE un): A giant hunter; frequent companion of Artemis and Leto; killed by a scorpion sent by Hera, who was offended by his boasts about his hunting skill.

Ornytion (or NI ti on): Son of Sisyphus and Merope; brother of Glaucus and Sinon.

Orpheus (OR fi us): Famed musician and poet; son of Apollo and Calliope; member of the *Argo*; husband of Eurydice; when she died, he journeyed to the Underworld to beg her return; lost her forever when he broke his promise not to look behind him to make sure she was following; torn apart by maenads after he rejected the rites of Dionysus and established his own cult.

Orthrus (OR thruss): Two-headed dog that guarded the cattle of Geryon; offspring of Typhon and Echidna; clubbed to death by Heracles.

Otreus (OH tryoos): King of Phrygia; Aphrodite disguised herself as his daughter in order to woo Anchises.

Otus (OH tuss): Giant son of Poseidon; twin brother of Ephialtes; trapped Ares in a jar for a year; after pursuing Artemis, tricked into killing Ephialtes, who killed him.

Ovid (OV id): A Roman poet during the Augustan Age at the dawn of the Christian Era.

Palaemon (puh LEE mon): A minor sea deity; formerly Melicertes, who was transformed when he leapt into the sea with his mother Ino.

Palamedes (pal uh MEE deez): Son of Nauplius who tricked Odysseus into revealing his sanity—and thus his fitness to join the Greek forces amassing for the Trojan War; later framed as a traitor by Odysseus and Diomedes; the Greeks stoned him to death.

Pales (PAY leez): Ancient Roman deity of cattle and pastures or of flocks and shepherds; gender uncertain; may even refer to twin deities.

Palinurus (pal i NYOO russ): Helmsman of Aeneas's flagship; swept overboard, he survived four days in the water, finally arriving on the shores of Italy only to be murdered by barbarians; Aeneas promised his ghost he would find and properly bury his body.

Pallas (PAL as): 1. Brother of Aegeus who tried to capture the throne of Athens with his army of 50 sons; thwarted more than once by his nephew Theseus, who ultimately killed him and all of his sons. 2. A son of Crius and Eurybia; brother of Astraeus; husband of Styx; father (by Styx) of Zelus, Nike, Cratus, and Bia. 3. A Giant slain by Athena during the war between the Giants and the Olympians. 4. Prince of Pallanteum; son of Evander; ally of Aeneas in his war with Turnus.

Pan (PAN): A god of shepherds, forests, wildlife, and fertility; half goat and half god; son of Hermes and a daughter of Dryops.

Pandareus (pan DER i us): Thief who may have stolen Zeus's golden dog, then gave it to Tantalus for safekeeping.

Pandia (PAN di uh): Beautiful daughter of Zeus and Selene.

Pandion (PAN di on; pan DIE on): King of Athens; father of Procne, Philomela, and Erechtheus; rewarded Tereus for helping him defeat King Labdacus of Thebes in a border dispute by giving him the hand of Procne; after losing both of his daughters to Tereus's treachery, he died of grief.

Pandora (pan DOE ruh): The first woman, created by the gods to punish mankind for receiving the gift of fire from Prometheus; though beautiful, she brought with her all the ills that have since plagued humankind.

Parcae (par SEE): The Roman Fates (in Greek, the Moirai).

Paris (PAR iss): Prince of Troy; son of Priam and Hecuba; judge in notorious beauty contest of the goddesses; abductor of Helen; instigator of the Trojan War; slayer of Achilles; killed by Philoctetes.

Pasiphaë (pa SIF ay ee): Queen of Crete; daughter of Helius and Perse; sister of Aeëtes and Circe; wife of Minos; lover of his prized white bull; mother (by Minos) of Androgeus, Ariadne, Deucalion, and Phaedra and (by the bull) of the monstrous Minotaur.

Patroclus (pa TROE kluss): Squire, best friend, and lover of Achilles; son of Menoetius; when Achilles withdrew from the fighting, Patroclus borrowed his armor, fought valiantly, and died at the hands of Hector; his death roused Achilles to return to battle in a fury.

Pausanias (paw SAY ni us): A Greek travelogue writer of the second century C.E.

Pegasus (PEG uh suss): Winged horse; offspring of Medusa and Poseidon.

Peirithous (pie RITH oh us): King of the Lapithae, a Thessalian tribe; son of Zeus or of Ixion; husband of Hippodameia; with his close friend Theseus, he attempted to kidnap Persephone from the Underworld to be his second bride; trapped by Hades in the Chairs of Forgetfulness; Heracles later freed Theseus, but could not free him.

Peitho (PIE thoe): Personification of persuasion.

Pelasgus (puh LAZ gus): According to Pelasgian myth, the first man—sprung up from the teeth that Eurynome kicked out of Ophion's mouth.

Peleus (PEE li us; PEE lyoos): King of Phthia; son of Aeacus; brother of Telamon; both brothers exiled from Aegina after killing their half-brother Phocus; husband of Antigone, daughter of King Eurytion of Phthia; accidentally killed Eurytion during Calydonian boar hunt, thus gaining the throne; a crew member on the *Argo*; after Antigone's death, husband of Thetis; father of Achilles.

Pelias (PEE li us): King of Iolcus; son of Tyro and Poseidon; usurped the throne from his half-brother Aeson; father of Acastus, Alcestis, and several other daughters; when Aeson's son Jason returned to Iolcus, he sent the young man on a dangerous quest for the Golden Fleece; tricked by Medea, who claimed to be able to restore his youth, was boiled alive by his daughters.

Pelops (PEE lops): Son of Tantalus and Dione; brother of Niobe and Broteas; restored to life by Zeus after his father carved and served him in a stew to the gods; husband of Hippodameia; father of Pittheus, Atreus, and Thyestes; also father of illegitimate son, Chrysippus.

Penelope (puh NELL uh pee): Faithful wife of Odysseus; daughter of Icarius; cousin of Helen; mother of Telemachus; remained chaste during his 20-year absence; warded off her many suitors by telling them to wait until she had finished weaving a shroud for Laertes, then secretly unraveling her work every night; after her husband's death, she married her stepson Telegonus.

Penthesileia (pen thuh si LEE uh): Amazon queen who fought on the side of the Trojans during the Trojan War; killed by Achilles, who fell in love with her as she died.

Pentheus (PEN thyoos): King of Thebes who disbelieved his cousin Dionysus's claims of godhood; son of Agave and Echion; tricked by Dionysus into dressing as a maenad to spy on their revels, he was discovered and torn to pieces by his mother and other revelers.

Periboea (per i BEE uh): 1. Daughter of Alcathous, king of Megara; cousin of Theseus; King Minos of Crete took a shine to her, but Theseus distracted him with an argument about their paternity. 2. Queen of Corinth; wife of Polybus; adoptive mother of Oedipus; also called Merope. 3. Wife of Telamon; mother of Ajax.

Periclymenus (per i KLIM uh nuss): A crew member on the *Argo;* shape-shifting son of Poseidon.

Perigune (per i GYOO nee): Daughter of Sinis (Pityocamptes); had a son, Melanippus, by Theseus, who had killed her father.

Periphetes (per i FEE teez): Lame son of Hephaestus and Anticleia who clubbed strangers over the head; nicknamed Corynetes ("Clubman"); clubbed to death by Theseus.

Perse (PER see): An Oceanid (sometimes called Perseis); daughter of Oceanus and Tethys; wife of Helius; mother (by Helius) of Aeëtes, Circe, and Pasiphaë.

Perseis (per SEE iss): *See* Perse.

Persephone (per SEF uh nee): Queen of the Underworld and wife of Hades; originally called Kore, daughter of Zeus and Demeter; abducted by Hades to be his bride; because she ate several pomegranate seeds while in the Underworld, she had to spend part of every year there; her descent (fall and winter) and reemergence (spring and summer) mark the passing of the seasons.

Perses (PER seez): 1. King and namesake of Persia; son of Perseus and Andromeda. 2. The father (by Asteria) of Hecate; son of Crius and Eurybia; brother of Astraeus and Pallas. 3. King of Colchis; deposed his brother Aeëtes; killed by Aeëtes' grandson, Medus. 4. The brother of Hesiod, whose *Works and Days* is addressed to him.

Perseus (PER si us; PER syoos): Hero who killed Medusa, freed Andromeda from a sea monster, and saved his mother from a human monster; son of Zeus and Danaë; faithful husband to Andromeda; father (by Andromeda) of Perses, Electryon, Alcaeus, Sthenelus, and three other children.

Phaea (FEE uh): Name of the Crommyonian sow slain by Theseus—or of the old woman who raised her; offspring of Typhon and Echidna.

Phaedra (FEE druh): Daughter of Minos and Pasiphaë; sister of Ariadne, Deucalion, and Androgeus; husband of Theseus; mother of Acamas and Demophon; fell in love with her stepson Hippolytus; when he rejected her, she committed suicide, but left a note accusing him of rape; the charge resulted in Hippolytus's death.

Phaëthon (FAY uh thon): 1. Son of Helius and Clymene; borrowed the chariot of the sun to prove his parentage and crashed it, nearly destroying the earth; killed by a thunderbolt hurled by Zeus. 2. A son of Eos and Cephalus.

Phaëthusa (fay uh THYOO suh): Daughter of Helius who, with her sister Lampetie, tended their father's cattle on the island of Thrinacia.

Phanes (FAY ness): An Orphic name for Eros.

Phanus (FAY nuss): A crew member on the *Argo*; son of Dionysus and Ariadne; brother of Thoas, Staphylus, and Oenopion.

Phemius (FEE mi us): A minstrel in the palace of Ithaca forced to serve Penelope's suitors; spared by Odysseus upon his return.

Philoctetes (fill ock TEE teez): Shepherd's son who lit Heracles' funeral pyre; Heracles rewarded him with his bow and arrows; became the greatest archer in Greece; recruited for Trojan War, but cruelly abandoned on Lemnos for nine years because a festering wound stank; later persuaded to rejoin war, in which he mortally wounded Paris of Troy.

Philoetius (fill EE shi us): A cowherd loyal to Odysseus, he helped his master slay Penelope's suitors.

Philomela (fill oh MEE luh): Daughter of Pandion; sister of Procne and Erechtheus; her brother-in-law Tereus raped her, cut out her tongue, and imprisoned her; got word to her sister by weaving her story into a robe; after feeding Tereus his son for supper, the sisters fled; transformed into a nightingale.

Phineus (FIN i us): 1. Prophet and king of Salmydessus; brother-in-law of Zetes and Calais; tormented by Harpies sent by Zeus to punish him for revealing too much of the future; grateful to his in-laws for driving the Harpies away, he foretold some of the future of the *Argo* and its crew. 2. Brother of Cepheus betrothed to his niece Andromeda; attempted to prevent wedding of Perseus and Andromeda, but Perseus turned him to stone; sometimes called Agenor.

Phobus (FOE bus): Personification of panic; son of Ares and Aphrodite; brother of Deimus and Harmonia.

Phocus (FOE kuss): Son of Aeacus; killed by his half-brothers, Peleus and Telamon.

Phoebe (FEE bee): One of the original Titans; daughter of Gaia and Uranus; mother (by Coeus) of Leto and Asteria.

Phoenix (FEE niks): King of the Dolopians, a tribe in Thessaly; teacher of young Achilles; persuaded Achilles to join the Greek forces during the Trojan War; later renamed Pyrrhus, Achilles' son, calling him Neoptolemus.

Pholus (FOE lus): A Centaur who showed Heracles great hospitality; died when he dropped one of Heracles' poisoned arrows on his foot.

Phorcys (FOR siss): A sea god; son of Gaia and Pontus; brother of Nereus, Thaumas, Ceto, and Eurybia; father (by Ceto) of the Graeae and the Gorgons.

Phrixus (FRICK suss): Son of Athamas and Nephele; brother of Helle; saved by a golden, winged ram from stepmother Ino's plot to have her new husband sacrifice him; the ram flew the boy safely to Colchis, then yielded the Golden Fleece.

Picus (PIE kuss): The woodpecker, a prophetic bird and attendant to Mars; son of Saturn; father of Faunus; grandfather of Latinus; turned into a woodpecker when he scorned Circe's love, instead devoting himself to a nymph named Canens.

Pindar (PIN der): A Greek poet of the fifth century B.C.E.

Pisastratus (piss uh STRAT us): King of Athens; father of Hippias, who succeeded him to the throne, and Hipparchus.

Pittheus (PITH yoos): King of Troezen; son of Pelops and Hippodameia; brother of Atreus and Thyestes; father of Aethra; grandfather of Theseus.

Pityocamptes (pit i oh KAMP teez): A nickname for Sinis.

Pleiades (PLEE uh deez; PLY uh deez): The seven daughters of Atlas and Pleione.

Pleione (ply OH nee; plee OH nee): An Oceanid (daughter of Oceanus and Tethys); mother (by Atlas) of the Pleiades.

Plutarch (PLOO tark): A Greek writer and biographer of the first and second century C.E.

Pluto (PLOO toe): 1. Roman god of the Underworld (in Greek, Hades); also called Dis or Orcus. 2. An Oceanid, mother (by Zeus) of Tantalus.

Plutus (PLOO tuss): Minor god of the earth's wealth; son of Demeter and Iasion.

Podaleirius (poe duh LIE ri us): Son of Asclepius, god of healing, and grandson of Apollo; brother of Machaon; cured the wound of Philoctetes near the end of the Trojan War.

Podarces (poe DAR seez): *See* Priam.

Pollux (POL uks): Roman name for Polydeuces.

Polybotes (pol i BOE teez): Giant crushed by Poseidon during the war between the Giants and the Olympians.

Polybus (POL i bus): King of Corinth; husband of Periboea (or Merope); adoptive father of Oedipus.

Polydectes (pol i DECK teez): King of Seriphus; brother of Dictys; fell in love with Danaë, sent her son Perseus to decapitate Medusa, and then attempted to ravish Danaë; turned to stone by Perseus, who returned with the horrifying head.

Polydeuces (pol i DYOO seez): A crew member on the *Argo*, an expert boxer; son of Zeus and Leda; brother of Castor, Helen, and Clytemnestra; helped rescue Helen after her abduction by Theseus.

Polydorus (pol i DOE russ): 1. King of Thebes; only son of Cadmus and Harmonia; brother of Ino, Agave, Autonoe, and Semele; established Thebes as Greek center of Dionysian worship. 2. Youngest son of Priam and Hecuba; sent to Thrace with a shipment of gold, he was murdered by Polymestor.

Polyhymnia (pol i HIM ni uh): One of the nine Muses; generally considered the Muse of sacred song and oratory; daughter of Zeus and Mnemosyne.

Polymede (pol i MEE dee): Daughter of Autolycus; according to some accounts, wife of Aeson and mother of Jason and Promachus; killed herself after Pelias killed Promachus.

Polymestor (pol i MESS tor): King of the Bistones, a tribe in Thrace; murdered Polydorus to steal his gold; when Polydorus's mother Hecuba found out, she blinded him and killed his infant sons.

Polyneices (pol i NIE seez): Son of Oedipus, king of Thebes; brother of Eteocles, Antigone, and Ismene; though his brother agreed to rule Thebes jointly after their father's exile, Eteocles seized the throne; their struggle led to the war of the Seven Against Thebes, in which the brothers killed each other.

Polypemon (pol i PEE mon): *See* Damastes.

Polyphemus (pol i FEE muss): One of the man-eating Cyclopes; son of Poseidon; blinded by Odysseus.

Polyxena (poe LICK see nuh): Daughter of Priam and Hecuba; sacrificed by Neoptolemus on the grave of his father, Achilles, at the end of the Trojan War.

Pomona (puh MOE nuh): Roman goddess of fruit and orchards; shy nymph who refused all suitors, but finally married Vertumnus, who tried many different guises to win her.

Pontus (PON tuss): Personification of the sea; son of Gaia; father (by Gaia) of Nereus, Phorcys, Thaumas, Ceto, and Eurybia.

Porphyrion (por FIR i on): Giant who attempted to rape Hera during the war between the Giants and the Olympians; killed by a bolt from Zeus and an arrow from the bow of Heracles.

Poseidon (puh SIE don): God of the sea, horses, and earthquakes; son of Rhea and Cronus; brother of Hestia, Demeter, Hera, Hades, and Zeus; husband of Amphitrite; father (by Amphitrite) of Triton, Rhode, and Benthesicyme, (by Aethra) of Theseus, (by Demeter) of Despoena and Arion, (by Medusa) of Chrysaor and Pegasus, and (by Theophane) of the golden-fleeced ram; also father of giants Polyphemus, Otus, and Ephialtes.

Priam (PRY um): King of Troy during the Trojan War; son of Laomedon; originally named Podarces, but name changed when chosen by sister Hesione to be spared when Heracles sacked Troy; husband of Hecuba; father of 50 sons and 12 daughters, including Hector, Paris, Helenus, Cassandra, Antiphus, Troilus, Isus, Lycaon, Astyoche, Creusa, Polydorus, and Polyxena; also father of 42 illegitimate children; dragged from the altar of Zeus and killed by Neoptolemus at the end of the war.

Priapus (pry AY pus): Incredibly ugly man with enormous genitals; son of Aphrodite and Dionysus.

Procne (PROCK nee): Daughter of Pandion; sister of Philomela and Erechtheus; wife of Tereus; mother of Itys; missed her sister so much she asked Tereus to bring her for a visit; when she discovered that Tereus had raped his sister and hidden her away, she killed her son and served him to his father for supper; while fleeing Tereus, she turned into a swallow.

Procris (PROCK riss): Wife of Cephalus; insulted when her husband tested her fidelity, she became a follower of Artemis; when they reconciled, Procris gave her husband the hound Laelaps and an unerring spear; rumors made her suspect his fidelity and follow him; hearing a rustling, Cephalus let fly his spear, killing her.

Proetus (pro EE tuss): King of Argos and later Tiryns; brother of Acrisius, who drove him from Argos to Tiryns; when his daughters refused to worship Dionysus, the god drove all Argive women mad, making them think they were cows; to rid the women of madness, he was forced to give away two thirds of his kingdom.

Promachus (PROM uh kuss): Son of Aeson and Alcimede (or Polymede); brother of Jason; killed in his boyhood by his uncle Pelias.

Prometheus (pro MEE thi us; pro MEE thyoos): Creator and divine friend of the human race; defied Zeus by bringing fire to humankind; punished by being chained to a rock, where an eagle devoured his liver every day; son of Iapetus and Clymene; brother of Atlas, Epimetheus, and Menoetius.

Proserpine (pro SER pi nuh): Roman Queen of the Underworld (in Greek, Persephone).

Protesilaus (pro tess i LAY us): Commander of 40 Phylacian ships during the Trojan War; killed by Hector, he was the first Greek to die on Trojan soil.

Psyche (SIE kee): Mortal loved by Cupid (Eros) and tormented by Venus because her beauty had caused people to stop worshipping the goddess; abandoned by Cupid when she ignored his demand that she not try to find out who he was; ultimately reconciled with Cupid and made immortal by Jupiter; mother (by Cupid) of Voluptas (Pleasure).

Pteleon (TEE lee un): According to Apollodorus, a man who seduced Procris, bribing her with a golden crown in her husband's absence.

Pygmalion (pig MAY li on): King of Tyre; brother of Dido; murdered his brother-in-law Sychaeus hoping to find his hidden wealth, but got nothing.

Pylades (PILL uh deez): Friend of Orestes who traveled to Tauris in an attempt to cure Orestes' madness.

Pyrrha (PURR uh): 1. A daughter of Epimetheus and Pandora; wife of Deucalion; after surviving the great flood, she and Deucalion repopulated the earth by throwing stones that turned into people. 2. Name adopted by Achilles when he disguised himself as a girl to hide among the daughters of King Lycomedes of Scyrus.

Pyrrhus (PURR us): Son of Achilles and Deidameia; later renamed Neoptolemus.

Pythia (PITH i uh): Apollo's priestess at Delphi; the prophetess.

Python (PIE thon): Serpent sent by Hera to torment Leto; killed by Apollo in the shrine at Delphi.

Quirinus (kwi RYE nuss): Minor Roman god of war; name given to Romulus after he ascended to heaven.

Remus (REE mus): Son of Rhea Silvia and Mars; twin brother of Romulus; tossed into the Tiber River by their treacherous grand-uncle Amulius, but saved by Mars and raised first by the woodpecker Picus and a she-wolf, then by Faustulus and Acca Larentia; when grown, they killed Amulius and restored their grandfather Numitor to the throne; tried to establish another city with his brother, but constant disagreements led to his death at the hands of Romulus's followers.

Rhea (REE uh): An ancient earth goddess; one of the original Titans; daughter of Gaia and Uranus; mother (by her brother Cronus) of six Olympians: Hestia, Demeter, Hera, Poseidon, Hades, and Zeus; engineered the plot that allowed Zeus to overthrow Cronus.

Rhea Silvia (REE uh SILL vi uh): Daughter of Numitor, deposed king of Alba Longa; also called Ilia; her uncle Amulius appointed her a Vestal Virgin in an attempt to prevent her from having legitimate heirs to the throne; but Mars seduced or raped her and she bore twin sons, Romulus and Remus; after their birth, Amulius imprisoned her and she was never seen again.

Rhesus (REE suss): King of Thrace; during Trojan War, Odysseus and Diomedes snuck into his camp, killed him and his 12 men, and stole his valuable horses.

Rhode (ROE dee): Nymph and namesake of the island of Rhodes; mother of seven sons by Poseidon.

Romulus (ROM yoo luss): Founder of Rome; son of Rhea Silvia and Mars; twin brother of Remus; tossed into the Tiber River by their treacherous grand-uncle Amulius, but saved by Mars and raised first by the woodpecker Picus and a she-wolf, then by Faustulus and Acca Larentia; when grown, they killed Amulius and restored their grandfather Numitor to the throne; though the brothers agreed to found another city, they disagreed on everything else, which led to Remus's death; after founding Rome, obtained wives by abducting women from the neighboring Sabine tribe; steadily expanded the city's boundaries; died (or disappeared) mysteriously; murdered by Rome's patricians or ascended to heaven, becoming Quirinus, a minor god of war.

Salmoneus (sal MOE ni us; sal MOE nyoos): King of Thessaly; son of Aeolus; brother of Sisyphus, Cretheus, and Athamas; usurped the throne from Sisyphus; killed by a thunderbolt of Zeus after he mocked the god and insisted his subjects call him by the god's name.

Saturn (SAT ern): Roman god of fertility, especially agriculture and sowing; more properly (in Latin) called Saturnus; associated with the Greek Cronus; but when dethroned by Jupiter, he fled to Italy; became an early king during the Golden Age of Latium; introduced agriculture and civilization to Italy; husband of Ops or Lua; father (by Venilia) of Picus.

Satyrs (SAY terz; SAT erz): Lively woodland spirits in the form of men with goat's legs, horse's tails, horns, and/or pointed ears; they had insatiable appetites for alcohol, sex, and revelry.

Scamander (skuh MAN der): River god who, finding his stream choked by the corpses of Achilles' victims, flooded the battlefield to drown Achilles, only to be thwarted by an enormous flame sent by Hephaestus.

Sciron (SKY ron): Murderer who killed travelers by kicking them over a cliff into the jaws of a man-eating turtle; killed when Theseus did the same to him.

Scylla (SILL uh): Long-necked, six-headed beast that lived in a cave on a cliff overlooking the Strait of Messina; once a beautiful maiden beloved by the sea god Glaucus, she had been transformed into a hideous monster by Circe.

Scyrius (SKER i us): King of Scyrus; father of Aegeus.

Selene (see LEE nee): Goddess of the moon; daughter of Hyperion and Theia; sister of Helius and Eos; mother (by Zeus) of Pandia and (by Endymion) of 50 daughters.

Semele (SEM uh lee): Daughter of Cadmus and Harmonia; sister of Ino, Agave, Autonoe, and Polydorus; mother (by Zeus) of Dionysus; goaded by jealous Hera, she asked to see Zeus in his full glory and was consumed by flames; name changed to Thyone after Dionysus descended to the Underworld and escorted her to Mount Olympus.

Seneca (SEN uh kuh): A Roman tragedian during the first century C.E.

Servius Tullius (SER vi us TULL i us): Sixth king of Rome; son of the god Vulcan (by Ocresia, a Latin slave of Tanaquil); raised by Tanaquil and Tarquinius Priscus; named regent after Tarquinius died, he secured power by exiling the sons of Ancus, who had murdered Tarquinius; later deposed by his son-in-law, Lucius Tarquinius Superbus; beaten by allies of Tarquinius, he died under the wheels of his treacherous daughter Tullia's chariot.

Shamash (SHAH mahsh): Sumerian sun god; protector of Gilgamesh and Enkidu.

Sibyl (Cumaean) (SIB ill): Aged prophetess, hundreds of years old when visited by Aeneas; Apollo gave her the power of prophecy as well as longevity, but not eternal youth; refused the god's offer of youth and beauty in return for becoming his mistress; led Aeneas through the Underworld to seek his father's counsel.

Side (SIE dee): First wife of Orion; sent to the Underworld by Hera after boasting that her own beauty outshone Hera's.

Sidero (sie DEE roe): Cruel stepmother of Tyro; killed by Tyro's son Pelias as she clung to the altar of Hera.

Siduri (see DOO ree): Old and wise fisher's wife met by Gilgamesh on his way to find Utanapishtim.

Silens (SIE lenz): Gods of the forest; half men, half goats; experts at music and prophecy; they had a great appetite for drink; followers of Pan or Dionysus.

Silenus (sie LEE nuss): Leader and namesake of the silens, minor woodland divinities.

Silvanus (sill VAY nus): Roman god of agriculture, especially of the woods.

Silvius (SILL vi us): First child of the new Roman race; son of Aeneas and Lavinia.

Sin (SIN): The Sumerian goddess of the moon.

Sinis (SIE niss; SIN iss): Robber who killed his victims by bending two trees and tying their arms to one tree, their legs to another, and then letting go; son of Damastes; father of Perigune; Theseus killed him the same way he killed others; nicknamed Pityocamptes ("Pine Bender").

Sinon (SIE non): Greek spy who allowed Trojans to capture him near the end of the Trojan War so that he could convince them to bring the Wooden Horse (secretly filled with Greek soldiers) inside the walls of Troy; son of Sisyphus and Merope; brother of Glaucus and Ornytion.

Sinope (si NOH pee): Nymph who escaped Apollo's pursuit by getting the god to agree to grant her any wish, then wishing for lifelong virginity.

Sirens (SIE renz): Winged women who used hauntingly sweet singing to lure sailors to their deaths; transfixed, the sailors would waste away from hunger.

Sisyphus (SISS i fuss): King (and perhaps founder) of Corinth known for his trickery; son of King Aeolus of Thessaly; brother of Salmoneus, who usurped the throne; husband of the Pleiad Merope; father (by Merope) of Glaucus, Ornytion, and Sinon and perhaps also (by Anticleia) of Odysseus; eternally punished for revealing that Zeus had abducted Aegina and for outwitting death (and prolonging his life) twice; endlessly pushed a boulder up an Underworld hill only to see it fall back to the bottom again.

Smyrna (SMER nuh): Beautiful daughter of Cinyras whom Aphrodite caused to fall in love with her father; mother (by Cinyras) of Adonis; transformed by Aphrodite into a myrrh tree.

Sol (SOL): Roman god of the sun (in Greek, Helius).

Sophocles (SOFF uh kleez): Greek tragedian of the fifth century B.C.E.

Spartoi (SPAR toy): An army of men who sprang from the earth when Cadmus sowed the teeth of a dragon; Cadmus managed to kill all but five; the survivors allied themselves with Cadmus and helped him found Thebes.

Spermo (SPER moe): Daughter of Anius; sister of Elais and Oino; could turn anything she touched to corn; kidnapped by the Greek forces on their way to the Trojan War; Dionysus turned the sisters into doves to allow them to escape.

Sphinx (SFINKS): Monster with the head of a woman, the body of a lion, the tail of a serpent, and the wings of an eagle; terrorized Thebes until Oedipus solved her riddle and she plunged to her death.

Staphylus (STAFF i luss): A crew member on the *Argo*; son of Dionysus and Ariadne; brother of Thoas, Phanus, and Oenopion.

Sterope (STER oh pee): Daughter of Acastus and Astydameia.

Steropes (STER oh peez): One of the Cyclopes; son of Gaia and Uranus; brother of Brontes and Arges; forgers of thunder and lightning for Zeus.

Sthenelus (STHEN uh luss): King of Argos; son of Perseus and Andromeda; brother of Electryon and Alcaeus; husband of Nicippe; father of Eurystheus; exiled his nephew Amphitryon for killing Electryon.

Stheno (STHEE noh; STHEN oh): One of the immortal Gorgons; sister of Euryale and Medusa.

Stymphalian birds (stim FAY li an BURDZ): Crane-sized, man-eating birds with brass claws, beaks, and wings; driven away from Arcadia by Heracles as his fifth labor.

Styx (STIKS): Goddess of the main river of the Underworld; first immortal to support Zeus and the Olympians in their battle with the Titans; an Oceanid (daughter of Oceanus and Tethys); mother (by Pallas) of Zelus, Nike, Cratus, and Bia.

Sychaeus (si KEE us): Priest of Heracles; husband of Dido; murdered by Pygmalion; his ghost warned his wife of her brother's treachery, allowing her to escape Tyre with his fortune.

Syrinx (SIR ingks): Nymph pursued by Pan; changed herself into marsh reeds to escape him; he tied several reeds together to form the first syrinx (panpipes).

Talus (TAY luss): 1. Last of the ancient race of bronze giants; Medea killed him by bewitching him and piercing his one vulnerable vein (near his ankle). 2. Talented nephew and apprentice of Daedalus; jealous of the boy's skill and inventiveness as an artisan, Daedalus pushed him off the roof of the temple of Athena.

Tanaquil (TAN uh kwill): Queen of Rome; wife of Lucius Tarquinius Priscus; ambitious woman who talked her husband into moving from Tarquinia to Rome; after his death, she orchestrated the succession to the throne of their son-in-law, Servius Tullius, by pretending Tarquinius was still alive and installing Servius as "acting regent," allowing him time to gain power and authority.

Tantalus (TAN tuh luss): King of Sipylus; son of Zeus and Pluto (an Oceanid); husband of the Pleiad Dione; father of Niobe, Broteas, and Pelops; eternally punished for attempting to serve his son Pelops to the Olympians for dinner; killed by Zeus; hanging forever in the Underworld just out of reach of food and drink.

Tarpeia (tar PEE uh): Daughter of a Roman commander who betrayed Rome to the Sabines led by Titus Tatius; killed by the Sabine soldiers as they entered the gate she had opened.

Tarquinius Collatinus, Lucius (LOO shuss tar KWIN i us kol uh TIE nus): Husband of Lucretia; after the king's son, Sextus Tarquinius, raped his wife, he and Lucius Junius Brutus overthrew the king; ruled jointly with Junius for a time, but the Romans, who no longer trusted any Tarquins, forced him into exile in Lavinium.

Tarquinius Priscus, Lucius (LOO shuss tar KWIN i us PRISS kuss): Fifth king of Rome; first Etruscan king of Rome; son of Demaratus; husband of Tanaquil; won popular election to succeed Ancus Marcius as king; assassinated by the sons of Ancus when he began grooming his son-in-law Servius Tullius as his successor.

Tarquinius Superbus, Lucius (LOO shuss tar KWIN i us soo PER bus): Seventh and last king of Rome; son of Lucius Tarquinius Priscus and Tanaquil; husband of Tullia; father of Sextus Tarquinius; killed his father-in-law, Servius Tullius, in order to gain the throne; later expelled from the city after his son brutally raped Lucretia, raising public sentiment against all Tarquins.

Tarquinius, Sextus (SEX tuss tar KWIN i us): Son of Lucius Tarquinius Superbus and Tullia, his brutal rape of Lucretia brought an end to the reign of Roman kings; Lucretia told her husband, Lucius Tarquinius Collatinus, of the crime; horrified, Collatinus and his friend Lucius Junius Brutus then led a popular revolt against Tarquinius, expelling the king and killing his son.

Tatia (TAY shuh): Queen of Rome; daughter of Titus Tatius; wife of Numa Pompilius.

Titus Tatius (TIE tuss TAY shuss): King of the Sabines; when Romans under Romulus abducted the Sabine women, he waged war on Rome; but when Sabine women defended their new Roman husbands, Romans and Sabines combined forces; shared rule with Romulus until his murder in an unrelated quarrel.

Taygete (tay JUH tee): One of the Pleiades (daughters of Atlas); mother (by Zeus) of Lacedaemon.

Teirisias (tie REE si us): Most renowned seer of classical mythology; magically spent seven years as a woman; blinded by Hera for taking Zeus's side in an argument about sexual pleasure; one of the few Thebans to accept Dionysus as a god; later warned Oedipus of his fate; after death, summoned by Odysseus for advice.

Telamon (TELL uh mon): King of Salamis; son of Aeacus; brother of Peleus; both brothers exiled from Aegina after killing their half-brother Phocus; crew member on the *Argo*; valiant ally of Heracles who helped him seize Troy; given the hand of Trojan princess Hesione as his reward; later husband of Periboea; father (by Hesione) of Teucer and (by Periboea) of Ajax.

Telegonus (tee LEG uh nuss): Son of Odysseus and Circe; killed Odysseus, not knowing that the man he had speared was his father; later married Penelope.

Telemachus (tuh LEM uh kuss): Son of Odysseus and Penelope; reunited with his father after a 20-year absence, he helped him rid the palace of Ithaca of the suitors for Penelope's hand who had lived off Odysseus's wealth for years; later married the sorceress Circe, who gave him immortality.

Telemus (TELL uh muss; TEE le muss): Seer who warned the Cyclops Polyphemus that a man named Odysseus would one day blind him.

Telephus (TELL uh fuss): Son of Heracles and Auge; husband of Priam's daughter Astyoche; wounded by Achilles while repelling Greek force that landed at Mysia; agreed to provide directions to Troy if Achilles cured him.

Tellus (TELL us): *See* Terra Mater.

Tenes (TEN eez): King of Tenedos; son of Apollo; killed by Achilles.

Tereus (TEE ri us; TEER yoos): King of Daulis; son of Ares; husband of Procne; father of Itys; raped his sister-in-law Philomela, cut her tongue out to prevent her from telling anyone, and locked her away in a cabin in the woods; after unknowingly eating his son, served to him by the two sisters, he stormed after them with sword drawn; he transformed into a hoopoe and the sisters became birds, too.

Terpsichore (terp SICK uh ree): One of the nine Muses; generally considered the Muse of dance; daughter of Zeus and Mnemosyne.

Terra Mater (TER uh MAY ter): Roman personification of the earth and the Roman goddess of the earth; also called Tellus or simply Terra (in Greek, Gaia); associated with both fertility and the dead.

Tethys (TEE thiss): An ancient sea goddess; one of the original Titans; daughter of Gaia and Uranus; mother (by Oceanus) of the world's rivers and the Oceanids.

Teucer (TYOO ser): An archer second in skill only to Philoctetes among the Greeks during the Trojan War; son of Telamon and Hesione; half-brother of Ajax; after the war, his father refused to allow him to land in Salamis because he had not prevented the Greeks' ill treatment of Ajax.

Thalia (thuh LIE uh): 1. One of the nine Muses; generally considered the Muse of comedy; daughter of Zeus and Mnemosyne. 2. One of the three Graces; daughter of Zeus and Eurynome; sister of Aglaia and Euphrosyne.

Thanatos (THAN uh toss): Personification of death; a son of Nyx.

Thaumas (THOW muss): A son of Gaia and Pontus; brother of Nereus, Phorcys, Ceto, and Eurybia; father (by the Oceanid Electra) of Iris.

Theia (THEE uh): One of the twelve original Titans; daughter of Gaia and Uranus; mother (by her brother Hyperion) of Helius, Selene, and Eos.

Themis (THEE miss): One of the original Titans; daughter of Gaia and Uranus; mother (by Zeus) of the Horae (Seasons) and Moirai (Fates).

Theophane (thee OFF uh nee): A beautiful maiden transformed into a ewe by Poseidon, who wanted to hide her from her many suitors; mother (by Poseidon) of the ram with the Golden Fleece.

Thersites (ther SIE teez): Soldier who won favor among the Greek ranks by lampooning their leaders; when he made fun of Achilles' infatuation with the dead Penthesileia, Achilles killed him with a single blow.

Theseus (THEE si us; THEE syoos): Hero and king of Athens; cleared the Isthmus of Corinth of predators; slew the Minotaur; introduced democratic reforms to government; son of Aethra and Poseidon (or Aegeus); husband of Phaedra; father (by Antiope) of Hippolytus and (by Phaedra) of Acamas and Demophon; died when pushed off a cliff by Lycomedes, king of Scyrus.

Thespius (THES pi us): King and namesake of Thespia; enticed (or tricked) Heracles into sleeping with 49 of his 50 daughters and conceiving 51 grandsons.

Thetis (THEE tiss): Ancient goddess of the sea; a Nereid (daughter of Nereus and Doris); wife of Peleus; mother of Achilles.

Thoas (THOE ass): 1. King of Lemnos; son of Dionysus and Ariadne; brother of Staphylus, Phanus, and Oenopion; his daughter Hypsipyle secretly spared him when the women of Lemnos killed all the other men on the island. 2. A Giant, brother of Agrius, beaten to death by the Fates in the war between the Giants and the Olympians.

Thyestes (THIGH ess teez): Son of Pelops and Hippodameia; brother of Pittheus and Atreus; committed adultery with Atreus's wife Aerope; father of Aegisthus; unwittingly ate his other children, who had been killed, cooked, and served by Atreus.

Thyone (THIGH oh nee): Semele's new name after her son Dionysus rescued her from the Underworld and brought her to Mount Olympus.

Tiamat (TEE ah maht): Babylonian mother of all things, primeval saltwater ocean; wife of Apsu; to avenge Apsu's death, declared war on her great-grandson Ea and the other gods; defeated by Marduk, who split her corpse to form earth and sky.

Tiberinus (tie ber EYE nuss): Eighth king of Alba Longa; drowned in the river Alba, which was renamed the Tiber in his honor.

Tiphys (TIFF iss): Helmsman of the *Argo;* died of illness before reaching Colchis.

Tisiphone (ti SIFF uh nee): One of the three Erinyes (Furies).

Titans (TIE tenz): Twelve children of Gaia and Uranus; six daughters (Theia, Rhea, Themis, Mnemosyne, Phoebe, and Tethys) and six sons (Oceanus, Coeus, Crius, Hyperion, Iapetos, and Cronus); also the descendants of these twelve.

Tithonus (ti THOE nuss): Lover of Eos; brother of Laomedon; father (by Eos) of Memnon and Emathion; at Eos's request, Zeus granted him immortality but not age-lessness; eventually shut away by Eos.

Tityus (TIT i us): Giant who attempted to rape Leto; killed by Artemis and Apollo; tormented eternally by having an eagle feast on his liver every day.

Tmolus (tee MOE luss): Woodland deity who judged Apollo the winner over Pan in a musical contest.

Triptolemus (trip TOL uh muss): Eleusian taught the art of agriculture by Demeter; traveled throughout the world to spread this teaching; perhaps a son of Celeus and Meteneira.

Triton (TRY ton): Minor sea god; son of Poseidon and Amphitrite; helped the *Argo* navigate a route from Lake Tritonis to the Mediterranean Sea.

Troilus (TROY luss; TROE i luss): Son of Priam and Hecuba ambushed and killed by Achilles.

Tros (TROHS): The king who gave his name to Troy.

Tullia (TULL i uh): Queen of Rome; violently ambitious daughter of Servius Tullius; wife of Lucius Tarquinius Superbus (after murdering his brother, her first husband, and talking him into murdering her sister, his first wife); goaded her husband into seizing the throne and murdering her father.

Tullus Hostilius (TULL us hos TILL i us): Third king of Rome; militant leader; conquered Alba Longa and neighboring Sabine tribes; died when struck by lightning (perhaps hurled by Jupiter).

Turnus (TER nuss): King of the Rutulian tribe; son of Daunus; brother of Juturna; after fighting a bloody war over the throne of Latium (and the hand of Lavinia), finally agreed to meet Aeneas in one-on-one combat to decide the issue; slain by Aeneas.

Tydeus (TIE di us; TIE dyoos): Calydonian warrior in the War of the Seven Against Thebes; mortally wounded, he slew his slayer and gorged on his brains, disgusting Athena.

Tyndareus (tin DER i us): King of Sparta; husband of Leda; father of Castor and Clytemnestra; foster father of Polydeuces and Helen, his wife's children by Zeus.

Typhon (TIE fone): Most frightening monster in classical mythology, with 100 serpentine heads and eyes that shot flames; fiercely battled Zeus in an attempt to overthrow the Olympians; ultimately crushed by Zeus under Mount Etna; also called Typhoeus.

Tyro (TIE roe): Daughter of Salmoneus violated by her uncle Sisyphus, who wanted revenge on his brother; Tyro killed the two sons that came from this union; later married Cretheus (another of her uncles); mother (by Cretheus) of Aeson and (by Poseidon) of Pelias.

Urania (yoo RAY ni uh): One of the nine Muses; generally considered the Muse of astronomy; daughter of Zeus and Mnemosyne.

Uranus (YOO ruh nuss; yoo RAY nuss): Personification of the sky; son of Gaia; father (by Gaia) of the Hundred-Handed Giants, the Cyclopes, and the Titans; castrated, overthrown, and imprisoned in Tartarus by his son Cronus.

Urshanabi (er shah NAH bee): Boatman of Utanapishtim; only man capable of safely sailing over the deep sea and Waters of Death.

Utanapishtim (oo tah nah PISH tim): In Sumerian myth, the sole survivor of the Great Flood; made immortal by Enlil.

Venus (VEE nuss): Roman goddess of love (in Greek, Aphrodite); originally a minor Italian fertility goddess; mother of Cupid (by Mercury) and Aeneas (by Anchises); grandmother of Iulus, thus the mother of all Rome.

Vergil (VER jill): Roman poet of the first century B.C.E.

Vertumnus (ver TUM nuss): Roman fertility god in charge of change: changing seasons, changes in vegetation, and so on; had the ability to assume any form; husband of fruit goddess Pomona, whom he wooed in a number of disguises before winning her love.

Vesta (VES tuh): Roman goddess of hearth and home (in Greek, Hestia); guardian of the hearth fire and patroness of all household activities; by extension, guardian of the community and of the entire state of Rome.

Virbius (VER bi us): Minor Roman god; a consort of Diana; reputed to be the devoted Hippolytus, brought back to life by Aesculapius after his horses dragged him to his death, then spirited away to Rome.

Voluptas (voe LUP tuhs): Personification of pleasure; daughter of Cupid and Psyche.

Vulcan (VULL ken): Roman god of fire and artisans, metal-working, and craftspeople who use fire; also called Mulciber (in Greek, Hephaestus); originally an ancient Italian god of uncontrolled fire (for example, volcanoes); father (by Ocresia, a slave) of Servius Tullius.

Xanthus (ZAN thuss): One of two immortal horses that the gods gave Peleus when he married Thetis; they wept at the death of Patroclus and warned Achilles of impending death.

Zagreus (ZAHG ri us; ZAHG ryoos): According to the Orphic cult, the horned son of Zeus and Persephone; given by Hera to the Titans, who ate him; Zeus swallowed his heart and reconceived (by Semele) the child as Dionysus.

Zelus (ZEE luss): Personification of zeal; son of Styx and Pallas; brother of Nike, Cratus, and Bia; he and his brothers became constant companions of Zeus.

Zephyrus (ZEF uh russ): The West Wind; son of Eos and Astraeus.

Zetes (ZEE teez): A crew member on the *Argo;* winged son of Boreas; twin brother of Calais; convinced crew not to turn back to retrieve Heracles, who had been left behind; chased Harpies away from brother-in-law Phineus; killed by Heracles after returning to Iolcus.

Zeus (ZYOOS; ZOOS): Most powerful of all Olympian gods; god of thunder; ruler of heaven, Earth, gods, and humans; son of Rhea and Cronus; unfaithful husband of Hera; brother of five Olympians: Hestia, Demeter, Hera, Hades, and Poseidon; father of Dionysus (by Semele) and five Olympians: Athena (by Metis), Ares (by Hera), Apollo and Artemis (by Leto), and Hermes (by Maia); also father of such heroes as Perseus (by Danaë) and Heracles (by Alcmene) as well as many other children by many other mistresses.

What's in a Name? Greek and Roman Gods and Heroes

The Romans freely borrowed gods and goddesses, as well as some heroes, from Greek mythology. The Roman names of these appropriated Greek figures are listed below.

Roman Name	Greek Name
The great gods:	
Jupiter	Zeus
Juno	Hera
Neptune	Poseidon
Minerva	Athena
Mars	Ares
Venus	Aphrodite
Vulcan	Hephaestus
Ceres	Demeter
Vesta	Hestia
Apollo (or Sol)	Apollo

Diana	Artemis
Mercury	Hermes
Pluto	Hades
Proserpine	Persephone
Bacchus (or Liber)	Dionysus

Other divinities:

Saturn	Cronus
Aurora	Eos
Lucifer	Eosphorus
Cupid or Amor	Eros
Discordia	Eris
Terra	Gaia
Juventas	Hebe
Latona	Leto
Mater Matuta	Leucothea
Nox	Nyx
Faunus	Pan
Ops	Rhea
Camenae	Muses
Parcae	Moirai

Heroes:

Hercules	Heracles
Ajax	Aias

Be Careful What You Wish For: The Fates of Mortals Who Slept with Gods or Goddesses

Ah, to be one of the lucky ones. How often have foolish mortals wished to have sex with the gods or goddesses? You, too, would no doubt give anything to have just one night of divine splendor—and leave to fate what it may bring. To lie down with a goddess, to give yourself to a god—what could bring greater pleasure?

But be careful what you wish for. Just consider the following couplings of mortals and gods, the offspring of this intercourse, and the price the mortals paid for their one night of divine splendor.

Mortal	Deity	Offspring	Aftermath
Semele	Zeus	Dionysus	Semele burned to a crisp when Zeus appeared to her in his full glory; Dionysus became a god.
Danaë	Zeus	Perseus	Danaë and Perseus survived her father's attempt to kill them; Perseus became a great hero.

Mortal	Deity	Offspring	Aftermath
Alcmene	Zeus	Heracles	Alcmene coupled just once more with her husband, who feared the god's jealousy; Heracles became the greatest of Greek heroes.
Leda	Zeus	Polydeuces	Polydeuces and his half-brother Castor became heroes on the *Argo*.
Leda	Zeus	Helen	Helen became the world's greatest beauty; her abduction sparked the Trojan War.
Callisto	Zeus	Arcas	Zeus transformed Callisto into a bear to protect her from Hera, but Artemis shot her; Arcas was carved and cooked by his grandfather Lycaon and served to Zeus, who reassembled him; Arcas would become king of Arcadia.
Io	Zeus	Epaphus	Hera sent a gadfly to torment Io, who had been transformed into a cow; Epaphus survived an attempted abduction by Hera to become king of Egypt.
Aegina	Zeus	Aeacus	Hera killed nearly all the inhabitants of Aegina's island refuge; Aeacus would become king of a new race created when Zeus transformed ants into people.
Europa	Zeus	Minos	Europa eventually married the king of Crete; Minos grew up to rule the island.
Europa	Zeus	Rhadymanthus	Rhadymanthus was driven from Crete by his brother Minos.
Europa	Zeus	Sarpedon	Sarpedon was also driven from Crete.
Ganymede	Zeus	None	Ganymede, a beautiful Trojan prince, was brought to Olympus by Zeus, who made the boy his cupbearer.
Aethra	Poseidon	Theseus	Theseus became a great hero.
Medusa	Poseidon	Chrysaor	Medusa was transformed into a Gorgon by Athena; Chrysaor became a giant warrior.
Medusa	Poseidon	Pegasus	Pegasus, a winged horse, carried thunderbolts for Zeus.

Mortal	Deity	Offspring	Aftermath
Theophane	Poseidon	Golden Ram	The ram saved Phrixus from the sacrificial altar and became the source of the fabled Golden Fleece.
Ixion	"Hera"	The Centaurs	Ixion did not actually sleep with Hera, but with a Hera-shaped cloud created by Zeus; he was then condemned to eternal torment.
Iasion	Demeter	Plutus	Iasion was killed by jealous Zeus; Plutus became a minor god of wealth.
Anchises	Aphrodite	Aeneas	Anchises was crippled by Zeus when he revealed the identity of Aeneas's mother; the hero, Aeneas, founded the Roman race.
Adonis	Aphrodite	None	Adonis was gored to death by a jealous Ares in the shape of a wild boar.
Hyacinthus	Apollo	None	Hyacinthus died when struck with a discus thrown by Apollo (and perhaps redirected by the jealous West Wind).
Chione	Apollo	Philammon	One of just two mortals to have slept with two different gods, Chione let it go to her head; she boasted of being more beautiful than Artemis, who shot her with an arrow; Philammon became a famed bard.
Chione	Hermes	Autolycus	Autolycus became a notorious thief.
Clytie	Hermes	Myrtilus	Myrtilus became the charioteer of King Oenomaus of Pisa; bribed by Pelops, he caused an accident that killed his master; Pelops killed him rather than honor his promise.
Clytie	Helius	None	Clytie, later spurned by Helius, wasted away and turned into a flower, the heliotrope.
Leucothoe	Helius	None	Jealous Clytie told Leucothoe's father what his daughter had done; he punished her by burying her alive; Helius transformed her into frankincense.

Mortal	Deity	Offspring	Aftermath
Endymion	Selene	50 daughters	Offered the chance by Zeus to determine his own fate, Endymion, foolish and vain, chose to sleep forever without aging a day.
Tithonus	Eos	Memnon	Tithonus, given immortality, became a wretched old man; Memnon, king of Ethiopia, died at the hands of Achilles.
Tithonus	Eos	Emathion	Emathion, king of Arabia, was killed by Heracles.
Cephalus	Eos	Phaethon	Aphrodite carried beautiful Phaethon away to serve in her temple.
Peleus	Thetis	Achilles	Thetis and Peleus broke up when Thetis tried to burn away her son's mortality; Achilles, greatest hero of the Trojan War, died in battle.

Read More About It

Nearly all of our knowledge of classical mythology—except for the information derived from vase painting and classical sculpture—comes from the following literary sources. All of these original sources are available in one or more translations at your local library or bookstore:

Aeschylus

Agamemnon*
The Eumenides*
The Libation Bearers*
The Persians
Prometheus Bound
Seven Against Thebes
The Suppliant Maidens

* These three tragedies by Aeschylus are often referred to collectively as the *Oresteia*.

Apollodorus

The Library

Apollonius Rhodius

Argonautica

Euripides

Alcestis
Andromache
Bacchae
The Cyclops
Electra
Hecuba
Helen
The Heracleidae
Heracles
Hippolytus
Ion
Iphigenia in Aulis
Iphigenia in Tauris
Medea
Orestes
The Phoenician Women
Rhesus
The Suppliant Women
The Trojan Women

Hesiod

Theogony
Works and Days

Homer

The Iliad
The Odyssey

Livy

The History of Rome from Its Foundation

Ovid

Fasti
Metamorphoses

Sophocles

Ajax
Antigone
Electra
Oedipus at Colonus
Oedipus the King
Philoctetes
The Women of Trachis

Vergil

The Aeneid

Anonymous

Homeric Hymns

Index

A

Acca Larentia, 287
Achilles, 204
  Calchas's prophecy, 217
  Cheiron's teachings, 217
  childhood, 214
  death, 206, 222
  disguise as girl, 218
  father, 214-215
  immortality, 216
  marriage of parents, 215
  Phoenix's teachings, 217
  Telephus's wounding, 202
  Trojan War
    admiral appointment, 218
    armor, 218
    battles, 219-220
    Briseis, 220
    Cycnus, death of, 219
    Hector, death of, 221
    King Tenes, death of, 219
    lending armor to Patroclus, 221
    Memnon, death of, 222
    Penthesileia, 222
    refusal to fight, 220
    returning to battle, 221
    Telephus, 219
    Thersites, death of, 222
Acrisius
  daughter, 124
  daughter/grandson banishment, 125
  death, 132
  sibling rivalry, 124
Adonis, 89, 136
Aeaea, 229
Aegean Sea, 194
Aegeus, 194
Aegipan, 102-103
Aeneas, 205, 274
  Anchises, death of, 278
  Anius's prophecy, 277
  Buthrotum, 278
  Crete, 277
  Creusa, 276
  Cumaean Sibyl, 280
  Delos, 277
  destiny, revealing, 281
  father, 274-275
  Harpies, 278
  immortality, 283
  Juno, 278-279
  Latinus's abdication, 282
  Latium war, 281-283
  Lavinia, 281-283
  leaving Troy, 276
  mother, 275
  Queen Dido, 279
  Sicily, 279
  son, 283
  Strophades Islands, 277
  Thrace, 277
  Trojan War, 275-276
  Underworld trip, 280-281
Aeneid, 51
Aeschylus, 10, 45
Aesculapius, 269
Aether, 16
aetiologies, 5-7
Agamemnon
  assembly of ships, 201
  death of, 211
  returning home, 211
  sacrifice of Iphigenia, 202
Agave, 147
Ajax of Locris, 205
Ajax of Salamis, 205

Alba Longa, 285-288
  Amulius, 286-288
  Faustulus, 287
  fight over city, 288
  mother, 286
  Numitor, 286
  Remus, 286-289
  reunion with grandfather, 287
  Romulus, 286-291
  she-wolf/woodpecker, 286
  Tiber River banishment, 286
Alcestis, 136
Alcmene, 158
Althaea, 119
Amazons, 166
  Penthesileia, 222
  Trojan War, 206
Amor, 270
Amphitrite, 75-76
Amphitryon, 158
Amulius, 286-288
Anchises, 274-275
ancient deities (Rome), 253
  Bellona, 272
  Camenae, 272
  Carmenta, 272
  Fauna, 270
  Faunus, 271
  Flora, 270
  Fornax, 272
  Fortuna, 272
  Ops, 272
  Pales, 272
  Silvanus, 272
  Vertumnus, 271

Ancient Theatre of Athens, 43-44
Ancus Marcius, 293
Andromeda, 129-130
Antigone, 155
Antiope, 195
Anu, 27
Aphrodite, 86-87
  Adonis, 89
  Aeneas, 275
  beauty, 88
  love for Hermes, 88
  marriage to Hephaestus, 87
  Poseidon's love for, 88
  relationships
    Ares, 87
    Dionysus, 88
  Trojan War, 203
Apollo, 89, 92-93
  Daphne, 93
  defending his mother, 90
  musical talents, 92
  Python, death of, 92
  Roman mythology, 266
  Sinope, 93
  Trojan War, 203
Apollodorus, 10, 49
Apollonius Rhodius, 48
Apsu, 27
Ara Maxima, 167
Ares, 86
  relationship with Aphrodite, 87
  Trojan War, 203
Arges, 58

Argo, 177
Argonautica, 49, 181
Argonauts, 173-185
Ariadne, 118, 194
Artemis, 89-92
  defending her mother, 90
  gifts, 90
  honoring, 91
  Trojan War, 203
  virginity, 91
ash tree nymphs, 60
Assyrians, 26
Astarte, 36
Athamas, 175-176
Athena, 82
  Athens dispute, 75
  birth, 82-83
  Erichthonius, 84
  Hephaestus, 83
  Perseus's assistance, 127
  revenge on Greeks, 210
  Trojan War, 203
  warfare, 83
Athens, Poseidon/Athena dispute, 75
Atlas, 65
Attica, 118
Augustan Age, 50
authors
  Apollodorus, 49
  Apollonius Rhodius, 48
  dramas
    Aeschylus, 45
    Euripides, 47-48
    Sophocles, 46-47
  Herodotus, 49

Hesiod
  life, 42-43
  performances, 40-41
  poetry, 40
  Shield, 42
  Theogony, 42
Homer
  Homeric Hymns, 42
  life, 41-42
  performances, 40-41
  poetry, 40
  The Iliad/The Odyssey, 42
Pausanias, 50
Pindar, 48
Plutarch, 49
Roman poets, 50-53
Autolycus, 138
Autonoe, 147

B

Babylonians, 26 29
Bacchus, 113
beauty contest, goddesses', 200
Bellona, 272
Bona Dea, 270
Briareus, 58
Brontes, 58
Bronze Age (mortals), 20
Broteas, 140

C

Cadmus, 146-148
Calliope, 72

Camenae, 272
Carmenta, 272
cattle of Geryon, 167
Centaurs, 171
Cerberus, 169
Ceres, 267
Ceryneian, 163, 170
Chaos (creation), 14-15
Charon, 139
Ciconians, 226
Clashing Rocks, 179
Clio, 71
Coeus, 59
Collatinus, 296
Cottus, 58
Creation
  Babylonian Genesis, 26-29
  Chaos, 14-15
  Creator (Ovid), 15
  Grcck/Babylonian myths compared, 30
  Hesiod, 15
  love, 15-17
  mortals, 21
    Bronze Age, 20
    Fire, 21-22
    Golden Age, 18-19
    Iron Age, 20
    Prometheus, 21
    Silver Age, 19-20
    women, 22-24
  Pelasgians, 17-18
Creator (Ovid), 15
Creon, 155
Cretan bull, 165
Crius, 59

Cronus, 59
  eating his children, 62
  Hundred-Handed Giants/Cyclopes imprisonment, 61
  vengeance of Zeus, 63
  war against, 63-65
cultures (myths), 11
Cupid, 270
Cyclopes, 58
  alliance with Zeus, 64
  Odysseus, 227-228

D

Daedalus tragedy, 244-246
daemons, 258
Danae, 124
dawn goddess, 100
Deianira, 171
Demeter, 78-80
  children, 79
  Eleusinian Mysteries, 79
  Persephone
    abduction, 79
    return, 135-136
    search for, 134-135
  relationship with Zeus, 71
  Trojan War, 203
Description of Greece, 50
destiny (myths), 11
Diana (Roman goddess), 266
Dictys, 125
Diomedes, 165, 204
Dionysus
  Argos, 117
  Attica, 118

Bacchants, 113
birth, 110-111
childhood, 111-112
children, 118
King Midas, 119
Lycurgus's attack, 114
madness, 112
marriage to Ariadne, 118
missionary work, 114-115
Oeneus, 119
Orchomenus, 117
Phrygia, 112
pirate kidnapping, 115-116
reaching Olympus, 119
rewarding followers, 117
Thebes homecoming, 116
wine, 113
dramas
Aeschylus, 45
chorus, 43-44
Euripides, 47-48
Sophocles, 46-47
Theatre of Dionysus, 43
dryads, 103
Dumuzi, 37

E

Ea, 27
Echo and Narcissus, 238-240
Eclogues, 51
elements (myths), 11
Eleusinian Mysteries, 79
Elysian Fields (Underworld), 281
Enkidu, 31
Enuma Elish, 26-29
Eos, 100
Erato, 72
Erebus, 16
Erigone, 118
Erinyes, 60
Eris, 17
Erymanthian boar, 163
Eteocles, 155
Euripides, 10, 47-48
Eurydice, 142-143
Eurynome, 17, 71
Euterpe, 71
extraordinary events (myths), 11

F

Fasti, 52
Father Liber, 267
Fauna, 270
Faunus, 271
fire, 21-22
Flora, 270
Fornax, 272
Fortuna, 272
fratricide, 289
Furies, 60

G

Gaia, children, 14
ash tree nymphs, 60
Cyclopes, 58
Erinyes, 60
Giants, 60
Hundred-Handed Giants, 58
Titans. *See* Titans
geniuses, 258
Giants, 60, 104-105
Porphyrion, 105
Talus, 184
Tityus, 140
war against, 105-106
Gilgamesh, 30
friendship with Enkidu, 31
gifts, 31
Humbaba, 32
immortality, 33-35
Ishtar, 32-33
Glaucus, 137
goddesses
Aphrodite, 86-87
Adonis, 89
Aeneas, 275
beauty, 88
Hermes' love, 88
marriage to Hephaestus, 87
Poseidon's love, 88
relationship with Ares, 87
relationship with Dionysus, 88
Trojan War, 203
Artemis, 89-92
defending her mother, 90
gifts, 90
honoring, 91
Trojan War, 203
virginity, 91

Athena, 82
  Athens dispute, 75
  birth, 82-83
  Erichthonius, 84
  Perseus's assistance, 127
  relationship with Hephaestus, 83
  revenge on Greeks, 210
  Trojan War, 203
  warfare, 83
Danae, 124
Demeter, 78-80
  children, 79
  Eleusinian Mysteries, 79
  Persephone, 79, 134-136
  relationship with Zeus, 71
  Trojan War, 203
Eos, 100
Eurynome, 17, 71
Great Goddess, 36-38
Hecate, 100-101
Hemera, 16
Hera
  beauty, 74
  Heracles, 159
  marriage to Zeus, 72-74
  sisters, 78
  Trojan War, 203
Hestia, 78-79, 203
Ishtar, 32-33, 36
Letus, 72
lovemaking dispute, 74

Metis
  Athena, birth of, 82
  relationship with Zeus, 70
Mnemosyne, 59, 71
myths, 11
Persephone
  abduction, 134
  Adonis, 136
  Alcestis, 136
  compromise, 135-136
  Demeter's search for, 134-135
  marriage to Hades, 136
  mercy, 136
  Sisyphus, 139
Phoebe, 59
Rhea, 59
Roman
  ancient, 253
  Bellona, 272
  Camenae, 272
  Carmenta, 272
  Ceres, 267
  daemons, 258
  daily rituals, 255-257
  Diana, 266
  dominions, 254
  Fauna, 270
  Flora, 270
  Fornax, 272
  Fortuna, 272
  geniuses, 258
  household, 257-258
  Juno, 262
  lares, 257
  manes, 258

  Mater Matuta, 269
  Minerva, 267
  Ops, 272
  Pales, 272
  pax deorum, 254
  penates, 257
  penates publici, 258
  petitioning, 255
  Pomona, 271
  Terra, 261
  Venus, 265-266
  Vesta, 262-263
Selene, 99
Styx, 102
Tethys, 16, 59
Theia, 59
Themis, 59, 71
Thetis, 215
  Achilles' girl disguise, 218
  family abandonment, 216
  marriage, 215
Tiamat, 27
Trojan War interventions, 203
gods
  Acrisius, 132
  Aether, 16
  Anu, 27
  Apollo, 89-93
  Apsu, 27
  Ares, 86
    relationship with Aphrodite, 87
    Trojan War, 203
  Coeus, 59
  Crius, 59

Cronus, 59
  eating his children, 62
  Hundred-Handed
    Giants/Cyclopes
    imprisonment, 61
  vengeance of Zeus, 63
  war against, 63-65
Dionysus
  Argos, 117
  Attica, 118
  Bacchants, 113
  birth, 110-111
  childhood, 111-112
  children, 118
  King Midas, 119
  Lycurgus's attack, 114
  madness, 112
  marriage to Ariadne,
    118
  missionary work,
    114-115
  Oeneus, 119
  Orchomenus, 117
  Phrygia, 112
  pirate kidnapping,
    115-116
  reaching Olympus, 119
  rewarding followers,
    117
  Thebes homecoming,
    116
  wine, 113
Dumuzi, 37
Ea, 27
Hades, 77
  abduction of
    Persephone, 134
  Trojan War, 203

Helius, 98-99, 246
Hephaestus
  acceptance, 85
  birth, 84
  creations, 85
  exile, 84
  marriage to Aphrodite,
    87
  relationship with
    Athena, 83
Hermes, 88, 94-96
Hyperion, 59
Iapetus, 59
Marduk, 28
myths, 11
Oceanus, 59
Olympian, 67
Pan, 102-103
Pontus, 16
Poseidon, 75
  Athens dispute, 75
  children, 76
  horses, 77
  infidelities, 76
  love for Aphrodite, 88
  relationship with
    Amphitrite, 75-76
  Trojan War, 203
Roman
  ancient, 253
  Apollo, 266
  Cupid, 270
  daemons, 258
  daily rituals, 255-257
  dominions, 254
  Faunus, 271
  geniuses, 258
  household, 257-258

Janus, 263-264
Jupiter, 261-262
lares, 257
Liber, 267
manes, 258
Mars, 264-265
Mercury, 268
Neptune, 268
Pales, 272
pax deorum, 254
penates, 257
penates publici, 258
petitioning, 255
Pluto, 268
Saturn, 260-261
Silvanus, 272
Vertumnus, 271
Vulcan, 268
Trojan War interventions,
  203
Uranus, 16
Zeus. *See* Zeus
Golden Age (mortals),
  18-19
Golden Apples (Garden
  of Hesperides), 168
Golden Fleece, Jason's
  quest, 175-176
  Aeëtes' challenge, 181
  Amycus's attacks, 179
  Argo trapping, 182
  bird attack, 180
  Circe's purification, 182
  Clashing Rocks, 179
  Drepane, 183
  fleece, 182
  help, 176-177
  homecoming, 184

Ionian Sea, 183
Lake Tritonis, 184
Lemnos, 177-178
Libyan coast, 183
Medea's help, 180
Mysia, 178
Pelias, death of, 185
Salmydessus, 179
Samothrace, 178
ship, 177
Sirens, 183
sons of Phrixus, 180
Talus, 184
tripod offering, 184
Graeae, 127
Great Goddess
(Mesopotamia), 36-38
Greeks (Trojan War), 202
Achilles. *See* Achilles
Agamemnon
assembly of ships, 201
death, 211
returning home, 211
sacrifice of Iphigenia,
202
Ajax of Locris, 205
Ajax of Salamis, 205
assembly of ships, 201
atrocities, committing,
209
capture of Helenus, 207
Diomedes, 204
diplomacy attempt, 202
end of war, 210
Menelaus
assembly of ships, 201
forgiving Helen, 209
marriage to Helen, 201

Odysseus. *See* Odysseus
Orestes, 212
Philoctetes, 202, 207
Protesilaus's death, 203
returning home, 210
sailing to Troy, 202
scavenger hunt, 207-208
surrounding town attacks,
203
survivors, 210
Teucer, 205
wooden horse, 208-209
Gyges, 58

H

Hades, 77
Persephone, 134-136
Trojan War, 203
Haemon, 155
hamadryads, 103
Hecate, 100-101
Hector, 204, 221
Hecuba, 226
Helen
abductions
Paris, 200-201
Theseus, 196
marriage to Menelaus,
201
suitors, 201
wooden horse, 208
Helius, 98-99, 246
Hemera, 16
Hephaestus
acceptance, 85
birth, 84

creations, 85
exile, 84
marriage to Aphrodite, 87
relationship with Athena,
83
Hera
beauty, 74
Heracles, 159
lovemaking dispute, 74
sisters, 78
Trojan War, 203
Zeus, 70-74
Heracles, 158
Ara Maxima, 167
birth, 158-159
burning, 172
children, 161
daughters of Thespius,
161
Deianira, 171
Eurytus, 169-171
finer arts teachings,
159-161
freeing Prometheus,
168
giants' attack on Mount
Olympus, 170
gifts, 160
Hera
acceptance, 172
suckling, 159
Hesione's rescue, 167
Jason and the Argonauts,
164
labors
cattle of Geryon, 167
Cerberus, 169
Ceryneian, 163

Cretan bull, 165
Erymanthian boar, 163
Golden Apples
    (Garden of
    Hesperides), 168
Hippolyta's golden
    girdle, 166
horses of Diomedes,
    165
Lernaean Hydra, 162
Nemean lion, 162
stables of Augeas, 164
Stymphalian birds, 164
madness, 161
Omphale, 170
parents, 158
poisoned shirt, 172
Rock of Gibraltar, 167
slavery, 169
Thebes/Minyans battle,
    161
vengeance of King
    Augeas/King
    Laomedon, 170
war against Giants, 105
warfare training, 159-161
Zeus's altar, 171
Hercules, 269
Hermes, 88, 94-96
Herodotus, 49
heroes
Achilles, 204
    Calchas's prophecy,
        217
    Cheiron's teachings,
        217
    creating, 214
    death, 206, 222

father, 214-215
girl disguise, 218
immortality, 216
marriage of parents,
    215
Phoenix's teachings,
    217
Telephus's wounding,
    202
Trojan War. *See*
    Achilles, Trojan War
Aeneas, 205
    Anchises, death of, 278
    Anius's prophecy, 277
    Buthrotum, 278
    Crete, 277
    Creusa, 276
    Cumaean Sibyl, 280
    Delos, 277
    destiny, 281
    Harpies, 278
    immortality, 283
    Juno, 278-279
    Latinus's abdication,
        282
    Latium war, 281-283
    Lavinia, 281-283
    leaving Troy, 276
    Queen Dido, 279
    Sicily, 279
    son, 283
    Strophades Islands,
        277
    Thrace, 277
    Trojan War, 275-276
    Underworld trip,
        280-281

Ajax of Locris, 205
Ajax of Salamis, 205
Diomedes, 204
Eurytus, 169
giants' attack on Mount
    Olympus, 170
Gilgamesh, 30
    friendship with
        Enkidu, 31
    gifts, 31
    Humbaba, 32
    immortality, 33-35
    Ishtar, 32-33
Hector, 204, 221
Heracles. *See* Heracles
Hercules, 269
myths, 8-9
Odysseus
    Aeaea, 229
    Aeolia, 228
    ancestors, 224
    Calypso, 232
    Ciconians, 226
    Circe, 229
    contest for Penelope,
        235
    crew, 232
    Cyclopes, 227-228
    death, 236
    Eumaeus, 233
    Hecuba, 226
    Ithaca, 233
    Laestrygonians, 228
    Leucothea's help, 233
    Lotus-Eaters, 226
    marriage to Penelope,
        224-225

Nausicaa, 233
returning to palace, 234
reunion with Penelope, 235
reunion with Telemachus, 234
shades of the dead, 230
Sirens, 231
Strait of Messina, 231
suitors of Helen, 224, 235
Thrinacia, 232
Trojan War, 204, 225
Zeus's help, 232
Perseus
Andromeda, 129-130
birth, 124
Dictys, 125
grandfather, 124, 132
Hesperides, 129
Medusa, death of, 126-128
return to Seriphus, 131
Tiryns, 132
wedding of Polydectes, 125
Teucer, 205
Theseus
Aegeus, death of, 194
Antiope, 195
Ariadne, 194
Athens, 191, 194
birth, 188
Cercyon, 190
Chairs of Forgetfulness, 197
conception, 188

death, 197
father's embrace, 192
Helen, 196
Heracles' Amazon victory, 195
Hippolytus, death of, 196
Marathonian bull, 191-192
marriage to Phaedra, 195
Minotaur, 193
Pallas's rebellion, 192
Perigune, 190
Periphetes, 189
Procrustes, 191
refuge, 197
Sciron, 190
Sinis, 189
Underworld escape, 197
tragic. See tragic heroes
Heroides, 52
Hesiod, 10
Creation, 15
life, 42-43
performances, 40-41
poetry, 40
Shield, 42
Theogony, 42
Hestia, 78-79, 203
Hippolytus, 166, 196
Homer, 9
Homeric Hymns, 42
life, 41-42
performances, 40-41
poetry, 40
The Iliad/The Odyssey, 42

Homeric Hymns, 42
Horace, 53
House of Cadmus, 147-148
household gods and goddesses (Roman), 257-258
human separation (myths), 11
humans. See mortals
Humbaba, 32
Hundred-Handed Giants, 58, 64
Hyperion, 59
Hypnos, 17

I

Iapetus, 21, 59
Icarius, 118
Iliad, The, 42
Inanna, 36
Ino, 147
Iphigenia, 202
Iron Age (mortals), 20
Ishtar, 32-33, 36
Ixion, 140

J

Janus, 263-264
Jason
Argonauts, 173-185
birth, 174
death, 186
Golden Fleece, retrieving
Aeëtes' challenge, 181
Amycus's attacks, 179
Argo trapping, 182
bird attack, 180

Circe's purification, 182
Clashing Rocks, 179
Drepane, 183
help, 176-177
homecoming, 184
Ionian Sea, 183
Lake Tritonis, 184
Lemnos, 177-178
Libyan coast, 183
Medea's help, 180
Mysia, 178
Pelias, death of, 185
Salmydessus, 179
Samothrace, 178
ship, 177
Sirens, 183
sons of Phrixus, 180
Talus, 184
tripod offering, 184
Heracles' assistance, 164
marriage to Glauce, 185
relationship with Medea, 185
return to Iolcus, 174-175
Jocasta, 148
death, 154
marriage to Oedipus, 152
Juno, 262
Jupiter, 261-262

K

Keres, The, 17
King Midas, 119
King Priam, 202

L

labors of Heracles
cattle of Geryon, 167
Cerberus, 169
Ceryneian, 163
Cretan bull, 165
Erymanthian boar, 163
Golden Apples (Garden of Hesperides), 168
Hippolyta's golden girdle, 166
horses of Diomedes, 165
Lernaean Hydra, 162
Nemean lion, 162
stables of Augeas, 164
Stymphalian birds, 164
Laestrygonians, 228
Laius, 148-150
lararia, 257
lares, 257
Latium, 261
Lavinia, 283
Lernaean Hydra, 162
Letus, 72
Liber, 267
Library, The, 49
Livy, 53
love (Creation), 15-17
Lucius Junius Brutus, 296
Lucius Tarquinius Priscus, 293-294
Lucius Tarquinius Superbus, 295-296
Lucretia, 295

M

maenads, 112
manes, 258
Marathonian bull, 191-192
Marduk, 28
Mars, 264-265
Mater Matuta, 269
Medea
Jason
Argo trapping, 182
Circe's purification, 182
fleece, 182
helping, 180
Ionian Sea, 183
Lake Tritonis, 184
Libyan coast, 183
marriage, 185
Pelias, death of, 185
revenge, 185
Sirens, 183
Talus, 184
tripod offering, 184
King Aegeus, 186
returning home, 186
Medusa, 126-128
meliae, 103
Melpomene, 72
Memnon, 206
Menelaus
assembly of ships, 201
diplomacy attempt, 202
Helen
forgiving, 209
marriage, 201

Mercury, 268
Merope, 137
Mesopotamia
    Assyrians, 26
    Babylonian Genesis,
        26-29
    Babylonians, 26
    Gilgamesh, 30
        friendship with
            Enkidu, 31
        gifts, 31
        Humbaba, 32
        immortality, 33-35
        Ishtar, 32-33
    Great Goddess, 36-38
    Sumerians, 26
Metamorphoses, 52
Metis
    Athena's birth, 82
    relationship with Zeus, 70
Midas, 119
Milky Way, 159
Minerva, 267
Minotaur, 192-193
Minyans, 161
Mnemosyne, 59, 71
Moirai, The, 17
monsters
    Cercyon, 190
    Minotaur, 192-193
    Periphetes, 189
    Procrustes, 191
    Sciron, 190
    Sinis, 189
Moros, 17
mortals. *See also* heroes
    Acca Larentia, 287
    Achilles. *See* Achilles

Aegeus, 194
Aeneas. *See* Aeneas
Aesculapius, 269
Agamemnon
    assembly of ships, 201
    death, 211
    Iphigenia sacrifice, 202
    returning home, 211
Agave, 147
Ajax of Locris, 205
Ajax of Salamis, 205
Alcmene, 158
Amazons, 166, 222
Amphitryon, 158
Amulius, 286-288
Anchises, 274-275
Ancus Marcius, 293
Andromeda, 129-130
Antigone, 155
Antiope, 195
Ariadne, 194
Autolycus, 138
Autonoe, 147
bronze, 20
Broteas, 140
Cadmus, 146
Ciconians, 226
Collatinus, 296
Creation, 21
Creon, 155
Deianira, 171
Diomedes, 204
Erigone, 118
Eteocles, 155
Eurydice, 142-143
fire, 21-22
Glaucus, 137

golden, 18-19
Haemon, 155
Hector, 204, 221
Hecuba, 226
Helen
    abduction by Paris,
        200-201
    abduction by Theseus,
        196
    capture, 207
    marriage to Menelaus,
        201
    suitors, 201
    wooden horse, 208
Helenus, 207
Heracles. *See* Heracles
Hippolytus, 196
House of Cadmus,
    147-148
Icarius, 118
Ino, 147
Iphigenia, 202
iron, 20
Ixion, 140
Jason. *See* Jason
Jocasta, 148
    death, 154
    marriage to Oedipus,
        152
King Priam, 202
Laius, 148-150
Lavinia, 283
Lucius Junius Brutus, 296
Lucius Tarquinius
    Priscus, 293-294
Lucius Tarquinius
    Superbus, 295-296
Lucretia, 295
Memnon, 206

Menelaus
  assembly of ships, 201
  diplomacy attempt, 202
  forgiving Helen, 209
  marriage to Helen, 201
Niobe, 140
Numa Pompilius, 292
Numitor, 286-288
Odysseus. *See* Odysseus
Oedipus. *See* Oedipus
Omphale, 170
Orestes, 211-212
Paris
  Achilles, death of, 206
  Helen, 200-201
Patroclus, 221
Peleus, 214-216
Pelops, 140
Penelope
  marriage to Odysseus,
    224-225
  reunion with Odysseus,
    235
  suitor contest, 235
Periboea and Polybus,
  149
Perigune, 190
Phaedra, 195
Philoctetes
  Heracles' bow and
    arrows, 172
  rescue, 207
  Trojan War, 202
Polyneices, 155
Prometheus, 21
Protesilaus, 203
Queen Dido, 279
relationship with Zeus, 69

Rhea Silvia, 286
Sabines, 290
Semele, 147
Servius, 294
Sextus Tarquinius, 295
silver, 19-20
Silvius, 283
Sinon, 137
Sisyphus, 137
  Autolycus's cattle thief,
    138
  cheating Death, 139
  children, 137
  confrontation with
    Zeus, 138
  eternal punishment,
    140
  marriage, 137
  tricking Persephone,
    139
Tantalus, 140-141
Teucer, 205
Theseus. *See* Theseus
Tullus Hostilius, 292
Turnus, 282-283
women, creating, 22-24
Mount Abyla, 167
Mount Atlas, 129
Mount Calpe, 167
Muses, 71-72
Mylitta, 36
myths, 12
  aetiologies, 5-7
  Chaos, 14-15
  Creation
    Creator (Ovid), 15
    Greeks/Babylonian,
      compared, 30

  Hesiod, 15
  love, 15-17
  Pelasgians, 17-18
culture, 11
destiny, 11
elements, 11
extraordinary events, 11
gods and goddesses, 11
heroes, 8-9
human separation, 11
Mesopotamia
  Babylonian Genesis,
    26-29
  Gilgamesh, 30-35
places, 11
recorders, 9-10
religions, 7-8
superhuman characters,
  11

N

naiads, 103
Narcissus and Echo,
  238-240
Nemean lion, 162
Nemesis, 17
Neptune, 268
Nessus, 171
Niobe, 140
Numa Pompilius, 292
Numitor, 286-288
nymphs, 103
  ash tree, 60
  Daphne, 93
  dryads, 103
  hamadryads, 103

meliae, 103
naiads, 103
oreads, 103
sea, 104
Nyx, 16

O

Oceanids, 104
Oceanus, 16, 59
odes, 48
Odysseus
  Aeaea, 229
  Aeolia, 228
  ancestors, 224
  Calypso, 232
  Ciconians, 226
  Circe, 229
  crew, 232
  Cyclopes, 227-228
  death, 236
  Eumaeus, 233
  Hecuba, 226
  Ithaca, 233
  Laestrygonians, 228
  Leucothea's help, 233
  Lotus-Eaters, 226
  Nausicaa, 233
  Penelope
    contest for, 235
    marriage to, 224-225
    reunion with, 235
  returning to palace, 234
  reunion with Telemachus,
    234
  shades of the dead, 230
  Sirens, 231
  Strait of Messina, 231

suitors of Helen, 224, 235
Thrinacia, 232
Trojan War, 204, 225
Zeus's assistance, 232
Odyssey, The, 42
Oedipus
  abandonment, 149
  ancestors, 146
  blindness, 154
  children, 152
  conception, 149
  father's murder, 150
  House of Cadmus,
    146-148
  Laius, 148-149
  marriage to mother, 152
  oracle consultation, 150
  Periboea and Polybus,
    149
  Polyneices' and Eteocles'
    rule of Thebes, 155
  reaching Athens, 154
  self-truth, 153
  Sphinx, 151-152
Olympians, 67
  Aphrodite, 86-87
    Adonis, 89
    Aeneas, 275
    beauty, 88
    Hermes' love, 88
    marriage to
      Hephaestus, 87
    Poseidon's love, 88
    relationship with Ares,
      87
    relationship with
      Dionysus, 88
    Trojan War, 203

Apollo, 89, 92-93
  Daphne, 93
  defending his mother,
    90
  musical talents, 92
  Python, death of, 92
  Sinope, 93
  Trojan War, 203
Ares, 86
  relationship with
    Aphrodite, 87
  Trojan War, 203
Artemis, 89, 92
  defending her
    mother, 90
  gifts, 90
  honoring, 91
  Trojan War, 203
  virginity, 91
Athena, 82
  birth, 82-83
  Erichthonius, 84
  relationship with
    Hephaestus, 83
  revenge on Greeks,
    210
  Trojan War, 203
  warfare, 83
Demeter, 79-80
  abduction of
    Persephone, 79
  children, 79
  Trojan War, 203
Hades, 77
  Persephone, 134-136
  Trojan War, 203
Helius, 246

Hephaestus
acceptance, 85
birth, 84
creations, 85
exile, 84
marriage to Aphrodite, 87
relationship with Athena, 83
Hera
beauty, 74
Heracles, 159
lovemaking dispute, 74
marriage to Zeus, 72-74
Trojan War, 203
Hermes, 88, 94-96
Hestia, 78-79, 203
Poseidon, 75
Athens dispute, 75
horses, 77
infidelities, 76
love for Aphrodite, 88
protecting children, 76
relationship with Amphitrite, 75-76
Trojan War, 203
war against Giants, 105-106
Zeus. *See* Zeus
Omphale, 170
On Make-Up, 52
Ops, 272
Orcus, 268
oreads, 103
Oresteia, 45
Orestes, 211-212
Orpheus, 142-143
Ovid, 10, 14-15, 52

P-Q

Pales, 272
Pan, 102-103
Pandora, 23-24
Parallel Lives, 49
Paris
Achilles, death of, 206
Helen, 200-201
Patroclus, 221
Pausanias, 50
pax deorum, 254
Pelasgians' Creation myths, 17-18
Peleus, 214-216
Pelops, 140
penates, 257
penates publici, 258
Penelope
Odysseus
marriage to, 224-225
reunion with, 235
suitor contest, 235
Penthesileia, 222
Periboea and Polybus, 149
Perigune, 190
Persephone, 89
abduction, 134
Adonis, 136
Alcestis, 136
compromise, 135-136
Demeter's search for, 134-135
marriage to Hades, 136
mercy, 136
Sisyphus, 139
Perses, 130

Perseus
Andromeda, 129-130
birth, 124
Dictys, 125
grandfather, 124, 132
Hesperides, 129
Medusa, death of, 126-128
Polydectes' wedding, 125
return to Seriphus, 131
Tiryns, ruling, 132
Phaedra, 195
Phaëthon, 246-247
Philoctetes
Heracles' bow and arrows, 172
rescue, 207
Trojan War, 202
Philomela and Procne, 240-242
Phoebe, 59
Phoenician Women, The, 154
pietas, 254
Pindar, 48
places (myths), 11
Plutarch, 49
Pluto, 268
poets
Apollonius Rhodius, 48
Hesiod
Creation, 15
life, 42-43
performances, 40-41
poetry, 40
Shield, 42
Theogony, 42
Homer, 9
Homeric Hymns, 42
life, 41-42

performances, 40-41
poetry, 40
The Iliad/The Odyssey,
    42
Orpheus, 142-143
Pindar, 48
Roman, 50-53
Polydectes' wedding, 125
Polyhymnia, 72
Polyneices, 155
Polyphemus, 227
Pomona, 271
Pontus, 16
Porphyrion, 105
Poseidon, 75
    Aphrodite, love for, 88
    Athens dispute, 75
    horses, 77
    infidelities, 76
    protecting children, 76
    relationship with
        Amphitrite, 75-76
    Trojan War, 203
Procne and Philomela,
    240-242
Procris, 242-244
Proetus, 124
Prometheus
    freeing, 168
    mortals, 21-22
    torture, 24
Protesilaus, 203

Queen Dido, 279

R

recorders (myths), 9-10
religions
    myths, 7-8
    Rome, 252
Remus and Romulus. *See*
    Romulus and Remus
Rhea, 59, 62, 286
rituals (Roman), 255-257
Rock of Gibraltar, 167
Roman mythology
    Aeneas, 274
        Anchises, death of, 278
        Anius's prophecy, 277
        Buthrotum, 278
        Crete, 277
        Creusa, 276
        Cumaean Sibyl, 280
        Delos, 277
        destiny, 281
        father, 274-275
        Harpies, 278
        immortality, 283
        Juno, 278-279
        Latinus's abdication,
            282
        Latium war, 281-283
        Lavinia, 281-283
        leaving Troy, 276
        mother, 275
        Queen Dido, 279
        Sicily, 279
        son, 283
        Strophades Islands,
            277
    Thrace, 277
    Trojan War, 275-276
    Underworld trip,
        280-281
Aesculapius, 269
ancient deities, 253,
    270-272
Apollo, 266
Ceres, 267
Cupid, 270
daily rituals, 255-257
deity dominions, 254
Diana, 266
Greek gods and
    goddesses, 253
Hercules, 269
household gods and
    goddesses, 257-258
influences, 252-253
Janus, 263-264
Juno, 262
Jupiter, 261-262
Liber, 267
Mars, 264-265
Mater Matuta, 269
Mercury, 268
Minerva, 267
Neptune, 268
pax deorum, 254
petitioning gods and
    goddesses, 255
pietas, 254
Pluto, 268
Pomona, 271
Rome
    boundary expansions,
        291

republican govern-
ment, 296
Romulus, death of, 291
Sabines, 290
seven kings, 292-296
women, 289
Romulus and Remus
Amulius, 286-288
death of Remus, 289
death of Romulus, 291
Faustulus, 287
fight over city, 288
mother, 286
Numitor, 286
reunion with grand-
father, 287
she-wolf/woodpecker,
286
Tiber River banish-
ment, 286
Saturn, 260-261
Terra, 261
Venus, 265-266
Vesta, 262-263
Vulcan, 268
Rome
boundaries, expanding,
291
finding women, 289
poets, 50-51
Horace, 53
Livy, 53
Ovid, 52
Seneca, 53
Vergil, 51
religious practices, 252
republican government,
296

rituals, 255-257
Romulus, death of, 291
Sabines, 290
Saturnalia, 261
seven kings, 294
Ancus Marcius, 293
Lucius Tarquinius
Priscus, 293-294
Lucius Tarquinius
Superbus, 295-296
Numa Pompilius, 292
Servius, 294
Tullus Hostilius, 292
Tarquins, banishing, 296
Vestal Virgins, 263
Romulus
death, 291
Rome
boundary expansions,
291
Sabines, 290
women, 289
Romulus and Remus
Amulius, 286-288
death of Remus, 289
death of Romulus, 291
Faustulus, 287
fight over city, 288
mother, 286
Numitor, 286
reunion with grandfather,
287
she-wolf/woodpecker,
286
Tiber River banishment,
286

S

Sabines, 290
Samothrace, 178
Saturn, 260-261
Saturnalia, 261
satyrs, 103
sea nymphs, 104
Selene, 99
Semele, 147
Dionysus, birth of, 111
reaching Olympus, 120
Seneca, 53
Servius, 294
Seven Against Thebes, 155
Sextus Tarquinius, 295
Shield, 42
silens, 103
Silvanus, 272
Silver Age (mortals), 19-20
Silvius, 283
Sinon, 137
Sirens, 142
Sisyphus, 137
Autolycus's cattle thief,
138
cheating Death, 139
children, 137
confrontation with Zeus,
138
eternal punishment, 140
marriage, 137
Persephone, 139
Sophocles, 10, 46-47
sparagmos, 113
stables of Augeas, 164
Steropes, 58
Stories of Changing Forms, 52

Stymphalian birds, 164
Styx, 102
Sumerians, 26
sun god, 98-99
superhuman characters, 11

T

Talus, 184
Tantalus, 140-141
Terpsichore, 72
Terra, 261
Tethys, 16, 59
Teucer, 205
Thalia, 72
Thanatos, 17
Theatre of Dionysus, 43-44
Thebes
    Cadmus, 146
    Creon, 155
    House of Cadmus,
        147-148
    Laius, 148-150
    Minyans' battle, 161
    plague, 153
    Polyneices/Eteocles, 155
    Seven Against Thebes, 155
    Sphinx, 151-152
Theia, 59
Themis, 59, 71
Theogony, 42
Theseus
    Aegeus, death of, 194
    Antiope, 195
    Ariadne, 194
    Athens throne, 194
    birth, 188
    Chairs of Forgetfulness,
        197

conception, 188
death, 197
father's embrace, 192
Helen, 196
Heracles' Amazon
    victory, 195
Hippolytus, death of, 196
Marathonian bull,
    191-192
marriage to Phaedra, 195
Minotaur, 193
monsters
    Athens arrival, 191
    Cercyon, 190
    Periphetes, 189
    Procrustes, 191
    Sciron, 190
    Sinis, 189
Perigune, 190
rebellion of Pallas, 192
refuge, 197
Underworld escape, 197
Thetis, 215
    Achilles' girl disguise, 218
    family abandonment, 216
    marriage, 215
Thyone. *See* Semele
Tiamat, 27
Titans, 59-60
    Atlas, 65
    Coeus, 59
    Crius, 59
    Cronus, 59
        eating his children, 62
        Hundred-Handed
            Giants/Cyclopes
            imprisonment, 61
        vengeance of Zeus, 63
        war against, 63-65

Hyperion, 59
Iapetus, 21, 59
    marriages, 61
Mnemosyne, 59
Oceanus, 59
Phoebe, 59
Prometheus
    freeing, 168
    mortals, 21-22
    torture, 24
Rhea, 59
Tethys, 59
Theia, 59
Themis, 59
Uranus's attack, 60-61
war against Cronus,
    63-65
Tityus, 140
tragedians
    Aeschylus, 45
    Euripides, 47-48
    Sophocles, 46-47
tragic heroes
    Daedalus, 244-246
    Echo and Narcissus,
        238-240
    Phaëthon, 246-247
    Procne and Philomela,
        240-242
    Procris, 242-244
tripods, 184
Trojan War
    Achilles, 204
        admiral appointment,
            218
        armor, 218
        battles, 219-220
        Briseis, 220
        Cycnus, death of, 219

death, 206, 222
Hector, death of, 221
King Tenes, death of, 219
lending armor to Patroclus, 221
Memnon, death of, 222
Penthesileia, 222
refusal to fight, 220
return to battle, 221
Telephus, 219
Thersites, death of, 222
Aeneas, 205, 275-276
Agamemnon, 211
Ajax of Locris, 205
Ajax of Salamis, 205
beauty contest, 200
capture of Helenus, 207
Diomedes, 204
diplomacy attempt, 202
end, 210
gods/goddesses interventions, 203
Greeks
assembly of ships, 201
atrocities, 209
attacking surrounding towns, 203
returning home, 210
sailing to Troy, 202
scavenger hunt, 207-208
survivors, 210
Hector, 204
Odysseus, 204, 225

Paris
abduction of Helen, 200-201
Achilles, death of, 206
beauty contest decision, 200
Philoctetes's abandonment, 202
Protesilaus, death of, 203
Telephus's wounding, 202
Teucer, 205
Trojan assistance, 206
wooden horse, 208-209
Trojans
Aeneas. *See* Aeneas
Amazon assistance, 206
capture of Helenus, 207
diplomacy attempt, 202
end of war, 210
Greek atrocities, 209
Hector, 204, 221
Memnon's assistance, 206
Paris
abduction of Helen, 201
Achilles, death of, 206
beauty contest, 200
Telephus's wounding, 202
wooden horse, 208-209
Tullus Hostilius, 292
Turnus, 282-283
Typhon, 106-107

U

Underworld
Elysian Fields, 281

Hades, 77
marriage to Persephone, 134-136
Trojan War, 203
Hecate, 100-101
Orpheus, 142-143
Persephone
abduction, 134
Adonis, 136
Alcestis, 136
compromise, 135-136
Demeter's search for, 134-135
marriage to Hades, 136
mercy, 136
Sisyphus, 139
Sisyphus's torture, 140
Styx, 102
Tantalus's torture, 141
Urania, 72
Uranus, children, 16
ash tree nymphs, 60
Cyclopes, 58
Erinyes, 60
Giants, 60
Hundred-Handed Giants, 58
Titans. *See* Titans
Utanapishtim, 33-35

V

Venus, 265-266
Vergil, 10, 51
Vertumnus, 271
Vesta, 262-263
Vestal Virgins, 263
Vulcan, 268

W-X-Y

water snake (Lernaean Hydra), 162
White Goddess, 269
women, 22-24
wooden horse (Trojan War), 208-209

Z

Zeus
    Athena, birth of, 82
    birth, 62
    confrontation with Sisyphus, 138
    infidelities, 73-74
    lovemaking dispute, 74
    lust, 70-72
    marriage to Hera, 72-73
    rebellion against, 70
    relationships
        Demeter, 71
        Eurynome, 71
        gods, 68
        Leto, 72
        Metis, 70
        Mnemosyne, 71
        mortals, 69
        Themis, 71
    responsibilities, 68
    Trojan War, 203
    Typhon battle, 106-107
    war against Cronus, 63-65

Check Out These
Best-Selling
COMPLETE IDIOT'S GUIDES®

Understanding **Catholicism**
SECOND EDITION
Bob O'Gorman, Ph.D. and Mary Faulkner, M.A.
1-59257-085-2
$18.95

Learning **Spanish**
THIRD EDITION
Gail Stein
0-02-864451-4
$18.95

The **Bible**
SECOND EDITION
James S. Bell Jr. and Stan Campbell
0-02-864382-8
$18.95

Being a **Groom**
Jennifer Lata Rung and Mark Rung
0-02-864456-5
$9.95

Grammar and **Style**
SECOND EDITION
Laurie E. Rozakis, Ph.D.
1-59257-115-8
$16.95

Playing the **Guitar**
SECOND EDITION
Frederick Noad
0-02-864244-9
$21.95 w/CD

Personal Finance in Your **20s & 30s**
SECOND EDITION
Sarah Young Fisher and Susan Shelly
0-02-864374-7
$19.95

Knitting and Crocheting
SECOND EDITION
Illustrated
Barbara Breiter and Gail Diven
1-59257-089-5
$16.95

The Perfect **Resume**
THIRD EDITION
Susan Ireland
0-02-864440-9
$14.95

Buying and Selling a **Home**
FOURTH EDITION
Shelley O'Hara and Nancy D. Lewis
1-59257-120-4
$18.95

Low-Carb Meals
Lucy Beale and Sandy G. Couvillon, M.S., L.D.N., R.D.
1-59257-180-8
$18.95

Calculus
W. Michael Kelley
0-02-864365-8
$18.95

More than *450* titles in *30* different categories
Available at booksellers everywhere

ALPHA